THE

100 BEST

MUTUAL FUNDS YOU CAN BUY 2003

▲

Gordon K. Williamson

Adams Media Corporation
Avon, Massachusetts

Also by Gordon K. Williamson
Big Decisions, Small Investor
Low Risk Investing
Making the Most of Your 401(k)

DEDICATION
This book is dedicated to all of my clients.
I would be nowhere without their trust and support.

ACKNOWLEDGMENTS
Special thanks (again) to Cynthia Shaffer for her computer skills. This is a truly
thankless job, and I appreciate everything she has done.

—··—··—··—··—··—··—··—··—··—··—··—

Published by Adams Media Corporation
57 Littlefield Street, Avon, MA 02322

ISBN: 1-58062-754-4

Printed in the United States of America.

J I H G F E D C B A

Library of Congress Cataloging-in-Publication Data
available from the publisher.

This publication is designed to provide accurate and authoritative information with regard
to the subject matter covered. It is sold with the understanding that the publisher is not
engaged in rendering legal, accounting, or other professional advice. If legal advice or other
expert assistance is required, the services of a competent professional person should be
sought.
   —From a *Declaration of Principles* jointly adopted by a Committee of the
American Bar Association and a Committee of Publishers and Associations

While due care has been taken to ensure accurate and current data, the ideas, principles, conclusions, and general suggestions contained in this volume are subject to the laws and regulations of local, state, and federal authorities, as well as to court cases and any revisions of
court cases. Due to the magnitude of the database and the complexity of the subject matter,
occasional errors are possible; the publisher assumes no liability direct or incidental for any
actions or investments made by readers of this book, and strongly suggests that readers seek
consultation with legal, financial, or accounting professionals before making any investment.

The data used to analyze the funds is current through December 31, 2001.

This book is available at quantity discounts for bulk purchases.
For information, call 1-800-872-5627 (in Massachusetts, 508-427-7100).

Visit our home page at *www.adamsmedia.com*

Contents

I.
About This Book

There are roughly 6 million business entities operating in the United States; close to 15,000 of these businesses are publicly held (meaning they have issued stock to the public). Of the 15,000 publicly traded companies, fewer than 4,000 are listed on the New York Stock Exchange (NYSE). The world's total stock market capitalization is approximately $18 trillion, almost one-half of which is represented by U.S. equities.

There are more than 13,000 mutual funds. There are well over three times as many mutual funds as there are stocks listed on the NYSE! The mutual fund industry is now the second largest financial institution in the nation, with assets exceeding $7 trillion, up from $1 trillion in 1991. By the beginning of the year 2000, U.S. households held 81 percent of mutual fund assets, up from 74 percent in 1990. Individual stocks and mutual funds accounted for 38 percent of U.S. households' financial assets, surpassing the previous all-time high of 34 percent in 1968. Just under 55 million households (52 percent of all households) own shares of one or more mutual funds, up from 4.6 million in 1980.

Mutual funds are the *best* investment vehicle that has been developed in the twentieth century. When properly selected, these vehicles combine professional management, ease of purchase and redemption, simple record-keeping, risk reduction, and superb performance, all in one type of investment. There are dozens of other types of investments, but none match the overall versatility of mutual funds.

A mutual fund is simply one method of investing. When you invest in a fund, your money is pooled with thousands of other investors' monies. This large pool of money is overseen by the fund's management, who place it in one or more types of investments. The universe of investments includes common stocks, preferred stocks, corporate bonds, tax-free municipal bonds, U.S. government obligations, zero-coupon bonds, convertible securities, gold, silver, foreign securities, and even real estate. The amount of money invested in one or more of these categories depends on the fund's objectives and restrictions and on management's perception of the economy.

The beauty of mutual funds is that once the investor decides on the *type* of investment desired there are several funds that fulfill that criterion. As an example, someone who needs current income would be attracted to bond funds (or a series of equity-oriented funds coupled with what is known as a "systematic withdrawal plan"—a monthly income program described in Appendix D). A person interested in appreciation would focus on an aggressive growth, growth and income, and/or international stock fund. A person who wanted some current income plus some growth to offset the effects of inflation should consider a balanced fund.

1

The track records of these funds can easily be obtained, as contrasted to the track records of stockbrokers, who are not ranked at all. A few mutual fund sources even look at a fund's risk-adjusted return, a standard of measurement that has not been sufficiently emphasized in the past.

This book was written to fill a void. There are already several mutual fund books and directories, but none deal exclusively with the very best funds. More important, *none of these publications measure risk properly*.

This is the thirteenth edition of this book. If you have read one or more of the previous editions, you will notice that this edition includes many funds not previously listed and that several of the *previous* "100 Best" are not included here. This does not mean that you should sell or transfer from a previous recommendation to one that appears in this edition. For the most part, mutual funds described in past editions are still excellent choices and should not be moved. There are a number of reasons a fund no longer appears in this, or previous, editions. These reasons are detailed in Chapter X.

Moving from one fund to another can often spell trouble. Since 1970, the average holding period for mutual funds has been reduced from over eleven years to just over two years. More recent studies indicate that it may now be closer to one year. Although the period from 1984 through 2000 was one of the strongest periods in history, many investors experienced significantly less performance than the market offered. While the Standard & Poor's 500 (S & P 500) Index returned an average of 16.3 percent per year from January 1984 through December 2000, the typical equity investor earned only 5.3 percent per year during the same period. The lesson from these numbers is simple: By jumping from investment to investment, investors lose out on the solid performance they are seeking.

Other sources give almost endless numbers and performance statistics for hundreds and hundreds of mutual funds, leaving readers to draw their own conclusions about what are the best funds. This book will save you a great deal of time because it has taken more than 13,000 existing funds and narrowed them down to the best 100, ranked by specific category and risk level. Even money market funds are included, a category rarely covered by any other publication.

Investors and financial advisors are not concerned with mediocre or poor performers; they simply want the best funds, *given certain parameters*. Personal investment considerations should include (in order of priority) your time horizon, risk tolerance, financial goals, existing portfolio, and tax bracket. Parameters within a given fund category include risk, performance, and consistency.

Current books and periodicals that cover funds focus on how a fund has performed in the past. Studies clearly point out that a fund whose performance is in the top half one year has a fifty-fifty chance of being in the bottom half the next year, or the year after that. Since there is little correlation between the past and the future when it comes to market returns, this book concentrates on consistency in management and the amount of risk assumed.

The model used to rank the 100 best is fully described in Chapter X. It is a logical, common-sense approach that cuts through the statistical jargon; it is also easy to understand. As my dad used to say, "There is nothing as uncommon as common sense."

II.
What Is a Mutual Fund?

A mutual fund is an investment company: an entity that makes investments on behalf of individuals and institutions that share common financial goals. The fund pools the money of many people, each with a different amount to invest. Professional money managers then use this pool of money to buy a variety of stocks, bonds, or money market instruments that, in their judgment, will help the fund's shareholders achieve their financial objectives.

Each fund has an investment objective, described in the fund's prospectus, that is important both to the manager and to the potential investor. The fund manager uses this objective as a guide when choosing investments for the fund's portfolio. Prospective investors use it to determine which funds are suitable for their own needs. The investment objectives of mutual funds cover a wide range. Some follow aggressive investment policies, involving greater risk, in search of higher returns; others seek current income from more conservative investments.

When the fund earns money, it distributes the earnings to its shareholders. Earnings come from stock dividends, interest paid by bonds or money market instruments, and gains from the sale of securities in the fund's portfolio. The dividends and capital gains produced are paid out in proportion to the number of fund shares owned. Thus, shareholders who invest a few hundred dollars get the same investment return per dollar as those who invest hundreds of thousands.

Mutual funds remain popular because they are convenient and efficient investment vehicles that give all individuals—even those with small sums to invest—access to a splendid array of opportunities. Mutual funds are uniquely democratic institutions. They can take a portfolio of giant blue-chip companies such as IBM, General Electric, and General Motors and slice it into small enough pieces so that almost anyone can buy.

Mutual funds allow you to participate in foreign stock and bond markets that might otherwise demand too much time, expertise, or expense to be worthwhile. International funds make investing across national borders no more difficult than investing across state lines. Over the next decade, as securities markets develop in the former Iron Curtain countries, mutual funds will no doubt give investors many opportunities to participate in those markets as well.

Mutual funds have opened up a world of fixed-income investing to people who, until recently, had few choices apart from passbook accounts and savings bonds. Through bond funds, shareholders can tap into the interest payments from any kind of fixed-income security they can imagine—and many they have never heard of. The range goes from U.S. Treasury bonds (T-bonds) to collateralized mortgage obligations (CMOs), adjustable-rate preferred stock, floating-rate notes, and even to other countries' debts—denominated both in U.S. dollars and in other currencies.

What is heavily marketed is not necessarily what is appropriate for you to invest in. A global biotechnology fund may be a great investment, but it may not be the right mutual fund for you. Buying what is "hot" rather than what is appropriate is one of the most common mistakes made by investors and an issue that is addressed throughout this book.

A reason to invest is to offset the effects of inflation. Over time, inflation can erode individuals' purchasing power. Mutual funds that invest primarily in common stocks may help keep you ahead of inflation over the long term.

	year	amount
first-class stamp	1934	3 cents
	1980	15 cents
	2002	34 cents
	Increase	1,133%
a new car	1934	$1,436
	1980	$6,200
	2002	$19,175
	Increase	1,335%
a day in the hospital	1934	$12
	1980	$344
	2002	$2,854
	Increase	23,783%

Sources: U.S. Postal Service, U.S. Census Bureau, and Wall Street Journal, April 30, 2002.

III.
How to Invest in a Mutual Fund

Investing in a mutual fund means buying shares of the fund. An investor becomes an owner of shares in the fund just as he or she might be an owner of shares of stock in a large corporation. The difference is that a fund's only business is investing in securities, and the price of its shares is directly related to the value of the securities held by the fund.

Mutual funds continually issue new shares for purchase by the public. The price per share for existing fund investors is not decreased by the ongoing issuance of new shares, since each share created is offset by the amount of new money coming in. Phrased another way, new money that comes into the fund is used to purchase additional securities in order not to dilute the income or value for existing shareholders.

A fund's share price can change from day to day, depending on the daily value of the securities held by the fund. The share price is called the net asset value, which is calculated as follows: The total value of the fund's investments at the end of the day, after expenses, is divided by the number of shares outstanding.

Newspapers report mutual fund activity every day. An example from the *Wall Street Journal* is shown here.

Everett Funds:

Evrt r	12.38	NL	-.01
MaxRtn	18.39	NL	+.06
ValTr	12.33	NL	-.01
LtdSl	17.71	NL	-.14
ExtrMid	2.82	2.95	-.02
ExJY p	7.24	7.60	+.01
FBK Gth t	11.06	11.06	..

FJA Funds:

Capit f	14.67	15.69	-.02
NwHrz	9.65	10.10	..
Permt	12.91	13.81	..
Perrin	20.96	22.42	-.02

The first column in the table is the fund's abbreviated name. Several funds under a single heading indicate a family of funds.

The second column is the net asset value (NAV) per share as of the close of the preceding business day. In some newspapers, the NAV is identified as the sell or the bid price; that is, the amount per share you would receive if you sold your shares. Each mutual fund determines its net asset value every business day by dividing the market value of its total assets, less liabilities, by the number of shares outstanding. On any given day, you can determine the value of your holdings by multiplying the NAV by the number of shares you own.

The third column is usually the offering price or, in some papers, the buy or the asked price; that is, the price you would pay if you purchased shares. The buy price is the NAV plus any sales charges. If there are no sales charges, an NL for no load appears in this column. In such a case, the buy price would be the same as the NAV.

The next column shows the change, if any, in the NAV from the preceding quotation—in other words, the change over the most recent one-day trading period. Thus, if you see a "+.06" in the newspaper next to your fund, *each* of your shares in the fund went up in value by six cents during the previous day.

A *p* following the abbreviated name of the fund denotes a fund that charges a fee that is subtracted from assets for marketing and distribution costs, also known as a 12b-1 plan (named after the federal government rule that permits such an expense). If the fund name is followed by an *r,* the fund has a contingent deferred sales load (CDSL) or a redemption fee. A CDSL is a charge incurred if shares are sold within a certain period; a redemption fee is a cost paid *whenever* shares are sold. An *f* indicates a fund that habitually enters the previous day's prices, instead of the current day's. A *t* designates a fund that has both a CDSL or a redemption fee and a 12b-1 plan.

IV.
How a Mutual Fund Operates

A mutual fund is owned by all of its shareholders, the people who purchased shares of the fund. The day-to-day operation of a fund is delegated to a management company.

The management company, often the organization that created the fund, may offer other mutual funds, financial products, and financial services as well. The management company usually serves as the fund's investment advisor.

The investment advisor manages the fund's portfolio of securities. The advisor is paid for its services in the form of a fee that is based on the total value of the fund's assets; fees average 0.5 percent. The advisor employs professional portfolio managers who invest the fund's money by purchasing a number of stocks or bonds or money market instruments, depending on what type of fund it is.

These fund professionals decide where to invest the fund's assets. The money managers make their investment decisions based on extensive, ongoing research into the financial performance of individual companies, taking into account general economic and market trends. In addition, they are backed up by economic and statistical resources. On the basis of their research, money managers decide what and when to buy, sell, or hold for the fund's portfolio, in light of the fund's specific investment objective.

In addition to the investment advisor, the fund may also contract with an underwriter that arranges for the distribution of the fund's shares to the investing public. The underwriter may act as a wholesaler, selling fund shares to security dealers, or it may retail directly to the public.

V.
Different Categories of Mutual Funds

Aggressive Growth. The investment objective of aggressive growth funds is max-imum capital gains, with little or no concern for dividends or income of any kind. What makes this category of mutual funds unique is that fund managers often have the ability to use borrowed money (leverage) to increase positions. Sometimes they deal in stock options and futures contracts (commodities). These trading techniques sound, and can be, scary, but such activities represent only a minor portion of the funds' holdings.

Because of their bullish dispositions, these funds will usually stay fully invested in the stock market. For investors, this means better-than-expected results during good (bull) markets and worse-than-average losses during bad (bear) market periods. Fortunately, the average bull market is almost four times as long as the typical bear market.

Do not be confused by economic conditions and stock market performance. There have been eight recessions since World War II. During seven of those eight recessions, U.S. stocks went up. During all eight recessions, stocks posted impres-sive gains in the second half of every recession. By the same token, do not under-estimate the impact of a loss. A 20 percent decline means that you must then have a gain of 25 percent just to break even.

A loss of 20 percent does not happen very often to aggressive growth funds, par-ticularly on a calendar year basis, but you should be aware that such extreme down-ward moves are possible, as was the case in 2001. Often brokers like to focus on the plus 45 percent, plus 50 percent, and plus 60 percent years, such as 1980, 1991, and 1999, while glossing over bad years, such as 1984 and 2001, when aggressive growth funds were down about 13 percent and 20 percent, respectively, on average.

One of the great wonders of the stock market is how volatility of returns is reduced when the investor's holding period is increased. Because of this, aggres-sive growth funds should only be owned by one of two kinds of investors: those who can live with high levels of daily, monthly, quarterly, and/or annual price per share fluctuations, and those who realize the importance of a diversified portfolio that cuts across several investment categories. The second kind of investor looks at how the entire package is performing, not just one segment.

The typical price-earnings (p/e) ratio for stocks in this category is 34, slightly more than the S & P 500 Index, which has an average p/e ratio of 31. This group of funds has an average beta of 1.3, making its *market-related* risk 30 percent higher than the S & P 500 (which always has a beta of 1.0, no matter what market conditions or levels are).

The standard deviation for aggressive growth funds is 37 percent. This means that the expected return for any given year would typically vary either way by 37 percent. In other words, since aggressive growth funds have averaged 4 percent over the past three years (ending December 31, 2001), annual returns are expected to range from negative 33.0 percent (4 - 37) to 41 percent (4 + 37). This would represent one standard deviation. A single standard deviation accounts for what you can expect two out of every three months (67 percent of the time or roughly two out of every three years). If you are looking for greater assurance, then two standard deviations must be used (multiply 37 percent times 2 in this case). This means that returns for about 95 percent of the time (two standard deviations) would be 4 percent plus or minus 74 percent; in other words, a range of -70 percent to 78 percent.

Small-company stocks have an average p/e ratio of 28. (The price-earnings ratio refers to the selling price of a stock in relation to its annual earnings. Thus, a fund category that has a p/e ratio of, say, 10 is comprised of mutual funds whose typical stock in the portfolio is selling for ten times what the corporation's earnings are for the year.) Small-company stock funds have a standard deviation of 31 percent and a beta of 1.0, figures that support the view that this category is less volatile than aggressive growth funds.

Historical returns over the past three, five, ten, and fifteen years for aggressive growth and small-company stock funds are shown here. All of the figures shown are *compound annual* rates of return (all periods ending December 31, 2001).

category	3 years	5 years	10 years	15 years
aggressive growth funds	3.9%	7.4%	9.7%	10.7%
small-company stock funds	15.4%	11.8%	15.6%	12.6%
S & P 500	-1.0%	10.7%	12.9%	13.7%
T-bills	4.8%	4.9%	4.6%	5.3%
CPI (rate of inflation)	2.5%	2.2%	2.5%	3.2%

Technology and service stocks dominate the aggressive growth fund category. Technology alone represents just over 26 percent of the typical aggressive growth fund's portfolio, followed by 21 percent in health and 17 percent in services. Small-company stocks are also dominated by technology (20 percent) and service issues (18 percent).

Balanced. This kind of fund invests in common stocks and corporate bonds. The weighting given to stocks depends on the fund manager's perception of, or belief in, the market. The more bullish the manager is, the more likely the portfolio will be loaded up with equities. Yet, no matter how strongly management feels about the stock market, it would be very rare to see stocks equal more than 67 percent of the portfolio. Similarly, no matter how bearish one becomes, it would be unlikely for a balanced fund to have more than 67 percent of its holdings represented by bonds. Often a fund's prospectus will outline the weighting ranges: The fund's managers must stay within these wide boundaries at all times. A small portion of these funds is made up of cash equivalents (T-bills, CDs, commercial paper, etc.), with a very small amount sometimes dedicated to preferred stocks and convertible securities.

Three other categories—multiasset global, convertible, and asset allocation— have been combined with balanced funds for the purposes of this book. This grouping is logical; because their overall objectives are largely similar, the general portfolio composition can be virtually identical in many cases, and the fund managers in each of these categories have the flexibility to load up heavily on stocks, bonds, preferreds, or convertible securities.

Multiasset global funds typically emphasize bonds more than stocks or cash. It is not uncommon to see a multiasset global fund that has 60 percent of its holdings in bonds, with 10 to 20 percent in stocks, and the remainder in foreign equities, preferred stocks, and cash. For the *stock* portion of this category, the average p/e ratio is 29. On the bond side, the average maturity of debt instruments in the portfolio is eight years. The standard deviation for this narrow category is 11 percent.

Convertible funds, as the name implies, are made up mostly of convertible preferred stocks and convertible bonds. The conversion feature allows the owner, the fund in this case, to convert or exchange securities for the corporation's common stock. Conversion and price appreciation take place during bull-market periods. Uncertain or down markets make conversion much less likely; instead, management falls back on the comparatively high dividend or interest payments that convertibles enjoy. The typical convertible fund has somewhere between two-thirds and three-quarters of its holdings in convertibles; the balance is in cash, stocks, and preferreds. For the stock portion of this category, the p/e ratio averages 29 and the standard deviation is 19 percent. On the bond side, the average maturity of debt instruments in the portfolio is seven years.

Asset allocation funds, like other categories that fall under the broad definition of "balanced," are hybrid in nature—part equity and part debt. These funds have a tendency to emphasize stocks over bonds. A fund manager who wants to take a defensive posture may stay on the sidelines by converting moderate or large parts of the portfolio into cash equivalents. The average asset allocation fund has somewhere between 50 and 65 percent of its portfolio in common stocks, with the remainder in bonds, foreign stocks, and cash. For the stock portion of this category, the typical p/e ratio is 28 and the standard deviation is 11 percent. On the bond side, the average maturity of debt instruments in the portfolio is eight years.

This group of funds has an average beta of 0.5, making its *market-related risk* 50 percent less than the S & P 500. Keep in mind that beta refers to a portfolio's *stock market-related* risk; it is not a meaningful way to measure bond or foreign security risk.

The standard deviation for balanced funds is 11 percent, which is under one-third the level of aggressive growth funds. This means that the expected return for any given year will vary by 11 percent. (For example, if you were expecting an annualized return of 7 percent, your actual return would range from -4 percent to 18 percent most of the time.)

Historical returns over the past three, five, ten, and fifteen years for balanced, multiasset global, convertible, and asset allocation funds are shown here. All of the figures are *compound annual* rates of return (all periods ending December 31, 2001).

category	3 years	5 years	10 years	15 years
balanced funds	2.2%	7.5%	9.3%	10.1%
multiasset global funds	3.2%	4.5%	7.7%	6.2%
asset allocation funds	2.4%	7.2%	9.0%	9.0%
convertible funds	6.5%	8.8%	10.9%	9.2%
utility funds	-0.6%	8.0%	9.2%	10.0%

Technology and financial stocks dominate the equity portion of the balanced fund category. These two groups represent over one-third of the typical balanced fund's stock portfolio. The other major equity sectors are industrial cyclicals, services, and health-care stocks.

Like other hybrid funds, balanced funds provide an income stream. The average yield of balanced, multiasset global, and asset allocation funds is under 2.5 percent. The typical yield for convertible securities funds is about 3.5 percent. High-tax-bracket investors who want to invest in these funds should consider using tax-sheltered money, if possible. Balanced, multiasset global, asset allocation, and convertible bond funds are particularly attractive within an individual retirement account (IRA), other qualified retirement plans, or variable annuities. (For more information about both fixed-rate and variable annuities, see two of my other books, *The 100 Best Annuities* and *Getting Started in Annuities*.)

Corporate Bonds. These funds invest in debt instruments (IOUs) issued by corporations, governments, and agencies of the U.S. government. Perhaps the typical corporate bond fund should be called a "government-corporate" fund.

All bonds have a maturity date; that is, a date when the issuer (the government, municipality, or corporation) pays back the *face value* of the bond (which is almost always $1,000 per bond) and stops paying interest. There are often hundreds of different securities in any given bond fund. Each one of these securities (bonds in this case) has a maturity date; these maturity dates can range from a few days up to thirty years.

Bond funds have a wide range of maturities. The name of the fund will often indicate whether it is made up of short-term or medium-term obligations. If the name of the fund does not include the words *short-term* or *intermediate,* then the fund most likely invests in bonds with average maturities over ten years. The greater the maturity, the more the fund's share value can change. There is an inverse relationship between interest rates and the value of a bond; when one moves up, the other goes down.

The weighted maturity date of the bonds within this group averages seven years, with a typical coupon rate of 6.5 percent. "Weighted maturity" refers to the time left until the average bond in the portfolio comes due (matures). The coupon rate represents the interest that the corporation or government pays out annually on a per-bond basis. The standard deviation for corporate bonds is 3.5 percent, less than one-third of that found with balanced funds. This means that the expected return for any given month, quarter, or year will be more predictable than almost any other category of mutual funds.

Using a beta measurement for bonds is of little value, because beta defines *stock market* risk and has nothing to do with interest-rate or financial risk.

Corporate bonds are rated in terms of their safety. The two major rating services are Moody's and Standard and Poor's. By reading the fund's prospectus or by telephoning the mutual fund company, you can find out how safe a corporate bond fund is, at least as far as financial or default risk is concerned. The vast majority of these funds are extremely conservative and safety (default) is not really an issue. U.S. government bonds are not rated since it is believed that there is no chance of default; unlike a corporation, the federal government can print money.

Historical returns over the past three, five, ten, and fifteen years for corporate bond funds are shown here. All of the figures shown are *compound annual* rates of return (all periods ending December 31, 2001).

category	3 years	5 years	10 years	15 years
corporate bond funds	5.2%	6.2%	6.5%	7.5%
government bond funds	5.3%	6.3%	6.2%	7.2%
municipal bond funds	3.4%	4.8%	5.8%	6.3%
world bond funds	4.4%	3.1%	4.7%	6.3%
CPI (rate of inflation)	2.5%	2.2%	2.5%	3.2%

Like income funds, corporate funds provide a high yield that is fully taxable and should be sheltered whenever possible. The average yield of these bond funds is just over 6 percent.

Financial Services. Financial sector funds invest in the common stock of banks, brokerage firms, insurance companies, consumer credit providers, as well as savings and loan associations. A large number of the portfolios in this industry group focus on a particular type of financial company, with banking being one of the more popular.

During the 2001 calendar year, the normally defensive financial services sector was affected by the volatility of the overall stock market. Although the group as a whole outperformed the S & P 500, the typical financial fund turned in negative results for the year. Despite short-term weakness, this sector remains one of the strongest.

Financial funds underperformed the S & P 500 by 17 percentage points during the last bull market (September 1998 to August 2000), but outperformed the S & P 500 by 29 percentage points during the last bear market (August 2000 to September 2001). Over the past twenty years, ending January 31, 2002, the average annualized return of financial funds was 17.3 percent vesus 15.2 percent for the S & P 500. During the past fourteen years, the best year for this sector was 1991 (59 percent) and the worst year was 1990 (-16 percent). Over the past five years, the best year was 1997 (44 percent) and the worst year was 2001 (-4 percent).

The typical p/e ratio for stocks in this category is 23 versus 30 for the S & P 500. This group of funds also has an average beta of 0.7, which means that it has 30 percent less *market risk* than the S & P 500.

The standard deviation for financial funds is 22 percent. Historical returns over the past three, five, ten, and fifteen years for financial stock funds are shown here. All of the figures shown are *compound annual* rates of return (all periods ending December 31, 2001).

category	3 years	5 years	10 years	15 years
financial funds	6.1%	13.0%	17.9%	15.8%
utility funds	-0.6%	8.0%	9.2%	10.0%
S & P 500	-1.0%	10.7%	12.9%	13.7%
growth & income funds	0.8%	9.0%	11.6%	11.6%
health-care funds	15.0%	15.2%	13.8%	17.5%

Global Stock. This category of mutual funds invests in equities issued by domestic and foreign firms. Fifteen of the twenty largest corporations in the world are located outside the United States. It makes sense to be able to invest in these and other corporations and industries—to be able to take advantage of opportunities wherever they appear. Global, also known as world, stock funds have the ability to invest in any country. Conceptually the more countries a fund is able to invest in, the lower its overall risk level can be; often return potential can also increase.

For the purposes of this book, the global stock category includes foreign and international equity funds. When it comes to investing in mutual funds, the words *foreign* and *international* are interchangeable. A foreign, or international, fund invests in securities outside the United States. Some foreign funds are broadly diversified, including stocks from European as well as Pacific Basin economies. Other international funds specialize in a particular region or country. A global fund invests in domestic as well as foreign securities. The portfolio manager of a global fund generally has more latitude in selecting securities, since either domestic or foreign securities can end up representing 50 percent or more of the portfolio, depending on management's view of the different markets, whereas a foreign or international fund is not allowed to invest in U.S. stocks or bonds.

The typical p/e ratio for stocks in this category is 28, a figure that is lower than that of the S & P 500 (p/e ratio of 31). This group of funds has an average beta of 0.9, meaning that its *U.S. market-related* risk is about 10 percent less than that of the general market, as measured by the S & P 500. The standard deviation for global stock funds is 21 percent, versus 24 percent for growth funds.

Foreign stock funds, which are exclusive of U.S. investments, have a p/e ratio of 28. Their standard deviation over the past three years has been 21 percent. Pacific Basin funds, a more narrowly focused type of foreign fund, have an average p/e ratio of 25 and a standard deviation of 30 percent. European funds, another type of specialized international fund, have a p/e ratio of 24 and a standard deviation of 21 percent.

Historical returns over the past three, five, ten, and fifteen years for global stocks are shown here. All of the figures shown are *compound annual* rates of return (all periods ending December 31, 2001).

category	3 years	5 years	10 years	15 years
global stock funds	1.3%	5.3%	8.4%	9.1%
foreign stock funds	-1.2%	2.2%	6.2%	7.2%
emerging markets funds	4.7%	-4.7%	0.9%	n/a
Pacific Basin funds	1.9%	-7.4%	0.4%	3.5%
European funds	-1.2%	5.4%	8.8%	7.1%

The four areas that dominate global (world) stock funds are the United States (44 percent of a typical fund's holdings), Europe (30 percent), Japan (7 percent), and the Pacific Rim (5 percent).

Government Bonds. These funds invest in securities issued by the U.S. government or one of its agencies (or former affiliates), such as the Government National Mortgage Association (GNMA), the Federal Home Loan Mortgage Corporation (FHLMC), or the Federal National Mortgage Association (FNMA). Investors are attracted to bond funds of all kinds for two reasons. First, bond funds have monthly distributions; individual bonds pay interest only semiannually. Second, effective management can control interest-rate risk by varying the average maturity of the fund's portfolio. If management believes that interest rates are moving downward, the fund will load up heavily on long-term obligations. If rates do decline, long-term bonds will appreciate more than their short- and medium-term counterparts. Conversely, if the manager anticipates rate hikes, average portfolio maturity can be pared down so there will be only modest principal deterioration if rates do go up.

Bond funds have portfolios with a wide range of maturities. Many funds use their names to characterize their maturity structure. Generally, "short term" means that the portfolio has a weighted average maturity of less than five years. "Intermediate" implies an average maturity of five to ten years, and "long term" is over ten years. The longer the maturity is, the greater the change in the fund's price per share (your principal) when interest rates change. Longer-term bond funds are riskier than short-term funds but tend to offer higher yields. The top holdings of government bond funds are GNMAs and U.S. Treasury notes (T-notes) of varying maturities.

The weighted maturity date of the bonds within this group averages six years, with a typical coupon rate of 6.3 percent (the coupon rate represents the interest that the corporation or government pays out annually on a per-bond basis)—figures that are virtually identical to the corporate bond category. These funds have a standard deviation of 3.4 percent—again the figure is almost identical to that for corporate bonds. This means that corporate and government bonds have similar volatilities.

Historical returns over the past three, five, ten, and fifteen years for government bond funds are shown here. All of the figures shown are *compound annual* rates of return (all periods ending December 31, 2001).

category	3 years	5 years	10 years	15 years
government bond funds	5.3%	6.3%	6.2%	7.2%
high-yield bond funds	-1.1%	1.4%	6.6%	6.6%
CPI (rate of inflation)	2.5%	2.2%	2.5%	3.2%
convertible funds	6.5%	8.8%	10.9%	9.2%
utility funds	-0.6%	8.0%	9.2%	10.0%

Like corporate bond funds, government funds provide a high yield that is fully taxable on the federal level and should be sheltered whenever possible. Interest from direct obligations of the U.S. government—T-bonds, T-notes, T-bills, EE bonds, HH bonds, and I bonds—are exempt from state and local income taxes. This means that a part of the income you receive from funds that include such securities is exempt from *state* taxes.

Growth. These funds seek capital appreciation with dividend income as a distant secondary concern. Investors who are attracted to growth funds are aiming to sell stock at a profit; they are not normally income oriented. If you are interested in current income you will want to look at Appendix D, "Systematic Withdrawal Plan."

Growth funds are attracted to equities from large well-established corporations. Unlike aggressive growth funds, growth funds may end up holding large cash positions during market declines or when investors are nervous about recent economic or market activities. The typical p/e ratio for stocks in this category is 31, the same as the S & P 500. This group of funds also has an average beta of 1, which means that it has the same *market risk* as the S & P 500.

The standard deviation for growth funds is 24 percent. This means that the expected return for any given year will vary by 24 percentage points. As an example, if you were expecting a 12 percent annual return, annual returns would probably range between negative 12 percent and positive 36 percent (12 percent plus or minus 24 percent).

Historical returns over the past three, five, ten, and fifteen years for growth and small-company stock funds are shown here. All of the figures shown are *compound annual* rates of return (all periods ending December 31, 2001).

category	3 years	5 years	10 years	15 years
growth funds	1.8%	9.3%	11.3%	12.3%
small-company stock funds	9.5%	9.2%	12.1%	12.3%
S & P 500	-1.0%	10.7%	12.9%	13.7%
growth & income funds	0.8%	9.0%	11.6%	11.6%
global stock funds	1.3%	5.3%	8.4%	9.1%

Technology (21 percent of the typical portfolio), service (14 percent), financial (17 percent), and health stocks (16 percent) dominate the composition of growth funds.

Growth and Income. With a name like this, you would think that this category of mutual funds is almost equally as concerned with income as it is with growth. The fact is, growth and income funds have an average dividend yield of just 0.6 percent. This boost in income is due to the small holdings in bonds and convertibles possessed by most growth and income funds.

The typical p/e ratio for stocks in this category is 28, versus 31 for the S & P 500. This group of funds has an average beta of 0.85, meaning that its *market-related risk* is 15 percent less than that of the general market, as measured by the S & P 500.

The standard deviation for growth and income funds is 17 percent, compared to 24 percent for the average growth fund. This means that, as a group, growth and income funds have slightly more predictable returns than growth funds.

For the purposes of this book, a second category, "equity-income funds," has been combined with growth and income. Equity-income funds have a lower standard deviation (14.5 percent compared to 17.1 percent for growth and income funds), a higher yield (1.3 percent compared to 0.6 percent), and a lower beta (0.63 compared to 0.85 for growth and income funds).

The typical growth and income fund is divided as follows: 88 percent in common stocks (4 percent of which is in foreign stock), 4 percent in cash, 3 percent in bonds, and 1 percent in other assets. The typical equity-income fund is divided as follows: 84 percent in common stocks (4 percent of which is in foreign stock), 9 percent in bonds, 4 percent in cash, and 3 percent in other assets. The typical p/e ratio for stocks in this category is 25.

Historical returns over the past three, five, ten, and fifteen years for growth and income funds are shown here. All of the figures shown are average *annual* rates of return (all periods ending December 31, 2001).

category	3 years	5 years	10 years	15 years
growth & income funds	0.8%	9.0%	11.6%	11.6%
equity-income funds	2.2%	8.5%	11.2%	11.1%
growth funds	1.8%	9.3%	11.3%	12.3%
balanced funds	2.2%	7.5%	9.3%	10.0%
foreign stock funds	-1.2%	2.2%	6.2%	7.2%

Technology, financial, industrial cyclicals, and service stocks dominate growth and income funds, representing over half of the typical portfolio.

Health Care. Health-care funds can invest in biotechnology, HMOs, pharmaceuticals, hospitals, nursing home care, and medical-device makers. A small number of the funds in this sector concentrate on one or two areas such as the riskier biotech or the more conservative service providers.

For the twelve months ending January 2002, the average health-care fund lost 8 percent even though the group outperformed the S & P 500 by more than 16 percentage points during this period. The past year was mixed-to-negative for this sector. At the beginning of 2001, pharmaceutical and biotechnology issues suffered as investors shifted money into more cyclical than value-oriented sectors. During the final months of 2001, the sector rallied but then fell again at the beginning of 2002. The most recent decline was most likely due to investors shying away from the more speculative biotech segment of health care, FDA delays in new-drug approval, as well as lost sales from generic competition. Despite these short-term negatives, this sector offers tremendous promise in the future.

Over the past twenty years, ending January 31, 2002, the average annualized return of health-care funds was 17.2 percent versus 15.2 percent for the S & P 500. During the past fourteen years, the best year for this sector was 2000 (47 percent) and the worst year was 1992 (-11 percent). Over the past five years, the best year was also 2000 (47 percent) and the worst year was 2001 (-6 percent).

The typical p/e ratio for stocks in this category is 40, a figure that is higher than the p/e ratio for the S & P 500. This group of funds also has an average beta of 0.4, which means that it has 60 percent less *market risk* than the S & P 500.

The standard deviation for health-care funds is 34 percent. Historical returns over the past three, five, ten, and fifteen years for health-care stock funds are shown here. All of the figures shown are *compound annual* rates of return (all periods ending December 31, 2001).

category	3 years	5 years	10 years	15 years
health-care funds	15.0%	15.2%	13.8%	17.5%
technology funds	-1.2%	9.2%	16.6%	16.7%
S & P 500	-1.0%	10.7%	12.9%	13.7%
aggressive growth	3.9%	7.4%	9.7%	10.7%
real estate funds	10.1%	6.2%	10.0%	8.9%

High-Yield. These funds generally invest in lower-rated corporate debt instruments. Bonds are characterized as either "bank quality," also known as "investment grade," or "junk." Investment-grade bonds are bonds rated AAA, AA, A, or BAA; junk bonds are instruments rated less than BAA: BA, B, CCC, CC, C, and D. High-yield bonds, also referred to as junk bonds, offer investors higher yields in exchange for the additional risk of default. High-yield bonds are subject to less interest-rate risk than regular corporate or government bonds. However, when the economy slows or people panic, these bonds can quickly drop in value.

The average weighted maturity date of the bonds within this group is just over six years, a figure similar to that for high-quality corporate and government bond funds. The typical coupon rate is 9 percent. (The coupon rate represents what the corporation pays out annually on a per-bond basis.) When it comes to high-yield bonds, investors would be wise to accept a lower yield in return for more stability of principal and appreciation potential. As with income funds, corporate funds provide a high yield that is fully taxable and should be sheltered whenever possible.

The standard deviation for high-yield bond funds is 8.6 percent, a figure that is more than twice the rate of corporate and government bond funds as a whole but less than balanced (11 percent) and more than global bond funds (8.0 percent). Historical returns over the past three, ten, and fifteen years for high-yield corporate bond funds are shown here. All of the figures shown are *compound annual* rates of return (all periods ending December 31, 2001).

category	3 years	5 years	10 years	15 years
high-yield bond funds	-1.1%	1.4%	6.6%	6.6%
corporate bond funds	5.2%	6.2%	6.5%	7.5%
government bond funds	5.3%	6.3%	6.2%	7.2%
world bond funds	4.4%	3.1%	4.7%	6.3%
balanced funds	2.2%	7.5%	9.3%	10.1%

Metals and Natural Resources. Metals funds invest in precious metals and mining stocks from around the world. The majority of these stocks are located in North America; South Africa and Australia are the only other major players. Most of these companies specialize in gold mining. Some funds own gold and silver bullion outright. Direct ownership of the metal is considered to be a more conservative posture than owning stocks of mining companies; these stocks are more volatile than the metal itself.

Metals funds, also known as gold funds, are the most speculative group represented in this book. They are considered to be a sector or specialty fund in that they are only able to invest in a single industry or country. Metals funds enjoy international diversification but are still narrowly focused; the limitations of the fund are what make it so unpredictable. Usually, fund management can invest in only three things: mining stocks, direct metal ownership (bullion or coins), and cash equivalents.

Despite their volatile nature, gold funds are included in the book because they can actually reduce portfolio risk. Why? The answer is that gold and other investments often move in opposite directions. For example, when government bonds are moving down in value, gold funds often increase in value. What could otherwise be viewed as a wild investment becomes somewhat tamer when included as part of a diversified portfolio.

The typical dividend for metal funds is 1.2 percent. The typical p/e ratio for stocks in this category is 22, about 30 percent less than the S & P 500 (p/e ratio of 31).

This group of funds has an average beta of 0.2, meaning that its stock market-related risk is modest—but do not let this fool you. We are only talking about stock market risk. Beta focuses on that portion of risk that investors cannot reduce by further diversification in U.S. stocks. Metals funds, as shown by their wild track record, are anything but conservative. A 0.2 beta indicates that movement in this category has little to do with the direction of the S & P 500; therefore, portfolio risk may be reduced by diversification into this category. The standard deviation for metals funds is 29 percent, versus a standard deviation of 60 percent for technology funds and 31 percent for emerging markets funds.

Another category, natural resources, has been combined with metals funds for this book. As the name implies, natural resources funds are commodity-driven, just as metals funds are heavily influenced by two commodities: gold and silver. In the case of natural resources funds, the prices of oil, gas, and timber are the driving force. Natural resources funds invest in companies that are involved with the discovery, exploration, development, refinement, storage, and transportation of one or more of these three natural resources. The standard deviation for this group is 32 percent, beta is 0.7, and the p/e ratio is 21.

Historical returns over the past three, five, ten, and fifteen years for metals and natural resources funds are shown here. All of the figures shown are *compound annual* rates of return (all periods ending December 31, 2001).

category	3 years	5 years	10 years	15 years
metals funds	1.7%	-11.7%	-3.2%	-1.3%
aggressive growth funds	3.9%	7.4%	9.7%	10.7%
natural resources funds	13.8%	3.1%	9.2%	8.6%
European funds	-1.2%	5.4%	8.8%	7.1%
CPI (rate of inflation)	2.5%	2.2%	2.5%	3.2%

Money Market. These funds invest in short-term money market instruments such as bank CDs, T-bills, and commercial paper. By maintaining a short average maturity and investing in high-quality instruments, money market funds are able to maintain a stable $1 net asset value. Since money market funds offer higher yields than a bank's insured money market deposit accounts, they are a very attractive haven for savings or temporary investment dollars. Like bond funds, money market funds come in both taxable and tax-free versions. Reflecting their tax-free status, municipal money market funds pay lower before-tax yields than taxable money market funds but can offer higher returns on an after-tax basis.

Since the price per share of taxable money market funds always stays at $1, interest is shown by the accumulation of additional shares. (For example, at the beginning of the year you may have 1,000 shares, and by the end of the year, 1,050. The fifty-share increase, or $50, represents interest.) There are no such things as capital gains or unrecognized gains in a money market fund. The entire return, or yield, is fully taxable (except in the case of a tax-free money market fund where your gain or return would always be exempt from federal taxes and possibly state income taxes as well).

These funds are designed as a place to park your money for a relatively short period, in anticipation of a major purchase such as a car or house, or until conditions appear more favorable for stocks, bonds, and/or real estate. There has only been one money market fund, now defunct, that has ever lost money for its investors (most of whom were bankers).

There are approximately 900 taxable money market funds and 450 tax-exempt money market funds. By far the largest money market fund is the Merrill Lynch CMA Money Fund ($68 billion). As of December 31, 2000, the ten largest money market funds controlled close to $350 billion and had an average maturity of fifty-eight days. The five highest-yielding taxable money market funds as of the middle of 2000 were Strong Investors Money Fund (5.6 percent over the past twelve months), Scudder Premium Money Market Shares (5.5 percent), OLDE Premium Plus MM Series (5.4 percent), Zurich YieldWise Government Money Fund (5.4 percent), and Aon Money Market Fund (5.4 percent).

The standard deviation for money market funds is lower than any other category of mutual funds and is well under 1 percent. Historical returns over the past three, five, ten, and fifteen years for taxable and tax-free money market funds are shown here. All of the figures shown are *compound annual* rates of return (all periods ending December 31, 2001).

category	3 years	5 years	10 years	15 years
money market funds	4.7%	4.8%	4.5%	n/a
tax-free money market funds	2.8%	2.9%	2.8%	n/a
government money market funds	4.6%	4.8%	4.4%	n/a
government bond funds	5.3%	6.3%	6.2%	7.2%
CPI (rate of inflation)	2.5%	2.2%	2.5%	3.2%

Municipal Bonds. Also known as tax-free, these funds are made up of tax-free debt instruments issued by states, counties, districts, or political subdivisions. Interest from municipal bonds is normally exempt from federal income tax. In almost all states, interest is also exempt from state and local income taxes if the portfolio is made up of issues from the investor's state of residence, a U.S. territory (Puerto Rico, the U.S. Virgin Islands, etc.), or the District of Columbia.

Until the early 1980s, municipal bonds were almost as sensitive to interest rate changes as corporate and government bonds. During the past several years, however, tax-free bonds have taken on a new personality. Now when interest rates change, municipal bonds exhibit only one-half to one-third the price change that occurs with similar funds comprised of corporate or government issues. This decreased volatility is due to a smaller supply of municipal bonds and the elimination of almost all tax shelters, which has increased the popularity of tax-free bonds.

Three kinds of events may result in tax liability for every mutual fund except money market funds. The first two events described are ones that cannot be controlled by the investor while the final event is determined solely by the shareholder or investor (you).

First, when bonds or stocks are sold in the fund portfolio for a profit (or loss), a capital gain (or capital loss) occurs. These gains and losses are passed down to the shareholder. Tax-free bond funds are not immune from capital gains taxes (or capital losses).

Second, interest and/or dividends paid by the securities within the fund are also passed on to shareholders (investors). As already mentioned, interest from municipal bonds is free from federal income taxes and, depending on the fund, may also be exempt from state income taxes. Municipal bond funds do not own stocks or convertibles, so they never throw off dividends.

Third, a taxable event may occur when you sell or exchange shares of a fund for cash or to go into another fund. As an example, suppose you bought into the fund at X dollars and cents per share. If you sell or exchange shares for X plus Y, then there will be a taxable gain (on Y, in this example). If you sell or exchange shares for a loss (X minus Y), then there will be a capital loss. Municipal bond funds are subject to such capital gains or losses. Fortunately, you are never required to sell off shares in any mutual fund, the decision about when and how much is always yours.

The standard deviation for municipal bond funds is 4 percent, meaning that this category's volatility is virtually identical to corporate bonds and government securities. Historical returns over the past three, five, ten, and fifteen years for municipal funds are shown here. All of the figures shown are *compound annual* rates of return (all periods ending December 31, 2001).

category	3 years	5 years	10 years	15 years
municipal bond funds	3.2%	4.6%	5.7%	6.3%
Calif. municipal bond funds	3.7%	5.0%	6.0%	6.3%
municipal bond funds				
(single state)	3.4%	4.8%	5.8%	6.3%
government bond funds	5.3%	6.3%	6.2%	7.2%
CPI (rate of inflation)	2.5%	2.2%	2.5%	3.2%

Real Estate. This specialized group of mutual funds mostly invests in real estate investment trusts (REITs) of various types (e.g., equity, mortgage-backed, and hybrid). There are a number of different types of REITs that are categorized by type and geographical location. The most common REITs are apartment, factory-outlet, health care, hotel, industrial, office, and shopping centers.

One of the more interesting ongoing debates is whether an investor should own real estate outright (rental property, strip shopping center, apartments, etc.) or indirectly through a mutual fund and/or REIT. Advocates of REITs point out that they have outperformed direct real estate investing over the past twenty years, although most of the difference is because REITs carry leverage of 30 percent or more, which adds to risk. Yet, even if the returns were the same, which they were from 1991 to 2001 according to a study by Wilshire Associates, direct ownership includes the following negatives: possible employees to manage the property, illiquidity (buying and selling can take months), lack of accountability (the appraisal process masks the volatility of direct investing), and lack of transparency of a public company.

Public and private pension funds have about $200 billion invested in real estate, versus a REIT industry capitalization of roughly $168 billion. According to Blumberg, the REIT Index had a return of -19 percent in 1998, -7 percent in 1999, 26 percent in 2000, and 16 percent in 2001.

For the twelve months ending January 2002, the average real-estate fund gained more than 8 percent. The sector outperformed the S & P 500 by 25 percentage points during this period. The bear market along with a low-interest-rate environment translated into an almost ideal environment for real estate and real estate investment trusts (REITs). Within the sector there was quite a bit of return disparity, the more conservative segment of the real-estate market rallied sporadically while the more speculative issues experienced large gains. During the first part of 2002, the sector was led by REITs that provided high income. Outlook for the next year or so remains mixed. Economic recovery should be a positive influence on rents while possible overbuilding by developers and the threat of rising interest rates are potential negatives. Regardless of one's outlook, REITs and real-estate funds remain a meaningful way to diversify a portfolio while enjoying a high current income stream.

Over the past ten years, ending January 31, 2002, the average annualized return of real estate funds was 9.8 percent versus 13.0 percent for the S & P 500. During the past fourteen years, the best year for this sector was 1991 (32 percent) and the worst year was 1998 (-17 percent). Over the past five years, the best year was also 2000 (24 percent) and the worst year was 1998 (-17 percent).

The typical p/e ratio for stocks in this category is 15, a figure that is much lower than the p/e ratio for the S & P 500. This group of funds also has an average beta of 0.2, which means that it has 80 percent less market risk than S & P 500.

The standard deviation for real estate funds is 15 percent. Historical returns over the past three, five, ten, and fifteen years for real estate funds are shown here. All of the figures shown are *compound annual* rates of return (all periods ending December 31, 2001).

category	3 years	5 years	10 years	15 years
real estate funds	10.1%	6.2%	10.0%	8.9%
technology funds	-1.2%	9.2%	16.6%	16.7%
S & P 500	-1.0%	10.7%	12.9%	13.7%
aggressive growth	3.9%	7.4%	9.7%	10.7%
health-care funds	15.0%	15.2%	13.8%	17.5%

Technology. It is difficult to identify a segment of the economy that has not been profoundly influenced by technology. From traditional manufacturers developing e-commerce strategies to emerging companies with revolutionary new products, technology is changing businesses and creating unprecedented opportunities for investors. Technology represents nearly half of all business equipment spending by U.S. companies. Consumer spending on information technology as a percentage of disposable income has nearly tripled in the past twelve years. Today, just over 19 percent of the S & P 500 Index is made up of technology stocks, up from just 7 percent in 1990.

Historically, because of its volatility, most investors have considered the technology sector a "speculative sector play." Consequently, they have either limited their holdings in this area to a small portion of their overall portfolios or avoided them altogether.

Having perfect twenty-twenty hindsight, this strategy would not have appeared to be misplaced for the years 2000 and 2001 when technology funds had returns of -31 percent and -38 percent, respectively. Keep in mind though, that avoiding this sector during the 1990s would have meant missing out on spectacular performance and nothing but positive returns, including 52 percent and 133 percent in 1998 and 1999, respectively.

These funds invest in common stocks of all aspects of technology, including computer hardware and software, telecommunications, semiconductor, networking, data storage, data security, fiber optics, wireless, and the Internet.

Technology is changing the way we work, live, and think. As the computer revolution evolves into the Internet and the wireless revolution, technology continues to amaze and dazzle us. This is true for investors in technology stocks as well. However, this excitement comes with significant risk.

The typical p/e ratio for stocks in this category is 46, versus 31 for the S & P 500. This group of funds has an average beta of 2.2, meaning that its market-related risk is over double that of the general market, as measured by the S & P 500. The standard deviation for technology funds is 60 percent, a figure that is significantly higher than any other category in the book. The next closest category, aggressive growth funds, has a standard deviation of 37. This means that, as a group, technology funds are expected to have less predictable returns than any other fund or category in the book.

Historical returns over the past three, five, ten, and fifteen years for technology funds are shown here. All of the figures shown are *compound annual* rates of return (all periods ending December 31, 2001).

category	3 years	5 years	10 years	15 years
technology funds	-1.2%	9.2%	16.6%	16.7%
aggressive growth funds	3.9%	7.4%	9.7%	10.7%
growth funds	1.8%	9.3%	11.3%	12.3%
S & P 500	-1.0%	10.7%	12.9%	13.7%
utility funds	-0.6%	8.0%	9.2%	10.0%

Utilities. These funds invest in common stocks of utility companies. A small percentage of the funds' assets are invested in bonds. Investors opposed to or in favor of nuclear power can seek out funds that avoid or buy into such utility companies by reviewing a fund's semiannual report or by telephoning the fund using its toll-free phone number.

If you like the usual stability of a bond fund but want more appreciation potential, then utility funds are for you. Since these funds are interest-rate sensitive, their performance somewhat parallels that of bonds but is also influenced by the stock market. The large dividend stream provided by utility funds makes them less risky than other categories of stock funds. Recession-resistant demand for electricity, gas, and other utilities translates into a comparatively steady stream of returns.

Since a healthy portion of the total return for utility funds (dividends) cannot be controlled by the investor, these funds are best suited for retirement plans or as part of some other tax-sheltered vehicle. But even if you do not have a qualified retirement plan such as an IRA, pension plan, or tax-sheltered annuity (TSA), utility funds can be a wise choice to lower overall portfolio volatility.

The average p/e ratio for this category is 19, with a standard deviation of 15 percent, a figure that is lower than that of growth and income funds. Utility funds have a beta of 0.5.

Historical returns over the past three, five, ten, and fifteen years for utilities funds are shown here. All of the figures shown are *compound annual* rates of return (all periods ending December 31, 2001).

category	3 years	5 years	10 years	15 years
utility funds	-0.6%	8.0%	9.2%	10.0%
balanced	2.2%	7.5%	9.3%	10.1%
multiasset global	3.2%	4.5%	7.7%	6.2%
asset allocation funds	2.4%	7.2%	9.0%	9.0%
convertible funds	6.5%	8.8%	10.9%	9.2%

World Bonds. Although the United States leads the world in outstanding debt, other countries and foreign corporations also issue IOUs as a way of financing projects and operations. As high as our debt seems, it is not out of line when compared to our gross national product (now called gross domestic product, GDP). The ratio of our debt to GDP is lower than any other member of the group of seven. (The other G-7 members are Germany, Japan, Canada, Italy, the United Kingdom, and France.)

International, also known as foreign, bond funds invest in fixed-income securities outside the United States. Global, or world, bond funds invest around the world, including the United States. Foreign bond funds normally offer higher yields than their domestic counterparts but also provide additional risk. Global bonds, on the other hand, provide less risk than a pure U.S. bond portfolio and also enjoy greater rates of return.

Global diversification reduces risk because the major economies around the world do not move up and down at the same time. As the United States climbs out of a recession, Japan may be just entering one, and Germany may still be in the middle of one. When Italy is trying to stimulate its economy by lowering interest rates, Canada may be raising its rates to curtail inflation. By investing in different world bond markets, you ensure that you will not be at the mercy of any one country's political environment or fiscal policy.

The weighted maturity date of the bonds within this group is just over nine years, about three years longer than U.S. government bond funds. Global bond funds have an average coupon rate of 6 percent. As with any investment that throws off a high current income, global and foreign bond funds should be part of a qualified retirement plan or variable annuity whenever possible.

The standard deviation for world bond funds is 8 percent, a low figure but still over twice the typical U.S. government bond fund. Historical returns over the past three, five, ten, and fifteen years for world bond funds are shown here. All of the figures shown are *compound annual* rates of return (all periods ending December 31, 2001).

category	3 years	5 years	10 years	15 years
world bond funds	4.4%	3.1%	4.7%	6.3%
government bond funds	5.3%	6.3%	6.2%	7.2%
corporate bond funds	5.2%	6.2%	6.5%	7.5%
high-yield bond funds	-1.1%	1.4%	6.6%	6.6%
CPI (rate of inflation)	2.5%	2.2%	2.5%	3.2%

All Categories. An inescapable conclusion we can draw from these different tables is that patience usually pays off. The single-digit performers over the past fifteen years have been corporate bonds, government bonds, high-yield bonds, metals (the only negative performer), money markets, municipal bonds, and natural resources. The most important thing left out of all of these tables is risk. However, we could make the case that stocks are not much riskier than bonds when the holding period is ten to fifteen years. The tables also do not take into account the tax advantages of certain investments. Government bonds are exempt from state and local income taxes. (*Note:* This is only true with direct obligations of the United States. It does not apply to GNMAs, FNMAs, or other government-agency issues.) Municipal bonds are exempt from federal income taxes and, depending on the type of tax-free fund as well as your state of residency, may also be exempt from any state or local taxes.

You should never consider money market funds as an investment. Money market funds, T-bills, and bank CDs are places to park your money temporarily. These accounts are best used to earn interest before you make a major purchase, while you are learning about investing in general, or until market conditions change. Almost all investors should avoid metals funds. The track record of this category is wild and usually negative. It is doubtful that a strong case can be made for metals. You can diversify and reduce your risk by owning other categories such as money market, one or more of the bond categories, and even possibly natural resources.

Compound Annual Returns for the 15-Year Period Ending December 31, 2001

category	15 years	category	15 years
aggressive growth	10.7%	growth & income	11.6%
asset allocation	9.0%	high-yield	6.6%
balanced	10.1%	metals (only)	-1.3%
convertible bond	9.2%	money market	6.0%
corporate bond	7.5%	multiasset global	6.2%
equity-income	11.1%	municipal bond	6.3%
European stocks	7.1%	natural resources	8.6%
foreign	7.2%	small company	12.6%
global equity	9.1%	technology	16.7%
government bond	7.2%	utilities	10.0%
growth	12.3%	world bond	6.3%
average for all categories 8.7%			

A common theme throughout this book is that, given time, equity (the different stock categories) always outperforms debt (the different bond categories). This does not mean that all of your money should be in the equity categories. Not everyone has the same level of patience or time horizon. It does mean that the great majority of investors need to review their portfolios and perhaps begin to emphasize domestic and even foreign stocks more.

VI.
Which Funds Are Best for You?

When asked what they are looking for, investors typically say, "I want the best." This could mean that they are looking for the most safety and greatest current income or the highest total return. There is no single "best" fund. The top-performing fund may have incredible volatility, causing shareholders to redeem their shares at the first sign of trouble. The "safest" fund may be devastated by risks not previously considered: inflation and taxes.

As you have already seen, there are several different categories of mutual funds, ranging from tax-free money market accounts to precious metals. During one period or another, each of these categories has dominated some periodical's "ten best funds" list. These impressive scores may only last a quarter, six months, or a year. The fact is that no one knows what the next best-performing category or individual fund will be.

For some fund groups—such as international stocks, growth, growth and income, and aggressive growth—the reign may last for several years. For other categories—such as money market, government bond, and precious metals—the glory may last a year or even less. Trying to outguess, chart, or follow a financial guru in order to determine the next trend is a fool's paradise. The notion that anyone has special insights into the marketplace is sheer nonsense. Countless neutral and lengthy studies attest to this fact. If this is the case, what should we do?

Step 1: Categories That Have Done Well Historically
The first step is to look at those generic categories of investments that have done well over long periods. A time frame of at least fifteen or twenty years is recommended. True, your investment horizon may be a fraction of this, but keep in mind two points. First, fifteen or twenty years includes good as well as bad times. Second, bad results cannot be hidden when you are studying the long term. Even the investor looking at a one- or two-year holding period should ask, "Do I want something that does phenomenally well one out of every five years, or do I want something that has a very good return in eight or nine out of every ten years?" Unless you are a gambler, the answer is obvious.

All investments can be categorized as either debt or equity instruments. Debt instruments in this book include corporate bonds, government bonds, high-yield bonds, international bonds, money market accounts, and municipal bonds. Equity instruments include growth, growth and income, international stocks, metals, and utility funds. Four other categories are hybrid instruments: asset allocation; balanced, convertible, and multiasset global funds. In this book, these four categories are combined under the heading "balanced."

Throughout history, equity has outperformed debt. The longer the time frame reviewed, the better equity vehicles look. Over the past half century, the worst fifteen-year holding period performance for stocks (+4.3 percent per year) was very similar to the average fifteen-year holding period performance for long-term government bonds (+4.9 percent per year). For twenty-year holding periods, the worst period for common stocks has been more than 40 percent better than the average for long-term government bonds. Indeed, stocks have outperformed bonds in every decade. Look at it this way: Would you rather have loaned Henry Ford or Bill Gates the money to start their companies, or would you rather have given them money in return for a piece of the action?

Step 2: Review Your Objectives

Decide what you are trying to do with your portfolio. Everyone wants one of the following: growth, current income, or a combination of growth and income. Don't assume that if you are looking for current income, your money should go into a bond or money market fund. There is a way to set up an equity fund so it will give you a high monthly income. This is known as a "systematic withdrawal plan" and is discussed in Appendix D. The growth-oriented investor, on the other hand, should consider certain categories of debt instruments or hybrid securities to help add more stability to a portfolio.

Objectives are certainly important, but so is the element of time. The shorter the time frame and the greater the need for assurances, the greater the likelihood that debt instruments should be used. A growth investor who is looking at a single-year time frame and wants a degree of safety is probably better off in a series of bond and/or money market accounts. On the other hand, the longer the commitment, the better equities look. Thus, even a cautious investor who has a life expectancy (or whose spouse has a life expectancy) of ten years or more should seriously consider having at least a moderate portion of his or her portfolio in equities.

A retired couple in their sixties should realize that one or both of them will probably live at least fifteen more years. Since this is the case, and since we know that equities have almost always outperformed bonds when looking at a horizon of ten years or more, their emphasis should be in this area.

The conservative investor may say that stocks are too risky. True, the day-to-day or year-to-year volatility of equities can be quite disturbing. However, it is also true that the medium- and long-term effects of inflation and the resulting diminished purchasing power of a fixed-income investment are even more devastating. At least with an equity there is a better than fifty-fifty chance that it will go up in value. In the case of inflation, what are the chances that the cost of goods and services will go down during the next one, three, five, or ten years? The answer is "not likely."

Step 3: Ascertain Your Risk Level

No investment is worthwhile if you stay awake at night worrying about it. If you do not already know or are uncertain about your risk level, contact your financial advisor. These professionals usually have some kind of questionnaire that you can answer. Your responses will give a good indication of which investments are proper for you and which should be avoided. If you do not deal with a financial advisor, take the following test. Your score, and what it means, are shown at the end of the questionnaire.

Test for Determining Your Risk Level

1.   "I invest for the long term, five to ten years or more. The final result is more important than daily, monthly, or annual fluctuations in value."

(10) Totally disagree. (20) Willing to accept some volatility, but not loss of principal. (30) Could accept a moderate amount of yearly fluctuation in return for a good total return. (40) Would accept an occasional negative year if the final results were good. (50) Agree.

2.   Rank the importance of current income.

(10) Crucial, the exact amount must be known. (20) Important, but I am willing to have the amount vary each period. (30) Fairly important, but other aspects of investing are also of concern. (40) Only a modest amount of income is needed. (50) Current income is unimportant.

3.   Rank the amount of loss you could tolerate in a single quarter.

(10) None. (20) A little, but over a year's time the total value of the investment should not decline. (30) Consistency of total return is more important than trying to get big gains. (40) One or two quarters of negative returns are the price you must pay when looking at the total picture. (50) Unimportant.

4.   Rank the importance of beating inflation.

(10) Factors such as preservation of principal and current income are much more important. (20) I am willing to have a slight variance in my returns, on a quarterly basis only, in order to have at least a partial hedge against inflation. (30) Could accept some annual volatility in order to offset inflation. (40) I consider inflation to be important, but have mixed feelings about how much volatility I could accept from one year to the next. (50) The long-term effects of inflation are devastating and should not be ignored by anyone.

5.   Rank the importance of beating the stock market over any given two-to-three-year period.

(10) Irrelevant. (20) A small concern. (30) Fairly important. (40) Very important. (50) Absolutely crucial.

Add up your score from questions 1 through 5. Your risk, as defined by your total point score, is as follows: 0–50 points = extremely conservative; 50–100 points =

somewhat conservative; 100–150 points = moderate; 150–200 points = somewhat aggressive; 200–250 points = very aggressive.

Step 4: Review Your Current Holdings

Everyone has heard the expression, "Don't put all your eggs in one basket." This advice also applies to investing. No matter how much we like investment *X*, if a third of our net worth is already in *X*, we probably should not add any more to this investment. After all, there is more than one good investment.

Since no single investment category is the top performer every year, it makes sense to diversify into several fundamentally good categories. By using proper diversification, we have an excellent chance of being number one with a portion of our portfolio every year. Babe Ruth may have hit more home runs than almost anyone, but he also struck out more. As investors, we should be content with consistently hitting doubles and triples.

Trying to hit a homer every time may result in financial ruin. Never lose track of the fact that losses always have a greater impact than gains. An investment that goes up 50 percent the first year and falls 50 percent the next year still has a net loss of 25 percent. This philosophy is emphasized throughout the book.

Step 5: Implementation

There is no such thing as the perfect time to invest. No matter how strongly you or some "expert" individual or publication believes that the market is going to go up or down, no one actually knows.

After you have properly educated yourself is the right time to invest. If you are afraid to take the big plunge, consider some form of dollar-cost averaging (see Appendix C). This is a disciplined approach to investing; it also reduces your risk exposure significantly.

Do read investment books and attend classes. Some people, however, may be tempted to remain on the sidelines indefinitely. For such people, there is no perfect time to invest. If the stock market drops 200 points, they are waiting for the next 100-point drop. If stocks or bonds are up 15 percent, they say things are peaking and they will invest as soon as it drops by 10 percent. If the stock or bond market does drop by that magical figure, these same investors are now certain that it will drop another 10 percent.

This "strategy" is frustrating. More important, it is wrong. You can look back in history and find lots of reasons not to have invested. But the fact is that all of the investments in this book have gone up almost every year. The "wait and see" approach is a poor one; the same reasons for not investing will still exist in the present and throughout the future.

Remember, your money is doing something right now. It is invested somewhere. If it is under the mattress, it is being eaten away by inflation. If it is in a "risk-free" investment, such as an insured savings account, bank CD, or U.S. Treasury bill, it is being subjected to taxation and the cumulative effects of reduced purchasing power. Do not think you can hide by having your money in some safe haven. Once you understand that there can be things worse than market swings, you will become an educated investor who knows there is no such thing as a truly risk-free place or investment.

If you are still not convinced, consider the story of Louie the loser. There is only one thing you can say about Louie's timing: It is always awful. So, it is no surprise that when he decided to invest $10,000 a year in Investment Company of America, he managed to pick the worst possible times. Every year for the past twenty years (1982–2001), he has invested on the very day that the stock market peaked. How has he done? He has over $889,830, which means his money has grown at an average rate of 13.5 percent a year (a cumulative investment of $200,000; twenty years times $10,000 invested each year).

If Louie had had "perfect timing," meaning he invested $10,000 on the worst day of the market each year for the past twenty years, his cumulative $200,000 investment would have grown to $1,114,860, or 14.9 percent annualized.

After asking you a series of questions, your investment advisor can give you a framework within which to operate. Investors who do not have a good advisor may wish to look at the different sample portfolios given here. These general recommendations will provide you with a sense of direction.

The Conservative Investor
15 percent balanced
10 percent utilities
15 percent growth and income (value oriented)
10 percent world bond
20 percent money market or short-term bonds
30 percent intermediate-term municipal or government bonds
    (depending on your tax bracket)

This portfolio would give you a weighting of 33 percent in equities (stocks) and 67 percent in debt instruments (bonds and cash equivalents). Investors who are not in a high federal income tax bracket may wish to avoid municipal bonds completely and use government bonds instead.

If your tax bracket is such that you are not sure whether you should own tax-free or taxable bonds (if, that is, the after-tax return on government bonds is similar to what a similarly maturing high-quality municipal bond pays), lean toward a municipal bond fund. These funds are almost always less volatile than a government bond fund that has the same or a similar average maturity.

The Moderate Investor
10 percent small-company growth (value oriented)
 5 percent balanced/convertibles
10 percent growth (value oriented)
15 percent growth and income (value oriented)
10 percent high-yield
10 percent short-term bonds
10 percent world bonds
15 percent global equities (value oriented)

10 percent health care
5 percent financial

This portfolio would give you a weighting of 67 percent in equities (common stocks) and 33 percent in debt instruments. The figures are a little misleading since high-yield bonds are more of a hybrid investment: part stock and part bond. The price, or value, of high-yield bonds is influenced by economic (macro and micro) news as well as interest rate changes. Whereas government, municipal, and high-quality corporate bonds often react favorably to bad economic news such as a recession, increases in the jobless rate, a slowdown in housing starts, and so on, high-yield bonds have a tendency to view such news positively. Thus, taking into account that high-yield bonds are about halfway between traditional bonds and stocks, the weighting distribution is more in the range of 72 percent equities and 28 percent bonds.

The Aggressive Investor
15 percent aggressive growth
20 percent small-company growth (value oriented)
20 percent growth (value oriented)
10 percent growth and income
15 percent health care
10 percent financial
10 percent real estate

This portfolio would give you a weighting of 100 percent in equities. Bond fund categories, with the possible exception of high-yield and international, are not recommended for the aggressive investor because they usually do not have enough appreciation potential.

Readers of the previous editions of this book may notice that this edition weighs equities (the different stock categories) less than it has in the past. This is because stock valuations as a whole are grossly out of line. The price-earnings ratios of the typical growth fund are at, or slightly higher than, the levels seen at the market's peak during the first quarter of 2000. Value-oriented equities are a much more attractive alternative to growth stocks, using current as well as historical comparisons.

Step 6: Review

After implementation, it is important that you keep track of how you are doing. One of the beauties of mutual funds is that, if you choose a fund with good management, managers will do their job and you can spend your time on something else. Nevertheless, review your situation at least quarterly. Once you feel comfortable with your portfolio, review it only semiannually or annually.

Daily or weekly tracking is pointless. If a particular investment goes up or down 5 percent, that does not mean you should rush out and buy more or sell off. That same investment may do just the opposite the following week or month. By watching your investments too closely, you will be defeating a major attribute of mutual funds: professional management. Presumably these fund managers know a lot more about their particular investments than you do. If they do not, you should either choose another fund or start your own mutual fund.

Step 7: Relax

If you do your homework by reading this book, you will be in fine shape. There are several thousand mutual funds. Some funds are just plain bad. Most mutual funds are mediocre. And, as with everything else in this world, a small portion are truly excellent. This book has taken those thousands of funds and eliminated all of the bad, mediocre, and fairly good. Only excellent mutual funds remain.

If you would like help designing a portfolio or picking a specific fund, telephone the Institute of Business & Finance (1-800-848-2029). The institute will be able to give you the names and telephone numbers of Certified Fund Specialists (CFS) in your area. To become a CFS, an individual must complete a rigorous, one-year educational program, pass a comprehensive exam, adhere to a professional code of ethics, and meet annual continuing education requirements.

VII.
Fund Features

Advantages of Mutual Funds

Listed here are some of the features of mutual funds—advantages not found in other kinds of investments.

Ease of Purchase. Mutual fund shares are easy to buy. For those who prefer to make investment decisions themselves, mutual funds are as close as the telephone or the mailbox. Those who would like help choosing a fund can draw on a wide variety of sources.

Many funds sell their shares through stockbrokers, financial planners, or insurance agents. These representatives can help you analyze your financial needs and objectives and recommend appropriate funds. For these professional services, you may be charged a sales commission, usually referred to as a "load." This charge is expressed as a percentage of the total purchase price of the fund shares. In some cases, there is no initial sales charge, or load, but there may be an annual fee and/or another charge if shares are redeemed during the first few years of ownership.

Other funds distribute their shares directly to the public. They may advertise in magazines and newspapers; most can be reached through toll-free telephone numbers. Because there are no sales agents involved, most of these funds, often called "no loads," charge a much lower fee or no sales commission at all. With these funds, it is generally up to you to do your investment homework.

In order to attract new shareholders, some funds have adopted 12b-1 plans (named after a federal government rule). These plans enable the fund to pay its own distribution costs. Distribution costs are those costs associated with marketing the fund, either through sales agents or through advertising. The 12b-1 fee is charged against fund assets and is paid indirectly by existing shareholders. Annual distribution fees of this type usually range between 0.1 percent and 1.25 percent of the value of the account.

Fees charged by a fund are described in the prospectus. In addition, a fee table listing all transactional fees and all annual fund expenses can be found at the front of the prospectus.

Access to Your Money (Marketability). Mutual funds, by law, must stand ready on any business day to redeem any or all of your shares at their current net asset value (NAV). Of course, the value may be greater or less than the price you originally paid, depending on the market.

To sell shares back to the fund, all you need to do is give the fund proper notification, as explained in the prospectus. Most funds will accept such notification by telephone; some funds require a written request. The fund will then send your check promptly. In most instances, the fund will issue a check when it receives the notification; by law, the fund must send you the check within seven business days. You receive the price your shares are worth on the day the fund gets proper notice of redemption from you. If you own a money market fund, you can also redeem shares by writing checks directly against your fund balance.

Disciplined Investment. The majority of funds allow you to set up what is known as a "check-o-matic plan." Under such a program, a set amount of money is automatically deducted from your checking account each month and sent directly to the mutual fund of your choice. Your bank (or credit union) will not charge you for this service. Mutual funds also offer such programs free of charge. Automatic investment plans can be changed or terminated at any time, again at no charge.

Exchange Privileges. As the economy or your own personal circumstances change, the kinds of funds you hold may no longer be the ones you need. Many mutual funds are part of a "family of funds" and offer a feature called an exchange privilege. Within a family of funds there may be several choices, each with a different investment objective, varying from highly conservative funds to more aggressive funds that carry a higher degree of risk. An exchange privilege allows you to transfer all or part of your money from one of these funds to another. Exchange policies vary from fund to fund. The fee for an exchange is nominal, five dollars or less. For the specifics about a fund's exchange privilege, check the prospectus.

Automatic Reinvestment. You can elect to have any dividends and capital gains distributions from your mutual fund investment turned back into the fund, automatically buying new shares and expanding your current holdings. Most shareholders opt for the reinvestment privilege. There is usually no cost or fee involved.

Automatic Withdrawal. You can make arrangements with the fund to automatically send you, or anyone you designate, checks from the fund's earnings or principal. This system works well for retirees, families who want to arrange for payments to their children at college, or anyone needing monthly income checks. See Appendix D for a more detailed example of how a systematic withdrawal plan works.

Detailed Record Keeping. The fund will handle all the paperwork and record keeping necessary to keep track of your investment transactions. A typical statement will note such items as your most recent investment or withdrawal and any dividends or capital gains paid to you in cash or reinvested in the fund. The fund will also report to you on the tax status of your earnings. If you lose any paperwork, the fund will send you copies of current or past statements.

Retirement Plans. Financial experts have long viewed mutual funds as appropriate vehicles for retirement investing; indeed, they are quite commonly used for this purpose. For retirees over the age of seventy and a half, mutual fund companies will recompute the minimum amount that needs to be taken out each year, as dictated by the IRS. Mutual funds are ideal for Keoghs, IRAs, 401(k) plans, and other employer-sponsored retirement plans. Many funds offer prototype retirement plans and standard IRA agreements. Having your own retirement plan drafted by a law firm would cost you thousands of dollars, not to mention the fees for the updates that would be needed every time the laws change. Mutual funds offer these plans and required updates for free.

Accountability. There are literally dozens of sources that track and monitor mutual funds. It is easy to determine a fund's track record and volatility over several different time periods. Federal regulatory bodies such as the NASD (National Association of Securities Dealers) and the SEC (Securities and Exchange Commission) have strict rules concerning performance figures and what appears in advertisements, brochures, and prospectuses.

Flexibility. Investment choices are almost endless: domestic stocks, foreign debt, international equities, government obligations, money market instruments, convertible securities, short- and intermediate-term bonds, real estate, gold, and natural resources. You are only limited by the choices offered by the fund family or families you are invested in. And because you can move part or all of your money from one mutual fund to another fund within the same family, usually for a minimal transfer fee, your portfolio can become more aggressive, conservative, or moderate with a simple phone call.

Economies of Scale. As a shareholder (investor) in a fund, you automatically get the benefit of reduced transaction charges. Since a fund often buys or sells thousands of shares of stock at a time, it is able to conduct its transactions at dramatically reduced costs. The fees a fund pays are far lower than what you would pay even if you were buying several hundred shares of a stock from a discount broker. The same is true when it comes to bonds. Funds are able to add them to their portfolio without any markup. When you buy a bond through a broker, even a discounter, there is always a markup; it is hidden in the price you pay and sell the bond for. The savings for bond investors ranges anywhere from less than 1 percent all the way up to 5 percent.

Risk Reduction: Importance of Diversification

If there is one ingredient to successful investing that is universally agreed on, it is the benefit of diversification. This concept is also backed by a great deal of research and market experience. The benefit provided by diversification is risk reduction. Risk to investors is frequently defined as volatility of return; in other words, how much an investment's return might vary. Investors prefer returns that are relatively predictable, which is to say, less volatile. On the other hand, they want returns to be high. Diversification eliminates most of the risk without reducing potential returns.

A fund's portfolio manager(s) will normally invest the fund's pool of money in 50 to 150 different securities to spread the fund's holdings over a number of investments. This diversification is an important principle in lessening the fund's overall investment risk. Such diversification is typically beyond the financial capacity of most individual investors. The following table shows the relationship between diversification and investment risk, defined as the variability of annual returns of a stock portfolio.

number of stocks	risk ratio
1	6.6
2	3.8
4	2.4
10	1.6
50	1.1
100	1.0

Note that the variability of return, or risk, associated with holding just one stock is more than six times that of a hundred-stock portfolio. Yet, the increased potential return found in a portfolio made up of a small number of stocks is minimal.

VIII.
Reading a Mutual Fund Prospectus

The purpose of the fund's prospectus is to provide the reader with full and complete disclosure. The prospectus covers the following key points:

- The fund's investment objective: what the managers are trying to achieve
- The investment methods it uses in trying to achieve this objective
- The name and address of its investment advisor and a brief description of the advisor's experience
- The level of investment risk the fund is willing to assume in pursuit of its investment objective
- Any investments the fund will not make (for example, real estate, options, or commodities)
- Tax consequences of the investment for the shareholder
- How to purchase shares of the fund, including the cost of investing
- How to redeem shares
- Services provided, such as IRAs, automatic investment of dividends and capital gains distributions, check writing, withdrawal plans, and any other features
- A condensed financial statement (in tabular form, covering the past ten years, or the period the fund has been in existence, if less than ten years) called "Per-Share Income and Capital Changes" (The fund's performance may be calculated from the information given in this table.)
- A tabular statement of any fees charged by the fund and their effect on earnings over time

IX.
Commonly Asked Questions

Q Are mutual funds a new kind of investment?

No. In fact, they have roots in eighteenth-century Scotland. The first U.S. mutual fund was organized in Boston in 1924. This fund, Massachusetts Investors Trust, is still in existence today. Several mutual fund companies have been in operation for over half a century.

Q. How much money do you need to invest in a mutual fund?

Literally anywhere from a few dollars to several million. Many funds have no minimum requirements for investing. A few funds are open to large institutional accounts only. The vast majority of funds require a minimum investment of between $250 and $1,000.

Q. Do mutual funds offer a fixed rate of return?

No. Mutual funds invest in securities such as stocks, bonds, and money market accounts whose yields and values fluctuate with market conditions.

Mutual funds can make money for their shareholders in three ways. First, they pay their shareholders dividends earned from the fund's investments. Second, if a security held by a fund is sold at a profit, funds pay their shareholders capital gains distributions. And third, if the value of the securities held by the fund increases, the value of each mutual fund share also increases.

In none of these cases, however, can a return be guaranteed. In fact, it is against the law for a mutual fund to make a claim as to its future performance. Ads quoting returns are based on past performance and should not be interpreted as a fixed rate yield. Past performance should not be taken as a predictor of future earnings.

Q. What are the risks of mutual fund investing?

Mutual funds are investments in financial securities with fluctuating values. The value of the securities in a fund's portfolio, for example, will rise and fall according to general economic conditions and the fortunes of the particular companies that issue those securities. Even the most conservative assets, such as U.S. government obligations, will fluctuate in value as interest rates change. These are risks that investors should be aware of when purchasing mutual fund shares.

Q. How can I evaluate a fund's long-term performance?

You can calculate a fund's performance by referring to the section in the prospectus headed "Per-Share Income and Capital Changes." This section will give you the figures you need to compute the annual rates of return earned by the fund each year for the past ten years (or for the life of the fund if less than ten years). There are also several periodicals that track the performance of funds on a regular basis. Or, you can telephone the fund, and they will give you performance figures.

Q. **What's the difference between yield and total return?**

Yield is the income per share paid to a shareholder from the dividends and interest over a specified period. Yield is expressed as a percentage of the current offering price per share.

Total return is a measure of the per-share change in total value from the beginning to the end of a specified period, usually a year, including distributions paid to shareholders. This measure includes income received from dividends and interest, capital gains distributions, and any unrealized capital gains or losses. Total return looks at the whole picture: appreciation (or loss) of principal plus any dividends or income. Total return provides the best measure of overall fund performance; do not be misled by an enticing yield.

Q. **How much does it cost to invest in a mutual fund?**

A mutual fund normally contracts with its management company to provide for most of the needs of a normal business. The management company is paid a fee for these services, which usually include managing the fund's investments.

In addition, the fund may pay directly for some of its costs, such as printing, mailing, accounting, and legal services. Typically, these two annual charges average 1.5 percent. In such a fund you would be paying $10 to $15 a year on every $1,000 invested.

Some fund directors have adopted plans (with the approval of the fund's shareholders) that allow them to pay certain distribution costs (the costs of advertising, for example) directly from fund assets. These costs may range from 0.1 percent to 1.25 percent annually.

There may also be other charges involved—for example, for exchanging shares. Some funds may charge a redemption fee when a shareholder redeems his or her shares, usually within five years of purchasing them. All costs and charges assessed by the fund organization are disclosed in its prospectus.

Q. **Is the management fee part of the sales charge?**

No, the management fee paid by the fund to its investment advisor is for services rendered in managing the fund's portfolio. An average fee ranges from 0.5 percent to 1.0 percent of the fund's total assets each year. As described earlier, the management fee and other business expenses generally total somewhere between 1.0 percent and 1.5 percent. These expenses are paid from the fund's assets and are reflected in the price of the fund shares. In contrast, most sales charges are deducted from your initial investment.

Q. **Is my money locked up for a certain period in a mutual fund?**

Unlike some other types of financial accounts, mutual funds are liquid investments. That means that any shares an investor owns may be redeemed freely on any day the fund is open for business. Since a mutual fund stands ready to buy back its shares at their current net asset value, you always have a buyer for your shares at current market value.

Q. **How often do I get statements from a mutual fund?**

Mutual funds ordinarily send immediate confirmation statements when an investor purchases or redeems (sells) shares. Statements alerting shareholders to reinvested dividends are sent out periodically. At least semiannually, investors also receive statements on the status of the fund's investments. Tax statements, referred to as "substitute 1099s," are mailed annually. Some funds automatically send out quarterly reports.

Q. **I've already purchased shares of a mutual fund. How can I tell how well my investment is doing?**

Figuring out how well your fund is faring is a two-step procedure. First, you need to know how many shares you now own. The *now* is emphasized because if you have asked the fund to plow any dividends and capital gains distributions back into the fund for you, it will do so by issuing you more shares, thereby increasing the value of your investment. Once you know how many shares you own, look up the fund's net assets value (sometimes called the sell or bid price) in the financial section of a major metropolitan daily newspaper. Next, multiply the net asset value by the number of shares you own to figure out the value of your investment as of that date. Compare today's value against your beginning value.

You will need to keep the confirmation statements you receive when you first purchase shares and as you make subsequent purchases in order to compare present value to the original purchase value. You will also need these statements for tax purposes.

Q. **Do investment experts recommend mutual funds for IRAs and other qualified plans?**

Financial experts view many mutual funds as compatible with the long-term objectives of saving for retirement. Indeed, fund shareholders cite this reason for investing more than any other. Many kinds of funds work best when allowed to ride out the ups and downs of market cycles over long periods.

Funds can also offer the owner of an IRA, Keogh, pension plan, 401(k), or 403(b) flexibility. By using the exchange privilege within a family of funds, the investor can shift investments from one kind of security to another in response to changes in personal finances or the economic outlook, or as retirement approaches.

Q. **Are money market funds a good investment?**

No. If I were to recommend an investment to you that lost money in seventeen of the past twenty-five calendar years (adjusted for income taxes and inflation), you would probably balk. Yet, this is the track record of CDs, money market accounts, and T-bills. Money market funds are an excellent place to park your money for the short-term; that is, some period less than two years.

Q. **Why don't more people invest in foreign (international) securities?**

Ignorance. The reality is that foreign securities (stocks and bonds), when added to domestic investments, actually reduce the portfolio's level of risk. Stock and bond markets around the world rarely move up and down at the same time. This random correlation is what helps lower risk and volatility: When U.S. stocks (or bonds) are going down, securities in other parts of the world may well be moving sideways or going up.

Q. **Is standard deviation the correct way to measure risk?**

No. Standard deviation measures volatility (or predictability) of returns. The standard deviation for each of the mutual funds in this book is ranked under the star system next to the heading "predictability of returns." The system used in this book for measuring risk is different, punishing funds for performance that is less than that offered by T-bills, a figure commonly referred to as the "risk-free rate of return." To me, this makes more sense than a system that punishes a fund for volatility by translating its high standard deviation figure as "high risk." This is what most financial writers do, whether the volatility the fund experienced was upward or downward volatility. I have yet to meet an investor who is upset that he or she did better than expected. No one minds upward volatility.

Q. **Why not simply invest in those funds that were the best performers over the past one, three, five, or ten years?**

This would be a big mistake. There is little relationship (or correlation) between the performance of one fund or fund category from one year to the next. This, by the way, is the way most investors and advisors select investments—making this one of the biggest and costliest mistakes one could make. Unfortunately, no one knows what the next best-performing fund or category will be.

Q. **What are you referring to when you talk about "common stocks"?**

Whenever you see the words *common stocks,* they refer to the Standard & Poor's 500 (S & P 500). The S & P 500 is comprised of 500 of many of the largest corporations in the United States, representing several industry groups. As of the middle of 1998, there had been seventy-five changes made to the S & P 500 since the beginning of 1995. The purpose of these changes is to make the index more representative of the U.S. economy and the stock market. As an example, financial stocks now represent 15 percent of the S & P 500 capitalization, up from 8 percent in 1990; technology stocks represent 14 percent, up from 7 percent in 1990 (Microsoft, which was added to the index in 1994, makes up 2.3 percent of the index). In short, the S & P 500 is higher growth, more global, less cyclical, and more diversified than it has ever been (and therefore deserves a higher p/e ratio than in the past).

Q. Speaking of common stocks, what are the odds of making money in the market?

If you think investing in the market is too risky, consider what the odds are for the following:

You will win a state lottery?	1 in 4 million
You will be dealt a royal flush poker hand?	1 in 649,739
Earth will be struck by a huge meteor during your lifetime?	1 in 9,000
You will be robbed this year?	1 in 500
The airlines will lose your luggage?	1 in 186
You will be audited by the IRS?	1 in 100
You will roll dice and get snake eyes?	1 in 36
You will go to Disney World this year?	1 in 9
The next bottled water you buy will be nothing more than tap water?	1 in 4
You will eat out today?	1 in 2
An investment in stocks will make money in any given year?	7 in 10
You will regain the weight you lost by dieting?	9 in 10

Source: *What the Odds Are,* by Les Krantz (Harper Perennial, 1992)

X.
How the 100 Best Funds Were Determined

With an entry field that numbers more than 13,000, it is no easy task to determine the 100 best mutual funds. Magazines and newspapers report on the "best" by relying on performance figures over a specific period, usually one, three, five, or ten years. Investors often rely on these sources and invest accordingly, only to be disappointed later.

Studies from around the world bear out what investors typically experience: that there is no correlation between the performance of a stock or bond from one year to the next. The same can be said for individual money managers—and sadly, for most mutual funds.

The criteria used to determine the 100 best mutual funds are unique and far-reaching. For a fund to be considered for this book, it had to pass several tests. First, all stock and bond funds that have had managers for less than five years were excluded; in the case of money market funds, the only remaining category, the criterion was liberalized since overhead costs have a much greater bearing on net returns than management's expertise.

This first step alone eliminated well over half the contenders. The reason for the cutoff is simple: A fund is often only as good as its manager. An outstanding ten-year track record may be cited in a periodical, but how relevant is this performance if the manager who oversaw the fund left a year or two ago? This criterion was liberalized in selecting money market funds because this category of funds normally requires less expertise.

Second, any fund that places in the bottom (worst) half of its category's risk ranking is excluded. No matter how profitable the finish line looks, the number of investors will be sparse if the fund demonstrates too much negative activity. In most cases, a little performance was gladly given up if a great deal of risk was eliminated. This reflects the book's philosophy that returns must be viewed in relation to the amount of risk that was taken. In most cases the funds described in the book possess outstanding risk management. Those few selected funds where risk control has been less than stellar have shown tremendous performance, and their risky nature has been highlighted to warn the reader.

Virtually all sources measure risk by standard deviation. Determining an investment's standard deviation is not as difficult as you might imagine. First, you calculate the asset's average annual return. Usually, the most recent three years are used, updated each quarter. Once an average annual rate of return is determined, a line is drawn on a graph, representing this return.

Next, the monthly returns are plotted on the graph. Since three years is a commonly accepted time period for such calculations, a total of thirty-six individual points are plotted—one for each month over the past three years. After these points are plotted, the standard deviation can be determined. Quite simply, standard deviation measures the variance of returns from the norm (the line drawn on a graph).

There is a problem in using standard deviation to determine the risk level of any investment, including a mutual fund. The shortcoming of this method is that standard deviation punishes good as well as bad results. An example will help expose the problem.

Suppose there were two different investments, X and Y. Investment X went up almost every month by exactly 1.5 percent but had a few months each year when it went down 1 percent. Investment Y went up only 1 percent most months, but it always went up 6 percent for each of the final months of the year. The standard deviation of Y would be substantially higher than X. It might be so high that we would avoid it because it was classified as "high risk." The fact is that we would love to own such an investment. No one ever minds upward volatility or surprises; it is only negative or downward volatility that is cause for alarm.

The system used for determining risk in this book is not widely used, but it is certainly a fairer and more meaningful measurement. The book's method for determining risk is to see how many months over the past three years a fund underperformed what is popularly referred to as a "risk-free vehicle," such as a bank CD or U.S. Treasury bill. The more months a fund falls below this safe return, the greater the fund will be punished in its risk ranking.

Third, the fund must have performed well for the past three and five years. A one- or two-year time horizon could be attributed to luck or nonrecurring events. A ten- or fifteen-year period would certainly be better, if not for the reality that the overwhelming majority of funds are managed by a different person today than they were even six years ago. More disturbing is the fact that investors do not stay with a fund for five years or more.

Finally, the fund must either possess an excellent risk-adjusted return or have had superior returns with no more than average levels of risk. It is assumed that most readers are equally concerned with risk and reward. Thus, the foundation of the text is based on which mutual funds have the best risk-adjusted returns.

Sadly, some funds were excluded, despite their superior performance and risk control, because they were either less than five years old, had new management, or were closed to new investors. A few funds in this edition have excellent returns with poorer-than-average levels of risk or had a risk level that was lower than its respective category average. The reasons that a handful of these funds were still included are evident when you read about them later in the book.

XI.
The 100 Best Funds

This section describes the 100 very best funds. As discussed, the methodology used to narrow down the universe of funds is based on performance, risk, and management.

Every one of these 100 funds is a superlative choice. However, there must still be a means to compare and rank each of the funds within its peer group. Each fund is first categorized by its investment objective. The category breakdown is as follows:

category of mutual fund	number
aggressive growth	10
balanced	8
corporate bond	6
financial	2
global equity	7
government bond	5
growth	10
growth & income	8
health care	2
high-yield bonds	5
metals/natural resources	5
money market	11
municipal bonds	9
real estate	2
technology	2
utilities	4
world bonds	4
total	**100 funds**

There are five areas to be ranked: total return, risk/volatility, management, tax minimization (current income in the case of bond, hybrid, and money market funds), and expense control. Of these five classifications, management, risk/volatility, and total return are the most important.

The track record of a fund is only as good as its management, which is why extensive space is given to this section for each fund. The areas of concern are the length of time the manager, or team, has overseen the fund, and management's background and investment philosophy.

The risk/volatility of the fund is the second biggest concern. Investors like to invest in things that have somewhat predictable results—that aren't up 60 percent one year and down 25 percent the next. A few such highly volatile funds are included, but the risk associated with such a fund is clearly highlighted, informing the prospective investor.

Total return was the third concern. When all is said and done, people like to make lots of money with an acceptable level of risk, or at least get decent returns by taking little, if any, risk. This is also known as the risk-adjusted return. So, although the very safest funds within each category were preferred, this safety had to be combined with impressive returns.

The fourth category, current income, was of lesser importance. Income is important to a lot of people but often gets in the way of selecting the proper investment; preservation of capital should also be considered. There is a better way to get current income than to rely on monthly dividend or interest checks. This is known as a systematic withdrawal plan (SWP). A sixty-six-year example of a SWP is shown in Appendix D. Current income-oriented investors will truly be amazed when they see how such a system works.

In the case of equity funds, "tax minimization" was substituted for the category "current income." This was done for two reasons. First, there is no reason a fund whose objective is capital appreciation should be punished simply because it does not throw off a high dividend. Once you are familiar with the benefits of using a systematic withdrawal plan, you will no longer care whether a certain aggressive growth or even growth and income fund pays much in the form of dividends. Second, unless your money is sheltered in a qualified retirement plan (IRA, pension plan, etc.), income taxes are a real concern. Funds should be rewarded for minimizing shareholder tax liability. This is why every mutual fund in the book is rated, one way or another, when it comes to personal income taxes.

Tax-conscious investors want to downplay current income as much as possible. For them, a high current income simply means paying more in taxes. For other categories—such as growth and income, utilities, and balanced—a healthy current income stream often translates into lower risk. And for still other categories—such as corporate bonds, government bonds, international bonds, money market, and municipal bonds—current income is, and rightfully should be, a major determinant for selection.

The final category, expenses, rates how effective management is in operating the fund. High expense ratios for a given category mean that the advisors are either too greedy or simply do not know or care about running an efficient operation. The actual expenses incurred by a fund are not directly seen by the client, but such costs are deducted from the portfolio's gross returns, which is important.

In addition to looking at the expense ratio of a fund, the turnover rate is studied. The turnover rate shows how often the fund buys and sells its securities. There is a real cost when such a transaction occurs. These transaction costs, also known as commissions, are borne by the fund and eat into the gross return figures. Expense ratios do not include transaction costs incurred when management decides to replace or add a security. Thus, expense ratios do not tell the whole story. By scrutinizing the turnover rate, the rankings take into account excessive trading. A fund's turnover rate may represent a larger true cost to the investor than the fund's expense ratio.

Each fund is ranked in each of these five categories. The rating ranges from zero to five points (stars) in each category. The points can be transcribed as follows: zero points = poor, one point = fair, two points = good, three points = very good, four points = superior, and five points = excellent.

All of the rankings for each fund are based on how the fund fared against its peer group category in the book. Thus, even though a given rating may only be fair or even poor, it is within the context of the category and its peers that have made the book—a category that only includes the very best. There is a strong likelihood that a fund in the book that is given a low score in one category would still rate as great when compared to the entire universe of funds or even compared to other funds within the same category but not included in this book.

Do not be fooled by a low rating for any fund in any of the five areas. All 100 of these funds are true winners. Keep in mind that only about one in 100 funds can appear in the book. The purpose of the ratings is to show the best of the best.

Aggressive Growth Funds

These funds focus strictly on appreciation, with no concern about generating income. Aggressive growth funds strive for maximum capital growth, frequently using trading strategies such as leveraging, purchasing restricted securities, or buying stocks of emerging growth companies. Portfolio composition is almost exclusively U.S. stocks.

Aggressive growth funds can go up in value quite rapidly during favorable market conditions. These funds will often outperform other categories of U.S. stocks during bull markets but suffer greater percentage losses during bear markets.

Over the past fifteen years (ending December 31, 2001), small stocks, which are included in the aggressive growth category, have *underperformed* common stocks by 1.1 percent per year, as measured by the Standard & Poor's 500 Stock Index. From 1987 through 2001, small stocks averaged 12.6 percent, while common stocks averaged 13.7 percent compounded per year. A $10,000 investment in small stocks grew to $59,264 over the past fifteen years; a similar initial investment in the S & P 500 grew to $68,924.

During the past twenty years, there have been sixteen 5-year periods (1982–1986, 1983–1987, etc.). The Small Stock Index, made up from the smallest 20 percent of companies listed on the NYSE, as measured by market capitalization, outperformed the S & P 500 in just five of those sixteen 5-year periods. During these same twenty years, there have been eleven 10-year periods (1982–1991, 1983–1992, etc.). The Small Stock Index has only outperformed the S & P 500 once of those eleven 10-year periods (1992–2001).

During the past thirty years, there have been eleven 20-year periods (1972–1991, 1973–1992, etc.). The Small Stock Index outperformed the S & P 500 in seven of those eleven 20-year periods.

Over the past fifty years, there have been forty-six 5-year periods (1952–1956, 1953–1957, etc.). The Small Stock Index outperformed the S & P 500 in twenty-eight of those forty-six 5-year periods. Over the past fifty years, there have been forty-one 10-year periods (1952–1961, 1953–1962, etc.). The Small Stock Index outperformed the S & P 500 in twenty-eight of those forty-one 10-year periods, the last such period being 1992–2001.

Ten thousand dollars invested in small stocks for the past fifty years grew to $8,401,975 by the end of 2001 (versus $2,889,360 for $10,000 invested in the S & P 500). For small stocks, this translates into an average compound return of 14.4 percent per year. Over the past fifty years, the worst year for small stocks was 1973, when a loss of 31 percent was suffered. Two years later, these same stocks posted a gain of almost 53 percent in one year. The best year so far has been 1967, when

Annual Returns - All Aggressive Growth and Small Co. Stock Funds

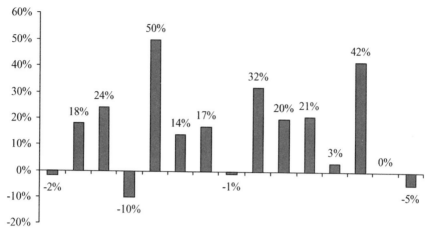

1987 1988 1989 1990 1991 1992 1993 1994 1995 1996 1997 1998 1999 2000 2001

small stocks posted a gain of 84 percent. The best five years in a row were 1975 to 1979, when the compounded annual rate of return was 39.8 percent per year. The worst five-year period over the past half-century has been 1969 to 1973, when this group lost an average compounded rate of -12.3 percent per year. For ten-year periods, the best has been 1975 to 1984 (compounded average rate of 30.4 percent per year); the worst has been 1965 to 1974 (compounded average rate of 3.2 percent per year).

To obtain the kinds of returns described here, investors would have needed quite a bit of patience and understanding. During the 1990s, small-company stocks had a standard deviation (variation of return) of 20.2 percent, compared to 15.8 percent for common stocks and 8.9 percent for long-term government bonds.

During the past three years, aggressive growth funds have outperformed the S & P 500 by 4.9 percent per year. Over the past five years, this fund category has underperformed the S & P 500 by an average of -3.3 percent per year. Average turnover during the past three years has been 139 percent.

The price-earnings (p/e) ratio is 34 for the typical aggressive growth fund, versus 31 for the S & P 500. The typical stock in these portfolios is only 21 percent the size of the average stock in the S & P 500. The average beta is 1.3, which means the group has a market-related risk that is 30 percent higher than the S & P 500. There is over $92 billion in all aggressive growth funds combined. The average aggressive growth fund throws virtually no annual income stream. The typical annual expense ratio for this group is 1.7 percent.

The p/e ratio for the typical small-company fund is 28, versus 31 for the S & P 500. The typical stock in these portfolios is only about 2 percent the size of the average stock in the S & P 500. The average beta is 0.96, which means the group's market-related risk is virtually the same as the S & P 500. There is about $195 billion in all small-company funds combined. The average small-company growth fund throws off an income stream of close to zero annually. The typical annual expense ratio for this group is 1.5 percent.

There are 245 funds that make up the aggressive growth category. The small-company stock category, which has 910 funds, has been combined with aggressive growth funds. Thus, for this section, there were a total of 1,155 possible candidates. Total market capitalization of these two categories combined is $288 billion.

Over the past three years, aggressive growth funds combined with small-company stock funds have had an average compound return of 8.5 percent per year (9.5 percent for small-company stock funds alone). The annual return has been 8.9 percent for the past five years (9.2 percent for small-company stock funds), 11.5 percent for the past decade (12.1 percent for small-company stock funds), and 11.8 percent for the past fifteen years (12.3 percent for small-company stock funds).

The standard deviation for this combined category (aggressive growth and small-company stock funds) has been 32.4 percent over the past three years— almost double the S & P 500 (standard deviation of 16.9 percent). This means that these funds have been more volatile than any other category except technology (standard deviation of 59.7 percent), and health care (standard deviation of 34.2 percent). Aggressive growth funds are certainly not for the faint of heart.

Fidelity Low-Priced Stock
82 Devonshire Street
Boston, MA 02109
(800) 544-8888
www.fidelity.com

total return	★★★
risk reduction	★★★★★
management	★★★★★
tax minimization	★★★★
expense control	★★★★★
symbol FLPSX	22 points
up-market performance	good
down-market performance	excellent
predictability of returns	excellent

Total Return ★★★

Over the past five years, Fidelity Low-Priced Stock has taken $10,000 and turned it into $20,120 ($16,020 over three years and $52,340 over the past ten years). This translates into an annualized return of 15 percent over the past five years, 17 percent over the past three years, and 18 percent for the decade. Over the past five years, this fund has outperformed 93 percent of all mutual funds; within its general category it has done better than 89 percent of its peers. Aggressive growth funds have averaged 9 percent annually over these same five years.

Risk/Volatility ★★★★★

Over the past five years, Fidelity Low-Priced Stock has been safer than 98 percent of all aggressive growth funds. Over the past decade, the fund has had no negative years, while the S & P 500 has had two (off 9 percent in 2000 and 12 percent in 2001); the Russell 2000 fell three times (off 2 percent in 1994, 3 percent in 1998, and 3 percent in 2000). The fund has underperformed the S & P 500 twice and the Russell 2000 three times in the past ten years. Consistency of *overperformance* for this fund has been good.

	past 5 years		past 7 years	
worst year	0.5%	1998	0.5%	1998
best year	26.7%	1997	29.0%	1992

Over the past five years, the fund's three worst quarters have been third quarter 1998 (-17 percent), third quarter 1999 (-7 percent), and third quarter 2001 (-7 percent). During the same period, the three best quarters have been second quarter 1999 (16 percent), second quarter 2001 (13 percent), and third quarter 1997 (13 percent). In the past, Fidelity Low-Priced Stock has done better than 34 percent of its peer group during the most recent bull market and outperformed 97 percent of its peer group during the most recent bear market. Consistency, or predictability, of returns for Fidelity Low-Priced Stock can be described as excellent. This fund's risk-related return ranks in the top quintile.

Management ★★★★★

There are 750 stocks in this $10.5 billion portfolio. The average aggressive growth fund today is $250 million in size. Close to 80 percent of the fund's holdings are in stocks. The stocks in this portfolio have an average p/e ratio of 19 and a median market capitalization of $775 million. The ten largest holdings compose 29 percent of the fund's total assets. The three largest sector weightings are industrial cyclicals (19 percent), financials (17 percent), and services (17 percent). The portfolio's equity holdings can be categorized as small-cap and a blend of growth and value stocks.

Joel Tillinghast has managed this fund for the past thirteen years. Manager Tillinghast's ability to keep the fund's average p/e ratio at roughly half that of the S & P 500's means that this portfolio is well positioned for the future. There are 154 funds besides Low-Priced Stock within the Fidelity family. Overall, the fund family's risk-adjusted performance can be described as very good.

Tax Minimization ★★★★

During the past five years, a $10,000 initial investment grew to $16,500 after taxes, assuming a 40 percent income tax bracket (state and federal combined) and a capital gains rate of 20 percent. This means that investors in this fund were able to preserve 82 percent of their total returns. Compared to other equity funds in the same category, this fund's tax savings are considered to be very good.

Expenses ★★★★★

Fidelity Low-Priced Stock's expense ratio is 1 percent; it has averaged 1 percent annually over the past three calendar years. The average expense ratio for the 1,200 funds in this category is 1.6 percent. This fund's turnover rate over the past year has been 44 percent, while its peer group average has been 117 percent.

Summary

Fidelity Low-Priced Stock, a small-cap value fund, has outperformed 98 percent of all mutual funds over the past ten years as well as 93 percent of its peer group over the same period. Returns over shorter periods have been equally impressive. Risk-adjusted returns have also been superb over the past three, five, and ten years. Within its peer group, the fund ranks number one when it comes to predictability of returns and ties for first place in the areas of low risk and low expenses. This portfolio's alpha, which measures excess returns per unit of risk taken, as measured against the fund's benchmark index, is quite appealing.

Profile

minimum initial investment $2,500	*IRA accounts available* . . . . yes
subsequent minimum investment . . $250	*IRA minimum investment* $500
available in all 50 states. . . . . yes	*date of inception.* . . . . Dec. 1989
telephone exchanges. . . . . yes	*dividend/income paid.* . . . . semiannually
number of funds in family 155	*largest sector weighting* indust. cyclicals

Fremont U.S. Micro-Cap

50 Beale Street, Suite 100
San Francisco, CA 94105
(800) 548-4539
www.fremontfunds.com

total return	★★★★
risk reduction	★★★
management	★★★
tax minimization	★★★
expense control	★★★
symbol FUSMX	16 points
up-market performance	excellent
down-market performance	fair
predictability of returns	poor

Total Return   ★★★★

Over the past five years, Fremont U.S. Micro-Cap has taken $10,000 and turned it into $23,870 ($21,470 over three years). This translates into an annualized return of 19 percent over the past five years and 29 percent over the past three years. Over the past five years, this fund has outperformed 99 percent of all mutual funds; within its general category, it has done better than 95 percent of its peers. Aggressive growth funds have averaged 9 percent annually over these same five years.

Risk/Volatility   ★★★

Over the past five years, Fremont U.S. Micro-Cap has been safer than 44 percent of all aggressive growth funds. Over the past decade, the fund has had one negative year, while the S & P 500 has had two (off 9 percent in 2000 and 12 percent in 2001); the Russell 2000 fell three times (off 2 percent in 1994, 3 percent in 1998, and 3 percent in 2000). The fund has underperformed the S & P 500 twice and the Russell 2000 twice in the last ten years. Consistency of *overperformance* for this fund has been outstanding.

	past 5 years		past 7 years	
worst year	-10.6%	2000	-10.6%	2000
best year	129.5%	1999	129.5%	1999

Over the past five years, the fund's three worst quarters have been third quarter 1998 (-29 percent), third quarter 2001 (-23 percent), and fourth quarter 2000 (-22 percent). During the same period, the three best quarters have been fourth quarter 1999 (50 percent), fourth quarter 1998 (44 percent), and second quarter 1999 (31 percent). In the past, Fremont U.S. Micro-Cap has done better than 84 percent of its peer group during the most recent bull market and outperformed 44 percent of its peer group during the most recent bear market. Consistency, or predictability, of returns for Fremont U.S. Micro-Cap can be described as poor. This fund's risk-related return ranks in the top quintile.

Management   ★★★

There are eighty stocks in this $715 million portfolio. The average aggressive growth fund today is $250 million in size. Close to 73 percent of the fund's holdings are in stocks. The stocks in this portfolio have an average p/e ratio of 36 and a median market capitalization of $315 million. The ten largest holdings compose 48 percent of the fund's total assets. The three largest sector weightings are technology (48 percent), health (17 percent), and services (12 percent). The portfolio's equity holdings can be categorized as small-cap and growth-oriented issues.

Robert Kern has managed this fund for the past five years. Manager Kern oversees the largest micro-cap fund in the nation, but there have been no signs of performance deterioration. Kern concentrates on the bottom 5 percent of stocks in terms of market capitalization, resulting in a universe of more than 4,000 stocks to choose from. There are nine funds besides U.S. Micro-Cap within the Fremont family. Overall, the fund family's risk-adjusted performance can be described as exceptional.

Tax Minimization   ★★★

During the past five years, a $10,000 initial investment grew to $17,900 after taxes, assuming a 40 percent income tax bracket (state and federal combined) and a capital gains rate of 20 percent. This means that investors in this fund were able to preserve 75 percent of their total returns. Compared to other equity funds in the same category, this fund's tax savings are considered to be good.

Expenses   ★★★

Fremont U.S. Micro-Cap's expense ratio is 1.6 percent; it has averaged 1.7 percent annually over the past three calendar years. The average expense ratio for the 1,200 funds in this category is 1.6 percent. This fund's turnover rate over the past year has been 117 percent, while its peer group average has also been 117 percent.

Summary

Freemont U.S. Micro-Cap, a small-cap growth fund, has outperformed 99 percent of all mutual funds over the past three and five years as well as 95 percent of its peer group over the same periods. Risk-adjusted returns have also been superb over the past three and five years. Within its peer group, the fund ranks in the top quartile when it comes to returns versus risk. Part of the reason risk-adjusted returns have been so great is due to the fund's ongoing large cash position, which not only reduces overall volatility but allows management to quickly pounce on attractive securities. This portfolio's alpha, which measures excess returns per unit of risk taken, as measured against the fund's benchmark index, is extremely appealing.

Profile

minimum initial investment $2,000	*IRA accounts available* . . . . yes
subsequent minimum investment . . $100	*IRA minimum investment* $1,000
available in all 50 states . . . . yes	*date of inception* . . . . June 1994
telephone exchanges . . . . yes	*dividend/income paid* . . . . annually
number of funds in family 10	*largest sector weighting* . . . technology

Meridian Growth
60 East Sir Francis Drake Boulevard #306
Larkspur, CA 94939
(800) 446-6662

total return	★★★
risk reduction	★★★★
management	★★★★
tax minimization	★★★
expense control	★★★★★
symbol MERDX	19 points
up-market performance	very good
down-market performance	very good
predictability of returns	very good

Total Return   ★★★
Over the past five years, Meridian Growth has taken $10,000 and turned it into $20,120 ($16,860 over three years and $37,080 over the past ten years). This translates into an annualized return of 15 percent over the past five years, 19 percent over the past three years, and 14 percent for the decade. Over the past five years, this fund has outperformed 96 percent of all mutual funds; within its general category, it has done better than 84 percent of its peers. Aggressive growth funds have averaged 9 percent annually over these same five years.

Risk/Volatility   ★★★★
Over the past five years, Meridian Growth has been safer than 98 percent of all aggressive growth funds. Over the past decade, the fund has had no negative years, while the S & P 500 has had two (off 9 percent in 2000 and 12 percent in 2001); the Russell 2000 fell three times (off 2 percent in 1994, 3 percent in 1998, and 3 percent in 2000). The fund has underperformed the S & P 500 twice and the Russell 2000 three times in the past ten years. Consistency of *overperformance* for this fund has been very good.

	past 5 years		past 10 years	
worst year	3.1%	1998	0.6%	1994
best year	28.2%	2000	28.2%	2000

Over the past five years, the fund's three worst quarters have been third quarter 1998 (-19 percent), third quarter 2001 (-15 percent), and second quarter 2001 (-5 percent). During the same period, the three best quarters have been second quarter 2001 (18 percent), fourth quarter 1998 (17 percent), and first quarter 2000 (14 percent). In the past, Meridian Growth has done better than 62 percent of its peer group during the most recent bull market and outperformed 78 percent of its peer group during the most recent bear market. Consistency, or predictability, of returns for Meridian Growth can be described as very good. This fund's risk-related return ranks in the top quintile.

Management   ★★★★

There are forty stocks in this $210 million portfolio. The average aggressive growth fund today is $250 million in size. Close to 100 percent of the fund's holdings are in stocks. The stocks in this portfolio have an average p/e ratio of 29 and a median market capitalization of $2 billion. The ten largest holdings compose 30 percent of the fund's total assets. The three largest sector weightings are services (31 percent), technology (26 percent), and retail (15 percent). The portfolio's equity holdings can be categorized as mid-cap and growth-oriented issues.

Richard Aster Jr. has managed this fund for the past eighteen years. Manager Aster avoids the common "growth-at-any-price" that so many of his peers fall victim to; his steady returns and temperate style are likely to suit investors well during the coming years. There is one other fund besides Growth within the Meridian family. Overall, the fund family's risk-adjusted performance can be described as exceptional.

Tax Minimization   ★★★

During the past five years, a $10,000 initial investment grew to $14,690 after taxes, assuming a 40 percent income tax bracket (state and federal combined) and a capital gains rate of 20 percent. This means that investors in this fund were able to preserve 73 percent of their total returns. Compared to other equity funds in the same category, this fund's tax savings are considered to be good.

Expenses   ★★★★★

Meridian Growth's expense ratio is 1 percent; it has averaged 1 percent annually over the past three calendar years. The average expense ratio for the 1,200 funds in this category is 1.6 percent. This fund's turnover rate over the past year has been 43 percent, while its peer group average has been 117 percent.

Summary

Meridian Growth, a medium-cap growth fund, has outperformed over 90 percent of all mutual funds over the past three, five, ten, and fifteen years as well as 91 percent of its peer group over the past decade. Returns over shorter periods have been equally impressive. Risk-adjusted returns have also been superb over the past three, five, and ten years. Within its peer group, the fund ranks number one when it comes to expense reduction. This portfolio's alpha, which measures excess returns per unit of risk taken, as measured against the fund's benchmark index, is quite appealing.

Profile

minimum initial investment $1,000	*IRA accounts available* . . . . yes
subsequent minimum investment . . . $50	*IRA minimum investment* $1,000
available in all 50 states. . . . . yes	*date of inception* . . . . Aug. 1984
telephone exchanges. . . . . yes	*dividend/income paid* . . . . annually
number of funds in family 2	*largest sector weighting* . . . . . . services

Merrill Lynch Small Cap Value B

P.O. Box 9011
Princeton, NJ 08543
(800) 995-6526
www.ml.com

total return	★★★★
risk reduction	★★★★
management	★★★
tax minimization	★★★
expense control	★★
symbol MBSPX	16 points
up-market performance	excellent
down-market performance	excellent
predictability of returns	good

Total Return   ★★★★

Over the past five years, Merrill Lynch Small Cap Value B has taken $10,000 and turned it into $22,880 ($19,540 over three years and $44,120 over the past ten years). This translates into an annualized return of 18 percent over the past five years, 25 percent over the past three years, and 16 percent for the decade. Over the past five years, this fund has outperformed 98 percent of all mutual funds; within its general category, it has done better than 92 percent of its peers. Aggressive growth funds have averaged 9 percent annually over these same five years.

Risk/Volatility   ★★★★

Over the past five years, Merrill Lynch Small Cap Value B has been safer than 51 percent of all aggressive growth funds. Over the past decade, the fund has had one negative year, while the S & P 500 has had two (off 9 percent in 2000 and 12 percent in 2001); the Russell 2000 fell three times (off 2 percent in 1994, 3 percent in 1998, and 3 percent in 2000). The fund has underperformed the S & P 500 twice and the Russell 2000 three times in the past ten years. Consistency of *overperformance* for this fund has been very good.

	past 5 years		past 10 years	
worst year	-6.6%	1998	-6.6%	1998
best year	31.9%	1999	31.9%	1999

Over the past five years, the fund's three worst quarters have been third quarter 1998 (-26 percent), third quarter 2001 (-17 percent), and fourth quarter 1997 (-11 percent). During the same period, the three best quarters have been second quarter 1999 (27 percent), fourth quarter 1999 (20 percent), and fourth quarter 1998 (16 percent). In the past, Merrill Lynch Small Cap Value B has done better than 86 percent of its peer group during the most recent bull market and outperformed 81 percent of its peer group during the most recent bear market. Consistency, or predictability, of returns for Merrill Lynch Small Cap Value B can be described as good. This fund's risk-related return ranks in the top quintile.

Management   ★★★

There are 140 stocks in this $750 million portfolio. The average aggressive growth fund today is $250 million in size. Close to 88 percent of the fund's holdings are in stocks. The stocks in this portfolio have an average p/e ratio of 26 and a median market capitalization of $830 million. The ten largest holdings compose 31 percent of the fund's total assets. The three largest sector weightings are technology (31 percent), industrials (17 percent), and services (16 percent). The portfolio's equity holdings can be categorized as small-cap and a blend of growth and value stocks.

Daniel Szemis has managed this fund for the past six years. Manager Szemis's ability to keep the fund's average p/e ratio at two-thirds that of the S & P 500's means that this portfolio is well positioned for the future. Management favors stocks that trade in the bottom quintile of their historical trading range. There are 247 funds besides Small Cap Value B within the Merrill Lynch family. Overall, the fund family's risk-adjusted performance can be described as good to very good.

Tax Minimization   ★★★

During the past five years, a $10,000 initial investment grew to $16,930 after taxes, assuming a 40 percent income tax bracket (state and federal combined) and a capital gains rate of 20 percent. This means that investors in this fund were able to preserve 74 percent of their total returns. Compared to other equity funds in the same category, this fund's tax savings are considered to be good.

Expenses   ★★

Merrill Lynch Small Cap Value B's expense ratio is 2.1 percent; it has averaged 2.1 percent annually over the past three calendar years. The average expense ratio for the 1,200 funds in this category is 1.6 percent. This fund's turnover rate over the past year has been 42 percent, while its peer group average has been 117 percent.

Summary

Merrill Lynch Small Cap Value B, a small-cap blend of both value and growth, has outperformed over 90 percent of all mutual funds over the past three and five years as well as 98 percent of its peer group over the same period. Returns over longer and shorter periods have been equally impressive. Risk-adjusted returns have also been outstanding over the past three, five, and ten years. Within its peer group, the fund ranks in the top quartile when it comes to return versus risk. This portfolio's alpha, which measures excess returns per unit of risk taken, as measured against the fund's benchmark index, is extremely appealing.

Profile

minimum initial investment $1,000	*IRA accounts available* . . . . yes
subsequent minimum investment . . . $50	*IRA minimum investment* $100
available in all 50 states. . . . . yes	*date of inception* . . . . Oct. 1988
telephone exchanges. . . . . yes	*dividend/income paid* . . . . annually
number of funds in family 248	*largest sector weighting* . . . technology

Quaker Aggressive Growth A

P.O. Box 844
Conshohocken, PA 19428-0844
(800) 220-8888
www.quakerfunds.com

total return	★★★★★
risk reduction	★★★★★
management	★★★★
tax minimization	★★★
expense control	★★★
symbol QUAGX	20 points
up-market performance	poor
down-market performance	excellent
predictability of returns	very good

Total Return   ★★★★★

Over the past five years, Quaker Aggressive Growth A has taken $10,000 and turned it into $33,040 ($20,980 over three years). This translates into an annualized return of 27 percent over the past five years and 28 percent over the past three years. Over the past five years, this fund has outperformed 99 percent of all mutual funds; within its general category, it has done better than 99 percent of its peers. Aggressive growth funds have averaged 9 percent annually over these same five years.

Risk/Volatility   ★★★★★

Over the past five years, Quaker Aggressive Growth A has been safer than 99 percent of all aggressive growth funds. Over the past decade, the fund has had one negative year, while the S & P 500 has had two (off 9 percent in 2000 and 12 percent in 2001); the Russell 2000 fell three times (off 2 percent in 1994, 3 percent in 1998, and 3 percent in 2000). The fund has underperformed the S & P 500 twice and the Russell 2000 twice in the past ten years. Consistency of *overperformance* for this fund has been outstanding.

	past 5 years		past 7 years	
worst year	-8.1%	2001	-8.1%	2001
best year	96.9%	1999	96.9%	1999

During the past five years, the fund's worst three quarters have been third quarter 1998 (-5 percent), fourth quarter 1997 (-5 percent), and first quarter 2001 (-4 percent). The three best-performing quarters over the same period have been fourth quarter 1999 (36 percent), first quarter 1999 (20 percent), and fourth quarter 1998 (19 percent). In the past, Quaker Aggressive Growth A has done better than just 3 percent of its peer group during the most recent bull market but outperformed 77 percent of its peer group during the most recent bear market. Consistency, or predictability, of returns for Quaker Aggressive Growth A can be described as very good. This fund's risk-related return ranks in the top quintile.

Management   ★★★★

There are fifty stocks in this $110 million portfolio. The average aggressive growth fund today is $250 million in size. Close to 56 percent of the fund's holdings are in stocks. The stocks in this portfolio have an average p/e ratio of 19 and a median market capitalization of $18 billion. The ten largest holdings compose 55 percent of the fund's total assets. The three largest sector weightings are energy (32 percent), financials (29 percent), and services (15 percent). The portfolio's equity holdings can be categorized as large-cap and value-oriented issues.

Manu Daftary has managed this fund for the past six years. Manager Daftary has an extremely flexible investment style, allowing the fund to be mostly cash if attractive stocks cannot be found. There are seven funds besides Aggressive Growth A within the Quaker family. Overall, the fund family's risk-adjusted performance can be described as very good to exceptional.

Tax Minimization   ★★★

During the past five years, a $10,000 initial investment grew to $26,100 after taxes, assuming a 40 percent income tax bracket (state and federal combined) and a capital gains rate of 20 percent. This means that investors in this fund were able to preserve 79 percent of their total returns. Compared to other equity funds in the same category, this fund's tax savings are considered to be good.

Expenses   ★★★

Quaker Aggressive Growth A's expense ratio is 1.4 percent; it has averaged 1.4 percent annually over the past three calendar years. The average expense ratio for the 1,200 funds in this category is 1.6 percent. This fund's turnover rate over the past year has been 124 percent, while its peer group average has been 117 percent.

Summary

Quaker Aggressive Growth A, a large-cap value fund, has outperformed over 99 percent of all mutual funds over the past three and five years and has done better than more than 99 percent of its peer group. Risk-adjusted returns have also been excellent over the past three and five years. The fund ranks in the top quintile when it comes to return versus risk. The portfolio ranks number one when it comes to performance within its peer group and ties for first when it comes to risk reduction. This fund has outperformed the S & P 500 by over 30 percentage points over the past three years. The stocks held in the portfolio have a p/e ratio that is only about two-thirds that of the S & P 500, positioning itself in an envious spot for the next few years. This portfolio's alpha, which measures excess returns per unit of risk taken, as measured against the fund's benchmark index, is extremely appealing.

Profile

minimum initial investment $2,000	*IRA accounts available* . . . . yes
subsequent minimum investment . $1,000	*IRA minimum investment* $1,000
available in all 50 states. . . . . yes	*date of inception* . . . . Nov. 1996
telephone exchanges. . . . . yes	*dividend/income paid* . . . . annually
number of funds in family 8	*largest sector weighting.* . . . . energy

Reserve Small-Cap Growth R
1250 Broadway, 32nd Floor
New York, NY 10001
(800) 637-1700
www.reservefunds.com

total return	★★★★
risk reduction	★
management	★★★
tax minimization	★★★★★
expense control	★★★★
symbol REGAX	17 points
up-market performance	excellent
down-market performance	poor
predictability of returns	poor

Total Return   ★★★★
Over the past five years, Reserve Small-Cap Growth R has taken $10,000 and turned it into $23,870 ($19,540 over three years). This translates into an annualized return of 19 percent over the past five years and 25 percent over the past three years. Over the past five years, this fund has outperformed 97 percent of all mutual funds; within its general category, it has done better than 90 percent of its peers. Aggressive growth funds have averaged 9 percent annually over these same five years.

Risk/Volatility   ★
Over the past five years, Reserve Small-Cap Growth R has been safer than 25 percent of all aggressive growth funds. Over the past decade, the fund has had three negative years, while the S & P 500 has had two (off 9 percent in 2000 and 12 percent in 2001); the Russell 2000 fell three times (off 2 percent in 1994, 3 percent in 1998, and 3 percent in 2000). The fund has underperformed the S & P 500 twice and the Russell 2000 twice in the past ten years.

	past 5 years		past 7 years	
worst year	-15.9%	2001	-15.9%	2001
best year	135.8%	1999	135.8%	1999

During the past five years, the fund's worst three quarters have been third quarter 2001 (-31 percent), first quarter 2001 (-24 percent), and first quarter 1997 (-17 percent). The three best-performing quarters over the same period have been fourth quarter 1999 (50 percent), fourth quarter 1998 (28 percent), and first quarter 2000 (27 percent). In the past, Reserve Small-Cap Growth R has done better than 97 percent of its peer group during the most recent bull market and outperformed 28 percent of its peer group during the most recent bear market. Consistency, or predictability, of returns for Reserve Small-Cap Growth R can be described as poor. This fund's risk-related return ranks in the top quintile.

Management   ★★★

There are forty-five stocks in this $65 million portfolio. The average aggressive growth fund today is $250 million in size. Close to 100 percent of the fund's holdings are in stocks. The stocks in this portfolio have an average p/e ratio of 31 and a median market capitalization of $840 million. The ten largest holdings compose 34 percent of the fund's total assets. The three largest sector weightings are technology (75 percent), health (8 percent), and services (8 percent). The portfolio's equity holdings can be categorized as mid-cap and growth-oriented issues.

A team has managed this fund for the past eight years. Comanagers Vroom, O'Connor, and Weisman try to buy companies whose management has an ownership stake. There are ten funds besides Small-Cap Growth R within the Reserve family. Overall, the fund family's risk-adjusted performance can be described as very good.

Tax Minimization   ★★★★★

During the past five years, a $10,000 initial investment grew to $23,390 after taxes, assuming a 40 percent income tax bracket (state and federal combined) and a capital gains rate of 20 percent. This means that investors in this fund were able to preserve 98 percent of their total returns. Compared to other equity funds in the same category, this fund's tax savings are considered to be exceptional.

Expenses   ★★★★

Reserve Small-Cap Growth R's expense ratio is 1.6 percent; it has averaged 1.6 percent annually over the past three calendar years. The average expense ratio for the 1,200 funds in this category is 1.6 percent. This fund's turnover rate over the past year has been 15 percent, while its peer group average has been 117 percent.

Summary

Reserve Small-Cap Growth R, a medium-cap growth fund, has outperformed over 97 percent of all mutual funds over the past three and five years and has outperformed over 90 percent of its peer group. Risk-adjusted returns have also been excellent over the past three and five years. The fund ranks in the top quintile when it comes to return versus risk. The portfolio ranks number two when it comes to tax efficiency, with an almost perfect score of 98 percent. In 1999, the fund outperformed the S & P 500 by an astounding 115 percentage points.

Profile

minimum initial investment $1,000	*IRA accounts available* . . . . yes
subsequent minimum investment . . $100	*IRA minimum investment* $250
available in all 50 states. . . . . yes	*date of inception* . . . . Nov. 1994
telephone exchanges. . . . . yes	*dividend/income paid* . . . . quarterly
number of funds in family 11	*largest sector weighting* . . . technology

Royce Micro-Cap Investor Shares
1414 Avenue of the Americas
New York, NY 10019
(800) 221-4268
www.roycefunds.com

total return	★★★
risk reduction	★★★★
management	★★★★
tax minimization	★★★★
expense control	★★★★
symbol RYOTX	19 points
up-market performance	very good
down-market performance	excellent
predictability of returns	very good

Total Return   ★★★
Over the past five years, Royce Micro-Cap Investor Shares has taken $10,000 and turned it into $20,120 ($16,430 over three years and $44,120 over the past ten years). This translates into an annualized return of 15 percent over the past five years, 18 percent over the past three years, and 16 percent for the decade. Over the past five years, this fund has outperformed 95 percent of all mutual funds; within its general category, it has done better than 85 percent of its peers. Aggressive growth funds have averaged 9 percent annually over these same five years.

Risk/Volatility   ★★★★
Over the past five years, Royce Micro-Cap Investor Shares has been safer than 45 percent of all aggressive growth funds. Over the past decade, the fund has had one negative year, while the S & P 500 has had two (off 9 percent in 2000 and 12 percent in 2001); the Russell 2000 fell three times (off 2 percent in 1994, 3 percent in 1998, and 3 percent in 2000). The fund has underperformed the S & P 500 twice and the Russell 2000 three times in the past ten years. Consistency of *overperformance* for this fund has been very good.

	past 5 years		past 10 years	
worst year	-3.3%	1998	-3.3%	1998
best year	24.7%	1997	29.4%	1992

During the past five years, the fund's worst three quarters have been third quarter 1998 (-21 percent), third quarter 2001 (-17 percent), and first quarter 1999 (-16 percent). The three best-performing quarters over the same period have been second quarter 1999 (23 percent), second quarter 2001 (21 percent), and third quarter 1997 (16 percent). In the past, Royce Micro-Cap Investor Shares has done better than 62 percent of its peer group during the most recent bull market and outperformed 84 percent of its peer group during the most recent bear market. Consistency, or predictability, of returns for Royce Micro-Cap Investor Shares can be described as very good. This fund's risk-related return ranks in the top quintile.

Management ★★★★

There are 160 stocks in this $170 million portfolio. The average aggressive growth fund today is $250 million in size. Close to 89 percent of the fund's holdings are in stocks. The stocks in this portfolio have an average p/e ratio of 23 and a median market capitalization of $270 million. The ten largest holdings compose 27 percent of the fund's total assets. The three largest sector weightings are industrial cyclicals (26 percent), technology (16 percent), and services (14 percent). The portfolio's equity holdings can be categorized as small-cap and a blend of growth and value stocks.

George Whitney has managed this fund for the past nine years. Manager Whitney's top holdings are companies that most of Wall Street has never heard of; stocks that are not researched by the vast majority of the brokerage houses. Management favors stocks that can be bought on the cheap and then proceed to improve the bottom line. There are twelve funds besides Micro-Cap Investor Shares within the Royce family. Overall, the fund family's risk-adjusted performance can be described as exceptional.

Tax Minimization ★★★★

During the past five years, a $10,000 initial investment grew to $17,300 after taxes, assuming a 40 percent income tax bracket (state and federal combined) and a capital gains rate of 20 percent. This means that investors in this fund were able to preserve 86 percent of their total returns. Compared to other equity funds in the same category, this fund's tax savings are considered to be very good.

Expenses ★★★★

Royce Micro-Cap Investor Shares's expense ratio is 1.5 percent; it has averaged 1.5 percent annually over the past three calendar years. The average expense ratio for the 1,200 funds in this category is 1.6 percent. This fund's turnover rate over the past year has been 71 percent, while its peer group average has been 117 percent.

Summary

Royce Micro-Cap Investor Shares, a small-cap value fund, has outperformed over 95 percent of all mutual funds over the past three and five years and has outperformed 85 percent of its peer group. Risk-adjusted returns have also been superb over the past three and five years. The fund ranks in the top third when it comes to return versus risk. The fund scores well in every category measured. This portfolio's alpha, which measures excess returns per unit of risk taken, as measured against the fund's benchmark index, is extremely appealing.

Profile

minimum initial investment $2,000	*IRA accounts available* . . . . yes
subsequent minimum investment . . . $50	*IRA minimum investment* $500
available in all 50 states. . . . . yes	*date of inception*. . . . . Dec. 1991
telephone exchanges. . . . . yes	*dividend/income paid* . . . . annually
number of funds in family 13	*largest sector weighting* indust. cyclicals

Smith Barney Aggressive Growth A

750 Washington Boulevard 11th Floor
Stamford, CT 10048
(800) 451-2010
www.salomonsmithbarney.com

total return	★★★★★
risk reduction	★★★
management	★★★★★
tax minimization	★★★★★
expense control	★★★★★
symbol SHRAX	23 points
up-market performance	very good
down-market performance	good
predictability of returns	good

Total Return   ★★★★★

Over the past five years, Smith Barney Aggressive Growth A has taken $10,000 and turned it into $31,760 ($18,610 over three years and $56,950 over the past ten years). This translates into an annualized return of 26 percent over the past five years, 23 percent over the past three years, and 19 percent for the decade. Over the past five years, this fund has outperformed 99 percent of all mutual funds; within its general category, it has done better than 99 percent of its peers. Aggressive growth funds have averaged 9 percent annually over these same five years.

Risk/Volatility   ★★★

Over the past five years, Smith Barney Aggressive Growth A has been safer than 81 percent of all aggressive growth funds. Over the past decade, the fund has had two negative years, while the S & P 500 has had two (off 9 percent in 2000 and 12 percent in 2001); the Russell 2000 fell three times (off 2 percent in 1994, 3 percent in 1998, and 3 percent in 2000). The fund has underperformed the S & P 500 twice and the Russell 2000 three times in the past ten years. Consistency of *overperformance* for this fund has been outstanding.

	past 5 years		past 10 years	
worst year	-5.0%	2001	-5.0%	2001
best year	63.7%	1999	63.7%	1999

Risk-adjusted returns have also been excellent over the past three, five, and ten years. During the past five years, the fund's worst three quarters have been third quarter 2001 (-22 percent), third quarter 1998 (-12 percent), and first quarter 2001 (-10 percent). The three best-performing quarters over the same period have been fourth quarter 1998 (38 percent), fourth quarter 1999 (29 percent), and third quarter 1997 (22 percent). In the past, Smith Barney Aggressive Growth A has done better than 46 percent of its peer group during the most recent bull market and outperformed 57 percent of its peer group during the most recent bear market.

Consistency, or predictability, of returns for Smith Barney Aggressive Growth A can be described as good. This fund's risk-related return ranks in the top quintile.

Management   ★★★★★
There are seventy-five stocks in this $2.2 billion portfolio. The average aggressive growth fund today is $250 million in size. Close to 97 percent of the fund's holdings are in stocks. The stocks in this portfolio have an average p/e ratio of 34 and a median market capitalization of $15 billion. The ten largest holdings compose 49 percent of the fund's total assets. The three largest sector weightings are health (46 percent), services (14 percent), and financials (12 percent). The portfolio's equity holdings can be categorized as large-cap and growth-oriented issues.

Richard Freeman has managed this fund for the past nineteen years. Management's ability to pick stocks in good and bad times is unequaled. There are 144 funds besides Aggressive Growth A within the Smith Barney family. Overall, the fund family's risk-adjusted performance can be described as good.

Tax Minimization   ★★★★★
During the past five years, a $10,000 initial investment grew to $31,440 after taxes, assuming a 40 percent income tax bracket (state and federal combined) and a capital gains rate of 20 percent. This means that investors in this fund were able to preserve 99 percent of their total returns. Compared to other equity funds in the same category, this fund's tax savings are considered to be exceptional.

Expenses   ★★★★★
Smith Barney Aggressive Growth A's expense ratio is 1.1 percent; it has averaged 1.1 percent annually over the past three calendar years. The average expense ratio for the 1,200 funds in this category is 1.6 percent. This fund's turnover rate over the past year has been 1 percent, while its peer group average has been 117 percent.

Summary
Smith Barney Aggressive Growth, a large-cap growth fund, has outperformed over 99 percent of all mutual funds over the past three, five, ten, and fifteen years and has whipped over 99 percent of its peer group over the same periods. This is an amazing accomplishment. The fund ranks in the top quintile when it comes to return versus risk. The fund ranks number one when it comes to tax efficiency. Expense reduction is also first rate. This portfolio's alpha, which measures excess returns per unit of risk taken, as measured against the fund's benchmark index, is extremely appealing. On a total point basis, this is the number-one fund for its category.

Profile
minimum initial investment $1,000	*IRA accounts available* . . . . yes
subsequent minimum investment . . . $50	*IRA minimum investment* $250
available in all 50 states. . . . . yes	*date of inception* . . . . Oct. 1983
telephone exchanges. . . . . yes	*dividend/income paid* . . . . annually
number of funds in family 145	*largest sector weighting* . . . . health

Tocqueville Small-Cap Value
1675 Broadway
New York, NY 10019
(800) 697-3863
www.tocqueville.com

total return	★★★
risk reduction	★★★
management	★★★
tax minimization	★★★
expense control	★★★
symbol TSCVX	15 points
up-market performance	good
down-market performance	excellent
predictability of returns	good

Total Return   ★★★
Over the past five years, Tocqueville Small-Cap Value has taken $10,000 and turned it into $21,010 ($17,720 over three years). This translates into an annualized return of 16 percent over the past five years and 21 percent over the past three years. Over the past five years, this fund has outperformed 97 percent of all mutual funds; within its general category, it has done better than 89 percent of its peers. Aggressive growth funds have averaged 9 percent annually over these same five years.

Risk/Volatility   ★★★
Over the past five years, Tocqueville Small-Cap Value has been safer than 31 percent of all aggressive growth funds. Over the past decade, the fund has had one negative year, while the S & P 500 has had two (off 9 percent in 2000 and 12 percent in 2001); the Russell 2000 fell three times (off 2 percent in 1994, 3 percent in 1998, and 3 percent in 2000). The fund has underperformed the S & P 500 twice and the Russell 2000 twice in the past ten years. Consistency of *overperformance* for this fund has been good.

	past 5 years		past 7 years	
worst year	-5.6%	1998	-5.6%	1998
best year	38.7%	1999	38.7%	1999

During the past five years, the fund's worst three quarters have been third quarter 1998 (-23 percent), third quarter 2001 (-16 percent), and first quarter 1999 (-13 percent). The three best-performing quarters over the same period have been second quarter 1999 (29 percent), first quarter 2000 (25 percent), and third quarter 1997 (17 percent). In the past, Tocqueville Small-Cap Value has done better than 26 percent of its peer group during the most recent bull market and outperformed 80 percent of its peer group during the most recent bear market. Consistency, or predictability, of returns for Tocqueville Small-Cap Value can be described as good. This fund's risk-related return ranks in the top quintile.

Management ★★★
There are forty stocks in this $50 million portfolio. The average aggressive growth fund today is $250 million in size. Close to 90 percent of the fund's holdings are in stocks. The stocks in this portfolio have an average p/e ratio of 27 and a median market capitalization of $500 million. The ten largest holdings compose 45 percent of the fund's total assets. The three largest sector weightings are technology (34 percent), industials (23 percent), and staples (13 percent). The portfolio's equity holdings can be categorized as small-cap and a blend of growth and value stocks.

Jean-Pierre Conreur has managed this fund for the past eight years. Manager Conreur oversees a fairly concentrated portfolio, favoring stronger growers that have temporarily stumbled. There are three funds besides Small-Cap Value within the Tocqueville Trust family. Overall, the fund family's risk-adjusted performance can be described as exceptional.

Tax Minimization ★★★
During the past five years, a $10,000 initial investment grew to $16,600 after taxes, assuming a 40 percent income tax bracket (state and federal combined) and a capital gains rate of 20 percent. This means that investors in this fund were able to preserve 79 percent of their total returns. Compared to other equity funds in the same category, this fund's tax savings are considered to be good.

Expenses ★★★
Tocqueville Small-Cap Value's expense ratio is 1.5 percent; it has averaged 1.5 percent annually over the past three calendar years. The average expense ratio for the 1,200 funds in this category is 1.6 percent. This fund's turnover rate over the past year has been 87 percent, while its peer group average has been 117 percent.

Summary
Tocqueville Small-Cap Value, a small-cap blend fund that invests in both value and growth, has outperformed over 98 percent of all mutual funds over the past three and five years and has done better than 90 percent of its peer group. Risk-adjusted returns have also been outstanding over the past three and five years. The fund ranks in the top third when it comes to return versus risk. The fund ranks well in every category measured. This portfolio's alpha, which measures excess returns per unit of risk taken, as measured against the fund's benchmark index, is below average.

Profile
minimum initial investment $1,000
subsequent minimum investment . . $100
available in all 50 states. . . . . yes
telephone exchanges. . . . . yes
number of funds in family 4

IRA accounts available . . . . yes
IRA minimum investment $250
date of inception . . . . Aug. 1994
dividend/income paid . . . . annually
largest sector weighting . . . technology

Wasatch Small-Cap Growth
150 Social Hall Avenue, 4th Floor
Salt Lake City, UT 84111
(800) 551-1700
www.wasatchfunds.com

total return	★★★★
risk reduction	★★★
management	★★★★
tax minimization	★★★★
expense control	★★★★
symbol WAAEX	19 points
up-market performance	excellent
down-market performance	excellent
predictability of returns	good

Total Return ★★★★
Over the past five years, Wasatch Small-Cap Growth has taken $10,000 and turned it into $27,030 ($20,490 over three years and $48,070 over the past ten years). This translates into an annualized return of 22 percent over the past five years, 27 percent over the past three years, and 17 percent for the decade. Over the past five years, this fund has outperformed 99 percent of all mutual funds; within its general category it has done better than 98 percent of its peers. Aggressive growth funds have averaged 9 percent annually over these same five years.

Risk/Volatility ★★★
Over the past five years, Wasatch Small-Cap Growth has been safer than 90 percent of all aggressive growth funds. Over the past decade, the fund has had no negative years, while the S & P 500 has had two (off 9 percent in 2000 and 12 percent in 2001); the Russell 2000 fell three times (off 2 percent in 1994, 3 percent in 1998, and 3 percent in 2000). The fund has underperformed the S & P 500 twice and the Russell 2000 three times in the past ten years. Consistency of *overperformance* for this fund has been outstanding.

	past 5 years		past 10 years	
worst year	11.2%	1998	4.7%	1992
best year	40.9%	1999	40.9%	1999

During the past five years, the fund's worst three quarters have been third quarter 1998 (-24 percent), third quarter 2001 (-15 percent), and first quarter 2001 (-11 percent). The three best-performing quarters over the same period have been fourth quarter 1998 (32 percent), second quarter 2001 (25 percent), and fourth quarter 1999 (24 percent). In the past, Wasatch Small-Cap Growth has done better than 92 percent of its peer group during the most recent bull market and outperformed 79 percent of its peer group during the most recent bear market. Consistency, or predictability, of returns for Wasatch Small-Cap Growth can be described as good. This fund's risk-related return ranks in the top quintile.

Management   ★★★★

There are eighty stocks in this $950 million portfolio. The average aggressive growth fund today is $250 million in size. Close to 80 percent of the fund's holdings are in stocks. The stocks in this portfolio have an average p/e ratio of 37 and a median market capitalization of $1 billion. The ten largest holdings compose 49 percent of the fund's total assets. The three largest sector weightings are health (37 percent), technology (23 percent), and services (19 percent). The portfolio's equity holdings can be categorized as small-cap and growth-oriented issues.

Jeff Cardon has managed this fund for the past sixteen years. Manager Cardon has taken a more conservative approach to equity selection than his peers. Yet, he sometimes takes a large position in a specific sector. There are six funds besides Small-Cap Growth within the Wasatch family. Overall, the fund family's risk-adjusted performance can be described as exceptional.

Tax Minimization   ★★★★

During the past five years, a $10,000 initial investment grew to $22,440 after taxes, assuming a 40 percent income tax bracket (state and federal combined) and a capital gains rate of 20 percent. This means that investors in this fund were able to preserve 83 percent of their total returns. Compared to other equity funds in the same category, this fund's tax savings are considered to be very good.

Expenses   ★★★★

Wasatch Small-Cap Growth's expense ratio is 1.4 percent; it has averaged 1.4 percent annually over the past three calendar years. The average expense ratio for the 1,200 funds in this category is 1.6 percent. This fund's turnover rate over the past year has been 40 percent, while its peer group average has been 117 percent.

Summary

Wasatch Small-Cap Growth, a small-cap growth fund, has outperformed over 98 percent of all mutual funds over the past five and ten years and has done better than over 99 percent of its peer group. Risk-adjusted returns have also been excellent over the past three, five, and ten years. The fund ranks good to very good in every category measured. This fund outperformed the S & P 500 by 41 percentage points in 1999. This portfolio's alpha, which measures excess returns per unit of risk taken, as measured against the fund's benchmark index, is extremely appealing.

Profile

minimum initial investment $2,000	*IRA accounts available* . . . . yes
subsequent minimum investment . . $100	*IRA minimum investment* $1,000
available in all 50 states. . . . . yes	*date of inception.* . . . . Dec. 1986
telephone exchanges. . . . . yes	*dividend/income paid* . . . . annually
number of funds in family 7	*largest sector weighting* . . . . health

Balanced Funds

The objective of balanced funds, also referred to as total return funds, is to provide both growth and income. Fund management purchases common stocks, bonds, and convertible securities. Portfolio composition is almost always exclusively U.S. securities. The weighting of stocks compared to bonds depends on the portfolio manager's perception of the stock market, interest rates, and risk levels. It is rare for less than 30 percent of the fund's holdings to be in either stocks or bonds.

Balanced funds offer neither the best nor the worst of both worlds. These funds will often outperform the different categories of bond funds during bull markets but suffer greater percentage losses during stock market declines. On the other hand, when interest rates are on the rise, balanced funds will typically decline less on a total return basis (current yield plus or minus principal appreciation) than a bond fund. When rates are falling, balanced funds will also outperform bond funds if stocks are also doing well.

Over the past ten years, the average balanced fund had 82 percent of the return of growth funds (9.3 percent versus 12.9 percent) with only 55 percent of the risk. Balanced funds are the perfect choice for the investor who cannot decide between stocks and bonds. This hybrid security is a middle-of-the-road approach, ideal for

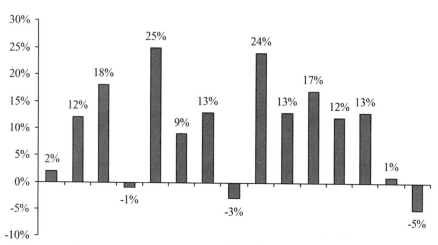

Annual Returns - Balanced Funds

someone who wants a fund manager to determine the portfolio's weighting of stocks, bonds, and convertibles.

More than 1,000 funds make up the entire balanced category, which consists of balanced only (493 funds), asset allocation (358 funds), multiasset global (88 funds), and convertibles (66 funds). Total market capitalization for this combined balanced category is $354 billion.

The price-earnings (p/e) ratio for stocks in a typical balanced fund is 28, roughly 10 percent lower than the S & P 500's p/e ratio of 31. The average beta is 0.54, which means that this group has only about half of the market-related risk of the S & P 500. During the past three years, balanced funds have surpassed the performance of the S & P 500 by nearly 4 percent annually. However, over the past five years, the S & P 500 has outperformed balanced funds by an average of 3.6 percent per year, and 3.7 percent annually for the past decade. Average turnover during the past three years has been 108 percent per annum. Balanced funds throw off an income stream of approximately 2.3 percent annually. The typical annual expense ratio for this group is 1.3 percent.

Calamos Convertible A
1111 E. Warrenville Road
Naperville, IL 60563
(800) 823-7386
www.calamos.com

total return	★★★★
risk reduction	★★★★
management	★★★★
current income	★★★★★
expense control	★★★
symbol CCVIX	20 points
up-market performance	good
down-market performance	very good
predictability of returns	good

Total Return   ★★★★
Over the past five years, Calamos Convertible A has taken $10,000 and turned it into $18,430 ($14,050 over three years and $33,950 over the past ten years). This translates into an annualized return of 13 percent over the past five years, 12 percent over the past three years, and 13 percent for the decade. Over the past five years, this fund has outperformed 94 percent of all mutual funds; within its general category, it has done better than 90 percent of its peers. Balanced funds have averaged 7 percent annually over these same five years.

During the past five years, a $10,000 initial investment grew to $16,660 after taxes, assuming a 40 percent income tax bracket (state and federal combined) and a capital gains rate of 20 percent. This means that investors in this fund were able to preserve 79 percent of their total returns. Compared to other hybrid funds in the same category, this fund's tax savings are considered to be very good.

Risk/Volatility   ★★★★
Over the past five years, Calamos Convertible A has been safer than 87 percent of all balanced funds. Over the past decade, the fund has had two negative years, while the S & P 500 has had two (off 9 percent in 2000 and 12 percent in 2001); the Lehman Brothers Aggregate Bond Index also fell twice (off 3 percent in 1994 and 1 percent in 1999). The fund has underperformed the S & P 500 twice and the Lehman Brothers Aggregate Bond Index three times in the past ten years. Consistency of *overperformance* for this fund has been outstanding.

	past 5 years		past 10 years	
worst year	-4.1%	2001	-7.0%	1994
best year	35.1%	1999	35.1%	1999

During the past five years, the fund's worst three quarters have been third quarter 1998 (-11 percent), third quarter 2001 (-7 percent), and first quarter 2001 (-6 percent). The three best-performing quarters over the same period have been fourth quarter 1999 (26 percent), fourth quarter 1998 (11 percent), and first quarter

1998 (11 percent). In the past, Calamos Convertible A has done better than 58 percent of its peer group during the most recent bull market and outperformed 64 percent of its peer group during the most recent bear market. Consistency, or predictability, of returns for Calamos Convertible A can be described as good. This fund's risk-related return ranks in the top third.

Management   ★★★★
There are seventy-five fixed-income securities in this $260 million portfolio. The average balanced fund today is $355 million in size. Close to 65 percent of this fund's holdings are in convertibles, 15 percent in bonds, and 10 percent in stocks. The stocks in this portfolio have an average p/e ratio of 25 and a median market capitalization of $11 million. The average maturity of the bonds in this account is five years; the weighted coupon rate averages 4 percent. The portfolio's equity holdings can be categorized as large-cap and value-oriented issues. The portfolio's fixed-income holdings can be categorized as medium quality.

John Calamos and Nick Calamos have managed this fund for the past sixteen years. Managers Calamos and Calamos have been investing in convertibles for more than fifteen and twenty years, respectively. There are eight funds besides Convertible A within the Calamos family. Overall, the fund family's risk-adjusted performance can be described as exceptional.

Current Income   ★★★★★
Over the past year, Calamos Convertible A had a twelve-month yield of 3.3 percent. During this same twelve-month period, the typical balanced fund had a yield that averaged 2.3 percent.

Expenses   ★★★
Calamos Convertible A's expense ratio is 1.2 percent; it has averaged 1.3 percent annually over the past three calendar years. The average expense ratio for the 1,100 funds in this category is 1.3 percent. This fund's turnover rate over the past year has been 93 percent, while its peer group average has been 108 percent.

Summary
Calamos Convertible A, a fund that mostly invests in convertibles with a modest weighting in bonds along with a minor amount of large-cap value stocks, has outperformed more than 93 percent of all mutual funds over the past three and five years and has done better than more than 91 percent of its peer group (99 percent over the past fifteen years). Risk-adjusted returns have also been very good. When it comes to convertibles, the Calamos clan could well be the best in the world.

Profile
minimum initial investment $500	IRA accounts available . . . . yes
subsequent minimum investment . . . $50	IRA minimum investment $500
available in all 50 states. . . . . yes	date of inception. . . . . June 1985
telephone exchanges. . . . . yes	dividend/income paid . . . . quarterly
number of funds in family 9	average bond quality . . . . BBB

Calamos Convertible Growth & Income A

1111 E. Warrenville Road
Naperville, IL 60563
(800) 823-7386
www.calamos.com

total return	★★★★★
risk reduction	★★★
management	★★★★
current income	★★★★
expense control	★★★
symbol CVTRX	19 points
up-market performance	very good
down-market performance	good
predictability of returns	fair

Total Return ★★★★★

Over the past five years, Calamos Convertible Growth & Income A has taken $10,000 and turned it into $22,880 ($15,610 over three years and $44,120 over the past ten years). This translates into an annualized return of 18 percent over the past five years, 16 percent over the past three years, and 16 percent for the decade. Over the past five years, this fund has outperformed 98 percent of all mutual funds; within its general category, it has done better than 99 percent of its peers. Balanced funds have averaged 7 percent annually over these same five years.

During the past five years, a $10,000 initial investment grew to $18,080 after taxes, assuming a 40 percent income tax bracket (state and federal combined) and a capital gains rate of 20 percent. This means that investors in this fund were able to preserve 79 percent of their total returns. Compared to other hybrid funds in the same category, this fund's tax savings are considered to be excellent.

Risk/Volatility ★★★

Over the past five years, Calamos Convertible Growth & Income A has been safer than 59 percent of all balanced funds. Over the past decade, the fund has had two negative years, while the S & P 500 has had two (off 9 percent in 2000 and 12 percent in 2001); the Lehman Brothers Aggregate Bond Index also fell twice (off 3 percent in 1994 and 1 percent in 1999). The fund has underperformed the S & P 500 twice and the Lehman Brothers Aggregate Bond Index three times in the past ten years. Consistency of *overperformance* for this fund has been outstanding.

	past 5 years		past 10 years	
worst year	-3.3%	2001	-5.3%	1994
best year	53.0%	1999	53.0%	1999

During the past five years, the fund's worst three quarters have been third quarter 1998 (-10 percent), third quarter 2001 (-7 percent), and first quarter 2001 (-7 percent). The three best-performing quarters over the same period have been fourth quarter 1999 (34 percent), fourth quarter 1998 (14 percent), and first quarter 1998 (13 percent). In the past, Calamos Convertible Growth & Income A has done better than 32 percent of its peer group during the most recent bull market and outperformed 57 percent of its peer group during the most recent bear market. Consistency, or predictability, of returns for Calamos Convertible Growth & Income A can be described as fair. This fund's risk-related return ranks in the top quintile.

Management   ★★★★
There are eighty fixed-income securities in this $180 million portfolio. The average balanced fund today is $355 million in size. Close to 70 percent of this fund's holdings are in convertibles, 20 percent in bonds, and 10 percent in stocks.

John Calamos and Nick Calamos have managed this fund for the past fourteen years. Managers Calamos and Calamos have been investing in convertibles for more than fifteen and twenty years, respectively. Unlike the Convertible Fund, this offering invests in "busted convertibles," securities that are so far out of the money that they trade more like bonds. There are eight funds besides Convertible Growth & Income A within the Calamos family. Overall, the fund family's risk-adjusted performance can be described as exceptional.

Current Income   ★★★★
Over the past year, Calamos Convertible Growth & Income A had a twelve-month yield of 2.6 percent. During this same twelve-month period, the typical balanced fund had a yield that averaged 2.3 percent.

Expenses   ★★★
Calamos Convertible Growth & Income A's expense ratio is 1.4 percent; it has averaged 1.7 percent annually over the past three calendar years. The average expense ratio for the 1,100 funds in this category is 1.3 percent. This fund's turnover rate over the past year has been 82 percent, while its peer group average has been 108 percent.

Summary
Calamos Convertible Growth & Income A, a fund that mostly invests in convertibles with a modest weighting in bonds along with a minor amount of large-cap growth stocks, has outperformed more than 97 percent of all mutual funds over the past three, five, and ten years and has done better than more than 99 percent of its peer group over the same periods. Risk-adjusted returns have been exceptional over the past three, five, and ten years. The portfolio ranks number one when it comes to performance over the past five years. The fund's performance has ranked in the top quartile of its category for each of the past five years—consistency that is rare in any category.

Profile

minimum initial investment $500	IRA accounts available . . . . yes
subsequent minimum investment . . . $50	IRA minimum investment $500
available in all 50 states. . . . . yes	date of inception . . . . Sept. 1988
telephone exchanges. . . . . yes	dividend/income paid . . . . quarterly
number of funds in family 9	average bond quality . . . . BBB

Dodge & Cox Balanced

One Sansome Street, 35th Floor
San Francisco, CA 94104
(800) 621-3979
www.dodgeandcox.com

total return	★★★★
risk reduction	★★★★★
management	★★★★★
current income	★★★★★
expense control	★★★★★
symbol DODBX	24 points
up-market performance	very good
down-market performance	excellent
predictability of returns	very good

Total Return   ★★★★

Over the past five years, Dodge & Cox Balanced has taken $10,000 and turned it into $18,430 ($14,050 over three years and $33,950 over the past ten years). This translates into an annualized return of 13 percent over the past five years, 12 percent over the past three years, and 13 percent for the decade. Over the past five years, this fund has outperformed 93 percent of all mutual funds; within its general category it has done better than 97 percent of its peers. Balanced funds have averaged 7 percent annually over these same five years.

During the past five years, a $10,000 initial investment grew to $16,330 after taxes, assuming a 40 percent income tax bracket (state and federal combined) and a capital gains rate of 20 percent. This means that investors in this fund were able to preserve 75 percent of their total returns. Compared to other hybrid funds in the same category, this fund's tax savings are considered to be very good.

Risk/Volatility   ★★★★★

Over the past five years, Dodge & Cox Balanced has been safer than 83 percent of all balanced funds. Over the past decade, the fund has had no negative years, while the S & P 500 has had two (off 9 percent in 2000 and 12 percent in 2001); the Lehman Brothers Aggregate Bond Index also fell twice (off 3 percent in 1994 and 1 percent in 1999). The fund has underperformed the S & P 500 twice and the Lehman Brothers Aggregate Bond Index twice in the past ten years. Consistency of *overperformance* for this fund has been very good.

	past 5 years		past 10 years	
worst year	6.7%	1998	2.0%	1994
best year	21.1%	1997	28.0%	1995

During the past five years, the fund's worst three quarters have been third quarter 1998 (-8 percent), third quarter 1999 (-5 percent), and third quarter 2001 (-5 percent). The three best-performing quarters over the same period have been second quarter 1997 (11 percent), and second quarter 1999 (10 percent), and fourth quarter 2000 (9 percent). In the past, the fund has done better than 74 percent of its peer group during the most recent bull market and outperformed 99 percent of its peer group during the most recent bear market. Consistency of returns for the fund is very good. This fund's risk-related return ranks in the top quintile.

Management   ★★★★★
There are eighty stocks and 130 fixed-income securities in this $5 billion portfolio. The average balanced fund today is $355 million in size. Close to 60 percent of this fund's holdings are in stocks and 35 percent in bonds. The stocks in this portfolio have an average p/e ratio of 25 and a median market capitalization of $10 billion. The average maturity of the bonds in this account is ten years; the weighted coupon rate averages 7 percent. The portfolio's equity holdings can be categorized as large-cap and value-oriented issues. The portfolio's fixed-income holdings can be categorized as long-term, high-quality debt.

A team has managed this fund for the past twenty-two years. Management has shown a consistency and level of patience not commonly found within the industry. Overall, the fund family's risk-adjusted performance can be described as exceptional.

Current Income   ★★★★★
Over the past year, Dodge & Cox Balanced had a yield of 3.2 percent. During this same period, the typical balanced fund had a 2.3 percent average yield.

Expenses   ★★★★★
Dodge & Cox Balanced's expense ratio is 0.5 percent; it has averaged 0.5 percent annually over the past three calendar years. The average expense ratio for the 1,100 funds in this category is 1.3 percent. This fund's turnover rate over the past year has been 23 percent, while its peer group average has been 108 percent.

Summary
Dodge & Cox, a balanced fund that invests mostly in medium-cap value stocks along with a lesser weighting in high-quality fixed-income, has outperformed more than 92 percent of all mutual funds over the past three and five years and has done better than more than 97 percent of its peer group over the last three, five, ten, and fifteen years. Risk-adjusted returns have also been excellent over the past three, five, and ten years. The fund rates between good and very good in every category measured and ties for first place as paying out the highest current income to investors. This portfolio's alpha, which measures excess returns per unit of risk taken, as measured against the fund's benchmark index, is quite appealing. On a total point basis, this is the number-one fund for its category.

Profile
minimum initial investment $2,500	*IRA accounts available* . . . . yes
subsequent minimum investment . . $100	*IRA minimum investment* $1,000
available in all 50 states. . . . . yes	*date of inception.* . . . . June 1931
telephone exchanges. . . . . yes	*dividend/income paid* . . . . quarterly
number of funds in family 4	*largest sector weighting* . . . . industrials

First Eagle SoGen Global A

1345 Avenue of the Americas
New York, NY 10105
(800) 334-2143
www.firsteaglesogen.com

total return	★★★
risk reduction	★★★★★
management	★★★★
current income	★★★★
expense control	★★★★
symbol SGENX	20 points
up-market performance	excellent
down-market performance	excellent
predictability of returns	very good

Total Return   ★★★

Over the past five years, First Eagle SoGen Global A has taken $10,000 and turned it into $15,390 ($14,430 over three years and $28,400 over the past ten years). This translates into an annualized return of 9 percent over the past five years, 13 percent over the past three years, and 11 percent for the decade. Over the past five years, this fund has outperformed 78 percent of all mutual funds; within its general category, it has done better than 87 percent of its peers. Balanced funds have averaged 7 percent annually over these same five years.

During the past five years, a $10,000 initial investment grew to $13,080 after taxes, assuming a 40 percent income tax bracket (state and federal combined) and a capital gains rate of 20 percent. This means that investors in this fund were able to preserve 57 percent of their total returns. Compared to other hybrid funds in the same category, this fund's tax savings are considered to be good.

Risk/Volatility   ★★★★★

Over the past five years, First Eagle SoGen Global A has been safer than 94 percent of all balanced funds. Over the past decade, the fund has had one negative year, while the S & P 500 has had two (off 9 percent in 2000 and 12 percent in 2001); the Lehman Brothers Aggregate Bond Index also fell twice (off 3 percent in 1994 and 1 percent in 1999). The fund has underperformed the S & P 500 twice and the Lehman Brothers Aggregate Bond Index twice in the past ten years. Consistency of *overperformance* for this fund has been good.

	past 5 years		past 10 years	
worst year	-0.3%	1998	-0.3%	1998
best year	20.0%	1999	26.2%	1993

During the past five years, the fund's worst three quarters have been third quarter 1998 (-11 percent), third quarter 2001 (-8 percent), and fourth quarter 1997 (-5 percent). The three best-performing quarters over the same period have been second quarter 1999 (9 percent), first quarter 1998 (8 percent), and second quarter

1997 (8 percent). In the past, First Eagle SoGen Global A has done better than 51 percent of its peer group during the most recent bull market and outperformed 99 percent of its peer group during the most recent bear market. Consistency, or predictability, of returns for First Eagle SoGen Global A can be described as very good. This fund's risk-related return ranks in the top quintile.

Management   ★★★★
There are 155 stocks and fifty-five fixed-income securities in this $1.6 billion portfolio. The average balanced fund today is $355 million in size. Close to 80 percent of this fund's holdings are in stocks and 15 percent in bonds. The stocks in this portfolio have an average p/e ratio of 19 and a median market capitalization of $1.5 billion. The portfolio's equity holdings can be categorized as mid-cap and value-oriented issues.

Jean-Marie Eveillard and Charles de Vaulx have managed this fund for the past nineteen years. Lead manager Eveillard is considered to be one of the most highly regarded money managers in the world and has a reputation that has remained untarnished for over two decades. There are six funds besides Global A within the First Eagle SoGen family. Overall, the fund family's risk-adjusted performance can be described as exceptional.

Current Income   ★★★★
Over the past year, First Eagle SoGen Global A had a twelve-month yield of 2.6 percent. During this same twelve-month period, the typical balanced fund had a yield that averaged 2.3 percent.

Expenses   ★★★★
First Eagle SoGen Global A's expense ratio is 1.3 percent; it has averaged 1.3 percent annually over the past three calendar years. The average expense ratio for the 1,100 funds in this category is 1.3 percent. This fund's turnover rate over the past year has been 12 percent, while its peer group average has been 108 percent.

Summary
First Eagle SoGen Global A, an international hybrid fund that invests mostly in foreign and domestic small-cap value stocks, has outperformed roughly three quarters of all mutual funds over the past five, ten, and fifteen years (92 percent over the past three years) and has done better than 99 percent of its peer group over the past fifteen years. Risk-adjusted returns have also been superb over the past three, five, and ten years. The fund rates between good and excellent in every category measured. It ties for first place when it comes to risk reduction.

Profile

minimum initial investment $1,000	*IRA accounts available* . . . . yes
subsequent minimum investment . . $100	*IRA minimum investment* $1,000
available in all 50 states . . . . yes	*date of inception* . . . . Apr. 1970
telephone exchanges . . . . yes	*dividend/income paid* . . . . annually
number of funds in family 7	largest country weighting . . . . U.S.

Gabelli ABC

One Corporate Center
Rye, NY 10580
(800) 422-3554
www.gabelli.com

total return	★★★
risk reduction	★★★★★
management	★★★★
current income	★★★
expense control	★★★
symbol GABCX	18 points
up-market performance	poor
down-market performance	excellent
predictability of returns	excellent

Total Return   ★★★

Over the past five years, Gabelli ABC has taken $10,000 and turned it into $16,110 ($12,600 over three years). This translates into an annualized return of 10 percent over the past five years and 8 percent over the past three years. Over the past five years, this fund has outperformed 83 percent of all mutual funds; within its general category, it has done better than 85 percent of its peers. Balanced funds have averaged 7 percent annually over these same five years.

During the past five years, a $10,000 initial investment grew to $13,730 after taxes, assuming a 40 percent income tax bracket (state and federal combined) and a capital gains rate of 20 percent. This means that investors in this fund were able to preserve 61 percent of their total returns. Compared to other hybrid funds in the same category, this fund's tax savings are considered to be good.

Risk/Volatility   ★★★★★

Over the past five years, Gabelli ABC has been safer than 99 percent of all balanced funds. Over the past decade, the fund has had no negative years, while the S & P 500 has had two (off 9 percent in 2000 and 12 percent in 2001); the Lehman Brothers Aggregate Bond Index also fell twice (off 3 percent in 1994 and 1 percent in 1999). The fund has underperformed the S & P 500 twice and the Lehman Brothers Aggregate Bond Index twice in the past ten years. Consistency of *overperformance* for this fund has been good.

	past 5 years		past 8 years	
worst year	4.6%	2001	4.5%	1994
best year	11.1%	1998	12.8%	1997

During the past five years, the fund's worst three quarters have been third quarter 1998 (-5 percent), third quarter 1999 (0 percent), and second quarter 1998 (0 percent). The three best-performing quarters over the same period have been: fourth quarter 1998 (12 percent), second quarter 1999 (6 percent), and second quarter 1997 (5 percent). In the past, Gabelli ABC has done better than just 3 percent of its peer group during the most recent bull market but outperformed 97 percent of its peer group during the most recent bear market. Consistency, or predictability, of returns for Gabelli ABC can be described as excellent. This fund's risk-related return ranks in the top third.

Management   ★★★★
There are fifty stocks and ten fixed-income securities in this $160 million portfolio. The average balanced fund today is $355 million in size. Close to 80 percent of this fund's holdings are in cash and 18 percent in stocks. The stocks in this portfolio have an average p/e ratio of 16 and a median market capitalization of $2 billion. The weighted coupon rate for the bond portion averages 5 percent. The portfolio's equity holdings can be categorized as mid-cap and a blend of growth and value stocks.

Mario Gabelli has managed this fund for the past nine years. Manager Gabelli buys shares of companies involved with acquisitions and mergers. He then takes advantage of the price difference between the accouncement and the deal's closing. Oftentimes, the fund has a moderate to very large cash position. Stock positions are frequently concentrated and may only be held for two months or less. There are twenty-one funds besides ABC within the Gabelli family. Overall, the fund family's risk-adjusted performance can be described as very good.

Current Income   ★★★
Over the past year, Gabelli ABC had a twelve-month yield of 0.9 percent. During this same twelve-month period, the typical balanced fund had a yield that averaged 2.3 percent.

Expenses   ★★★
Gabelli ABC's expense ratio is 1.5 percent; it has averaged 1.5 percent annually over the past three calendar years. The average expense ratio for the 1,100 funds in this category is 1.3 percent. This fund's turnover rate over the past year has been 312 percent, while its peer group average has been 108 percent.

Summary
Gabelli ABC, a balanced fund, has outperformed more than 85 percent of all mutual funds over the past three and five years and has done better than 95 percent of its peer group. Risk-adjusted returns have been very good over the past three and five years. The fund ranks in the top quintile when it comes to return versus risk. The portfolio ranks number one when it comes to risk reduction and predictability of returns within its peer group. This portfolio's alpha, which measures excess returns per unit of risk taken, as measured against the fund's benchmark index, is appealing.

Profile

minimum initial investment $2,500	*IRA accounts available* . . . . yes
subsequent minimum investment $1	*IRA minimum investment* $250
available in all 50 states. . . . . yes	*date of inception*. . . . . May 1993
telephone exchanges. . . . . yes	*dividend/income paid* . . . . annually
number of funds in family 22	*largest sector weighting*. . . . . . . energy

Nations Convertible Securities Investor A

One Bank of America Plaza, 33rd Floor
Charlotte, NC 28255
(800) 321-7854
www.bankofamerica.com

total return	★★★
risk reduction	★★★★
management	★★★★
current income	★★★★★
expense control	★★★
symbol PACIX	19 points
up-market performance	good
down-market performance	poor
predictability of returns	good

Total Return ★★★

Over the past five years, Nations Convertible Securities Investor A has taken $10,000 and turned it into $17,630 ($13,310 over three years and $37,080 over the past ten years). This translates into an annualized return of 12 percent over the past five years, 10 percent over the past three years, and 14 percent for the decade. Over the past five years, this fund has outperformed 90 percent of all mutual funds; within its general category, it has done better than 73 percent of its peers. Balanced funds have averaged 7 percent annually over these same five years.

During the past five years, a $10,000 initial investment grew to $14,280 after taxes, assuming a 40 percent income tax bracket (state and federal combined) and a capital gains rate of 20 percent. This means that investors in this fund were able to preserve 56 percent of their total returns. Compared to other hybrid funds in the same category, this fund's tax savings are considered to be good.

Risk/Volatility ★★★★

Over the past five years, Nations Convertible Securities Investor A has been safer than 82 percent of all balanced funds. Over the past decade, the fund has had two negative years, while the S & P 500 has had two (off 9 percent in 2000 and 12 percent in 2001); the Lehman Brothers Aggregate Bond Index also fell twice (off 3 percent in 1994 and 1 percent in 1999). The fund has underperformed the S & P 500 twice and the Lehman Brothers Aggregate Bond Index three times in the past ten years. Consistency of *overperformance* for this fund has been outstanding.

	past 5 years		past 10 years	
worst year	-7.9%	2001	-7.9%	2001
best year	26.8%	1999	26.8%	1999

During the past five years, the fund's worst three quarters have been third quarter 1998 (-9 percent), first quarter 2001 (-9 percent), and third quarter 2001 (-8 percent). The three best-performing quarters over the same period have been fourth quarter 1999 (17 percent), first quarter 2000 (13 percent), and second quarter 1997

(13 percent). In the past, Nations Convertible Securities Investor A has done better than 41 percent of its peer group during the most recent bull market and outperformed 61 percent of its peer group during the most recent bear market. Consistency, or predictability, of returns for Nations Convertible Securities Investor A can be described as good. This fund's risk-related return ranks in the top third.

Management   ★★★★
There are seventy-five fixed-income securities in this $320 million portfolio. The average balanced fund today is $355 million in size. Close to 45 percent of this fund's holdings are in bonds, 30 percent in convertibles, and 20 percent in stocks. The stocks in this portfolio have an average p/e ratio of 21 and a median market capitalization of $9 billion. The weighted coupon rate for the bond portion averages 4 percent. The portfolio's equity holdings can be categorized as large-cap and value-oriented issues.

Ed Cassens has managed this fund for the past eight years. Manager Cassens makes sure the portfolio stays well diversified by sector as well as by individual issues. There are 186 funds besides Convertible Securities Investor A within the Nations family. Overall, the fund family's risk-adjusted performance can be described as very good.

Current Income   ★★★★★
Over the past year, Nations Convertible Securities Investor A had a twelve-month yield of 3.3 percent. During this same twelve-month period, the typical balanced fund had a yield that averaged 2.3 percent.

Expenses   ★★★
Nations Convertible Securities Investor A's expense ratio is 1.2 percent; it has averaged 1.2 percent annually over the past three calendar years. The average expense ratio for the 1,100 funds in this category is 1.3 percent. This fund's turnover rate over the past year has been 73 percent, while its peer group average has been 108 percent.

Summary
Nations Convertible Securities Investor A, a balanced fund that invests in lower-rated bonds, convertibles, and large-cap growth stocks, has outperformed 88 percent of all mutual funds over the past three, five, and ten years. Risk-adjusted returns have also been very good over the past three, five, and ten years. The fund scores well in every category measured and ranks number one as paying out more current income to investors than any of its peers. Returns have been similar to those of the S & P 500 but with far greater risk.

Profile

minimum initial investment $1,000	*IRA accounts available* . . . . yes
subsequent minimum investment . . $100	*IRA minimum investment* $500
available in all 50 states. . . . . yes	*date of inception* . . . . Sept. 1987
telephone exchanges. . . . . yes	*dividend/income paid* . . . . quarterly
number of funds in family 187	*average bond quality*. . . . . BB

Oakmark Equity & Income I

Two North LaSalle Street
Chicago, IL 60602
(800) 625-6275
www.oakmark.com

total return	★★★★★
risk reduction	★★★★★
management	★★★★
current income	★
expense control	★★★
symbol OAKBX	18 points
up-market performance	very good
down-market performance	excellent
predictability of returns	very good

Total Return   ★★★★★

Over the past five years, Oakmark Equity & Income I has taken $10,000 and turned it into $21,930 ($15,210 over three years). This translates into an annualized return of 17 percent over the past five years and 15 percent over the past three years. Over the past five years, this fund has outperformed 98 percent of all mutual funds; within its general category, it has done better than 99 percent of its peers. Balanced funds have averaged 7 percent annually over these same five years.

During the past five years, a $10,000 initial investment grew to $20,500 after taxes, assuming a 40 percent income tax bracket (state and federal combined) and a capital gains rate of 20 percent. This means that investors in this fund were able to preserve 88 percent of their total returns. Compared to other hybrid funds in the same category, this fund's tax savings are considered to be excellent.

Risk/Volatility   ★★★★★

Over the past five years, Oakmark Equity & Income I has been safer than 91 percent of all balanced funds. Over the past decade, the fund has had no negative years, while the S & P 500 has had two (off 9 percent in 2000 and 12 percent in 2001); the Lehman Brothers Aggregate Bond Index also fell twice (off 3 percent in 1994 and 1 percent in 1999). The fund has underperformed the S & P 500 twice and the Lehman Brothers Aggregate Bond Index once in the past ten years. Consistency of *overperformance* for this fund has been very good.

	past 5 years		past 6 years	
worst year	7.9%	1999	7.9%	1999
best year	26.6%	1997	26.6%	1997

During the past five years, the fund's worst three quarters have been third quarter 1998 (-7 percent), third quarter 2001 (-3 percent), and second quarter 2000 (0 percent). The three best-performing quarters over the same period have been fourth quarter 1998 (11 percent), second quarter 1997 (11 percent), and third quarter 2000 (10 percent). In the past, Oakmark Equity & Income I has done better than 71 percent of its peer group during the most recent bull market and outper-formed more than 99 percent of its peer group during the most recent bear market. Consistency, or predictability, of returns for Oakmark Equity & Income I can be described as very good. This fund's risk-related return ranks in the top quintile.

Management   ★★★★
There are forty stocks and twenty-five fixed-income securities in this $770 million port-folio. The average balanced fund today is $355 million in size. Close to 65 percent of this fund's holdings are in stocks and 30 percent in bonds. The stocks in this portfolio have an average p/e ratio of 24 and a median market capitalization of $4 billion. The weighted coupon rate for the bond portion averages 7 percent. The portfolio's equity holdings can be categorized as mid-cap and a blend of growth and value stocks.

Clyde McGregor and Edward Studzinski have managed this fund for the past five years. Managers McGregor and Studzinski target cash-rich companies that are selling at a discount. There are eight funds besides Equity & Income I within the Oakmark family. Overall, the fund family's risk-adjusted performance can be described as very good to exceptional.

Current Income   ★
Over the past year, Oakmark Equity & Income I had a twelve-month yield of 0.8 percent. During this same twelve-month period, the typical balanced fund had a yield that averaged 2.3 percent.

Expenses   ★★★
Oakmark Equity & Income I's expense ratio is 1.2 percent; it has averaged 1.2 per-cent annually over the past three calendar years. The average expense ratio for the 1,100 funds in this category is 1.3 percent. This fund's turnover rate over the past year has been 81 percent, while its peer group average has been 108 percent.

Summary
Oakmark Equity & Income, a balanced fund that mostly invests in medium-cap value stocks, has outperformed more than 97 percent of all mutual funds over the past three and five years and has done better than 99 percent of its peer group over the same periods. Risk-adjusted returns have also been exceptional. The fund ranks in the top quintile when it comes to return versus risk. The portfolio ranks number two when it comes to peer group performance and ties for number one for risk reduction. It is also the most tax-efficient fund in its category. The bond portion is high quality. This portfolio's alpha, which measures excess returns per unit of risk taken, as measured against the fund's benchmark index, is quite appealing.

Profile
minimum initial investment $1,000	*IRA accounts available* . . . . yes
subsequent minimum investment . . $100	*IRA minimum investment* $1,000
available in all 50 states. . . . . yes	*date of inception* . . . . Nov. 1995
telephone exchanges. . . . . yes	*dividend/income paid* . . . . annually
number of funds in family 9	*largest sector weighting* . . . . financials

Oppenheimer Global Growth & Income A

P.O. Box 5270
Denver, CO 80217
(800) 525-7048
www.oppenheimerfunds.com

total return	★★★★★
risk reduction	★
management	★★★★
current income	★★
expense control	★★★★
symbol OPGIX	14 points
up-market performance	excellent
down-market performance	poor
predictability of returns	poor

Total Return   ★★★★★

Over the past five years, Oppenheimer Global Growth & Income A has taken $10,000 and turned it into $21,930 ($14,820 over three years and $37,080 over the past ten years). This translates into an annualized return of 17 percent over the past five years, 14 percent over the past three years, and 14 percent for the decade. Over the past five years, this fund has outperformed 97 percent of all mutual funds; within its general category, it has done better than 99 percent of its peers. Balanced funds have averaged 7 percent annually over these same five years.

During the past five years, a $10,000 initial investment grew to $19,430 after taxes, assuming a 40 percent income tax bracket (state and federal combined) and a capital gains rate of 20 percent. This means that investors in this fund were able to preserve 79 percent of their total returns. Compared to other hybrid funds in the same category, this fund's tax savings are considered to be very good.

Risk/Volatility   ★

Over the past decade, Oppenheimer Global Growth & Income A has had four negative years, while the S & P 500 has had two (off 9 percent in 2000 and 12 percent in 2001); the Lehman Brothers Aggregate Bond Index also fell twice (off 3 percent in 1994 and 1 percent in 1999). The fund has underperformed the S & P 500 twice and the Lehman Brothers Aggregate Bond Index three times in the past ten years. Consistency of *overperformance* for this fund has been outstanding.

	past 5 years		past 10 years	
worst year	-16.3%	2001	-16.3%	2001
best year	86.6%	1999	86.6%	1999

During the past five years, the fund's worst three quarters have been third quarter 2001 (-25 percent), third quarter 1998 (-17 percent), and first quarter 2001 (-15 percent). The three best-performing quarters over the same period have been fourth quarter 1999 (32 percent), second quarter 1999 (24 percent), and fourth quarter 1998 (21 percent). In the past, Oppenheimer Global Growth & Income A has done better than 81 percent of its peer group during the most recent bull market and outperformed 36 percent of its peer group during the most recent bear market. Consistency, or predictability, of returns for Oppenheimer Global Growth & Income A can be described as poor. This fund's risk-related return ranks in the top quintile.

Management   ★★★★
There are fifty stocks in this $1.4 billion portfolio. The average balanced fund today is $355 million in size. Close to 95 percent of this fund's holdings are in stocks. The stocks in this portfolio have an average p/e ratio of 28 and a median market capitalization of $3 billion. The portfolio's equity holdings can be categorized as mid-cap and a blend of growth and value stocks.

Frank Jennings has managed this fund for the past seven years. Manager Jennings has a knack for finding equity opportunities in various asset categories. He has a "flexible, go anywhere approach." There are 215 funds besides Global Growth & Income A within the Oppenheimer family. Overall, the fund family's risk-adjusted performance can be described as good to very good.

Current Income   ★★
Over the past year, Oppenheimer Global Growth & Income A had a twelve-month yield of 0.1 percent. During this same twelve-month period, the typical balanced fund had a yield that averaged 2.3 percent.

Expenses   ★★★★
Oppenheimer Global Growth & Income A's expense ratio is 1.2 percent; it has averaged 1.2 percent annually over the past three calendar years. The average expense ratio for the 1,100 funds in this category is 1.3 percent. This fund's turnover rate over the past year has been 48 percent, while its peer group average has been 108 percent.

Summary
Oppenheimer Global Growth & Income A, a multiasset international fund that invests in medium-cap growth as well as value stocks, has outperformed roughly 95 percent of all mutual funds over the past three and five years and has done better than 99 percent of its peer group. Risk-adjusted returns have been excellent over the past three, five, and ten years. The fund ranks in the top third when it comes to return versus risk. The fund outperformed the S & P 500 by 66 percentage points in 1999. This portfolio's alpha, which measures excess returns per unit of risk taken, as measured against the fund's benchmark index, is quite appealing.

Profile
minimum initial investment $1,000	*IRA accounts available* . . . . yes
subsequent minimum investment . . . $25	*IRA minimum investment* $250
available in all 50 states. . . . . yes	*date of inception* . . . . Oct. 1990
telephone exchanges. . . . . yes	*dividend/income paid* . . . . annually
number of funds in family 216	*largest sector weighting* . . . technology

Corporate Bond Funds

Traditionally, bond funds are held by investors who require high current income and low risk. Interest income is normally paid on a monthly basis. Corporate bond funds are made up primarily of bonds issued by domestic corporations; government securities often represent a moderate part of these funds. Portfolio composition is almost always exclusively U.S. issues.

Bonds are normally purchased because of their income stream; the principal in a bond fund fluctuates. The major influence on bond prices, and therefore on the value of the fund's shares, is interest rates. There is an inverse relationship between interest rates and bond values; whatever one does, the other does the opposite. If interest rates rise, the price per share of a bond fund will fall, and vice versa.

The amount of appreciation or loss of a corporate bond fund depends primarily on the average maturity of the bonds in the portfolio. The cumulative amount of interest-rate movement and the typical yield of the bonds in the fund's portfolio are distant secondary concerns. *Short-term* bond funds, made up of debt instruments with an average maturity of five years or less, are subject to very little interest-rate risk or reward. *Medium-term* bond funds, with maturities averaging between six and ten years, are subject to one-third to one-half the risk level of long-term funds. A long-term corporate bond fund will average an 8 percent increase or decrease in share price for every cumulative 1 percent change in interest rates.

Often investors can tell what kind of corporate bond fund they are purchasing by its name. Unless the fund includes the term *short* in its title, chances are that it is a medium- or long-term bond fund. Investors would be wise to contact the fund or meet with an investment advisor to learn more about the portfolio's average maturity; most bond funds will dramatically reduce their portfolio's average maturity during periods of interest-rate uncertainty.

The average weighted maturity for the bonds in these funds is just under seven years, the average coupon rate is 6.5 percent, and the average weighted price is $985 (meaning that the bonds are worth $15 less than face value, on average). A price, or value, of par ($1,000 per bond) means that the bonds in a portfolio are worth face value and are not currently being traded at a discount (a price less than $1,000 per bond) or at a premium (some figure above $1,000). The portfolio of the *average* corporate bond fund is made up of securities purchased at a $15-per-bond discount ($985 versus $1,000 for bonds bought at face value). A portfolio manager purchases bonds at a discount for one of two reasons: to decrease the portfolio's current income, or to slightly increase the fund's volatility (the lower the coupon rate, the more susceptible a bond is to the effects of interest-rate changes).

Annual Returns - Corporate Bond Funds

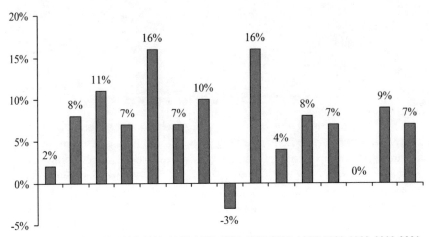

1987 1988 1989 1990 1991 1992 1993 1994 1995 1996 1997 1998 1999 2000 2001

During the past ten years, corporate bond funds have underperformed the Lehman Brothers Aggregate Bond Index by a little less than 1 percent per year. Over the past three and five years, the gap widens to a little over 1 percent. Average turnover during the past three years has been 156 percent, a surprisingly high figure given the general belief that stocks are traded (turned over) much more frequently than bonds. (The typical growth fund has a turnover rate of 114 percent annually.) The average corporate bond fund throws off an annual income stream of about 5.5 percent. The typical annual expense ratio for this group is just under 1 percent.

Over the past fifteen years (ending December 31, 2001), individual corporate bonds have underperformed common stocks by 4.8 percent per year. From 1987 through 2001, long-term corporate bonds averaged 8.9 percent compounded per year, compared to 13.7 percent for common stocks and 12.3 percent for small stocks. A $10,000 investment in corporate bonds grew to $35,756 over the past fifteen years; a similar initial investment in common stocks grew to $68,924 and $59,264 for small stocks.

Over the past half-century, corporate bonds have only outpaced inflation on a pretax basis. A dollar invested in corporate bonds at the beginning of 1952 grew to $22.78 by the end of 2001. This translates into an average compound return of 6.5 percent per year. During this same period, $1 inflated to $6.67; this translates into an average annual inflation rate of 4 percent. This creates an inflation-adjusted rate of return of just 2.5 percent for corporate bonds. Factoring in taxes that would have been paid on the interest as it was received year by year lowers the *real* rate of return. This often results in flat and even negative real rates of return to the investor, especially for those in higher tax brackets.

Over the past fifty years, the worst year for long-term corporate bonds, on a total return basis (yield plus or minus principal appreciation or loss), was 1969, when a loss of 8 percent was suffered. The best year so far has been 1982, when corporate bonds posted a gain of 43 percent.

More than 950 funds make up the corporate bonds category. Total market capitalization of this category is $305 billion. Over the past three and five years, corporate bond funds have had an average compound return of 5.2 percent and 6.2 percent per year, respectively. For the decade, corporate bond funds have averaged 6.5 percent per year and 7.5 percent per annum for the past fifteen years. All of these figures represent total returns. This means that bond appreciation (or depreciation) was added (or subtracted) from current yield.

The standard deviation for corporate bond funds has been 3.5 percent over the past three years. As you may recall, a low standard deviation means a greater predictability of returns (fewer surprises—for better or worse). If a fund, or fund category, such as corporate bonds, has an average annual return of 10 percent and a standard deviation of 3 percent, this means that returns for every two out of three years should be roughly 10 percent, plus or minus 3 percent (one standard deviation). If you want to increase certainty of returns, then you must look at two standard deviations. This means that returns, for about 95 percent of the time, would be 10 percent plus or minus 6 percent (or +4 percent to +16 percent). These funds have been less volatile than any equity fund and have shown similar return variances (volatility) as government bond funds.

Dodge & Cox Income

One Sansome Street, 35th Floor
San Francisco, CA 94104
(800) 621-3979
www.dodgeandcox.com

total return	★★★★★
risk reduction	★★★★
management	★★★★★
current income	★★★★
expense control	★★★★★
symbol DODIX	23 points
up-market performance	very good
down-market performance	excellent
predictability of returns	good

Total Return   ★★★★★

Over the past five years, Dodge & Cox Income has taken $10,000 and turned it into $14,700 ($12,250 over three years and $21,590 over the past ten years). This translates into an annualized return of 8 percent over the past five years, 7 percent over the past three years, and 8 percent for the decade. Over the past five years, this fund has outperformed 71 percent of all mutual funds; within its general category, it has done better than 93 percent of its peers. Corporate bond funds have averaged 6 percent annually over these same five years.

During the past five years, a $10,000 initial investment grew to $13,060 after taxes, assuming a 40 percent income tax bracket (state and federal combined) and a capital gains rate of 20 percent. This means that investors in this fund were able to preserve 65 percent of their total returns. Compared to other hybrid funds in the same category, this fund's tax savings are considered to be excellent.

Risk/Volatility   ★★★★

Over the past five years, Dodge & Cox Income has been safer than 76 percent of all corporate bond funds. Over the past decade, the fund has had two negative years, while the Lehman Brothers Aggregate Bond Index has had two (off 3 percent in 1994 and 1 percent in 1999). The fund has underperformed the Lehman Brothers Aggregate Bond Index twice over the past ten years. Consistency of *overperformance* for this fund has been outstanding.

	past 5 years		past 10 years	
worst year	-0.8%	1999	-2.9%	1994
best year	10.7%	2000	20.2%	1995

During the past five years, the fund's worst three quarters have been second quarter 1999 (-1 percent), first quarter 1997 (-1 percent), and first quarter 1999 (0 percent). The three best-performing quarters over the same period have been third quarter 2001 (4 percent), fourth quarter 2000 (4 percent), and first quarter 2001 (4 percent). In the past, Dodge & Cox Income has done better than 81 percent of its peer group during the most recent bull market and outperformed 94 percent of its peer group during the most recent bear market. Consistency, or predictability, of returns for Dodge & Cox Income can be described as good. This fund's risk-related return ranks in the top quintile.

Management   ★★★★★

There are 130 fixed-income securities in this $1.2 billion portfolio. The average corporate bond fund today is $320 million in size. Close to 95 percent of the fund's holdings are in bonds. The average maturity of the bonds in this account is ten years; the weighted coupon rate averages 7 percent. The portfolio's fixed-income holdings can be categorized as intermediate-term, high-quality debt.

A team has managed this fund for the past eleven years. Management focuses on security selection instead of expected changes in interest rates or the yield curve. There are three funds besides Income within the Dodge & Cox family. Overall, the fund family's risk-adjusted performance can be described as exceptional.

Current Income   ★★★★

Over the past year, Dodge & Cox Income had a twelve-month yield of 6 percent. During this same twelve-month period, the typical corporate bond fund had a yield that averaged 5.5 percent.

Expenses   ★★★★★

Dodge & Cox Income's expense ratio is 0.5 percent; it has averaged 0.5 percent annually over the past three calendar years. The average expense ratio for the 1,000 funds in this category is 1.0 percent. This fund's turnover rate over the past year has been 34 percent, while its peer group average has been 156 percent.

Summary

Dodge & Cox Income, which has the majority of its assets in U.S. government securities, has outperformed more than 70 percent of all mutual funds over the past five years and has done better than more than 93 percent of its peer group over the past three, five, and ten years. Risk-adjusted returns have ranged between very good and excellent over the past three, five, and ten years. The fund ranks in the top quintile when it comes to return versus risk. The portfolio ranks number one for controlling expenses and number two for performance. Over half the portfolio is in U.S. Treasury or agency-backed issues. The fund has landed in the top half of performance for each of the past eleven years—a rarity for a fund in any category. This portfolio's alpha, which measures excess returns per unit of risk taken, as measured against the fund's benchmark index, is appealing. On a total point basis, this is the number-one fund for its category.

Profile

minimum initial investment $2,500	*IRA accounts available* . . . . yes
subsequent minimum investment . . $100	*IRA minimum investment* $1,000
available in all 50 states. . . . . yes	*date of inception* . . . . Jan. 1989
telephone exchanges. . . . . yes	*dividend/income paid* . . . . quarterly
number of funds in family 4	*average credit quality*. . . . . AA

FPA New Income
11400 West Olympic Boulevard, Suite 1200
Los Angeles, CA 90064
(800) 982-4372

total return	★★★★★
risk reduction	★★★★
management	★★★★★
current income	★★★★
expense control	★★★★★
symbol FPNIX	23 points
up-market performance	very good
down-market performance	excellent
predictability of returns	good

Total Return   ★★★★★

Over the past five years, FPA New Income has taken $10,000 and turned it into $14,030 ($12,600 over three years and $21,590 over the past ten years). This translates into an annualized return of 7 percent over the past five years, 8 percent over the past three years, and 8 percent for the decade. Over the past five years, this fund has outperformed 70 percent of all mutual funds; within its general category, it has done better than 90 percent of its peers. Corporate bond funds have averaged 6 percent annually over these same five years.

During the past five years, a $10,000 initial investment grew to $12,460 after taxes, assuming a 40 percent income tax bracket (state and federal combined) and a capital gains rate of 20 percent. This means that investors in this fund were able to preserve 61 percent of their total returns. Compared to other bond funds in the same category, this fund's tax savings are considered to be excellent.

Risk/Volatility   ★★★★

Over the past five years, FPA New Income has been safer than 99 percent of all corporate bond funds. Over the past decade, the fund has had no negative years, while the Lehman Brothers Aggregate Bond Index has had two (off 3 percent in 1994 and 1 percent in 1999). The fund has underperformed the Lehman Brothers Aggregate Bond Index twice over the past ten years. Consistency of *overperformance* for this fund has been good.

	past 5 years		past 10 years	
worst year	3.4%	1999	1.5%	1994
best year	12.3%	2001	14.4%	1995

During the past five years, the fund's worst three quarters have been second quarter 2000 (-1 percent), fourth quarter 1999 (0 percent), and third quarter 1999 (0 percent). The three best-performing quarters over the same period have been first quarter 2001 (6 percent), third quarter 2000 (4 percent), and third quarter 2001 (3 percent). In the past, FPA New Income has done better than 92 percent of its peer group during the most recent bull market and outperformed more than 99 percent of its peer group during the most recent bear market. Consistency, or predictability, of returns for FPA New Income can be described as good. This fund's risk-related return ranks in the top quintile.

Management ★★★★★
There are sixty-five fixed-income securities in this $705 million portfolio. The average corporate bond fund today is $320 million in size. Close to 80 percent of the fund's holdings are in bonds. The average maturity of the bonds in this account is nine years; the weighted coupon rate averages 6 percent. The portfolio's fixed-income holdings can be categorized as intermediate-term, high-quality debt.

Robert Rodriguez has managed this fund for the past eighteen years. Manager Rodriguez has been particularly adept at shortening maturities before expected interest rate increases. As simple as this may sound, few of his peers have been this successful. There are three funds besides New Income within the FPA family. Overall, the fund family's risk-adjusted performance can be described as good to very good.

Current Income ★★★★
Over the past year, FPA New Income had a twelve-month yield of 5.8 percent. During this same twelve-month period, the typical corporate bond fund had a yield that averaged 5.5 percent.

Expenses ★★★★★
FPA New Income's expense ratio is 0.6 percent; it has averaged 0.6 percent annually over the past three calendar years. The average expense ratio for the 1,000 funds in this category is 1.0 percent. This fund's turnover rate over the past year has been 21 percent, while its peer group average has been 156 percent.

Summary
FPA New Income, a corporate bond fund that has three quarters of its assets in U.S. government securities, has outperformed over 70 percent of all mutual funds over the past five years and has done better than over 93 percent of its peer group over the past five years and has outshined 99 percent of its category for the past fifteen years. Risk-adjusted returns have ranged between very good and excellent over the past three, five, and ten years. The fund ranks in the top quintile when it comes to return versus risk. The fund receives top marks when it comes to returns and expense control. This portfolio's alpha, which measures excess returns per unit of risk taken, as measured against the fund's benchmark index, is quite appealing.

Profile

minimum initial investment $1,500	*IRA accounts available* . . . . yes
subsequent minimum investment . . $100	*IRA minimum investment* $100
available in all 50 states. . . . . yes	*date of inception.* . . . . Apr. 1969
telephone exchanges. . . . . yes	*dividend/income paid* . . . . quarterly
number of funds in family 4	*average credit quality* . . . . AAA

Fremont Bond
50 Beale Street, Suite 100
San Francisco, CA 94105
(800) 548-4539
www.fremontfunds.com

total return	★★★★★
risk reduction	★★★★
management	★★★★
current income	★★
expense control	★★★
symbol FBDFX	18 points
up-market performance	good
down-market performance	excellent
predictability of returns	good

Total Return   ★★★★★

Over the past five years, Fremont Bond has taken $10,000 and turned it into $14,700 ($12,250 over three years). This translates into an annualized return of 8 percent over the past five years and 7 percent over the past three years. Over the past five years, this fund has outperformed 74 percent of all mutual funds; within its general category, it has done better than 99 percent of its peers. Corporate bond funds have averaged 6 percent annually over these same five years.

During the past five years, a $10,000 initial investment grew to $13,010 after taxes, assuming a 40 percent income tax bracket (state and federal combined) and a capital gains rate of 20 percent. This means that investors in this fund were able to preserve 64 percent of their total returns. Compared to other funds in the same category, this fund's tax savings are considered to be excellent.

Risk/Volatility   ★★★★

Over the past five years, Fremont Bond has been safer than 61 percent of all corporate bond funds. Over the past decade, the fund has had two negative years, while the Lehman Brothers Aggregate Bond Index has had two (off 3 percent in 1994 and 1 percent in 1999). The fund has underperformed the Lehman Brothers Aggregate Bond Index twice over the past ten years. Consistency of *overperformance* for this fund has been outstanding.

	past 5 years		past 8 years	
worst year	-1.2%	1999	-4.0%	1994
best year	12.8%	2000	21.3%	1995

During the past five years, the fund's worst three quarters have been second quarter 1999 (-2 percent), first quarter 1997 (-1 percent), and first quarter 1999 (0 percent). The three best-performing quarters over the same period have been third quarter 2001 (6 percent), third quarter 1998 (5 percent), and fourth quarter 2000 (4 percent). In the past, Fremont Bond has done better than 40 percent of its peer group during the most recent bull market and outperformed 96 percent of its peer group during the most recent bear market. Consistency, or predictability, of returns for Fremont Bond can be described as good. This fund's risk-related return ranks in the top quintile.

Management   ★★★★
There are 325 fixed-income securities in this $790 million portfolio. The average corporate bond fund today is $320 million in size. Close to 80 percent of the fund's holdings are in bonds. The average maturity of the bonds in this account is seven years; the weighted coupon rate averages 6 percent. The portfolio's fixed-income holdings can be categorized as intermediate-term, high-quality debt.

William Gross has managed this fund for the past eight years. Legendary manager Gross is willing to make large bets on the direction of interest rates as well as concentrated industry groups. There are nine funds besides Bond within the Fremont family. Overall, the fund family's risk-adjusted performance can be described as exceptional.

Current Income   ★★
Over the past year, Fremont Bond had a twelve-month yield of 5.2 percent. During this same twelve-month period, the typical corporate bond fund had a yield that averaged 5.5 percent.

Expenses   ★★★
Fremont Bond's expense ratio is 0.6 percent; it has averaged 0.6 percent annually over the past three calendar years. The average expense ratio for the 1,000 funds in this category is 1.0 percent. This fund's turnover rate over the past year has been 176 percent, while its peer group average has been 156 percent.

Summary
Fremont Bond, a corporate bond fund that has over three-fourths of its assets in securities rated AAA, has outperformed more than 82 percent of all mutual funds over the past five years, and has done better than more than 99 percent of its peer group over the past three, five, and ten years. Risk-adjusted returns have ranged between very good and excellent over the past three and five years. The fund ranks in the top third when it comes to return versus risk. The portfolio ranks number one when it comes to performance and also rates highly in risk reduction. The fund's returns have been in the top quartile of its category for almost every year since its inception. Bill Gross is considered one of the very best, if not the best, bond fund managers in the country. This portfolio's alpha, which measures excess returns per unit of risk taken, as measured against the fund's benchmark index, is appealing.

Profile

minimum initial investment $2,000	*IRA accounts available* . . . . yes
subsequent minimum investment . . $100	*IRA minimum investment* $1,000
available in all 50 states. . . . . yes	*date of inception*. . . . . Apr. 1993
telephone exchanges. . . . . yes	*dividend/income paid*. . . . . monthly
number of funds in family 10	*average credit quality* . . . . AAA

Harbor Bond

One SeaGate
Toledo, OH 43666
(800) 422-1050
www.harborfunds.com

total return	★★★★★
risk reduction	★★★★
management	★★★★★
current income	★★★★
expense control	★
symbol HABDX	19 points
up-market performance	very good
down-market performance	very good
predictability of returns	good

Total Return   ★★★★★

Over the past five years, Harbor Bond has taken $10,000 and turned it into $14,700 ($12,250 over three years and $21,590 over the past ten years). This translates into an annualized return of 8 percent over the past five years, 7 percent over the past three years, and 8 percent for the decade. Over the past five years, this fund has outperformed 72 percent of all mutual funds; within its general category, it has done better than 96 percent of its peers. Corporate bond funds have averaged 6 percent annually over these same five years.

During the past five years, a $10,000 initial investment grew to $13,110 after taxes, assuming a 40 percent income tax bracket (state and federal combined) and a capital gains rate of 20 percent. This means that investors in this fund were able to preserve 66 percent of their total returns. Compared to other funds in the same category, this fund's tax savings are considered to be excellent.

Risk/Volatility   ★★★★

Over the past five years, Harbor Bond has been safer than 71 percent of all corporate bond funds. Over the past decade, the fund has had two negative years, while the Lehman Brothers Aggregate Bond Index has had two (off 3 percent in 1994 and 1 percent in 1999). The fund has underperformed the Lehman Brothers Aggregate Bond Index twice over the past ten years. Consistency of *overperformance* for this fund has been outstanding.

	past 5 years		past 10 years	
worst year	-0.3%	1999	-3.8%	1994
best year	11.3%	2000	19.2%	1995

During the past five years, the fund's worst three quarters have been second quarter 1999 (-1 percent), first quarter 1997 (-1 percent), and fourth quarter 1999 (0 percent). The three best-performing quarters over the same period have been third quarter 1998 (5 percent), third quarter 2001 (5 percent), and fourth quarter 2000 (4 percent). In the past, Harbor Bond has done better than 90 percent of its peer group during the most recent bull market and outperformed 52 percent of its peer group during the most recent bear market. Consistency, or predictability, of returns for Harbor Bond can be described as good. This fund's risk-related return ranks in the top quintile.

Management   ★★★★★

There are 275 fixed-income securities in this $1 billion portfolio. The average corporate bond fund today is $320 million in size. Close to 50 percent of the fund's holdings are in bonds. The average maturity of the bonds in this account is seven years; the weighted coupon rate averages 6 percent. The portfolio's fixed-income holdings can be categorized as intermediate-term, high-quality debt.

William Gross has managed this fund for the past fifteen years. Manager Gross uses the Lehman Brothers Aggregate Bond index to determine the portfolio's sector and interest rate exposure. There are ten funds besides Harbor Bond within the Harbor family. Overall, the fund family's risk-adjusted performance can be described as very good to exceptional.

Current Income   ★★★★

Over the past year, Harbor Bond had a twelve-month yield of 4.6 percent. During this same twelve-month period, the typical corporate bond fund had a yield that averaged 5.5 percent.

Expenses   ★

Harbor Bond's expense ratio is 0.6 percent; it has averaged 0.6 percent annually over the past three calendar years. The average expense ratio for the 1,000 funds in this category is 1.0 percent. This fund's turnover rate over the past year has been 494 percent, while its peer group average has been 156 percent.

Summary

Harbor Bond, a corporate bond fund that has roughly two-thirds of its assets in fixed-income securities rated AAA, has outperformed more than 80 percent of all mutual funds over the past three years and has done better than 95 percent of its peer group over the past five and ten years. Risk-adjusted returns have ranged between very good and excellent over the past three, five, and ten years. This is the most tax-efficient corporate bond fund in the book. The fund ranks number two in performance and also does quite well at minimizing risk. The fund's returns have been in the top half of performance for each of the past twelve years, frequently in the top quartile—a rarity for a fund in any category. This portfolio's alpha, which measures excess returns per unit of risk taken, as measured against the fund's benchmark index, is appealing.

Profile

minimum initial investment $1,000	IRA accounts available . . . . yes
subsequent minimum investment . . $500	IRA minimum investment $500
available in all 50 states. . . . . yes	date of inception. . . . . Dec. 1987
telephone exchanges. . . . . yes	dividend/income paid . . . . quarterly
number of funds in family 11	average credit quality. . . . . AA

Stein Roe Intermediate Bond

P.O. Box 804058
Chicago, IL 60680
(800) 338-2550
www.steinroe.com

total return	★★★★★
risk reduction	★★★★
management	★★★★★
current income	★★★★★
expense control	★★★
symbol SRBFX	19 points
up-market performance	very good
down-market performance	excellent
predictability of returns	good

Total Return   ★★★★★

Over the past five years, Stein Roe Intermediate Bond has taken $10,000 and turned it into $14,030 ($12,250 over three years and $19,680 over the past ten years). This translates into an annualized return of 7 percent over the past five years, 7 percent over the past three years, and 7 percent for the decade. Over the past five years, this fund has outperformed 70 percent of all mutual funds; within its general category, it has done better than 92 percent of its peers. Corporate bond funds have averaged 6 percent annually over these same five years.

During the past five years, a $10,000 initial investment grew to $12,460 after taxes, assuming a 40 percent income tax bracket (state and federal combined) and a capital gains rate of 20 percent. This means that investors in this fund were able to preserve 61 percent of their total returns. Compared to other funds in the same category, this fund's tax savings are considered to be excellent.

Risk/Volatility   ★★★★

Over the past five years, Stein Roe Intermediate Bond has been safer than 88 percent of all corporate bond funds. Over the past decade, the fund has had one negative year, while the Lehman Brothers Aggregate Bond Index has had two (off 3 percent in 1994 and 1 percent in 1999). The fund has underperformed the Lehman Brothers Aggregate Bond Index twice over the past ten years. Consistency of *over-performance* for this fund has been outstanding.

	past 5 years		past 10 years	
worst year	1.3%	1999	-2.6%	1994
best year	10.8%	2000	16.8%	1995

During the past five years, the fund's worst three quarters have been second quarter 1999 (-1 percent), first quarter 1997 (0 percent), and fourth quarter 1999 (0 percent). The three best-performing quarters over the same period have been first quarter 2001 (4 percent), second quarter 1997 (4 percent), and third quarter 2000 (3 percent). In the past, Stein Roe Intermediate Bond has done better than 66 percent of its peer group during the most recent bull market and outperformed 69 percent of its peer group during the most recent bear market. Consistency, or predictability, of returns for Stein Roe Intermediate Bond can be described as good. This fund's risk-related return ranks in the top quintile.

Management ★★★★★
There are 130 fixed-income securities in this $650 million portfolio. The average corporate bond fund today is $320 million in size. Close to 97 percent of the fund's holdings are in bonds. The average maturity of the bonds in this account is seven years; the weighted coupon rate averages 8 percent. The portfolio's fixed-income holdings can be categorized as intermediate-term, medium-quality debt.

Michael Kennedy has managed this fund for the past fourteen years. Manager Kennedy has long believed that high-quality corporate issues will trump similar-maturing Treasuries. He is able to add value by sector rotation, which can include government bonds as well as agency-backed securities. There are twenty funds besides Intermediate Bond within the Stein Roe family. Overall, the fund family's risk-adjusted performance can be described as good to very good.

Current Income ★★★★★
Over the past year, Stein Roe Intermediate Bond had a twelve-month yield of 6.8 percent. During this same twelve-month period, the typical corporate bond fund had a yield that averaged 5.5 percent.

Expenses ★★★
Stein Roe Intermediate Bond's expense ratio is 0.7 percent; it has averaged 0.7 percent annually over the past three calendar years. The average expense ratio for the 1,000 funds in this category is 1.0 percent. This fund's turnover rate over the past year has been 356 percent, while its peer group average has been 156 percent.

Summary
Stein Roe Intermediate Bond, an intermediate-term, medium-quality corporate bond fund that has an average maturity of seven years, has outperformed over 83 percent of all mutual funds over the past three years and has done better than 98 percent of its peer group. Risk-adjusted returns have ranged between very good and excellent over the past three, five, and ten years. The fund ranks in the top quintile when it comes to return versus risk. The portfolio rates well in almost every category measured and rates number one when it comes to current income. This portfolio's alpha, which measures excess returns per unit of risk taken, as measured against the fund's benchmark index, is quite appealing.

Profile
minimum initial investment $2,500
subsequent minimum investment . . $100
available in all 50 states. . . . . yes
telephone exchanges. . . . . yes
number of funds in family 21

IRA accounts available . . . . yes
IRA minimum investment $500
date of inception. . . . . Dec. 1978
dividend/income paid. . . . . monthly
average credit quality . . . . A

Strong Ultra-Short Income Investor Class

P.O. Box 2936
Milwaukee, WI 53201
(800) 368-1030
www.estrong.com

total return	★★★
risk reduction	★★★★★
management	★★★★
current income	★★★★
expense control	★★★★
symbol STADX	21 points
up-market performance	very good
down-market performance	fair
predictability of returns	excellent

Total Return   ★★★

Over the past five years, Strong Ultra-Short Income Investor Class has taken $10,000 and turned it into $13,390 ($11,580 over three years and $17,910 over the past ten years). This translates into an annualized return of 6 percent over the past five years, 5 percent over the past three years, and 6 percent for the decade. Over the past five years, this fund has outperformed 50 percent of all mutual funds; within its general category, it has done better than 49 percent of its peers. Corporate bond funds have averaged 6 percent annually over these same five years.

During the past five years, a $10,000 initial investment grew to $11,900 after taxes, assuming a 40 percent income tax bracket (state and federal combined) and a capital gains rate of 20 percent. This means that investors in this fund were able to preserve 56 percent of their total returns. Compared to other funds in the same category, this fund's tax savings are considered to be very good.

Risk/Volatility   ★★★★★

Over the past five years, Strong Ultra-Short Income Investor Class has been safer than 40 percent of all corporate bond funds. Over the past decade, the fund has had no negative years, while the Lehman Brothers Aggregate Bond Index has had two (off 3 percent in 1994 and 1 percent in 1999). The fund has underperformed the Lehman Brothers Aggregate Bond Index twice over the past ten years. Consistency of *overperformance* for this fund has been very good.

	past 5 years		past 10 years	
worst year	4.3%	2001	3.6%	1994
best year	6.8%	2000	8.4%	1992

During the past five years, the fund's worst three quarters have been third quarter 2001 (0 percent), fourth quarter 1998 (1 percent), and second quarter 1999 (1 percent). Consistency, or predictability, of returns for Strong Ultra-Short Income Investor Class can be described as excellent. This fund's risk-related return ranks in the top quintile.

Management   ★★★★

There are 355 fixed-income securities in this $3 billion portfolio. The average corporate bond fund today is $320 million in size. Close to 95 percent of the fund's holdings are in bonds. The average maturity of the bonds in this account is just one year; the weighted coupon rate averages 7 percent. The portfolio's fixed-income holdings can be categorized as short-term, high-quality debt.

Jeffery Koch and Thomas Sontag have managed this fund for the past eight years. Managers Koch and Sontag believe in owning the more generous interest-earning BBB and below. But the portfolio also has almost half of its assets in the highest-rated issues. There are 101 funds besides Advantage Investor Class within the Strong family. Overall, the fund family's risk-adjusted performance can be described as good.

Current Income   ★★★★

Over the past year, Strong Ultra-Short Income Investor Class had a twelve-month yield of 5.7 percent. During this same twelve-month period, the typical corporate bond fund had a yield that averaged 5.5 percent.

Expenses   ★★★★

Strong Ultra-Short Income Investor Class's expense ratio is 0.8 percent; it has averaged 0.8 percent annually over the past three calendar years. The average expense ratio for the 1,000 funds in this category is 1.0 percent. This fund's turnover rate over the past year has been 48 percent, while its peer group average has been 156 percent.

Summary

Strong Advantage Investor, a corporate bond fund that invests in ultra-short-term, high-quality issues, has outperformed 70 percent of all mutual funds over the past three years and has done better than 99 percent of its peer group over the past ten years. Risk-adjusted returns have been superb over the past three, five, and ten years. The fund ranks in the top half when it comes to return versus risk for ultra-short bonds; it would rank in the top quintile if it were rated against traditional fixed-income portfolios. The fund ranks number one when it comes to risk minimization and predictability of returns. This fund is a good alternative to money market account investors who are willing to accept just a tad more risk. This portfolio's alpha, which measures excess returns per unit of risk taken, as measured against the fund's benchmark index, is appealing.

Profile

minimum initial investment $2,500	*IRA accounts available* . . . . yes
subsequent minimum investment . . . $50	*IRA minimum investment* $250
available in all 50 states. . . . . yes	*date of inception* . . . . Nov. 1988
telephone exchanges. . . . . yes	*dividend/income paid*. . . . . monthly
number of funds in family 102	*average credit quality*. . . . . AA

Financial Funds

A potential problem with including sector funds is that investors may be tempted to get away from diversification and go right into one or more specialized plays. Indeed, the following bar chart shows the top-performing sector each year from 1989 through the end of 2000. As you can see, one can make a convincing case for sector funds.

Over the past fifteen years (ending December 31, 2001), financial funds have outperformed common stocks by 1.4 percent per year, as measured by the S & P 500. From 1987–2001, financial funds averaged 15.8 percent, while common stocks averaged 13.7 percent compounded per year. A $10,000 investment in financial funds grew to $90,290 over the past fifteen years; while $10,000 invested in the S & P 500 grew to $68,900.

During the past three years, financial funds have outperformed the S & P 500 by 7.1 percent per year. Over the past five years, this fund category has outperformed the S & P 500 by an average of 2.3 percent per year. Average turnover during the past three years has been 147 percent.

The p/e ratio is 22 for the typical financial fund, versus 31 for the S & P 500. The typical stock in these portfolios is only 35 percent the size of the average stock in the S & P 500. The average beta is 0.7, which means the group has a market-related risk that is 30 percent lower than the S & P 500. There is more than $16 billion in all financial funds combined. The average financial fund throws off roughly one-half of 1 percent annual income stream. The typical annual expense ratio for this group is 1.7 percent.

Over the past three years, financial funds have averaged a compound return of 6.1 percent per year. The annual return has been 13.0 percent for the past five years, 17.9 percent for the past decade, and 15.8 percent for the past fifteen years. The standard deviation has been 22 percent over the past three years, versus 17 percent for the S & P 500.

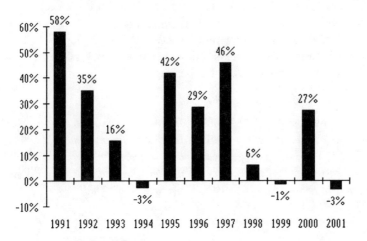

Century Shares Trust

1 Liberty Square
Boston, MA 02109
(800) 321-1928
www.centuryfunds.com

total return	★★★★★
risk reduction	★★★★
management	★★★★
tax minimization	★★★★
expense control	★★★★★
symbol CENSX	22 points
up-market performance	good
down-market performance	excellent
predictability of returns	good

Total Return   ★★★★★

Over the past five years, Century Shares Trust has taken $10,000 and turned it into $21,930 ($13,680 over three years and $44,120 over the past ten years). This translates into an annualized return of 17 percent over the past five years, 11 percent over the past three years, and 16 percent for the decade. Over the past five years, this fund has outperformed 95 percent of all mutual funds; within its general category, it has done better than 76 percent of its peers. Financial funds have averaged 13 percent annually over these same five years.

Risk/Volatility   ★★★★

Over the past five years, Century Shares Trust has been safer than 38 percent of all financial funds. Over the past decade, the fund has had three negative years, while the S & P 500 has had two (off 9 percent in 2000 and 12 percent in 2001); the Wilshire 5000 also fell twice (off 11 percent in 2000 and 11 percent in 2001). The fund has underperformed the S & P 500 twice and the Wilshire 5000 three times in the past ten years. Consistency of *overperformance* for this fund has been good.

	past 5 years		past 10 years	
worst year	-12.4%	1999	-12.4%	1999
best year	50.1%	1997	50.1%	1997

During the past five years, the fund's worst three quarters have been third quarter 1999 (-20 percent), third quarter 1998 (-17 percent), and first quarter 2001 (-8 percent). The three best-performing quarters over the same period have been third quarter 2000 (27 percent), second quarter 1997 (20 percent), and fourth quarter 2000 (10 percent). In the past, Century Shares Trust has done better than 20 percent of its peer group during the most recent bull market and outperformed 81 percent of its peer group during the most recent bear market. Consistency, or predictability, of returns for Century Shares Trust can be described as good. This fund's risk-related return ranks in the top third.

Management   ★★★★

There are fifty-five stocks in this $325 million portfolio. The average financial fund today is $150 million in size. Close to 100 percent of the fund's holdings are in stocks. The stocks in this portfolio have an average p/e ratio of 29 and a median market capitalization of $11 billion. The ten largest holdings compose 53 percent of the fund's total assets. The portfolio's equity holdings can be categorized as large-cap and value-oriented issues.

Allan Fulkerson and Alexander Thorndike have managed this fund for the past fifteen years. Managers Fulkerson and Thorndike have concentrated the holdings in insurance companies. There are two funds besides Shares Trust within the Century family.

Tax Minimization   ★★★★

During the past five years, a $10,000 initial investment grew to $18,640 after taxes, assuming a 40 percent income tax bracket (state and federal combined) and a capital gains rate of 20 percent. This means that investors in this fund were able to preserve 85 percent of their total returns. Compared to other equity funds in the same category, this fund's tax savings are considered to be very good.

Expenses   ★★★★★

Century Shares Trust's expense ratio is 0.8 percent; it has averaged 0.8 percent annually over the past three calendar years. The average expense ratio for the 105 funds in this category is 1.7 percent. This fund's turnover rate over the past year has been 17 percent, while its peer group average has been 147 percent.

Summary

Century Shares Trust, a sector fund that invests in medium- and large-cap value stocks, has outperformed more than 95 percent of all mutual funds over the past five years and has done better than more than 75 percent of its peer group. Risk-adjusted returns have ranged between good and very good over the past three to ten years. The fund ranks in the top half when it comes to return versus risk. The portfolio ranks number one within its sector group when it comes to returns and expense reduction. This fund outperformed the S & P 500 by over 46 percentage points in 2000 and underperformed the index by more than 33 percentage points in 1999. This portfolio's alpha, which measures excess returns per unit of risk taken, as measured against the fund's benchmark index, is quite appealing. On a total point basis, this is the number-one fund for its category.

Profile

minimum initial investment $1,000	*IRA accounts available* . . . . yes
subsequent minimum investment . . . $50	*IRA minimum investment* $1,000
available in all 50 states. . . . . yes	*date of inception*. . . . . Mar. 1928
telephone exchanges. . . . . yes	*dividend/income paid* . . . semi-annually
number of funds in family 3	*largest sector weighting* . . . . financials

Davis Financial A

2949 E. Elvira Road, Suite 101
Tucson, AZ 85706
(800) 279-0279
www.davisfunds.com

total return	★★★
risk reduction	★★★★
management	★★★★
tax minimization	★★★★★
expense control	★★★★
symbol RPFGX	20 points
up-market performance	excellent
down-market performance	poor
predictability of returns	good

Total Return   ★★★

Over the past five years, Davis Financial A has taken $10,000 and turned it into $19,260 ($11,910 over three years and $56,950 over the past ten years). This translates into an annualized return of 14 percent over the past five years, 6 percent over the past three years, and 19 percent for the decade. Over the past five years, this fund has outperformed 95 percent of all mutual funds; within its general category, it has done better than 80 percent of its peers. Financial funds have averaged 13 percent annually over these same five years.

Risk/Volatility   ★★★★

Over the past five years, Davis Financial A has been safer than 87 percent of all financial funds. Over the past decade, the fund has had three negative years, while the S & P 500 has had two (off 9 percent in 2000 and 12 percent in 2001); the Wilshire 5000 also fell twice (off 11 percent in 2000 and 11 percent in 2001). The fund has underperformed the S & P 500 twice and the Wilshire 5000 three times in the past ten years. Consistency of *overperformance* for this fund has been very good.

	past 5 years		past 10 years	
worst year	-9.1%	2001	-9.1%	2001
best year	44.5%	1997	50.5%	1995

During the past five years, the fund's worst three quarters have been third quarter 2001 (-16 percent), third quarter 1998 (-16 percent), and third quarter 1999 (-13 percent). The three best-performing quarters over the same period have been fourth quarter 1998 (20 percent), third quarter 2000 (18 percent), and second quarter 1997 (17 percent). In the past, Davis Financial A has done better than 94 percent of its peer group during the most recent bull market and outperformed 42 percent of its peer group during the most recent bear market. Consistency, or predictability, of returns for Davis Financial A can be described as good. This fund's risk-related return ranks in the top quintile.

Management   ★★★★
There are forty stocks in this $600.4 million portfolio. The average financial fund today is $150 million in size. Close to 100 percent of the fund's holdings are in stocks. The stocks in this portfolio have an average p/e ratio of 30 and a median market capitalization of $10 billion. The ten largest holdings compose 53 percent of the fund's total assets. The portfolio's equity holdings can be categorized as large-cap and value-oriented issues.

Christopher Davis and Kenneth Feinberg have managed this fund for the past eight years. Managers Davis and Feinberg enjoy fine reputations because of their stock selection abilities. There are twenty-six funds besides Financial A within the Davis family. Overall, the fund family's risk-adjusted performance can be described as good to very good.

Tax Minimization   ★★★★★
During the past five years, a $10,000 initial investment grew to $18,100 after taxes, assuming a 40 percent income tax bracket (state and federal combined) and a capital gains rate of 20 percent. This means that investors in this fund were able to preserve 94 percent of their total returns. Compared to other equity funds in the same category, this fund's tax savings are considered to be exceptional.

Expenses   ★★★★
Davis Financial A's expense ratio is 1.1 percent; it has averaged 1.1 percent annually over the past three calendar years. The average expense ratio for the 105 funds in this category is 1.7 percent. This fund's turnover rate over the past year has been 35 percent, while its peer group average has been 147 percent.

Summary
Davis Financial A, a sector fund that invests in large-cap value stocks, has outperformed more than 95 percent of all mutual funds over the past five years and 99 percent over the past ten years. Within its peer group, the fund has outshone 80 percent of its competitors. Risk-adjusted returns have ranged between good and excellent over the past three to ten years. The fund ranks in the top half when it comes to return versus risk. More than half of the fund's assets are in ten stocks. This fund outperformed the S & P 500 by more than 41 percentage points in 2000 and underperformed the index by 22 percentage points in 1999. This portfolio's alpha, which measures excess returns per unit of risk taken, as measured against the fund's benchmark index, is quite appealing.

Profile

minimum initial investment $1,000	*IRA accounts available* . . . . yes
subsequent minimum investment . . . $25	*IRA minimum investment* $250
available in all 50 states. . . . . yes	*date of inception*. . . . . May 1991
telephone exchanges. . . . . yes	*dividend/income paid*. . . . semiannually
number of funds in family 27	*largest sector weighting* . . . . financials

Global Equity (Stock) Funds

International, also known as "foreign," funds invest only in stocks of foreign companies, while global funds invest in both foreign and U.S. stocks. For the purposes of this book, the universe of global equity funds shown encompasses both foreign (international) and world (global) portfolios.

The economic outlook of foreign countries is the major factor in mutual fund management's decision about which nations and industries are to be favored. A secondary concern is the future anticipated value of the U.S. dollar relative to foreign currencies. A strong or weak dollar can detract or add to an international fund's overall performance. A strong dollar will lower a foreign portfolio's return; a weak dollar will enhance international performance. Trying to gauge the direction of any currency is as difficult as trying to figure out what the U.S. stock market will do tomorrow, next week, or the following year.

Investors who do not wish to be subjected to currency swings may wish to use a fund family that practices currency hedging for their foreign holdings. Currency hedging means that management is buying a kind of insurance policy that pays off in the event of a strong U.S. dollar. Basically, the foreign or international fund that is being hurt by the dollar is making a killing in currency futures contracts. When done properly, the gains in the futures contracts, the insurance policy, offset some, most, or all security losses attributable to a strong dollar. Some people may feel that buying currency contracts is risky business for the fund; it is not.

Like automobile insurance, currency hedging only pays off if there is an accident; that is, if the U.S. dollar increases in value against the currencies represented by the portfolio's securities. If the dollar remains level or decreases in value, so much the better, the foreign securities increase in value and the currency contracts become virtually worthless. The price of these contracts becomes a cost of doing business; as with car insurance, the protection is simply renewed. In the case of a currency contract, the contract expires and a new one is purchased, covering another period.

It is wise to consider investing abroad, since different economies experience prosperity and recession at different times. During the 1980s, foreign stocks were the number-one performing investment, averaging a compound return of over 22 percent per year, compared to 18 percent for U.S. stocks and 5 percent for residential real estate. But during the past ten years (ending December 31, 2001), U.S. stocks, as measured by the S & P 500, have outperformed foreign stocks, as measured by the MSCI EAFE index, 12.9 percent versus 4.5 percent (compounded annual rates of return). Over the past fifteen years (ending December 31, 2001), U.S. stocks have had an average compound annual return of 13.7 percent versus

5.9 percent for foreign stocks. To give you a broader perspective, take a look at how U.S. securities have fared against their foreign counterparts over each of the past twenty-five years.

Why Global Stocks and Bonds Deserve a Place in Every Investor's Portfolio
The following table shows the total return for each investment category in each of the past thirty years.

Year	U.S. Stocks	U.S. Gov. Bonds	Non-U.S. Stocks	Non-U.S. Bonds
1972	+19.0	+7.3	+37.4	+4.4
1973	-14.6	+2.3	-14.2	+6.3
1974	-26.5	+0.2	-22.1	+5.3
1975	+37.2	+12.3	+37.0	+8.8
1976	+24.0	+15.6	+3.8	+10.5
1977	-7.2	+3.0	+19.4	+38.9
1978	+6.5	+1.2	+34.3	+18.5
1979	+18.6	+2.3	+6.2	-5.0
1980	+32.3	+3.1	+24.4	+13.7
1981	-5.0	+7.3	-1.0	-4.6
1982	+21.5	+31.1	-0.9	+11.9
1983	+22.6	+8.0	+24.6	+4.3
1984	+6.3	+15.0	+7.9	-2.0
1985	+31.7	+21.3	+56.7	+37.2
1986	+18.6	+15.6	+67.9	+33.9
1987	+5.3	+2.3	+24.9	+36.1
1988	+16.6	+7.6	+28.6	+3.0
1989	+31.6	+14.2	+10.8	-4.5
1990	-3.1	+8.3	-14.9	+14.1
1991	+30.4	+16.1	+12.5	+17.9
1992	+7.7	+8.1	-12.2	+7.1
1993	+10.1	+18.2	+32.6	+15.1
1994	+1.3	-7.8	+7.8	+6.7
1995	+37.4	+31.7	+11.2	+19.6
1996	+23.1	-0.9	+6.1	+4.1
1997	+33.3	+16.0	+1.8	-4.3
1998	+28.6	+13.1	+20.0	+17.8
1999	+21.0	-9.0	+27.0	-5.1
2000	-9.1	+21.5	-14.2	-2.6
2001	-11.9	+3.7	-21.4	-3.5

Number of years this category achieved the best results

U.S. Stocks	U.S. Gov. Bonds	Non-U.S. Stocks	Non-U.S. Bonds
10	6	9	5

Increasing your investment returns and reducing portfolio risk are two reasons to consider adding global/foreign funds to your portfolio. Global investing allows you to maximize your returns by investing in some of the world's best-managed and most profitable companies. Japan, for example, is the world's leading producer of sophisticated electronics goods; Germany is the leading producer of heavy machinery; the United States is the leading producer of biotechnology; and Southeast Asia is the leading producer of commodity-manufactured goods.

Diversification reduces investment risk: Recent studies have once again proved this most basic investment principle. A 1996 study showed that the least volatile investment portfolio over the twenty-five-year period (1972–1996) would have been composed of 60 percent U.S. equities and 40 percent foreign equities. These results reflect the importance of balancing a portfolio between U.S. and foreign equities.

Japan, the most economically mature country in the Pacific Basin, has become the dominant force behind the development of the newly industrialized countries (NICs) of Hong Kong, Korea, Thailand, Singapore, Malaysia, and Taiwan. As demand for Japanese products has grown and costs in Japan have risen, the search for affordable production of goods has caused Japanese investment to flow into neighboring countries, fostering their development as economically independent and prosperous nations.

The NICs, with some of the cheapest labor forces and richest untapped natural resources in the world, have recently experienced an enormous influx of international investment capital and today represent the world's fastest growing source of low-cost manufacturing. The Pacific Region (which includes Japan, Hong Kong, Korea, Taiwan, Thailand, Singapore, Malaysia, and Australia) has experienced outstanding economic growth and today represents 25 percent of the world's stock market capital—nearly double what it was fifteen years ago.

The newly industrialized countries are favored locations for the manufacture and assembly of consumer electronics products. Displaced from high-cost countries such as the United States and Japan, electronics factories in these developing countries significantly benefit from reduced labor costs. Today, in fact, Korea is the world's third-largest manufacturer of semiconductors.

The Pacific Region yields yet another country with strong economic growth: China. Opportunities to benefit from the industrialization of China come from firms listed on the Hong Kong Stock Exchange, in such basic areas as electricity, construction materials, public transportation, and fundamental telecommunications. Indeed, these low-tech and essential industries, once growth industries in the United States, are now the foundation of a natural growth progression occurring in the NICs of Southeast Asia.

Companies such as China Light and Power (Hong Kong), Siam Cement (Thailand), and Hyundai (Korea) offer much the same profit potential today as their northern European counterparts did 100 years ago, their U.S. counterparts forty years ago, and their Japanese counterparts as recently as twenty years ago.

Investors have long been familiar with the names of many of Europe's major producers: Nestlé, Olivetti, Shell, Bayer, Volkswagen, and Perrier, to name just a few. Europe's impressive manufacturing capacity, diverse industrial base, quality

Annual Returns - Global Equity (Stock) Funds

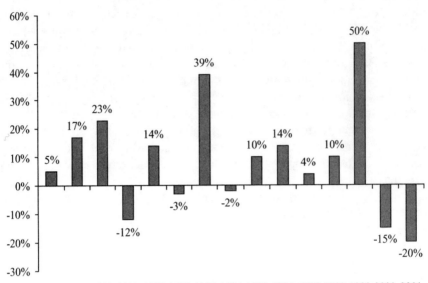

labor pools, and many leading, multinational, blue-chip corporations make it an environment for growth, accessible to you through foreign funds.

With economic deregulation and the elimination of internal trade barriers, many European companies are, for the first time in history, investing in and competing for exposure to the whole European market. Companies currently restricted to manufacturing and distributing within their national boundaries will soon be able to locate facilities anywhere in Europe, maximizing the efficient employment of labor, capital, and raw materials.

The global stock category is made up of over 1,500 funds (308 "World," 898 "Foreign," 177 "European," and 203 "Pacific"). Total market capitalization of this entire category is $363 billion. These funds typically throw off a dividend of less than 1 percent and have an expense ratio of 1.8 percent. The price-earnings (p/e) ratio is 25, versus a p/e ratio of 31 for the typical stock in the S & P 500.

Over the past three years, global equity funds have had an average compound return of -0.2 percent per year. The annual return for the past five years has been 1.8 percent, 6.3 percent for the past ten years, and 7.4 percent for the past fifteen years. The standard deviation for global equity funds has been 22.2 percent over the past three years. This means that global equity funds have experienced about 10 percent less volatility than growth funds.

Artisan International
P.O. Box 8412
Boston, MA 02266
(800) 344-1770
www.artisanfunds.com

total return	★★★★
risk reduction	★★★
management	★★★★
tax minimization	★★★★
expense control	★★★★
symbol ARTIX	19 points
up-market performance	excellent
down-market performance	good
predictability of returns	good

Total Return ★★★★

Over the past five years, Artisan International has taken $10,000 and turned it into $18,430 ($13,680 over three years). This translates into an annualized return of 13 percent over the past five years and 11 percent over the past three years. Over the past five years, this fund has outperformed 94 percent of all mutual funds; within its general category, it has done better than 97 percent of its peers. Global equity funds have averaged 2 percent annually over these same five years.

Risk/Volatility ★★★

Over the past five years, Artisan International has been safer than 47 percent of all global equity funds. Over the past decade, the fund has had two negative years, while the S & P 500 has had two (off 9 percent in 2000 and 12 percent in 2001); the EAFE fell three times (off 12 percent in 1992, 14 percent in 2000, and 21 percent in 2001). The fund has underperformed the S & P 500 twice and the EAFE Index twice in the past ten years. Consistency of *overperformance* for this fund has been outstanding.

	past 5 years		past 6 years	
worst year	-15.9%	2001	-15.9%	2001
best year	81.3%	1999	81.3%	1999

During the past five years, the fund's worst three quarters have been third quarter 1998 (-19 percent), first quarter 2001 (-13 percent), and third quarter 2000 (-11 percent). The three best-performing quarters over the same period have been fourth quarter 1999 (49 percent), fourth quarter 1998 (25 percent), and first quarter 1998 (20 percent). In the past, Artisan International has done better than 77 percent of its peer group during the most recent bull market and outperformed 72 percent of its peer group during the most recent bear market. Consistency, or predictability, of returns for Artisan International can be described as good. This fund's risk-related return ranks in the top quintile.

Management   ★★★★
There are eighty-five stocks in this $4.7 billion portfolio. The average global equity fund today is $330 million in size. Close to 98 percent of the fund's holdings are in stocks. The stocks in this portfolio have an average p/e ratio of 21 and a median market capitalization of $24 billion. The ten largest holdings compose 33 percent of the fund's total assets. The three largest sector weightings are financials (39 percent), services (22 percent), and staples (15 percent). The portfolio's equity holdings can be categorized as mid-cap and a blend of growth and value stocks.

Mark Yockey has managed this fund for the past seven years. Manager Yockey has been quite successful at manuvering in and out of different sectors and countries. There are three funds besides International within the Artisan family. Overall, the fund family's risk-adjusted performance can be described as exceptional.

Tax Minimization   ★★★★
During the past five years, a $10,000 initial investment grew to $15,110 after taxes, assuming a 40 percent income tax bracket (state and federal combined) and a capital gains rate of 20 percent. This means that investors in this fund were able to preserve 82 percent of their total returns. Compared to other equity funds in the same category, this fund's tax savings are considered to be very good.

Expenses   ★★★★
Artisan International's expense ratio is 1.2 percent; it has averaged 1.3 percent annually over the past three calendar years. The average expense ratio for the 1,700 funds in this category is 1.8 percent. This fund's turnover rate over the past year has been 72 percent, while its peer group average has been 99 percent.

Summary
Artisan International, a foreign stock fund that invests in large-cap value and growth stocks outside of the United States, has outperformed 95 percent of all mutual funds over the past five years and has done better than more than 97 percent of its peer group. Risk-adjusted returns have been exceptional over the past three, five, and ten years. The fund ranks in the top quintile when it comes to return versus risk. The portfolio ranks highly in every category measured. This fund outperformed the S & P 500 by over 60 percentage points in 1999. This portfolio's alpha, which measures excess returns per unit of risk taken, as measured against the fund's benchmark index, is quite appealing.

Profile
minimum initial investment $1,000	*IRA accounts available* . . . . yes
subsequent minimum investment . . . $50	*IRA minimum investment* $1,000
available in all 50 states. . . . . yes	*date of inception.* . . . . Dec. 1995
telephone exchanges. . . . . yes	*dividend/income paid* . . . . annually
number of funds in family 4	*largest sector weighting* . . . . financials

First Eagle SoGen Overseas A
1345 Avenue of the Americas
New York, NY 10105
(800) 334-2143
www.firsteaglesogen.com

total return	★★
risk reduction	★★★★★
management	★★★★
tax minimization	★
expense control	★★★★★
symbol SGOVX	17 points
up-market performance	good
down-market performance	excellent
predictability of returns	excellent

Total Return   ★★
Over the past five years, First Eagle SoGen Overseas A has taken $10,000 and turned it into $15,390 ($14,820 over three years). This translates into an annualized return of 9 percent over the past five years and 14 percent over the past three years. Over the past five years, this fund has outperformed 78 percent of all mutual funds; within its general category, it has done better than 90 percent of its peers. Global equity funds have averaged 2 percent annually over these same five years.

Risk/Volatility   ★★★★★
Over the past five years, First Eagle SoGen Overseas A has been safer than 99 percent of all global equity funds. Over the past decade, the fund has had no negative years, while the S & P 500 has had two (off 9 percent in 2000 and 12 percent in 2001); the EAFE fell three times (off 12 percent in 1992, 14 percent in 2000, and 21 percent in 2001). The fund has underperformed the S & P 500 twice and the EAFE Index twice in the past ten years. Consistency of *overperformance* for this fund has been good.

	past 5 years		past 8 years	
worst year	2.5%	1998	2.5%	1998
best year	33.2%	1999	33.2%	1999

During the past five years, the fund's worst three quarters have been third quarter 1998 (-14 percent), third quarter 2001 (-9 percent), and fourth quarter 1997 (-8 percent). The three best-performing quarters over the same period have been second quarter 1999 (15 percent), first quarter 1998 (11 percent), and fourth quarter 1999 (8 percent). In the past, First Eagle SoGen Overseas A has done better than 46 percent of its peer group during the most recent bull market and outperformed 99 percent of its peer group during the most recent bear market. Consistency, or predictability, of returns for First Eagle SoGen Overseas A can be described as excellent. This fund's risk-related return ranks in the top quintile.

Management   ★★★★
There are 125 stocks in this $450 million portfolio. The average global equity fund today is $330 million in size. Close to 92 percent of the fund's holdings are in stocks. The stocks in this portfolio have an average p/e ratio of 19 and a median market capitalization of $920 million. The ten largest holdings compose 29 percent of the fund's total assets. The three largest sector weightings are industrial cyclicals (41 percent), financials (17 percent), and services (15 percent). The portfolio's equity holdings can be categorized as small-cap and value-oriented issues.

Jean-Marie Eveillard and Charles de Vaulx have managed this fund for the past nine years. Managers Eveillard and Vaulx have remained steadfast in their commitment to deeply discounted securities, despite strong pressure and temptation to invest elsewhere. There are six funds besides Overseas A within the First Eagle SoGen Funds family. Overall, the fund family's risk-adjusted performance can be described as exceptional.

Tax Minimization   ★
During the past five years, a $10,000 initial investment grew to $8,930 after taxes, assuming a 40 percent income tax bracket (state and federal combined) and a capital gains rate of 20 percent. This means that investors in this fund were able to preserve 58 percent of their total returns. Compared to other equity funds in the same category, this fund's tax savings are considered to be poor.

Expenses   ★★★★★
First Eagle SoGen Overseas A's expense ratio is 1.3 percent; it has averaged 1.3 percent annually over the past three calendar years. The average expense ratio for the 1,700 funds in this category is 1.8 percent. This fund's turnover rate over the past year has been 17 percent, while its peer group average has been 99 percent.

Summary
First Eagle SoGen Overseas A, a foreign stock fund that invests in small-cap value stocks outside of the United States, has outperformed 93 percent of all mutual funds over the past three years and has done better than more than 97 percent of its peer group. Risk-adjusted returns have been exceptional over the past three and five years. The fund ranks in the top quintile when it comes to return versus risk. The portfolio receives the highest marks possible when it comes to low risk, expense control, and predictability of returns. For patient and conservative equity investors, this offering is hard to beat. This portfolio's alpha, which measures excess returns per unit of risk taken, as measured against the fund's benchmark index, is quite appealing.

Profile
minimum initial investment $1,000	IRA accounts available . . . . yes
subsequent minimum investment . . $100	IRA minimum investment $1,000
available in all 50 states. . . . . yes	date of inception . . . . Aug. 1993
telephone exchanges. . . . . yes	dividend/income paid . . . . annually
number of funds in family 7	largest sector weighting indust. cyclicals

Merrill Lynch Global Small Cap D

P.O. Box 9011
Princeton, NJ 08543
(800) 995-6526
www.ml.com

total return	★★★★★
risk reduction	★★★★
management	★★★★★
tax minimization	★★★★★
expense control	★★
symbol MDGCX	21 points
up-market performance	excellent
down-market performance	good
predictability of returns	fair

Total Return   ★★★★★

Over the past five years, Merrill Lynch Global Small Cap D has taken $10,000 and turned it into $20,120 ($20,980 over three years). This translates into an annualized return of 15 percent over the past five years and 28 percent over the past three years. Over the past five years, this fund has outperformed 96 percent of all mutual funds; within its general category, it has done better than 96 percent of its peers. Global equity funds have averaged 2 percent annually over these same five years.

Risk/Volatility   ★★★★

Over the past five years, Merrill Lynch Global Small Cap D has been safer than 44 percent of all global equity funds. Over the past decade, the fund has had two negative years, while the S & P 500 has had two (off 9 percent in 2000 and 12 percent in 2001); the EAFE fell three times (off 12 percent in 1992, 14 percent in 2000, and 21 percent in 2001). The fund has underperformed the S & P 500 twice and the EAFE Index twice in the past ten years. Consistency of *overperformance* for this fund has been outstanding.

	past 5 years		past 7 years	
worst year	-9.8%	2001	-9.8%	2001
best year	106.7%	1999	106.7%	1999

During the past five years, the fund's worst three quarters have been third quarter 1998 (-20 percent), third quarter 2001 (-18 percent), and fourth quarter 1997 (-16 percent). The three best-performing quarters over the same period have been fourth quarter 1999 (64 percent), first quarter 2000 (21 percent), and fourth quarter 1998 (18 percent). In the past, Merrill Lynch Global Small Cap D has done better than 77 percent of its peer group during the most recent bull market and outperformed 81 percent of its peer group during the most recent bear market. Consistency, or predictability, of returns for Merrill Lynch Global Small Cap D can be described as fair. This fund's risk-related return ranks in the top quintile.

Management   ★★★★★

There are 170 stocks in this $55 million portfolio. The average global equity fund today is $330 million in size. Close to 70 percent of the fund's holdings are in stocks. The stocks in this portfolio have an average p/e ratio of 23 and a median market capitalization of $1.3 billion. The ten largest holdings compose 43 percent of the fund's total assets. The three largest sector weightings are industrial cyclicals (22 percent), financials (18 percent), and services (12 percent). The portfolio's equity holdings can be categorized as mid-cap and a blend of growth and value stocks.

Kenneth Chiang has managed this fund for the past eight years. Manager Chiang makes bold sector moves that pay off more often than not. He is constantly reworking and revising large portions of the portfolio. There are 247 funds besides Global Small Cap D within the Merrill Lynch family. Overall, the fund family's risk-adjusted performance can be described as good to very good.

Tax Minimization   ★★★★★

During the past five years, a $10,000 initial investment grew to $17,700 after taxes, assuming a 40 percent income tax bracket (state and federal combined) and a capital gains rate of 20 percent. This means that investors in this fund were able to preserve 88 percent of their total returns. Compared to other equity funds in the same category, this fund's tax savings are considered to be excellent.

Expenses   ★★

Merrill Lynch Global Small Cap D's expense ratio is 1.5 percent; it has averaged 1.8 percent annually over the past three calendar years. The average expense ratio for the 1,700 funds in this category is 1.8 percent. This fund's turnover rate over the past year has been 180 percent, while its peer group average has been 99 percent.

Summary

Merrill Lynch Global Small Cap D, a global stock fund that invests in mid-cap value and growth stocks around the world, has outperformed 99 percent of all mutual funds over the past three years and has done better than 96 percent of its peer group. Risk-adjusted returns have been exceptional over the past three and five years. The fund ranks in the top quintile when it comes to return versus risk. This is the second most tax-efficient fund in its category. The fund outperformed the S & P 500 by more than 85 percentage points in 1999. This portfolio's alpha, which measures excess returns per unit of risk taken, as measured against the fund's benchmark index, is extremely appealing.

Profile

minimum initial investment $1,000	IRA accounts available . . . . yes
subsequent minimum investment . . . $50	IRA minimum investment $100
available in all 50 states. . . . . yes	date of inception . . . . Aug. 1994
telephone exchanges. . . . . yes	dividend/income paid . . . . annually
number of funds in family 248	largest sector weighting indust. cyclicals

Oppenheimer Global A
P.O. Box 5270
Denver, CO 80217
(800) 525-7048
www.oppenheimerfunds.com

total return	★★★★★
risk reduction	★★★★
management	★★★★★
tax minimization	★★★★
expense control	★★★★★
symbol OPPAX	23 points
up-market performance	excellent
down-market performance	good
predictability of returns	very good

Total Return   ★★★★★
Over the past five years, Oppenheimer Global A has taken $10,000 and turned it
into $20,120 ($14,430 over three years and $31,060 over the past ten years). This
translates into an annualized return of 15 percent over the past five years, 13 percent over the past three years, and 12 percent for the decade. Over the past five
years, this fund has outperformed 96 percent of all mutual funds; within its general
category, it has done better than 97 percent of its peers. Global equity funds have
averaged 2 percent annually over these same five years.

Risk/Volatility   ★★★★
Over the past five years, Oppenheimer Global A has been safer than 71 percent of
all global equity funds. Over the past decade, the fund has had three negative years,
while the S & P 500 has had two (off 9 percent in 2000 and 12 percent in 2001);
the EAFE fell three times (off 12 percent in 1992, 14 percent in 2000, and 21 percent in 2001). The fund has underperformed the S & P 500 twice and the EAFE
Index three times in the past ten years. Consistency of *overperformance* for this
fund has been outstanding.

	past 5 years		past 10 years	
worst year	-11.8%	2001	-14.2%	1992
best year	58.5%	1999	58.5%	1999

During the past five years, the fund's worst three quarters have been third
quarter 2001 (-18 percent), third quarter 1998 (-17 percent), and first quarter 2001
(-14 percent). The three best-performing quarters over the same period have been
fourth quarter 1999 (36 percent), fourth quarter 1998 (21 percent), and first quarter
2000 (13 percent). In the past, Oppenheimer Global A has done better than 78 percent of its peer group during the most recent bull market and outperformed 78 percent of its peer group during the most recent bear market. Consistency, or
predictability, of returns for Oppenheimer Global A can be described as very good.
This fund's risk-related return ranks in the top quintile.

Management   ★★★★★
There are 110 stocks in this $6 billion portfolio. The average global equity fund today is $330 million in size. Close to 90 percent of the fund's holdings are in stocks. The stocks in this portfolio have an average p/e ratio of 28 and a median market capitalization of $9 billion. The ten largest holdings compose 31 percent of the fund's total assets. The three largest sector weightings are technology (21 percent), health (19 percent), and financials (18 percent). The portfolio's equity holdings can be categorized as large-cap and growth-oriented issues.

William Wilby has managed this fund for the past ten years. Manager Wilby uses a theme-based approach to selecting equities, while avoiding region and country bets. There are 215 funds besides Global A within the Oppenheimer family. Overall, the fund family's risk-adjusted performance can be described as good to very good.

Tax Minimization   ★★★★
During the past five years, a $10,000 initial investment grew to $16,100 after taxes, assuming a 40 percent income tax bracket (state and federal combined) and a capital gains rate of 20 percent. This means that investors in this fund were able to preserve 80 percent of their total returns. Compared to other equity funds in the same category, this fund's tax savings are considered to be very good.

Expenses   ★★★★★
Oppenheimer Global A's expense ratio is 1.1 percent; it has averaged 1.1 percent annually over the past three calendar years. The average expense ratio for the 1,700 funds in this category is 1.8 percent. This fund's turnover rate over the past year has been 62 percent, while its peer group average has been 99 percent.

Summary
Oppenheimer Global A, a world stock fund that invests in large-cap growth stocks around the world, has outperformed 96 percent of all mutual funds over the past five years and has done better than 97 percent of its peer group. Risk-adjusted returns have been superb over the past three, five, and ten years. The fund ranks in the top quintile when it comes to return versus risk. The portfolio receives the highest marks possible when it comes to performance and controlling expenses. Close to half of the portfolio is in mid-cap issues. Oppenheimer remains one of the leaders when it comes to global investing. This portfolio's alpha, which measures excess returns per unit of risk taken, as measured against the fund's benchmark index, is quite appealing. On a total point basis, this is the number-one fund for its category.

Profile
minimum initial investment $1,000
subsequent minimum investment . . . $25
available in all 50 states. . . . . yes
telephone exchanges. . . . . yes
number of funds in family 216
IRA accounts available . . . . yes
IRA minimum investment $250
date of inception. . . . . Dec. 1969
dividend/income paid . . . . annually
largest sector weighting . . . technology

Pilgrim International Small Cap A
7337 East Doubletree Ranch Road
Scottsdale, AZ 85258
(800) 334-3444
www.ingfunds.com

total return	★★★★★
risk reduction	★★★
management	★★★★
tax minimization	★★★★★
expense control	★★★
symbol NIGRX	20 points
up-market performance	fair
down-market performance	fair
predictability of returns	fair

Total Return   ★★★★★
Over the past five years, Pilgrim International Small Cap A has taken $10,000 and turned it into $21,010 ($13,310 over three years). This translates into an annualized return of 16 percent over the past five years and 10 percent over the past three years. Over the past five years, this fund has outperformed 97 percent of all mutual funds; within its general category, it has done better than 99 percent of its peers. Global equity funds have averaged 2 percent annually over these same five years.

Risk/Volatility   ★★★
Over the past five years, Pilgrim International Small Cap A has been safer than 19 percent of all global equity funds. Over the past decade, the fund has had two negative years, while the S & P 500 has had two (off 9 percent in 2000 and 12 percent in 2001); the EAFE fell three times (off 12 percent in 1992, 14 percent in 2000, and 21 percent in 2001). The fund has underperformed the S & P 500 twice and the EAFE Index twice in the past ten years.

	past 5 years		past 7 years	
worst year	-27.5%	2001	-27.5%	2001
best year	121.9%	1999	121.9%	1999

During the past five years, the fund's worst three quarters have been first quarter 2001 (-19 percent), third quarter 2001 (-17 percent), and third quarter 1998 (-15 percent). The three best-performing quarters over the same period have been fourth quarter 1999 (53 percent), first quarter 1998 (25 percent), and fourth quarter 1998 (19 percent). In the past, Pilgrim International Small Cap A has done better than 25 percent of its peer group during the most recent bull market and outperformed 26 percent of its peer group during the most recent bear market. Consistency, or predictability, of returns for Pilgrim International Small Cap A can be described as fair. This fund's risk-related return ranks in the top quintile.

Management   ★★★★

There are 155 stocks in this $160 million portfolio. The average global equity fund today is $330 million in size. Close to 100 percent of the fund's holdings are in stocks. The stocks in this portfolio have an average p/e ratio of 28 and a median market capitalization of $2 billion. The ten largest holdings compose 12 percent of the fund's total assets. The three largest sector weightings are industrial cyclicals (21 percent), services (13 percent), and financials (12 percent). The portfolio's equity holdings can be categorized as mid-cap and growth-oriented issues.

A team has managed this fund for the past eight years. Management favors fast-growing smaller companies that have improving fundamentals. The managers use a momentum-driven strategy. There are 122 funds besides International Small Cap A within the ING Pilgrim family. Overall, the fund family's risk-adjusted performance can be described as very good.

Tax Minimization   ★★★★★

During the past five years, a $10,000 initial investment grew to $18,700 after taxes, assuming a 40 percent income tax bracket (state and federal combined) and a capital gains rate of 20 percent. This means that investors in this fund were able to preserve 89 percent of their total returns. Compared to other equity funds in the same category, this fund's tax savings are considered to be excellent.

Expenses   ★★★

Pilgrim International Small Cap A's expense ratio is 1.7 percent; it has averaged 1.7 percent annually over the past three calendar years. The average expense ratio for the 1,700 funds in this category is 1.8 percent. This fund's turnover rate over the past year has been 56 percent, while its peer group average has been 99 percent.

Summary

Pilgrim International Small Cap Growth Portfolio A, a foreign stock fund that invests in mid-cap growth stocks outside of the United States, has outperformed 97 percent of all mutual funds over the past five years and has done better than 99 percent of its peer group. Risk-adjusted returns have been exceptional over the past three and five years. The fund ranks in the top quintile when it comes to return versus risk. The portfolio is rated number one when it comes to performance. The fund outperformed the S & P 500 by more than 100 percentage points in 1999. This portfolio's alpha, which measures excess returns per unit of risk taken, as measured against the fund's benchmark index, is quite appealing.

Profile

minimum initial investment $1,000	*IRA accounts available* . . . . yes
subsequent minimum investment . . $100	*IRA minimum investment* $250
available in all 50 states. . . . . yes	*date of inception* . . . . Aug. 1994
telephone exchanges. . . . . yes	*dividend/income paid* . . . . annually
number of funds in family 123	*largest sector weighting* indust. cyclicals

Tweedy, Browne Global Value

350 Park Avenue
New York, NY 10022
(800) 432-4789
www.tweedy.com

total return	★★★★
risk reduction	★★★★★
management	★★★★★
tax minimization	★★★★
expense control	★★★★★
symbol TBGVX	23 points
up-market performance	fair
down-market performance	very good
predictability of returns	excellent

Total Return ★★★★

Over the past five years, Tweedy, Browne Global Value has taken $10,000 and turned it into $18,430 ($13,310 over three years). This translates into an annualized return of 13 percent over the past five years and 10 percent over the past three years. Over the past five years, this fund has outperformed 93 percent of all mutual funds; within its general category, it has done better than 97 percent of its peers. Global equity funds have averaged 2 percent annually over these same five years.

Risk/Volatility ★★★★★

Over the past five years, Tweedy, Browne Global Value has been safer than 99 percent of all global equity funds. Over the past decade, the fund has had one negative year, while the S & P 500 has had two (off 9 percent in 2000 and 12 percent in 2001); the EAFE fell three times (off 12 percent in 1992, 14 percent in 2000, and 21 percent in 2001). The fund has underperformed the S & P 500 twice and the EAFE Index twice in the past ten years. Consistency of *overperformance* for this fund has been outstanding.

	past 5 years		past 8 years	
worst year	-4.7%	2001	-4.7%	2001
best year	25.3%	1999	25.3%	1999

Risk-adjusted returns have been exceptional over the past three and five years. During the past five years, the fund's worst three quarters have been third quarter 1998 (-18 percent), third quarter 2001 (-13 percent), and first quarter 2001 (-2 percent). The three best-performing quarters over the same period have been fourth quarter 1998 (16 percent), first quarter 1998 (16 percent), and second quarter 1999 (15 percent). In the past, Tweedy, Browne Global Value has done better than 22 percent of its peer group during the most recent bull market and outperformed 97 percent of its peer group during the most recent bear market. Consistency, or predictability, of returns for Tweedy, Browne Global Value can be described as excellent. This fund's risk-related return ranks in the top quintile.

Management   ★★★★★
There are 195 stocks in this $3.8 billion portfolio. The average global equity fund today is $330 million in size. Close to 86 percent of the fund's holdings are in stocks. The stocks in this portfolio have an average p/e ratio of 21 and a median market capitalization of $4 billion. The ten largest holdings compose 35 percent of the fund's total assets. The three largest sector weightings are financials (22 percent), staples (21 percent), and health (19 percent). The portfolio's equity holdings can be categorized as mid-cap and value-oriented issues.

A team has managed this fund for the past nine years. Managers Browne, Browne, and Spears look for ideas where few dare to tread. Positions are usually held for a long time. There is one other fund besides Global Value within the Tweedy, Browne family. Overall, the fund family's risk-adjusted performance can be described as exceptional.

Tax Minimization   ★★★★
During the past five years, a $10,000 initial investment grew to $14,560 after taxes, assuming a 40 percent income tax bracket (state and federal combined) and a capital gains rate of 20 percent. This means that investors in this fund were able to preserve 79 percent of their total returns. Compared to other equity funds in the same category, this fund's tax savings are considered to be very good.

Expenses   ★★★★★
Tweedy, Browne Global Value's expense ratio is 1.4 percent; it has averaged 1.4 percent annually over the past three calendar years. The average expense ratio for the 1,700 funds in this category is 1.8 percent. This fund's turnover rate over the past year has been 12 percent, while its peer group average has been 99 percent.

Summary
Tweedy, Browne Global Value, a foreign stock fund that invests in mid-cap value stocks outside of the United States, has outperformed 93 percent of all mutual funds over the past five years and has done better than 97 percent of its peer group. The fund ties for first place when it comes to risk reduction and has a lower turnover rate than any of its peer group. This portfolio's alpha, which measures excess returns per unit of risk taken, as measured against the fund's benchmark index, is appealing. On a total point basis, this is the number-one fund for its category.

Profile

minimum initial investment $2,500	*IRA accounts available* . . . . yes
subsequent minimum investment . . $250	*IRA minimum investment* $500
available in all 50 states. . . . . yes	*date of inception*. . . . . June 1993
telephone exchanges. . . . . yes	*dividend/income paid* . . . . annually
number of funds in family 2	*largest sector weighting* . . . . financials

William Blair International Growth N

222 West Adams Street, 34th Floor
Chicago, IL 60606
(800) 742-7272
www.wmblair.com

total return	★★★★
risk reduction	★★★★
management	★★★★
tax minimization	★★★★
expense control	★★★
symbol WBIGX	19 points
up-market performance	very good
down-market performance	good
predictability of returns	very good

Total Return   ★★★★

Over the past five years, William Blair International Growth N has taken $10,000
and turned it into $18,430 ($15,610 over three years). This translates into an annualized return of 13 percent over the past five years and 16 percent over the past
three years. Over the past five years, this fund has outperformed 95 percent of all
mutual funds; within its general category, it has done better than 97 percent of its
peers. Global equity funds have averaged 2 percent annually over these same five
years.

Risk/Volatility   ★★★★

Over the past five years, William Blair International Growth N has been safer than
72 percent of all global equity funds. Over the past decade, the fund has had three
negative years, while the S & P 500 has had two (off 9 percent in 2000 and 12 percent in 2001); the EAFE fell three times (off 12 percent in 1992, 14 percent in
2000, and 21 percent in 2001). The fund has underperformed the S & P 500 twice
and the EAFE Index twice in the past ten years. Consistency of *overperformance*
for this fund has been very good.

	past 5 years		past 10 years	
worst year	-13.7%	2001	-13.7%	2001
best year	96.3%	1999	96.3%	1999

During the past five years, the fund's worst three quarters have been third
quarter 1998 (-17 percent), third quarter 2001 (-16 percent), and first quarter 2001
(-11 percent). The three best-performing quarters over the same period have been
fourth quarter 1999 (43 percent), first quarter 1998 (17 percent), and fourth quarter
1998 (17 percent). In the past, William Blair International Growth N has done better
than 66 percent of its peer group during the most recent bull market and outperformed 76 percent of its peer group during the most recent bear market. Consistency,
or predictability, of returns for William Blair International Growth N can be
described as very good. This fund's risk-related return ranks in the top quintile.

Management   ★★★★

There are 130 stocks in this $190 million portfolio. The average global equity fund today is $330 million in size. Close to 88 percent of the fund's holdings are in stocks. The stocks in this portfolio have an average p/e ratio of 32 and a median market capitalization of $5 billion. The ten largest holdings compose 26 percent of the fund's total assets. The three largest sector weightings are financials (25 percent), services (18 percent), and health (17 percent). The portfolio's equity holdings can be categorized as mid-cap and growth-oriented issues.

W. George Greig has managed this fund for the past six years. Manager Greig focuses on companies whose earnings grow at 17 percent or more per year. He frequently goes after mid- and small- cap issues. There are eleven funds besides International Growth N within the William Blair family. Overall, the fund family's risk-adjusted performance can be described as fair to good.

Tax Minimization   ★★★★

During the past five years, a $10,000 initial investment grew to $14,190 after taxes, assuming a 40 percent income tax bracket (state and federal combined) and a capital gains rate of 20 percent. This means that investors in this fund were able to preserve 77 percent of their total returns. Compared to other equity funds in the same category, this fund's tax savings are considered to be very good.

Expenses   ★★★

William Blair International Growth N's expense ratio is 1.6 percent; it has averaged 1.5 percent annually over the past three calendar years. The average expense ratio for the 1,700 funds in this category is 1.8 percent. This fund's turnover rate over the past year has been 116 percent, while its peer group average has been 99 percent.

Summary

William Blair International Growth N, a foreign stock fund that invests in large-cap growth stocks outside of the United States, has outperformed 95 percent of all mutual funds over the past five years and has done better than 97 percent of its peer group. Risk-adjusted returns have been superb over the past three and five years. The fund ranks in the top quintile when it comes to return versus risk. The portfolio scores very well in all categories measured. The fund outperformed the S & P 500 by over 75 percentage points in 1999. This portfolio's alpha, which measures excess returns per unit of risk taken, as measured against the fund's benchmark index, is extremely appealing.

Profile

minimum initial investment $5,000	*IRA accounts available* . . . . yes
subsequent minimum investment . $1,000	*IRA minimum investment* $2,000
available in all 50 states. . . . . yes	*date of inception* . . . . Oct. 1992
telephone exchanges. . . . . yes	*dividend/income paid* . . . . annually
number of funds in family 12	*largest sector weighting* . . . . financials

Government Bond Funds

These funds invest in direct and indirect U.S. government obligations. Government bond funds are made up of one or more of the following: T-bills, T-notes, T-bonds, and mortgage-backed securities such as GNMAs (Government National Mortgage Association) and FNMAs (Federal National Mortgage Association). Treasury bills, notes, and bonds make up the entire marketable debt of the U.S. government. Such instruments are exempt from state income taxes.

Although GNMAs are considered an indirect obligation of the government, they are still backed by the full faith and credit of the United States. FNMAs are not issued by the government but are considered virtually identical in safety to GNMAs. Both instruments are subject to state and local income taxes. All of the securities in a government bond fund are subject to federal income taxes.

The average maturity of securities found in government bond funds varies broadly depending on the type of fund as well as on management's perception of risk and the future direction of interest rates. A more thorough discussion of interest rates and the volatility of bond fund prices can be found in the introduction to the corporate bond section, beginning on page 89.

Over the past fifteen years (1987–2001), government bonds have returned an average compound return of 9.1 percent—versus 8.9 percent for corporate bonds. A $10,000 investment in U.S. government bonds grew to $36,858 over the past fifteen years; a similar initial investment in corporate bonds grew to $35,756.

Over the past fifty years, the worst year for government bonds was 1967, when a loss of 9 percent was suffered. The second worst year was 1999, when the bonds suffered a loss of just less than 9 percent. The best year so far has been 1982, when government bonds posted a gain of 40 percent. All of these figures are based on total return (current yield plus or minus any appreciation or loss of principal). The second best year was 1995, when these debt instruments had a total return of just less than 32 percent.

Over the past fifty years, there have been forty-six 5-year periods (1952–1956, 1953–1957, etc.). On a pretax basis, government bonds have outperformed inflation during twenty-seven of the forty-six 5-year periods (59 percent of the time). The last 5-year period in which inflation outperformed long-term government bonds was 1979–1983 (8.4 percent versus 6.4 percent for bonds). Over the past fifty years, there have been forty-one 10-year periods (1952–1961, 1953–1962, etc.). On a pretax basis, government bonds have outperformed inflation during twenty-three of the forty-one 10-year periods, including the past seventeen in a row. The last 10-year period in which inflation outperformed long-term government bonds was 1975–1984 (7.3 percent versus 7.0 percent for bonds). Over

Annual Returns - U.S. Government Bond Funds

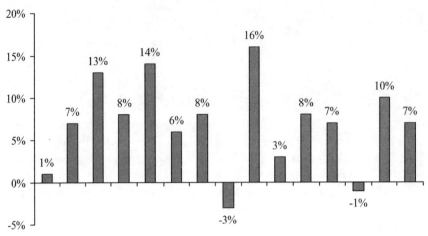

the past half-century, there have been thirty-one 20-year periods (1952–1971, 1953–1972, etc.). On a pretax basis, government bonds have outperformed inflation during the past sixteen consecutive 20-year periods (out of the possible thirty-one 20-year periods starting in 1952). Inflation outperformed long-term government bonds every other 20-year period starting with 1952–1971 through 1966–1985 (6.4 percent versus 6.0 percent for U.S. government bonds).

Over 550 funds make up the government bonds category. Total market capitalization of this category is $129 billion.

Over the past three and five years (all periods ending December 31, 2000), government funds have had an average compound annual return of 5.3 percent. For the decade, these funds have averaged 6.2 percent per year, over the past fifteen years, 7.2 percent a year. The standard deviation for government bond funds has been 3.4 percent over the past three years. This means that these funds have been less volatile than any other category except money market funds.

Government bond funds are the perfect choice for the conservative investor who wants to avoid any possibility of default. However, these securities should be avoided by even conservative investors who are in a high tax bracket or who are unable to shelter such an investment in a retirement plan or annuity. Such investors should first look at the advantages of municipal bond funds that pay interest that is generally nontaxable. Over the past fifty years, government bonds have had a compound average rate of return of 6.1 percent. with inflation running 3.9 percent over the same period. Always remember that government and corporate bonds are generally not a good investment once inflation and taxes are factored in. The investor who appreciates the cumulative effects of even low levels of inflation should probably avoid government and corporate bonds except as part of a retirement plan when nearing retirement.

Franklin U.S. Government Securities A

One Franklin Parkway
San Mateo, CA 94403
(800) 342-5236
www.franklintempleton.com

total return	★★★★★
risk reduction	★★★★
management	★★★★★
current income	★★★★★
expense control	★★★★
symbol FKUSX	23 points
up-market performance	very good
down-market performance	very good
predictability of returns	very good

Total Return   ★★★★★

Over the past five years, Franklin U.S. Government Securities A has taken $10,000 and turned it into $14,030 ($11,910 over three years and $19,680 over the past ten years). This translates into an annualized return of 7 percent over the past five years, 6 percent over the past three years, and 7 percent for the decade. Over the past five years, this fund has outperformed 67 percent of all mutual funds; within its general category, it has done better than 86 percent of its peers. Government bond funds have averaged 6 percent annually over these same five years.

During the past five years, a $10,000 initial investment grew to $12,420 after taxes, assuming a 40 percent income tax bracket (state and federal combined) and a capital gains rate of 20 percent. This means that investors in this fund were able to preserve 60 percent of their total returns. Compared to other funds in the same category, this fund's tax savings are considered to be very good.

Risk/Volatility   ★★★★

Over the past five years, Franklin U.S. Government Securities A has been safer than 93 percent of all government bond funds. Over the past decade, the fund has had one negative year, while the Lehman Brothers Aggregate Bond Index had two (off 3 percent in 1994 and 1 percent in 1999). The fund has underperformed the Lehman Brothers Aggregate Bond Index twice and the Lehman Brothers Government Bond Index twice in the past ten years. Consistency of *overperformance* for this fund has been outstanding.

	past 5 years		past 10 years	
worst year	0.8%	1999	-2.7%	1994
best year	10.6%	2000	16.7%	1995

During the past five years, the fund's worst three quarters have been second quarter 1999 (-1 percent), fourth quarter 1999 (0 percent), and fourth quarter 1998 (0 percent). The three best-performing quarters over the same period have been: third quarter 2001 (4 percent), fourth quarter 2000 (4 percent), and third quarter

2001 (4 percent). In the past, Franklin U.S. Government Securities A has done better than 73 percent of its peer group during the most recent bull market and outperformed 62 percent of its peer group during the most recent bear market. Consistency, or predictability, of returns for Franklin U.S. Government Securities A can be described as very good. This fund's risk-related return ranks in the top third.

Management   ★★★★★
There are 20,400 fixed-income securities in this $7.2 billion portfolio. The average government bond fund today is $230 million in size. Close to 97 percent of the fund's holdings are in bonds. The average maturity of the bonds in this account is eight years; the weighted coupon rate averages 7 percent. The portfolio's fixed-income holdings can be categorized as short-term, high-quality debt.

A team has managed this fund for the past thirteen years. Managers Lemein, Coffey, and Bayston have determined that GNMAs boast one of the most attractive risk/return profiles of any fixed-income instrument. Management favors a buy-and-hold approach. There are 209 funds besides U.S. Government Securities A within the Franklin Templeton family. Overall, the fund family's risk-adjusted performance can be described as very good.

Current Income   ★★★★★
Over the past year, Franklin U.S. Government Securities A had a twelve-month yield of 6.4 percent. During this same twelve-month period, the typical government bond fund had a yield that averaged 5.0 percent.

Expenses   ★★★★
Franklin U.S. Government Securities A's expense ratio is 0.7 percent; it has averaged 0.7 percent annually over the past three calendar years. The average expense ratio for the 600 funds in this category is 1.1 percent. This fund's turnover rate over the past year has been 4 percent, while its peer group average has been 212 percent.

Summary
Franklin U.S. Government Seccurities, a government bond fund that invests in GNMAs, has outperformed two-thirds of all mutual funds over the past five years and has done better than 86 percent of its peer group. Risk-adjusted returns have been very good for the past three, five, and ten years. The portfolio ranks receives ratings of very good and excellent in every category measured and is number one when it comes to paying out current income to investors.

Profile

minimum initial investment $1,000	*IRA accounts available* . . . . yes
subsequent minimum investment . . . $50	*IRA minimum investment* $250
available in all 50 states. . . . . yes	*date of inception.* . . . . May 1970
telephone exchanges. . . . . yes	*dividend/income paid.* . . . . monthly
number of funds in family 210	*average credit quality* . . . . AAA

Pilgrim GNMA Income A

7337 East Doubletree Ranch Road
Scottsdale, AZ 85258
(800) 992-0180
www.ingfunds.com

total return	★★★★★
risk reduction	★★★
management	★★★★
current income	★★★★
expense control	★★★
symbol LEXNX	19 points
up-market performance	good
down-market performance	excellent
predictability of returns	good

Total Return   ★★★★★

Over the past five years, Pilgrim GNMA Income A has taken $10,000 and turned it into $14,030 ($12,250 over three years and $19,680 over the past ten years). This translates into an annualized return of 7 percent over the past five years, 7 percent over the past three years, and 7 percent for the decade. Over the past five years, this fund has outperformed 71 percent of all mutual funds; within its general category, it has done better than 98 percent of its peers. Government bond funds have averaged 6 percent annually over these same five years.

During the past five years, a $10,000 initial investment grew to $12,700 after taxes, assuming a 40 percent income tax bracket (state and federal combined) and a capital gains rate of 20 percent. This means that investors in this fund were able to preserve 67 percent of their total returns. Compared to other funds in the same category, this fund's tax savings are considered to be excellent.

Risk/Volatility   ★★★

Over the past five years, Pilgrim GNMA Income A has been safer than 72 percent of all government bond funds. Over the past decade, the fund has had one negative year, while the Lehman Brothers Aggregate Bond Index had two (off 3 percent in 1994 and 1 percent in 1999). The fund has underperformed the Lehman Brothers Aggregate Bond Index twice and the Lehman Brothers Government Bond Index twice in the past ten years. Consistency of *overperformance* for this fund has been outstanding.

	past 5 years		past 10 years	
worst year	0.6%	1999	-2.1%	1994
best year	10.4%	2000	15.9%	1995

During the past five years, the fund's worst three quarters have been fourth quarter 1999 (-1 percent), first quarter 1997 (0 percent), and second quarter 1999 (0 percent). The three best-performing quarters over the same period have been third quarter 2001 (5 percent), first quarter 2001 (4 percent), and second quarter

1997 (4 percent). In the past, Pilgrim GNMA Income A has done better than just 17 percent of its peer group during the most recent bull market but outperformed 96 percent of its peer group during the most recent bear market. Consistency, or predictability, of returns for Pilgrim GNMA Income A can be described as good. This fund's risk-related return ranks in the top third.

Management   ★★★★
There are 230 fixed-income securities in this $510 million portfolio. The average government bond fund today is $230 million in size. Close to 94 percent of the fund's holdings are in bonds. The average maturity of the bonds in this account is nine years; the weighted coupon rate averages 7 percent. The portfolio's fixed-income holdings can be categorized as intermediate-term, high-quality debt.

Dennis Jamison and Roseann McCarthy have managed this fund for the past sixteen years. Managers Jamison and McCarthy concentrate on multifamily mortgage-backed securities issued by GNMA that limit prepayments (what are referred to as "lockout periods"). There are 122 funds besides GNMA Income A within the ING Pilgrim Group family. Overall, the fund family's risk-adjusted performance can be described as very good.

Current Income   ★★★★
Over the past year, Pilgrim GNMA Income A had a twelve-month yield of 5.8 percent. During this same twelve-month period, the typical government bond fund had a yield that averaged 5.0 percent.

Expenses   ★★★
Pilgrim GNMA Income A's expense ratio is 1.1 percent; it has averaged 1.1 percent annually over the past three calendar years. The average expense ratio for the 600 funds in this category is 1.1 percent. This fund's turnover rate over the past year has been 65 percent, while its peer group average has been 212 percent.

Summary
Pilgrim GNMA Income A, a government bond fund that invests in intermediate-term GNMAs and U.S. Treasury bonds, has outperformed 82 percent of all mutual funds over the past five years and has done better than 98 percent of its peer group. Risk-adjusted returns have ranged between good and very good for the past three, five, and ten years. The fund ranks as the number-one performer in its category in the areas of total return and tax efficiency. This portfolio's alpha, which measures excess returns per unit of risk taken, as measured against the fund's benchmark index, is appealing.

Profile
minimum initial investment $1,000
subsequent minimum investment . . $100
available in all 50 states. . . . . yes
telephone exchanges. . . . . yes
number of funds in family 123

IRA accounts available . . . . yes
IRA minimum investment $250
date of inception . . . . Oct. 1973
dividend/income paid. . . . . monthly
average credit quality . . . . AAA

Sit U.S. Government Securities

4600 Norwest Center
90 South 7th Street
Minneapolis, MN 55402
(800) 332-5580
www.sitfunds.com

total return	★★★★
risk reduction	★★★★★
management	★★★★★
current income	★★★★
expense control	★★★★
symbol SNGVX	22 points
up-market performance	excellent
down-market performance	very good
predictability of returns	excellent

Total Return   ★★★★

Over the past five years, Sit U.S. Government Securities has taken $10,000 and turned it into $14,030 ($11,910 over three years and $17,910 over the past ten years). This translates into an annualized return of 7 percent over the past five years, 6 percent over the past three years, and 6 percent for the decade. Over the past five years, this fund has outperformed 64 percent of all mutual funds; within its general category, it has done better than 97 percent of its peers. Government bond funds have averaged 6 percent annually over these same five years.

During the past five years, a $10,000 initial investment grew to $12,580 after taxes, assuming a 40 percent income tax bracket (state and federal combined) and a capital gains rate of 20 percent. This means that investors in this fund were able to preserve 64 percent of their total returns. Compared to other funds in the same category, this fund's tax savings are considered to be excellent.

Risk/Volatility   ★★★★★

Over the past five years, Sit U.S. Government Securities has been safer than 57 percent of all government bond funds. Over the past decade, the fund has had no negative years, while the Lehman Brothers Aggregate Bond Index had two (off 3 percent in 1994 and 1 percent in 1999). The fund has underperformed the Lehman Brothers Aggregate Bond Index twice and has outperformed the Lehman Brothers Government Bond Index every year for the past ten years. Consistency of *over-performance* for this fund has been outstanding.

	past 5 years		past 10 years	
worst year	1.3%	1999	1.3%	1999
best year	9.1%	2000	11.5%	1995

During the past five years, the fund's worst three quarters have been first quarter 1999 (0 percent), second quarter 1999 (0 percent), and first quarter 1997 (0 percent). The three best-performing quarters over the same period have been fourth quarter 2000 (3 percent), third quarter 2001 (3 percent), and third quarter 1997 (3 percent). In the past, Sit U.S. Government Securities has done better than 95 percent of its peer group during the most recent bull market and outperformed 57 percent of its peer group during the most recent bear market. Consistency, or predictability, of returns for Sit U.S. Government Securities can be described as excellent. This fund's risk-related return ranks in the top quintile.

Management   ★★★★★
There are 500 fixed-income securities in this $210 million portfolio. The average government bond fund today is $230 million in size. Close to 98 percent of the fund's holdings are in bonds. The average maturity of the bonds in this account is five years; the weighted coupon rate averages 8 percent. The portfolio's fixed-income holdings can be categorized as short-term, high-quality debt.

Michael Brilley and Bryce Doty have managed this fund for the past eleven years. Managers Brilley and Doty sort out pockets of securities that are too small for most institutional players, such as the GNMA mobile home subsector and VA Vendee mortgages. There are ten funds besides U.S. Government Securities within the Sit family. Overall, the fund family's risk-adjusted performance can be described as very good.

Current Income   ★★★★
Over the past year, Sit U.S. Government Securities had a twelve-month yield of 5.6 percent. During this same twelve-month period, the typical government bond fund had a yield that averaged 5.0 percent.

Expenses   ★★★★
Sit U.S. Government Securities's expense ratio is 0.8 percent; it has averaged 0.8 percent annually over the past three calendar years. The average expense ratio for the 600 funds in this category is 1.1 percent. This fund's turnover rate over the past year has been 56 percent, while its peer group average has been 212 percent.

Summary
Sit U.S. Government Securities, a government bond fund that invests in very high quality, short-term securities, has outperformed 80 percent of all mutual funds over the past three years and has done better than 99 percent of its peer group over the past decade. Risk-adjusted returns have been superb for the past three, five, and ten years. The fund receives the highest possible marks when it comes to risk minimization and predictability of returns. This portfolio's alpha, which measures excess returns per unit of risk taken, as measured against the fund's benchmark index, is appealing.

Profile
minimum initial investment $2,000	*IRA accounts available* . . . . yes
subsequent minimum investment . . $100	*IRA minimum investment* $1
available in all 50 states. . . . . yes	*date of inception.* . . . . June 1987
telephone exchanges. . . . . yes	*dividend/income paid.* . . . . monthly
number of funds in family 11	*average credit quality* . . . . AAA

Strong Government Securities Investor Shares

P.O. Box 2936
Milwaukee, WI 53201
(800) 368-1030
www.strongfunds.com

total return	★★★★★
risk reduction	★★★
management	★★★
current income	★★★
expense control	★
symbol STVSX	15 points
up-market performance	excellent
down-market performance	excellent
predictability of returns	good

Total Return   ★★★★★

Over the past five years, Strong Government Securities Investor Shares has taken $10,000 and turned it into $14,030 ($11,910 over three years and $21,590 over the past ten years). This translates into an annualized return of 7 percent over the past five years, 6 percent over the past three years, and 8 percent for the decade. Over the past five years, this fund has outperformed 69 percent of all mutual funds; within its general category, it has done better than 94 percent of its peers. Government bond funds have averaged 6 percent annually over these same five years.

During the past five years, a $10,000 initial investment grew to $12,620 after taxes, assuming a 40 percent income tax bracket (state and federal combined) and a capital gains rate of 20 percent. This means that investors in this fund were able to preserve 65 percent of their total returns. Compared to other funds in the same category, this fund's tax savings are considered to be excellent.

Risk/Volatility   ★★★

Over the past five years, Strong Government Securities Investor Shares has been safer than 60 percent of all government bond funds. Over the past decade, the fund has had two negative years, while the Lehman Brothers Aggregate Bond Index had two (off 3 percent in 1994 and 1 percent in 1999). The fund has underperformed the Lehman Brothers Aggregate Bond Index twice and the Lehman Brothers Government Bond Index once in the past ten years. Consistency of *overperformance* for this fund has been very good.

	past 5 years		past 10 years	
worst year	-1.1%	1999	-3.4%	1994
best year	11.3%	2000	19.9%	1995

During the past five years, the fund's worst three quarters have been second quarter 1999 (-1 percent), first quarter 1999 (1 percent), and fourth quarter 1999 (0 percent). The three best-performing quarters over the same period have been third quarter 2001 (5 percent), fourth quarter 2000 (4 percent), and third quarter 1998

(4 percent). In the past, Strong Government Securities Investor Shares has done better than 78 percent of its peer group during the most recent bull market and outperformed 89 percent of its peer group during the most recent bear market. Consistency, or predictability, of returns for Strong Government Securities Investor Shares can be described as good. This fund's risk-related return ranks in the top quintile.

Management   ★★★
There are 310 fixed-income securities in this $1.6 billion portfolio. The average government bond fund today is $230 million in size. Close to 97 percent of the fund's holdings are in bonds. The average maturity of the bonds in this account is six years; the weighted coupon rate averages 7 percent. The portfolio's fixed-income holdings can be categorized as intermediate-term, high-quality debt.

Bradley Tank and Thomas Sontag have managed this fund for the past eight years. Managers Tank and Sontag have determined that GNMAs boast one of the most attractive risk/return profiles of any fixed-income instrument. Management has done a particularly good job of being sensitive to sector allocations and maturity dates. There are 101 funds besides Government Securities Investor Shares within the Strong family. Overall, the fund family's risk-adjusted performance can be described as good.

Current Income   ★★★
Over the past year, Strong Government Securities Investor Shares had a twelve-month yield of 5.2 percent. During this same twelve-month period, the typical government bond fund had a yield that averaged 5.0 percent.

Expenses   ★
Strong Government Securities Investor Shares's expense ratio is 0.9 percent; it has averaged 0.9 percent annually over the past three calendar years. The average expense ratio for the 600 funds in this category is 1.1 percent. This fund's turnover rate over the past year has been 373 percent, while its peer group average has been 212 percent.

Summary
Strong Government Securities Investor Shares, a government bond fund that invests in intermediate-term agency-backed and direct obligations, has outperformed 80 percent of all mutual funds over the past three years and has done better than 98 percent of its peer group during the past fifteen years. Risk-adjusted returns have ranged from very good to excellent for the past three, five, and ten years.

Profile
minimum initial investment $2,500	*IRA accounts available* . . . . yes
subsequent minimum investment . . . $50	*IRA minimum investment* $250
available in all 50 states. . . . . yes	*date of inception* . . . . Oct. 1986
telephone exchanges. . . . . yes	*dividend/income paid*. . . . . monthly
number of funds in family 102	*average credit quality* . . . . AAA

Vanguard GNMA

Vanguard Financial Center
P.O. Box 2600
Valley Forge, PA 19482
(800) 662-7447
www.vanguard.com

total return	★★★★★
risk reduction	★★★★
management	★★★★★
current income	★★★★★
expense control	★★★★★
symbol VFIIX	24 points
up-market performance	very good
down-market performance	very good
predictability of returns	very good

Total Return   ★★★★★

Over the past five years, Vanguard GNMA has taken $10,000 and turned it into $14,030 ($12,250 over three years and $19,680 over the past ten years). This translates into an annualized return of 7 percent over the past five years, 7 percent over the past three years, and 7 percent for the decade. Over the past five years, this fund has outperformed 69 percent of all mutual funds; within its general category, it has done better than 95 percent of its peers. Government bond funds have averaged 6 percent annually over these same five years.

During the past five years, a $10,000 initial investment grew to $12,460 after taxes, assuming a 40 percent income tax bracket (state and federal combined) and a capital gains rate of 20 percent. This means that investors in this fund were able to preserve 61 percent of their total returns. Compared to other funds in the same category, this fund's tax savings are considered to be very good.

Risk/Volatility   ★★★★

Over the past five years, Vanguard GNMA has been safer than 60 percent of all government bond funds. Over the past decade, the fund has had one negative year, while the Lehman Brothers Aggregate Bond Index had two (off 3 percent in 1994 and 1 percent in 1999). The fund has underperformed the Lehman Brothers Aggregate Bond Index twice and the Lehman Brothers Government Bond Index twice in the past ten years. Consistency of *overperformance* for this fund has been outstanding.

	past 5 years		past 10 years	
worst year	0.8%	1999	-1.0%	1994
best year	7.9%	2001	17.0%	1995

During the past five years, the fund's worst three quarters have been second quarter 1999 (-1 percent), first quarter 1997 (0 percent), and fourth quarter 1999 (0 percent). The three best-performing quarters over the same period have been third quarter 2001 (4 percent), second quarter 1997 (4 percent), and fourth quarter 2000

(4 percent). In the past, Vanguard GNMA has done better than 68 percent of its peer group during the most recent bull market and outperformed 75 percent of its peer group during the most recent bear market. Consistency, or predictability, of returns for Vanguard GNMA can be described as very good. This fund's risk-related return ranks in the top quintile.

Management   ★★★★★

There are 23,500 fixed-income securities in this $16 billion portfolio. The average government bond fund today is $230 million in size. Close to 97 percent of the fund's holdings are in bonds. The average maturity of the bonds in this account is six years; the weighted coupon rate averages 7 percent. The portfolio's fixed-income holdings can be categorized as short-term, high-quality debt.

Paul Kaplan has managed this fund for the past eight years. Manager Kaplan has a big advantage over his typical competitor: overhead costs that are a half point lower than the industry norm. Additionally, he seeks out undervalued securities coupled with a reduction in prepayment risk. There are 154 funds besides GNMA within the Vanguard family. Overall, the fund family's risk-adjusted performance can be described as very good.

Current Income   ★★★★★

Over the past year, Vanguard GNMA had a twelve-month yield of 6.3 percent. During this same twelve-month period, the typical government bond fund had a yield that averaged 5.0 percent.

Expenses   ★★★★★

Vanguard GNMA's expense ratio is 0.3 percent; it has averaged 0.3 percent annually over the past three calendar years. The average expense ratio for the 600 funds in this category is 1.1 percent. This fund's turnover rate over the past year has been 8 percent, while its peer group average has been 212 percent.

Summary

Vanguard GNMA, a government bond fund that pretty much exclusively invests in GNMAs, has outperformed more than 80 percent of all mutual funds over the past three years and has done better than 95 percent of its peer group. Risk-adjusted returns have been outstanding for the past five and ten years. The portfolio receives ratings of very good to excellent in every category measured. It rates number one when it comes to current income and low expenses, and also has the lowest turnover rate. On a total point basis, this is the number-one fund for its category.

Profile

minimum initial investment $3,000	*IRA accounts available* . . . . yes
subsequent minimum investment . . $100	*IRA minimum investment* $1,000
available in all 50 states. . . . . yes	*date of inception*. . . . . June 1980
telephone exchanges. . . . . yes	*dividend/income paid*. . . . . monthly
number of funds in family 155	*average credit quality* . . . . AAA

Growth Funds

These funds generally seek capital appreciation, with current income as a distant secondary concern. Growth funds typically invest in U.S. common stocks, while avoiding speculative issues and aggressive trading techniques. The goal of most of these funds is long-term growth. The approaches used to attain this appreciation can vary significantly among growth funds.

Over the past fifteen years, U.S. stocks have outperformed both corporate and government bonds. From 1987 through 2001, common stocks have averaged 13.7 percent compounded per year, compared to 8.9 percent for corporate bonds and 9.1 percent for government bonds. A $10,000 investment in stocks, as measured by the S & P 500, grew to over $68,924 over the past fifteen years; a similar initial investment in corporate bonds grew to only $35,760.

Looking at a longer time frame, you do even better: $10,000 invested in stocks at the beginning of 1952 would have grown to $2,889,360 by the end of 2001. This translates into an average compound return of 12.9 percent per year. Over the past fifty years, the worst year for common stocks was 1974, when a loss of 26 percent was suffered. One year later, these same stocks posted a gain of 37 percent. The best year so far has been 1954, when growth stocks posted a gain of 53 percent.

Growth stocks have outperformed bonds in every single decade. If George Washington had invested $1 in common stocks with an average return of 12 percent, his investment would be worth over $455 billion today. If he had averaged 14 percent, his portfolio would be large enough to pay our national debt five times over!

The following table covers 129 years and shows the odds of making money (a positive return) over each of several different time periods.

Standard & Poor's Composite 500 Stock Index
Various periods, 1871–1977 (dividends not included)

length of period	total number of periods	number of periods in which stock prices			percentage opportunity for profit (not including dividends)
		rose	declined	unchanged	
1 year	129	84	45	65	65
5 years	125	100	25	80	80
10 years	120	108	12	90	90
15 years	116	107	9	92	92
20 years	110	107	3	97	97
25 years	105	104	1	99	99
30 years	100	100	0	100	100

More than 3,100 funds make up the growth category. Total market capitalization is $1.1 trillion. The standard deviation is 24.4 percent; beta (stock market-related risk) is 1.0, the same as the overall market, as measured by the S & P 500. The typical portfolio is divided into 90 percent U.S. stocks, 4 percent foreign stocks, and the balance in money market instruments. The average turnover rate for all growth funds is 114 percent per year. The yield on growth funds averages about 0.2 percent annually. Fund expenses average 1.4 percent per year.

Volatility (standard deviation) in today's markets is unprecedented. As this chart shows, nearly half of the past year's 105 trading days (through May 31, 2000) saw changes of 1 percent. Nearly one-quarter saw changes greater than 2 percent. Finally, all but six days experienced at least a 1 percent change between the intraday low and high.

Percentage of Time S & P 500 Had 1–2% Daily Changes (1990–2000)
Percentage of trading days with changes of positive or negative

Year	S & P 500	1%	2%	1% intraday	2% intraday
1990	-3.2%	29.6	5.1	60.1	14.7
1991	30.6%	23.3	3.6	50.2	7.1
1992	7.7%	11.0	0.0	28.0	0.8
1993	10.0%	6.7	0.4	14.6	1.6
1994	1.3%	10.7	0.8	27.0	1.6
1995	37.4%	5.2	0.0	17.9	1.2
1996	23.1%	15.0	1.2	39.4	4.4
1997	33.4%	32.0	5.9	70.8	15.1
1998	28.6%	31.4	9.1	69.1	22.2
1999	21.1%	36.5	9.1	77.0	21.0
2000 *	-2.8%	48.1	22.1	94.2	44.2

* through May 31, 2000

Annual Returns - Growth Funds

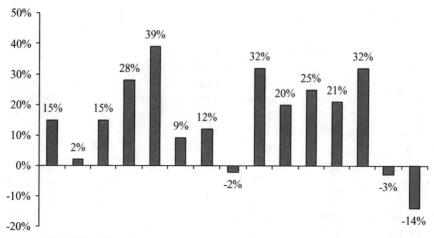

Historical returns over the past three, five, ten, and fifteen years for growth funds are shown here. All of the figures shown are *compound annual* rates of return (all periods ending December 31, 2001).

3 years	5 years	10 years	15 years
1.8%	9.3%	11.3%	12.3%

Calamos Growth A

1111 E. Warrenville Road
Naperville, IL 6053
(800) 823-7386
www.calamos.com

total return	★★★★
risk reduction	★★★
management	★★★★
tax minimization	★★★★
expense control	★★★
symbol CVGRX	18 points
up-market performance	very good
down-market performance	fair
predictability of returns	poor

Total Return   ★★★★

Over the past five years, Calamos Growth A has taken $10,000 and turned it into $33,040 ($20,980 over three years and $56,950 over the past ten years). This translates into an annualized return of 27 percent over the past five years, 28 percent over the past three years, and 19 percent for the decade. Over the past five years, this fund has outperformed 99 percent of all mutual funds; within its general category, it has done better than 99 percent of its peers. Growth funds have averaged 9 percent annually over these same five years.

Risk/Volatility   ★★★

Over the past five years, Calamos Growth A has been safer than 78 percent of all growth funds. Over the past decade, the fund has had two negative years, while the S & P 500 has had two (off 9 percent in 2000 and 12 percent in 2001). The fund has underperformed the S & P 500 three times in the past ten years. Consistency of *overperformance* for this fund has been outstanding.

	past 5 years		past 10 years	
worst year	-7.7%	2001	-7.7%	2001
best year	77.7%	1999	77.7%	1999

During the past five years, the fund's worst three quarters have been third quarter 1998 (-18 percent), third quarter 2001 (-15 percent), and fourth quarter 2000 (-13 percent). The three best-performing quarters over the same period have been fourth quarter 1999 (48 percent), first quarter 2000 (35 percent), and fourth quarter 1998 (31 percent). In the past, Calamos Growth A has done better than 45 percent of its peer group during the most recent bull market and outperformed 68 percent of its peer group during the most recent bear market. Consistency, or predictability, of returns for Calamos Growth A can be described as poor. This fund's risk-related return ranks in the top quintile.

Management   ★★★★

There are ninety stocks in this $650 million portfolio. The average growth fund today is $365 million in size. Close to 100 percent of the fund's holdings are in stocks. The stocks in this portfolio have an average p/e ratio of 27 and a median market capitalization of $1.5 billion. The ten largest holdings compose 20 percent of the fund's total assets. The three largest sector weightings are services (29 percent), health (17 percent), and retail (11 percent). The portfolio's equity holdings can be categorized as small-cap and growth-oriented issues.

John Calamos and John Calamos Jr. have managed this fund for the past ten years. Managers Calamos and Calamos use a proprietary quantitative model to target fast-growing companies. Management then buys attractively valued issues, based on historical and industry comparisons. Once a stock reaches its price target or its fundamentals weaken, it is quickly jettisoned. There are eight funds besides Growth A within the Calamos family. Overall, the fund family's risk-adjusted performance can be described as exceptional.

Tax Minimization   ★★★★

During the past five years, a $10,000 initial investment grew to $28,090 after taxes, assuming a 40 percent income tax bracket (state and federal combined) and a capital gains rate of 20 percent. This means that investors in this fund were able to preserve 85 percent of their total returns. Compared to other equity funds in the same category, this fund's tax savings are considered to be very good.

Expenses   ★★★

Calamos Growth A's expense ratio is 1.5 percent; it has averaged 1.5 percent annually over the past three calendar years. The average expense ratio for the 3,300 funds in this category is 1.4 percent. This fund's turnover rate over the past year has been 91 percent, while its peer group average has been 114 percent.

Summary

Calamos Growth A, a small-cap growth fund, has outperformed more than 99 percent of all mutual funds over the past three, five, and ten years and has done better than 99 percent of its peer group during the same periods. Risk-adjusted returns have also been excellent over the past three, five, and ten years. The fund ranks in the top quintile when it comes to return versus risk. The portfolio scores well when it comes to performance, risk reduction, and expense control. In 1999, the fund outperformed the S & P 500 by 57 percentage points. This portfolio's alpha, which measures excess returns per unit of risk taken, as measured against the fund's benchmark index, is extremely appealing.

Profile

minimum initial investment $500	*IRA accounts available* . . . . yes
subsequent minimum investment . . . $50	*IRA minimum investment* $500
available in all 50 states. . . . . yes	*date of inception* . . . . Sept. 1990
telephone exchanges. . . . . yes	*dividend/income paid* . . . . quarterly
number of funds in family 9	*largest sector weighting* . . . . . . services

FMI Focus
225 East Mason Street
Milwaukee, WI 53202
(800) 811-5311

total return	★★★★★
risk reduction	★★★
management	★★★★
tax minimization	★★★★★
expense control	★
symbol FMIOX	18 points
up-market performance	excellent
down-market performance	fair
predictability of returns	fair

Total Return   ★★★★★

Over the past five years, FMI Focus has taken $10,000 and turned it into $44,840 ($19,540 over three years). This translates into an annualized return of 35 percent over the past five years and 25 percent over the past three years. Over the past three years, this fund has outperformed 99 percent of all mutual funds; within its general category, it has done better than 91 percent of its peers. Growth funds have averaged 9 percent annually over these same five years.

Risk/Volatility   ★★★

Over the past three years, FMI Focus has been safer than 87 percent of all growth funds. Over the past decade, the fund has had no negative years, while the S & P 500 has had two (off 9 percent in 2000 and 12 percent in 2001). The fund has underperformed the S & P 500 twice in the past ten years.

	past 5 years		past 10 years	
worst year	2.5%	2001	2.5%	2001
best year	69.8%	1997	69.8%	1997

During the past five years, the fund's worst three quarters have been third quarter 2001 (-21 percent), fourth quarter 2000 (-12 percent), and first quarter 2001 (-10 percent). The three best-performing quarters over the same period have been fourth quarter 1999 (38 percent), third quarter 1997 (32 percent), and fourth quarter 1998 (32 percent). In the past, FMI Focus has done better than 97 percent of its peer group during the most recent bull market and outperformed 68 percent of its peer group during the most recent bear market. Consistency, or predictability, of returns for FMI Focus can be described as fair. This fund's risk-related return ranks in the top quintile.

Management   ★★★★

There are 110 stocks in this $300 million portfolio. The average growth fund today is $365 million in size. Close to 87 percent of the fund's holdings are in stocks. The stocks in this portfolio have an average p/e ratio of 19 and a median market capitalization of $1.4 billion. The ten largest holdings compose 35 percent of the fund's total assets. The three largest sector weightings are financials (23 percent), industrials (19 percent), and technology (18 percent). The portfolio's equity holdings can be categorized as small-cap and a blend of growth and value stocks.

Ted Kellner and Richard Lane have managed this fund for the past six years. Managers Kellner and Lane are not averse to owning traditionally valued issues. Management is willing to load up on certain industry groups and has a tendency to move in and out of a number of stocks during the course of any given year. FMI Focus is the only fund within the FMI family.

Tax Minimization   ★★★★★

During the past three years, a $10,000 initial investment grew to $18,300 after taxes, assuming a 40 percent income tax bracket (state and federal combined) and a capital gains rate of 20 percent. This means that investors in this fund were able to preserve 87 percent of their total returns. Compared to other equity funds in the same category, this fund's tax savings are considered to be excellent.

Expenses   ★

FMI Focus's expense ratio is 1.8 percent; it has averaged 1.8 percent annually over the past three calendar years. The average expense ratio for the 3,300 funds in this category is 1.4 percent. This fund's turnover rate over the past year has been 239 percent, while its peer group average has been 114 percent.

Summary

FMI Focus, a small-cap portfolio that invests in both value and growth, has outperformed over 99 percent of all mutual funds over the past three years and has done better than 91 percent of its peer group during the same period. Risk-adjusted returns have also been outstanding over the same period. The fund ranks as the best performer in its category. This portfolio's alpha, which measures excess returns per unit of risk taken, as measured against the fund's benchmark index, is extremely appealing.

Profile

minimum initial investment $1,000	*IRA accounts available* . . . . yes
subsequent minimum investment . . $100	*IRA minimum investment* $1,000
available in all 50 states. . . . . yes	*date of inception.* . . . . Dec. 1996
telephone exchanges. . . . . yes	*dividend/income paid* . . . . quarterly
number of funds in family 1	*largest sector weighting* . . . . financials

Fountainhead Special Value

431 N. Pennsylvania Street
Indianapolis, IN 46204
(800) 868-9535

total return	★★★★
risk reduction	★★★
management	★★★★
tax minimization	★★★★★
expense control	★★★
symbol KINGX	19 points
up-market performance	very good
down-market performance	good
predictability of returns	fair

Total Return   ★★★★

Over the past five years, Fountainhead Special Value has taken $10,000 and turned it into $23,870 ($18,160 over three years). This translates into an annualized return of 19 percent over the past five years and 22 percent over the past three years. Over the past three years, this fund has outperformed 98 percent of all mutual funds; within its general category, it has done better than 97 percent of its peers. Growth funds have averaged 9 percent annually over these same five years.

Risk/Volatility   ★★★

Over the past three years, Fountainhead Special Value has been safer than 80 percent of all growth funds. Over the past decade, the fund has had three negative years, while the S & P 500 has had two (off 9 percent in 2000 and 12 percent in 2001). The fund has underperformed the S & P 500 twice in the past ten years.

	past 5 years		past 10 years	
worst year	-15.7	2000	-15.7	2000
best year	133.4%	1999	133.4%	1999

During the past five years, the fund's worst three quarters have been third quarter 1998 (-25 percent), third quarter 2001 (-24 percent), and second quarter 2000 (-10 percent). The three best-performing quarters over the same period have been fourth quarter 1999 (52 percent), second quarter 1999 (22 percent), and first quarter 1999 (16 percent). In the past, Fountainhead Special Value has done better than 52 percent of its peer group during the most recent bull market and outperformed 75 percent of its peer group during the most recent bear market. Consistency, or predictability, of returns for Fountainhead Special Value can be described as fair. This fund's risk-related return ranks in the top quintile.

Management   ★★★★

There are thirty-five stocks in this $20 million portfolio. The average growth fund today is $365 million in size. Close to 100 percent of the fund's holdings are in stocks. The stocks in this portfolio have an average p/e ratio of 28 and a median market capitalization of $3 billion. The ten largest holdings compose 48 percent of the fund's total assets. The three largest sector weightings are services (55 percent), health (25 percent), and financials (12 percent). The portfolio's equity holdings can be categorized as mid-cap and a blend of growth and value stocks.

Roger King has managed this fund for the past six years. Manager King uses a bottom-up approach that identifies companies that are selling at a discount to their private market value. He is not afraid to load up on a specific sector. There is one other fund besides Special Value within the Fountainhead family.

Tax Minimization ★★★★★
During the past three years, a $10,000 initial investment grew to $17,350 after taxes, assuming a 40 percent income tax bracket (state and federal combined) and a capital gains rate of 20 percent. This means that investors in this fund were able to preserve 90 percent of their total returns. Compared to other equity funds in the same category, this fund's tax savings are considered to be excellent.

Expenses ★★★
Fountainhead Special Value's expense ratio is 1.4 percent; it has averaged 1.4 percent annually over the past three calendar years. The average expense ratio for the 3,300 funds in this category is 1.4 percent. This fund's turnover rate over the past year has been 125 percent, while its peer group average has been 114 percent.

Summary
Fountainhead Special Value, a mid-cap portfolio that invests in both value and growth, has outperformed more than 98 percent of all mutual funds over the past three years and has done better than 97 percent of its peer group during the same period. Risk-adjusted returns have also been outstanding over the same period. The fund scores well in every category measured and ranks number one for tax efficiency. In 1999, the fund outperformed the S & P 500 by 112 percentage points. This portfolio's alpha, which measures excess returns per unit of risk taken, as measured against the fund's benchmark index, is extremely appealing.

Profile

minimum initial investment $5,000	IRA accounts available . . . . yes
subsequent minimum investment . $1,000	IRA minimum investment $2,000
available in all 50 states. . . . . yes	date of inception. . . . . Dec. 1996
telephone exchanges. . . . . yes	dividend/income paid . . . . annually
number of funds in family 2	largest sector weighting. . . . . . services

Hartford Capital Appreciation A
P.O. Box 219054
Kansas City, MO 64121
(888) 843-7824
www.thehartford.com

total return	★★★★
risk reduction	★★★
management	★★★★
tax minimization	★★★★★
expense control	★★★
symbol ITHAX	19 points
up-market performance	very good
down-market performance	good
predictability of returns	fair

Total Return ★★★★

Over the past five years, Hartford Capital Appreciation A has taken $10,000 and turned it into $27,030 ($16,860 over three years). This translates into an annualized return of 22 percent over the past five years and 19 percent over the past three years. Over the past five years, this fund has outperformed 99 percent of all mutual funds; within its general category, it has done better than 98 percent of its peers. Growth funds have averaged 9 percent annually over these same five years.

Risk/Volatility ★★★

Over the past five years, Hartford Capital Appreciation A has been safer than 86 percent of all growth funds. Over the past decade, the fund has had one negative year, while the S & P 500 has had two (off 9 percent in 2000 and 12 percent in 2001). The fund has underperformed the S & P 500 twice in the past ten years. Consistency of *overperformance* for this fund has been outstanding.

	past 5 years		past 10 years	
worst year	-6.9%	2001	-6.9%	2001
best year	66.8%	1999	66.8%	1999

During the past five years, the fund's worst three quarters have been third quarter 1998 (-22 percent), second quarter 2001 (-20 percent), and fourth quarter 1997 (-6 percent). The three best-performing quarters over the same period have been fourth quarter 1999 (52 percent), second quarter 1997 (32 percent), and fourth quarter 1998 (26 percent). In the past, Hartford Capital Appreciation A has done better than 63 percent of its peer group during the most recent bull market and outperformed 74 percent of its peer group during the most recent bear market. Consistency, or predictability, of returns for Hartford Capital Appreciation A can be described as fair. This fund's risk-related return ranks in the top quintile.

Management ★★★★
There are 135 stocks in this $1.6 billion portfolio. The average growth fund today is $365 million in size. Close to 100 percent of the fund's holdings are in stocks. The stocks in this portfolio have an average p/e ratio of 26 and a median market capitalization of $6 billion. The ten largest holdings compose 19 percent of the fund's total assets. The three largest sector weightings are industrial cyclicals (21 percent), services (17 percent), and health (15 percent). The portfolio's equity holdings can be categorized as mid-cap and value-oriented issues.

Saul Pannell has managed this fund for the past six years. Manager Pannell is on the constant lookout for underappreciated equities. He employs a "go any-where" approach that strict stylists may find troublesome. There are seventy-nine funds besides Capital Appreciation A within the Hartford family. Overall, the fund family's risk-adjusted performance can be described as good to very good.

Tax Minimization ★★★★★
During the past five years, a $10,000 initial investment grew to $23,520 after taxes, assuming a 40 percent income tax bracket (state and federal combined) and a capital gains rate of 20 percent. This means that investors in this fund were able to preserve 87 percent of their total returns. Compared to other equity funds in the same category, this fund's tax savings are considered to be excellent.

Expenses ★★★
Hartford Capital Appreciation A's expense ratio is 1.3 percent; it has averaged 1.3 percent annually over the past three calendar years. The average expense ratio for the 3,300 funds in this category is 1.4 percent. This fund's turnover rate over the past year has been 169 percent, while its peer group average has been 114 percent.

Summary
Hartford Capital Appreciation A, a mid-cap portfolio that invests in value equities, has outperformed 99 percent of all mutual funds over the past three years and has done better than 98 percent of its peer group during the same period. Risk-adjusted returns have also been outstanding over the past three and five years. The fund scores well in every category measured. In 1999, the fund outperformed the S & P 500 by 46 percentage points. This portfolio's alpha, which measures excess returns per unit of risk taken, as measured against the fund's benchmark index, is extremely appealing.

Profile
minimum initial investment $500	IRA accounts available . . . . yes
subsequent minimum investment . . . $25	IRA minimum investment $250
available in all 50 states. . . . . yes	date of inception . . . . July 1996
telephone exchanges. . . . . yes	dividend/income paid . . . . annually
number of funds in family 80	largest sector weighting indust. cyclicals

Lord Abbett Mid-Cap Value A

90 Hudson Street
Jersey City, NJ 07302
(800) 201-6984
www.lordabbett.com

total return	★★★
risk reduction	★★★★★
management	★★★★
tax minimization	★★★★
expense control	★★★
symbol LAVLX	19 points
up-market performance	very good
down-market performance	excellent
predictability of returns	very good

Total Return ★★★

Over the past five years, Lord Abbett Mid-Cap Value A has taken $10,000 and turned it into $22,880 ($17,280 over three years and $44,120 over the past ten years). This translates into an annualized return of 18 percent over the past five years, 20 percent over the past three years, and 16 percent for the decade. Over the past five years, this fund has outperformed 98 percent of all mutual funds; within its general category, it has done better than 90 percent of its peers. Growth funds have averaged 9 percent annually over these same five years.

Risk/Volatility ★★★★★

Over the past five years, Lord Abbett Mid-Cap Value A has been safer than 89 percent of all growth funds. Over the past decade, the fund has had two negative years, while the S & P 500 has had two (off 9 percent in 2000 and 12 percent in 2001). The fund has underperformed the S & P 500 twice in the past ten years. Consistency of *overperformance* for this fund has been very good.

	past 5 years		past 10 years	
worst year	-0.5%	1998	-3.3%	1994
best year	53.3%	2000	53.3%	2000

During the past five years, the fund's worst three quarters have been third quarter 1998 (-17 percent), third quarter 2001 (-8 percent), and third quarter 1999 (-8 percent). The three best-performing quarters over the same period have been second quarter 1999 (18 percent), fourth quarter 2000 (15 percent), and second quarter 1997 (14 percent). In the past, Lord Abbett Mid-Cap Value A has done better than 57 percent of its peer group during the most recent bull market and outperformed 99 percent of its peer group during the most recent bear market. Consistency, or predictability, of returns for Lord Abbett Mid-Cap Value A can be described as very good. This fund's risk-related return ranks in the top quintile.

Management ★★★★
There are fifty-two stocks in this $1 billion portfolio. The average growth fund today is $365 million in size. Close to 100 percent of the fund's holdings are in stocks. The stocks in this portfolio have an average p/e ratio of 25 and a median market capitalization of $4 billion. The ten largest holdings compose 27 percent of the fund's total assets. The three largest sector weightings are industrial cyclicals (23 percent), health (19 percent), and financials (13 percent). The portfolio's equity holdings can be categorized as mid-cap and a blend of growth and value stocks.

Edward von der Linde and Howard Hansen have managed this fund for the past ten years. Managers von der Linde and Hansen favor stability and limiting downside risk more than anything else. Management uses a dividend discount model to find attractively valued stocks. There are 100 funds besides Mid-Cap Value A within the Lord Abbett family. Overall, the fund family's risk-adjusted performance can be described as good.

Tax Minimization ★★★★
During the past five years, a $10,000 initial investment grew to $18,760 after taxes, assuming a 40 percent income tax bracket (state and federal combined) and a capital gains rate of 20 percent. This means that investors in this fund were able to preserve 82 percent of their total returns. Compared to other equity funds in the same category, this fund's tax savings are considered to be very good.

Expenses ★★★
Lord Abbett Mid-Cap Value A's expense ratio is 1.4 percent; it has averaged 1.4 percent annually over the past three calendar years. The average expense ratio for the 3,300 funds in this category is 1.4 percent. This fund's turnover rate over the past year has been 78 percent, while its peer group average has been 114 percent.

Summary
Lord Abbett Mid-Cap Value A, a mid-cap portfolio that invests in both growth and value equities, has outperformed 97 percent of all mutual funds over the past three, five, and ten years and has done better than 90 percent of its peer group. Risk-adjusted returns have also been superb over the past three, five, and ten years. The fund ranks in the top quintile when it comes to return versus risk. The fund scores between good and excellent in every category measured. At times, the fund will concentrate on a small handful of industry groups. This portfolio's alpha, which measures excess returns per unit of risk taken, as measured against the fund's benchmark index, is quite appealing.

Profile

minimum initial investment $1,000	*IRA accounts available* . . . . yes
subsequent minimum investment $1	*IRA minimum investment* $250
available in all 50 states. . . . . yes	*date of inception*. . . . . June 1983
telephone exchanges. . . . . yes	*dividend/income paid* . . . . annually
number of funds in family 101	*largest sector weighting* indust. cyclicals

Meridian Value

60 E. Sir Francis Drake Boulevard, #306
Larkspur, CA 94939
(800) 446-6662

total return	★★★★
risk reduction	★★★★★
management	★★★★★
tax minimization	★★★★★
expense control	★★★★★
symbol MVALX	24 points
up-market performance	excellent
down-market performance	excellent
predictability of returns	very good

Total Return   ★★★★

Over the past five years, Meridian Value has taken $10,000 and turned it into $30,520 ($20,980 over three years). This translates into an annualized return of 25 percent over the past five years and 28 percent over the past three years. Over the past five years, this fund has outperformed 99 percent of all mutual funds; within its general category, it has done better than 99 percent of its peers. Growth funds have averaged 9 percent annually over these same five years.

Risk/Volatility   ★★★★★

Over the past five years, Meridian Value has been safer than 96 percent of all growth funds. Over the past decade, the fund has had no negative years, while the S & P 500 has had two (off 9 percent in 2000 and 12 percent in 2001). The fund has underperformed the S & P 500 twice in the past ten years. Consistency of *over-performance* for this fund has been outstanding.

	past 5 years		past 10 years	
worst year	11.7%	2001	11.7%	2001
best year	38.3%	1999	38.3%	1999

During the past five years, the fund's worst three quarters have been third quarter 1998 (-17 percent), third quarter 2001 (-11 percent), and fourth quarter 1997 (-9 percent). The three best-performing quarters over the same period have been second quarter 1999 (25 percent), fourth quarter 1998 (18 percent), and first quarter 2000 (16 percent). In the past, Meridian Value has done better than 77 percent of its peer group during the most recent bull market and outperformed 97 percent of its peer group during the most recent bear market. Consistency, or predictability, of returns for Meridian Value can be described as very good. This fund's risk-related return ranks in the top quintile.

Management   ★★★★★

There are seventy-five stocks in this $1.1 billion portfolio. The average growth fund today is $365 million in size. Close to 90 percent of the fund's holdings are in stocks. The stocks in this portfolio have an average p/e ratio of 29 and a median market capitalization of $3 billion. The ten largest holdings compose 31 percent of the fund's total assets. The three largest sector weightings are services (25 percent), technology (21 percent), and health (18 percent). The portfolio's equity holdings can be categorized as mid-cap and a blend of growth and value stocks.

Kevin O'Boyle and Richard Aster Jr. have managed this fund for the past eight years. Managers O'Boyle and Aster are considered stock-picking pros. Management looks for beaten-down growth stocks that have some type of catalyst in place that will trigger a turnaround. There is one other fund besides Value within the Meridian family. Overall, the fund family's risk-adjusted performance can be described as exceptional.

Tax Minimization ★★★★★
During the past five years, a $10,000 initial investment grew to $27,470 after taxes, assuming a 40 percent income tax bracket (state and federal combined) and a capital gains rate of 20 percent. This means that investors in this fund were able to preserve 90 percent of their total returns. Compared to other equity funds in the same category, this fund's tax savings are considered to be excellent.

Expenses ★★★★★
Meridian Value's expense ratio is 1.1 percent; it has averaged 1.1 percent annually over the past three calendar years. The average expense ratio for the 3,300 funds in this category is 1.4 percent. This fund's turnover rate over the past year has been 76 percent, while its peer group average has been 114 percent.

Summary
Meridian Value, a mid-cap portfolio that invests in both growth and value equities, has outperformed 99 percent of all mutual funds over the past three and five years and has done better than 99 percent of its peer group. Risk-adjusted returns have also been exceptional over the past three and five years. The fund ranks in the top quintile when it comes to return versus risk. The fund scores between very good and excellent in every category measured. It is also the most tax-efficent fund within its category. In 2000, the fund outperformed the S & P 500 by 46 percentage points. This portfolio's alpha, which measures excess returns per unit of risk taken, as measured against the fund's benchmark index, is extremely appealing. On a total point basis, this is the number-one fund for its category.

Profile
minimum initial investment $1,000	*IRA accounts available* . . . . yes
subsequent minimum investment . . . $50	*IRA minimum investment* $1,000
available in all 50 states. . . . . yes	*date of inception* . . . . Feb. 1994
telephone exchanges. . . . . yes	*dividend/income paid* . . . . annually
number of funds in family 2	*largest sector weighting* . . . . . . services

Olstein Financial Alert C

4 Manhattanville Road, Suite 102
Purchase, NY 10577
(800) 799-2113
www.olsteinfunds.com

total return	★★★★
risk reduction	★★★★
management	★★★
tax minimization	★★★
expense control	★
symbol OFALX	15 points
up-market performance	excellent
down-market performance	very good
predictability of returns	good

Total Return   ★★★★

Over the past five years, Olstein Financial Alert C has taken $10,000 and turned it into $28,160 ($17,720 over three years). This translates into an annualized return of 23 percent over the past five years and 21 percent over the past three years. Over the past five years, this fund has outperformed 99 percent of all mutual funds; within its general category, it has done better than 99 percent of its peers. Growth funds have averaged 9 percent annually over these same five years.

Risk/Volatility   ★★★★

Over the past five years, Olstein Financial Alert C has been safer than 35 percent of all growth funds. Over the past decade, the fund has had no negative years, while the S & P 500 has had two (off 9 percent in 2000 and 12 percent in 2001). The fund has underperformed the S & P 500 twice in the past ten years. Consistency of *over-performance* for this fund has been outstanding.

	past 5 years		past 10 years	
worst year	12.9%	2000	12.9%	2000
best year	34.9%	1999	34.9%	1999

During the past five years, the fund's worst three quarters have been third quarter 2001 (-22 percent), third quarter 1998 (-16 percent), and second quarter 1998 (-7 percent). The three best-performing quarters over the same period have been fourth quarter 1998 (28 percent), second quarter 1999 (22 percent), and second quarter 2001 (20 percent). In the past, Olstein Financial Alert C has done better than 95 percent of its peer group during the most recent bull market and outperformed 92 percent of its peer group during the most recent bear market. Consistency, or predictability, of returns for Olstein Financial Alert C can be described as good. This fund's risk-related return ranks in the top quintile.

Management   ★★★

There are 100 stocks in this $785 million portfolio. The average growth fund today is $365 million in size. Close to 95 percent of the fund's holdings are in stocks. The stocks in this portfolio have an average p/e ratio of 22 and a median market capitalization of $3 billion. The ten largest holdings compose 23 percent of the fund's total assets. The three largest sector weightings are technology (26 percent), industrials (17 percent), and financials (15 percent). The portfolio's equity holdings can be categorized as mid-cap and value-oriented issues.

Bob Olstein has managed this fund for the past seven years. Manager Olstein is constantly on the lookout for inexpensive companies that have a strong balance sheet. Management has a fast-moving disciplined strategy, which means quick sales when a stock falls from Olstein's grace. There is one other fund besides Financial Alert C within the Olstein family.

Tax Minimization   ★★★

During the past five years, a $10,000 initial investment grew to $21,120 after taxes, assuming a 40 percent income tax bracket (state and federal combined) and a capital gains rate of 20 percent. This means that investors in this fund were able to preserve 75 percent of their total returns. Compared to other equity funds in the same category, this fund's tax savings are considered to be good.

Expenses   ★

Olstein Financial Alert C's expense ratio is 2.2 percent; it has averaged 2.2 percent annually over the past three calendar years. The average expense ratio for the 3,300 funds in this category is 1.4 percent. This fund's turnover rate over the past year has been 158 percent, while its peer group average has been 114 percent.

Summary

Olstein Financial Alert C, a mid-cap portfolio that invests value stocks, has outperformed 99 percent of all mutual funds over the past three and five years and has done better than 99 percent of its peer group. Risk-adjusted returns have also been exceptional over the past three and five years. The fund ranks in the top quintile when it comes to return versus risk. The fund scores between very good and excellent in every category measured. This portfolio's alpha, which measures excess returns per unit of risk taken, as measured against the fund's benchmark index, is extremely appealing.

Profile

minimum initial investment $1,000	IRA accounts available . . . . yes
subsequent minimum investment . . $100	IRA minimum investment $250
available in all 50 states. . . . . yes	date of inception . . . . Sept. 1995
telephone exchanges. . . . . yes	dividend/income paid . . . . annually
number of funds in family 2	largest sector weighting . . . technology

Parnassus

One Market Stewart Tower, Suite 1600
San Francisco, CA 94105
(800) 999-3505
www.parnassus.com

total return	★★★
risk reduction	★★★★
management	★★★★
tax minimization	★★★★
expense control	★★★★★
symbol PARNX	20 points
up-market performance	very good
down-market performance	good
predictability of returns	fair

Total Return   ★★★
Over the past five years, Parnassus has taken $10,000 and turned it into $21,040 ($16,430 over three years and $44,120 over the past ten years). This translates into an annualized return of 16 percent over the past five years, 18 percent over the past three years, and 16 percent for the decade. Over the past five years, this fund has outperformed 98 percent of all mutual funds; within its general category, it has done better than 95 percent of its peers. Growth funds have averaged 9 percent annually over these same five years.

Risk/Volatility   ★★★★
Over the past five years, Parnassus has been safer than 20 percent of all growth funds. Over the past decade, the fund has had no negative years, while the S & P 500 has had two (off 9 percent in 2000 and 12 percent in 2001). The fund has underperformed the S & P 500 twice in the past ten years. Consistency of *over-performance* for this fund has been outstanding.

	past 5 years		past 10 years	
worst year	1.4%	1998	0.6%	1995
best year	47.7%	1999	47.7%	1999

During the past five years, the fund's worst three quarters have been third quarter 1998 (-24 percent), fourth quarter 1997 (-13 percent), and second quarter 1998 (-13 percent). The three best-performing quarters over the same period have been fourth quarter 1998 (45 percent), fourth quarter 1999 (27 percent), and first quarter 2000 (27 percent). In the past, Parnassus has done better than 58 percent of its peer group during the most recent bull market and outperformed 76 percent of its peer group during the most recent bear market. Consistency, or predictability, of returns for Parnassus can be described as fair. This fund's risk-related return ranks in the top quintile.

Management   ★★★★
There are twenty stocks in this $380 million portfolio. The average growth fund today is $365 million in size. Close to 38 percent of the fund's holdings are in stocks. The stocks in this portfolio have an average p/e ratio of 27 and a median market capitalization of $28 billion. The ten largest holdings compose 91 percent of the fund's total assets. The three largest sector weightings are technology (44 percent), financials (43 percent), and retail (8 percent). The portfolio's equity holdings can be categorized as large-cap and value-oriented issues.

Jerome Dodson has managed this fund for the past eighteen years. Manager Dodson has a "go anywhere" approach to investing that has certainly paid off, as evidenced by his well-timed portfolio changes. Management is not afraid of having a concentrated portfolio or a majority of assets in cash from time to time. There are three funds besides Parnassus within the Parnassus family. Overall, the fund family's risk-adjusted performance can be described as exceptional.

Tax Minimization   ★★★★
During the past five years, a $10,000 initial investment grew to $16,600 after taxes, assuming a 40 percent income tax bracket (state and federal combined) and a capital gains rate of 20 percent. This means that investors in this fund were able to preserve 79 percent of their total returns. Compared to other equity funds in the same category, this fund's tax savings are considered to be very good.

Expenses   ★★★★★
Parnassus's expense ratio is 0.9 percent; it has averaged 0.9 percent annually over the past three calendar years. The average expense ratio for the 3,300 funds in this category is 1.4 percent. This fund's turnover rate over the past year has been 121 percent, while its peer group average has been 114 percent.

Summary
Parnassus, a large-cap value fund, has outperformed 98 percent of all mutual funds over the past three, five, and ten years and has done better than 98 percent of its peer group. Risk-adjusted returns have also been exceptional over the past three and five years. The fund ranks in the top quintile when it comes to return versus risk. The fund scores between good and excellent in every category measured. It has lower expenses than any fund in its category. This portfolio's alpha, which measures excess returns per unit of risk taken, as measured against the fund's benchmark index, is extremely appealing.

Profile
minimum initial investment $2,000	IRA accounts available . . . . yes
subsequent minimum investment . . . $50	IRA minimum investment $500
available in all 50 states. . . . . yes	date of inception. . . . . Dec. 1984
telephone exchanges. . . . . yes	dividend/income paid . . . . annually
number of funds in family 4	largest sector weighting . . . technology

Thompson Plumb Growth
1200 John Q. Hammons Drive
5th Floor
Madison, WI 53717
(800) 999-0887
www.thompsonplumb.com

total return	★★★★
risk reduction	★★★★★
management	★★★★★
tax minimization	★★★★
expense control	★★★★
symbol THPGX	22 points
up-market performance	excellent
down-market performance	excellent
predictability of returns	very good

Total Return   ★★★★
Over the past five years, Thompson Plumb Growth has taken $10,000 and turned it into $24,890 ($16,020 over three years). This translates into an annualized return of 20 percent over the past five years and 17 percent over the past three years. Over the past five years, this fund has outperformed 99 percent of all mutual funds; within its general category, it has done better than 99 percent of its peers. Growth funds have averaged 9 percent annually over these same five years.

Risk/Volatility   ★★★★★
Over the past five years, Thompson Plumb Growth has been safer than 90 percent of all growth funds. Over the past decade, the fund has had no negative years, while the S & P 500 has had two (off 9 percent in 2000 and 12 percent in 2001). The fund has underperformed the S & P 500 twice in the past ten years. Consistency of *over-performance* for this fund has been very good.

	past 5 years		past 10 years	
worst year	6.4%	1999	0.4%	1994
best year	32.4%	1997	33.1%	1996

During the past five years, the fund's worst three quarters have been third quarter 1998 (-15 percent), third quarter 1999 (-11 percent), and third quarter 2001 (-8 percent). The three best-performing quarters over the same period have been fourth quarter 1998 (25 percent), second quarter 1997 (17 percent), and fourth quarter 2000 (12 percent). In the past, Thompson Plumb Growth has done better than 83 percent of its peer group during the most recent bull market and outperformed more than 99 percent of its peer group during the most recent bear market. Consistency, or predictability, of returns for Thompson Plumb Growth can be described as very good. This fund's risk-related return ranks in the top quintile.

Management   ★★★★★

There are seventy-five stocks in this $330 million portfolio. The average growth fund today is $365 million in size. Close to 99 percent of the fund's holdings are in stocks. The stocks in this portfolio have an average p/e ratio of 31 and a median market capitalization of $13 billion. The ten largest holdings compose 29 percent of the fund's total assets. The three largest sector weightings are financials (22 percent), technology (19 percent), and services (19 percent). The portfolio's equity holdings can be categorized as large-cap and a blend of growth and value stocks.

John Thompson and Clint Oppermann have managed this fund for the past six years. Managers Thompson and Oppermann often make large sector bets that can result in quite a bit of volatility—most of which has been the good kind, upward. There are two funds besides Growth within the Thompson Plumb family. Overall, the fund family's risk-adjusted performance can be described as exceptional.

Tax Minimization   ★★★★

During the past five years, a $10,000 initial investment grew to $20,660 after taxes, assuming a 40 percent income tax bracket (state and federal combined) and a capital gains rate of 20 percent. This means that investors in this fund were able to preserve 83 percent of their total returns. Compared to other equity funds in the same category, this fund's tax savings are considered to be very good.

Expenses   ★★★★

Thompson Plumb Growth's expense ratio is 1.3 percent; it has averaged 1.3 percent annually over the past three calendar years. The average expense ratio for the 3,300 funds in this category is 1.4 percent. This fund's turnover rate over the past year has been 64 percent, while its peer group average has been 114 percent.

Summary

Thompson Plumb Growth, a large-cap portfolio that invests in both growth and value equities, has outperformed 99 percent of all mutual funds over the past five years and has done better than 99 percent of its peer group. Risk-adjusted returns have also been exceptional over the past three and five years. The fund ranks in the top quintile when it comes to return versus risk. The fund scores between very good and excellent in every category measured. In 2000, the fund outperformed the S & P 500 by 35 percentage points. This portfolio's alpha, which measures excess returns per unit of risk taken, as measured against the fund's benchmark index, is extremely appealing.

Profile

minimum initial investment $1,000	*IRA accounts available* . . . . yes
subsequent minimum investment . . $100	*IRA minimum investment* $250
available in all 50 states. . . . . yes	*date of inception* . . . . Feb. 1992
telephone exchanges. . . . . yes	*dividend/income paid* . . . . annually
number of funds in family 3	*largest sector weighting* . . . . financials

Wasatch Core Growth
150 Social Hall Avenue, 4th Floor
Salt Lake City, UT 84111
(800) 551-1700
www.wasatchfunds.com

total return	★★★★
risk reduction	★★★★
management	★★★★
tax minimization	★★★★
expense control	★★★★
symbol WGROX	20 points
up-market performance	excellent
down-market performance	excellent
predictability of returns	good

Total Return   ★★★★
Over the past five years, Wasatch Core Growth has taken $10,000 and turned it into $27,030 ($20,980 over three years and $52,340 over the past ten years). This translates into an annualized return of 22 percent over the past five years, 28 percent over the past three years, and 18 percent for the decade. Over the past five years, this fund has outperformed 99 percent of all mutual funds; within its general category, it has done better than 97 percent of its peers. Growth funds have averaged 9 percent annually over these same five years.

Risk/Volatility   ★★★★
Over the past five years, Wasatch Core Growth has been safer than 76 percent of all growth funds. Over the past decade, the fund has had no negative years, while the S & P 500 has had two (off 9 percent in 2000 and 12 percent in 2001). The fund has underperformed the S & P 500 twice in the past ten years. Consistency of *over-performance* for this fund has been very good.

	past 5 years		past 10 years	
worst year	1.6%	1998	1.6%	1998
best year	37.4%	2000	40.4%	1995

During the past five years, the fund's worst three quarters have been third quarter 1998 (-23 percent), third quarter 2001 (-17 percent), and fourth quarter 1997 (-2 percent). The three best-performing quarters over the same period have been second quarter 2001 (31 percent), fourth quarter 1998 (21 percent), and second quarter 1997 (17 percent). In the past, Wasatch Core Growth has done better than 75 percent of its peer group during the most recent bull market and outperformed more than 99 percent of its peer group during the most recent bear market. Consistency, or predictability, of returns for Wasatch Core Growth can be described as good. This fund's risk-related return ranks in the top quintile.

Management   ★★★★
There are fifty stocks in this $1.2 billion portfolio. The average growth fund today is $365 million in size. Close to 94 percent of the fund's holdings are in stocks. The stocks in this portfolio have an average p/e ratio of 25 and a median market capitalization of $2 billion. The ten largest holdings compose 55 percent of the fund's total assets. The three largest sector weightings are services (32 percent), health (28 percent), and financials (16 percent). The portfolio's equity holdings can be categorized as small-cap and growth-oriented issues.

Taylor Stewart Jr. has managed this fund for the past ten years. Manager Stewart only buy stocks with low p/e ratios in comparison to their earnings-growth rates. A large number of the companies in the portfolio have annual growth rates in the 15- to 25-percent range. There are six funds besides Core Growth within the Wasatch family. Overall, the fund family's risk-adjusted performance can be described as exceptional.

Tax Minimization   ★★★★
During the past five years, a $10,000 initial investment grew to $24,060 after taxes, assuming a 40 percent income tax bracket (state and federal combined) and a capital gains rate of 20 percent. This means that investors in this fund were able to preserve 89 percent of their total returns. Compared to other equity funds in the same category, this fund's tax savings are considered to be excellent.

Expenses   ★★★★
Wasatch Core Growth's expense ratio is 1.3 percent; it has averaged 1.3 percent annually over the past three calendar years. The average expense ratio for the 3,300 funds in this category is 1.4 percent. This fund's turnover rate over the past year has been 51 percent, while its peer group average has been 114 percent.

Summary
Wasatch Core Growth, a small-cap portfolio that invests in growth stocks, has outperformed between 98 and 99 percent of all mutual funds over the past three, five, and ten years and has done better than 99 percent of its peer group. Risk-adjusted returns have also been exceptional over the past three, five, and ten years. The fund ranks in the top quintile when it comes to return versus risk. The fund scores very well in every category measured. In 2000, the fund outperformed the S & P 500 by 46 percentage points. This portfolio's alpha, which measures excess returns per unit of risk taken, as measured against the fund's benchmark index, is extremely appealing.

Profile
minimum initial investment $2,000	*IRA accounts available* . . . . yes
subsequent minimum investment . . $100	*IRA minimum investment* $1,000
available in all 50 states. . . . . yes	*date of inception*. . . . . Dec. 1986
telephone exchanges. . . . . yes	*dividend/income paid* . . . . annually
number of funds in family 7	*largest sector weighting*. . . . . . services

Growth and Income Funds

These funds attempt to produce both capital appreciation and current income, giving priority to the appreciation potential in the stocks purchased. Growth and income fund portfolios include seasoned, well-established firms that pay comparatively high cash dividends. But do not let this category's name mislead you. The average growth and "income" fund has an annual yield of just 0.7 percent, versus 0.2 percent for the typical growth fund. The goal of these funds is to provide long-term growth without excessive volatility in share price. Portfolios are almost always composed exclusively of U.S. stocks, with an emphasis on financial, technology, industrial cyclical, services, health, and energy stocks.

Over the past fifty years (ending December 31, 2001), common stocks have outperformed inflation, on average, 68 percent of the time over one-year periods, 84 percent of the time over five-year periods, 86 percent of the time over ten-year periods, 92 percent of the time over fifteen-year periods, and 100 percent of the time over any given twenty-year period. Over the same period, high-quality, long-term corporate bonds have outperformed inflation, on average, 62 percent of the time over one-year periods, 66 percent of the time over five-year periods, 70 percent of the time over ten-year periods, 78 percent of the time over fifteen-year periods, and 82 percent over any given twenty-year period.

Annual Returns - Growth and Income Funds

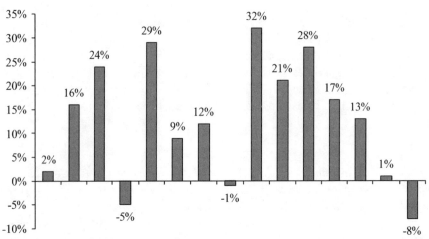

More than 1,200 funds make up the growth and income category. Total market capitalization of this category is close to $1 trillion.

Another category, "equity-income" funds, has been combined with growth and income. Equity-income funds have had a standard deviation of 14.5 percent, an average annual dividend yield of 1.5 percent, a 70 percent turnover rate, and an average annual expense ratio of 1.4 percent. Over the past three years, equity-income funds have had a compounded annualized return of 2.2 percent, 8.5 percent over the past five years, 11.2 percent for ten years, and 11.5 percent for the past fifteen years.

Over the past three and five years, growth and income funds have had an average compound return of 0.8 and 9.0 percent per year, respectively. These funds have averaged 11.6 percent annually over the past ten years and 11.6 percent annually for the past fifteen years. The standard deviation for growth and income funds has been 17.1 percent over the past three years (compared to 14.5 for equity-income and 24.4 percent for growth funds). This means that growth and income funds have been 43 percent more predictable than growth funds but have been about 15 percent less predictable than pure equity-income funds.

American Century Equity Income Investor Shares

4500 Main Street
P.O. Box 419200
Kansas City, MO 64141
(800) 345-2021
www.americancentury.com

total return	★★★
risk reduction	★★★★★
management	★★★★
tax minimization	★★
expense control	★★★
symbol TWEIX	17 points
up-market performance	good
down-market performance	excellent
predictability of returns	excellent

Total Return   ★★★

Over the past five years, American Century Equity Income Investor Shares has taken $10,000 and turned it into $19,260 ($13,680 over three years). This translates into an annualized return of 14 percent over the past five years and 11 percent over the past three years. Over the past five years, this fund has outperformed 96 percent of all mutual funds; within its general category, it has done better than 79 percent of its peers. Growth and income funds have averaged 9 percent annually over these same five years.

Risk/Volatility   ★★★★★

Over the past five years, American Century Equity Income Investor Shares has been safer than 98 percent of all growth and income funds. Over the past decade, the fund has had one negative year, while the S & P 500 has had two (off 9 percent in 2000 and 12 percent in 2001). The fund has underperformed the S & P 500 twice in the past ten years. Consistency of *overperformance* for this fund has been very good.

	past 5 years		past 10 years	
worst year	-0.2%	1999	-0.2%	1999
best year	28.3%	1997	29.6%	1995

Over the past five years, the fund's three worst quarters have been third quarter 1998 (-6 percent), third quarter 1999 (-6 percent), and first quarter 1999 (-5 percent). During the same period, the three best quarters have been fourth quarter 1998 (14 percent), second quarter 1997 (13 percent), and second quarter 1999 (13 percent). In the past, American Century Equity Income Investor Shares has done better than 46 percent of its peer group during the most recent bull market and outperformed 99 percent of its peer group during the most recent bear market. Consistency, or predictability, of returns for American Century Equity Income Investor Shares can be described as excellent. This fund's risk-related return ranks in the top quintile.

Management ★★★★
There are sixty stocks in this $840 million portfolio. The average growth and income fund today is $720 million in size. Close to 75 percent of the fund's holdings are in stocks. The stocks in this portfolio have an average p/e ratio of 20 and a median market capitalization of $5 billion. The ten largest holdings compose 33 percent of the fund's total assets. The three largest sector weightings are industrial cyclicals (21 percent), financials (17 percent), and energy (14 percent). The portfolio's equity holdings can be categorized as mid-cap and value-oriented issues.

Philip Davidson and Scott Moore have managed this fund for the past six years. Managers Davidson and Moore want to make sure that investors receive decent income along with growth, unlike most of their competitors who appear to be concerned only with capital appreciation. There are 109 funds besides Equity Income Investor Shares within the American Century Investments family. Overall, the fund family's risk-adjusted performance can be described as very good.

Tax Minimization ★★
During the past five years, a $10,000 initial investment grew to $12,130 after taxes, assuming a 40 percent income tax bracket (state and federal combined) and a capital gains rate of 20 percent. This means that investors in this fund were able to preserve 63 percent of their total returns. Compared to other equity funds in the same category, this fund's tax savings are considered to be fair.

Expenses ★★★
The fund's expense ratio is 1 percent; it has averaged 1 percent annually over the past three calendar years. The average expense ratio for the 1,400 funds in this category is 1.3 percent. This fund's turnover rate over the past year has been 169 percent, while its peer group average has been 79 percent.

Summary
American Century Equity Income Investor Shares, a mid-cap value fund, has outperformed 96 percent of all mutual funds over the past five years as well as 80 percent of its peer group over the same period. Risk-adjusted returns have ranged between very good and excellent over the past three and five years. Within its peer group, the fund ranks as one of the lowest risk growth and income funds and is one of the most predictable when it comes to returns. On a year-by-year basis, this fund's performance has been in the top half or quartile six out of the past seven years. This portfolio outperformed the S & P 500 in 2000 by more than 31 percentage points. This portfolio's alpha, which measures excess returns per unit of risk taken, as measured against the fund's benchmark index, is appealing.

Profile
minimum initial investment $2,500	*IRA accounts available* . . . . yes
subsequent minimum investment . . . $50	*IRA minimum investment* $1,000
available in all 50 states . . . . yes	*date of inception* . . . . Aug. 1994
telephone exchanges . . . . yes	*dividend/income paid* . . . . quarterly
number of funds in family 110	*largest sector weighting* indust. cyclicals

Ameristock

1301 East Ninth Street
36th Floor
Cleveland, OH 44114
(800) 394-5064
www.ameristock.com

total return	★★★★★
risk reduction	★★★★
management	★★★★★
tax minimization	★★★★★
expense control	★★★★★
symbol AMSTX	24 points
up-market performance	good
down-market performance	excellent
predictability of returns	good

Total Return   ★★★★★

Over the past five years, Ameristock has taken $10,000 and turned it into $21,930 ($12,600 over three years). This translates into an annualized return of 17 percent over the past five years and 8 percent over the past three years. Over the past five years, this fund has outperformed 98 percent of all mutual funds; within its general category, it has done better than 99 percent of its peers. Growth and income funds have averaged 9 percent annually over these same five years.

Risk/Volatility   ★★★★

Over the past five years, Ameristock has been safer than 88 percent of all growth and income funds. Over the past decade, the fund has had no negative years, while the S & P 500 has had two (off 9 percent in 2000 and 12 percent in 2001). The fund has underperformed the S & P 500 twice in the past ten years. Consistency of *over-performance* for this fund has been outstanding.

	past 5 years		past 10 years	
worst year	1.3%	2001	1.3%	2001
best year	32.9%	1997	32.9%	1997

Over the past five years, the fund's three worst quarters have been third quarter 2001 (-10 percent), third quarter 1999 (-8 percent), and third quarter 1998 (-6 percent). During the same period, the three best quarters have been fourth quarter 1998 (19 percent), third quarter 2000 (14 percent), and second quarter 1997 (14 percent). In the past, Ameristock has done better than 40 percent of its peer group during the most recent bull market and outperformed 95 percent of its peer group during the most recent bear market. Consistency, or predictability, of returns for Ameristock can be described as good. This fund's risk-related return ranks in the top quintile.

Management   ★★★★★

There are fifty stocks in this $870 million portfolio. The average growth and

income fund today is $720 million in size. Close to 90 percent of the fund's hold-
ings are in stocks. The stocks in this portfolio have an average p/e ratio of 31 and
a median market capitalization of $59 billion. The ten largest holdings compose 45
percent of the fund's total assets. The three largest sector weightings are technology (20 percent), financials (18 percent), and health (14 percent). The portfolio's equity holdings can be categorized as large-cap and value-oriented issues.

Nicholas Gerber and Angrew Ngim have managed this fund for the past five
years. Managers Gerber and Ngim are patient investors with strong convictions
about sticking with a mix of fallen growth stocks and traditional value.
Management is cautious and slow moving, avoiding the knee-jerk reactions that
frequently plague Wall Street. There are two funds besides Ameristock within the
Ameristock Mutual Fund family.

Tax Minimization ★★★★★
During the past five years, a $10,000 initial investment grew to $20,610 after taxes,
assuming a 40 percent income tax bracket (state and federal combined) and a capital gains rate of 20 percent. This means that investors in this fund were able to preserve 94 percent of their total returns. Compared to other equity funds in the same
category, this fund's tax savings are considered to be exceptional.

Expenses ★★★★★
Ameristock's expense ratio is 0.8 percent; it has averaged 0.9 percent annually over
the past three calendar years. The average expense ratio for the 1,400 funds in this
category is 1.3 percent. This fund's turnover rate over the past year has been 6 percent, while its peer group average has been 79 percent.

Summary
Ameristock, a large-cap value fund, has outperformed 98 percent of all mutual
funds over the past ten years as well as 99 percent of its peer group over the same
period. Returns over shorter periods have also been impressive. Risk-adjusted
returns have ranged between very good and excellent over the past three and five
years. By category, the fund ranks in the top quartile when it comes to returns
versus risk. Within its peer group, the fund ranks number two when it comes to performance and ties for first place in expenses and low turnover. This portfolio's
alpha, which measures excess returns per unit of risk taken, as measured against
the fund's benchmark index, is quite appealing. On a total point basis, this is the
number-one fund for its category.

Profile
minimum initial investment $1,000
subsequent minimum investment . . $100
available in all 50 states. . . . . yes
telephone exchanges. . . . . yes
number of funds in family 3

IRA accounts available . . . . yes
IRA minimum investment $1,000
date of inception . . . . Aug. 1995
dividend/income paid . . . . quarterly
largest sector weighting . . . technology

Dodge & Cox Stock

One Sansome Street
35th Floor
San Francisco, CA 94104
(800) 621-3979
www.dodgeandcox.com

total return	★★★★
risk reduction	★★★★★
management	★★★★★
tax minimization	★★★★
expense control	★★★★★
symbol DODGX	23 points
up-market performance	very good
down-market performance	excellent
predictability of returns	good

Total Return   ★★★★

Over the past five years, Dodge & Cox Stock has taken $10,000 and turned it into $21,010 ($15,210 over three years and $48,070 over the past ten years). This translates into an annualized return of 16 percent over the past five years, 15 percent over the past three years, and 17 percent for the decade. Over the past five years, this fund has outperformed 97 percent of all mutual funds; within its general category it has done better than 97 percent of its peers. Growth and income funds have averaged 9 percent annually over these same five years.

Risk/Volatility   ★★★★★

Over the past five years, Dodge & Cox Stock has been safer than 91 percent of all growth and income funds. Over the past decade, the fund has had no negative years, while the S & P 500 has had two (off 9 percent in 2000 and 12 percent in 2001). The fund has underperformed the S & P 500 twice in the past ten years. Consistency of *overperformance* for this fund has been very good.

	past 5 years		past 10 years	
worst year	5.4%	1998	5.2%	1994
best year	28.4%	1997	33.4%	1995

Over the past five years, the fund's three worst quarters have been third quarter 1998 (-14 percent), third quarter 2001 (-10 percent), and third quarter 1999 (-8 percent). During the same period, the three best quarters have been second quarter 1999 (17 percent), second quarter 1997 (15 percent), and fourth quarter 1998 (13 percent). In the past, Dodge & Cox Stock has done better than 83 percent of its peer group during the most recent bull market and outperformed 96 percent of its peer group during the most recent bear market. Consistency, or predictability, of returns for Dodge & Cox Stock can be described as good. This fund's risk-related return ranks in the top quintile.

Management   ★★★★★
There are eighty stocks in this $6.3 billion portfolio. The average growth and income fund today is $720 million in size. Close to 88 percent of the fund's holdings are in stocks. The stocks in this portfolio have an average p/e ratio of 25 and a median market capitalization of $10 billion. The ten largest holdings compose 29 percent of the fund's total assets. The three largest sector weightings are industrial cyclicals (24 percent), financials (20 percent), and energy (12 percent). The portfolio's equity holdings can be categorized as large-cap and value-oriented issues.

A team has managed this fund for the past twenty-three years. Management has maintained a value approach from which they have never deviated. This bargain-hunting approach has certainly paid off over the medium- and long-term. There are three funds besides Dodge & Cox Stock within the Dodge & Cox Funds family. Overall, the fund family's risk-adjusted performance can be described as exceptional.

Tax Minimization   ★★★★
During the past five years, a $10,000 initial investment grew to $17,230 after taxes, assuming a 40 percent income tax bracket (state and federal combined) and a capital gains rate of 20 percent. This means that investors in this fund were able to preserve 82 percent of their total returns. Compared to other equity funds in the same category, this fund's tax savings are considered to be very good.

Expenses   ★★★★★
Dodge & Cox Stock's expense ratio is 0.5 percent; it has averaged 0.5 percent annually over the past three calendar years. The average expense ratio for the 1,400 funds in this category is 1.3 percent. This fund's turnover rate over the past year has been 32 percent, while its peer group average has been 79 percent.

Summary
Dodge & Cox Stock, a large-cap value fund, has outperformed 97 percent of all mutual funds over the past five and ten years as well as 97 percent of its peer group over the same period. Returns over shorter and longer periods have been equally impressive. Risk-adjusted returns have also been outstanding over the past three, five, and ten years. Within its peer group, the fund receives high marks in the areas of return, low risk, expense control, and turnover. It ranks number one for low expenses. This portfolio's alpha, which measures excess returns per unit of risk taken, as measured against the fund's benchmark index, is extremely appealing.

Profile
minimum initial investment . . . . . $2,500   *IRA accounts available* . . . . yes
subsequent minimum investment . . $100   *IRA minimum investment* $1,000
available in all 50 states. . . . . yes   *date of inception* . . . . Jan. 1965
telephone exchanges. . . . . yes   *dividend/income paid* . . . . quarterly
number of funds in family 4   *largest sector weighting* indust. cyclicals

FPA Perennial
11400 W. Olympic Boulevard, Suite 1200
Los Angeles, CA 90064
(800) 982-4372

total return	★★★★★
risk reduction	★★★
management	★★★★
tax minimization	★★★★
expense control	★★★★
symbol FPPFX	19 points
up-market performance	excellent
down-market performance	excellent
predictability of returns	fair

Total Return   ★★★★★
Over the past five years, FPA Perennial has taken $10,000 and turned it into
$21,930 ($16,860 over three years and $31,080 over the past ten years). This trans-
lates into an annualized return of 17 percent over the past five years, 19 percent
over the past three years, and 14 percent for the decade. Over the past five years,
this fund has outperformed 98 percent of all mutual funds; within its general category, it has done better than 90 percent of its peers. Growth and income funds have
averaged 9 percent annually over these same five years.

Risk/Volatility   ★★★
Over the past five years, FPA Perennial has been safer than 67 percent of all growth
and income funds. Over the past decade, the fund has had one negative year, while
the S & P 500 has had two (off 9 percent in 2000 and 12 percent in 2001). The fund
has underperformed the S & P 500 twice in the past ten years. Consistency of *overperformance* for this fund has been very good.

	past 5 years		past 10 years	
worst year	4.8%	1998	0%	1994
best year	25.3%	1999	25.3%	1999

Over the past five years, the fund's three worst quarters have been third
quarter 1998 (-20 percent), third quarter 2001 (-13 percent), and first quarter 1999
(-10 percent). During the same period, the three best quarters have been second
quarter 1999 (29 percent), second quarter 2001 (22 percent), and fourth quarter
1998 (21 percent). In the past, FPA Perennial has done better than 97 percent of its
peer group during the most recent bull market and outperformed 91 percent of its
peer group during the most recent bear market. Consistency, or predictability, of
returns for FPA Perennial can be described as fair. This fund's risk-related return
ranks in the top quintile.

Management   ★★★★

There are thirty-five stocks in this $55 million portfolio. The average growth and income fund today is $720 million in size. Close to 100 percent of the fund's holdings are in stocks. The stocks in this portfolio have an average p/e ratio of 26 and a median market capitalization of $2 billion. The ten largest holdings compose 39 percent of the fund's total assets. The three largest sector weightings are industrial cyclicals (37 percent), technology (19 percent), and retail (11 percent). The portfolio's equity holdings can be categorized as mid-cap and a blend of growth and value stocks.

Eric Ende and Steven Geist have managed this fund for the past five years. Managers Ende and Geist have a conservative approach to money management: corporations with high returns on equity, strong financials plus modest valuations. There are three funds besides Perennial within the FPA family. Overall, the fund family's risk-adjusted performance can be described as good to very good.

Tax Minimization   ★★★★

During the past five years, a $10,000 initial investment grew to $17,320 after taxes, assuming a 40 percent income tax bracket (state and federal combined) and a capital gains rate of 20 percent. This means that investors in this fund were able to preserve 79 percent of their total returns. Compared to other equity funds in the same category, this fund's tax savings are considered to be very good.

Expenses   ★★★★

FPA Perennial's expense ratio is 1.3 percent; it has averaged 1.3 percent annually over the past three calendar years. The average expense ratio for the 1,400 funds in this category is 1.3 percent. This fund's turnover rate over the past year has been 16 percent, while its peer group average has been 79 percent.

Summary

FPA perennial, a mid-cap fund that invests in growth and value stocks, has outperformed 98 percent of all mutual funds over the past three and five years as well as 90 percent of its peer group over the same period. Risk-adjusted returns have also been exceptional over the past three and five years. By category, the fund ranks in the top quartile when it comes to returns versus risk. Within its peer group, the fund ranks number one when it comes to performance; expense control and low turnover figures are also impressive. This portfolio's alpha, which measures excess returns per unit of risk taken, as measured against the fund's benchmark index, is quite appealing.

Profile

minimum initial investment $1,500	*IRA accounts available* . . . . yes
subsequent minimum investment . . $100	*IRA minimum investment* $100
available in all 50 states. . . . . yes	*date of inception.* . . . . Apr. 1984
telephone exchanges. . . . . yes	*dividend/income paid.* . . . . semiannually
number of funds in family 4	*largest sector weighting* indust. cyclicals

MFS Value A
P.O. Box 2281
Boston, MA 02107
(800) 637-2929
www.mfs.com

total return	★★★
risk reduction	★★★★
management	★★★★
tax minimization	★★★★
expense control	★★★
symbol MEIAX	18 points
up-market performance	good
down-market performance	very good
predictability of returns	very good

Total Return   ★★★
Over the past five years, MFS Value A has taken $10,000 and turned it into $20,120 ($12,600 over three years). This translates into an annualized return of 15 percent over the past five years and 8 percent over the past three years. Over the past five years, this fund has outperformed 96 percent of all mutual funds; within its general category, it has done better than 96 percent of its peers. Growth and income funds have averaged 9 percent annually over these same five years.

Risk/Volatility   ★★★★
Over the past five years, MFS Value A has been safer than 97 percent of all growth and income funds. Over the past decade, the fund has had one negative year, while the S & P 500 has had two (off 9 percent in 2000 and 12 percent in 2001). The fund has underperformed the S & P 500 twice in the past ten years. Consistency of *over-performance* for this fund has been outstanding.

	past 5 years		past 10 years	
worst year	-7.8%	2001	-7.8%	2001
best year	33.9%	1997	33.9%	1997

Over the past five years, the fund's three worst quarters have been third quarter 2001 (-11 percent), first quarter 2001 (-8 percent), and third quarter 1999 (-7 percent). During the same period, the three best quarters have been second quarter 1997 (14 percent), fourth quarter 1998 (12 percent), and third quarter 2000 (11 percent). In the past, MFS Value A has done better than 41 percent of its peer group during the most recent bull market and outperformed 82 percent of its peer group during the most recent bear market. Consistency, or predictability, of returns for MFS Value A can be described as very good. This fund's risk-related return ranks in the top quintile.

Management   ★★★★

There are 100 stocks in this $1 billion portfolio. The average growth and income fund today is $720 million in size. Close to 96 percent of the fund's holdings are in stocks. The stocks in this portfolio have an average p/e ratio of 24 and a median market capitalization of $24 billion. The ten largest holdings compose 23 percent of the fund's total assets. The three largest sector weightings are financials (21 percent), services (17 percent), and industrials (14 percent). The portfolio's equity holdings can be categorized as large-cap and value-oriented issues.

Lisa Nurme has managed this fund for the past six years. Manager Nurme tends to favor dividend-paying equities, making her approach different from the competition. By emphasizing more traditional companies, management has been able to reduce volatility. There are 196 funds besides Value A within the MFS family. Overall, the fund family's risk-adjusted performance can be described as very good.

Tax Minimization   ★★★★

During the past five years, a $10,000 initial investment grew to $17,300 after taxes, assuming a 40 percent income tax bracket (state and federal combined) and a capital gains rate of 20 percent. This means that investors in this fund were able to preserve 86 percent of their total returns. Compared to other equity funds in the same category, this fund's tax savings are considered to be very good.

Expenses   ★★★

MFS Value A's expense ratio is 1.2 percent; it has averaged 1.3 percent annually over the past three calendar years. The average expense ratio for the 1,400 funds in this category is 1.3 percent. This fund's turnover rate over the past year has been 63 percent, while its peer group average has been 79 percent.

Summary

MFS Value A, a large-cap value fund, has outperformed 96 percent of all mutual funds over the past five years as well as 96 percent of its peer group over the same period. Returns over shorter periods have been equally impressive. Risk-adjusted returns have ranged between very good and exceptional over the past three and five years. By category, the fund ranks in the top quartile when it comes to returns versus risk. Within its peer group, the fund scores well in every category measured. This portfolio's alpha, which measures excess returns per unit of risk taken, as measured against the fund's benchmark index, is quite appealing.

Profile

minimum initial investment $1,000	*IRA accounts available* . . . . yes
subsequent minimum investment . . . $50	*IRA minimum investment* $250
available in all 50 states. . . . . yes	*date of inception* . . . . Jan. 1996
telephone exchanges. . . . . yes	*dividend/income paid* . . . . quarterly
number of funds in family 197	*largest sector weighting* . . . . financials

Muhlenkamp

3000 Stonewood Drive, Suite 300
Wexford, PA 15090
(800) 860-3863
www.muhlenkamp.com

total return	★★★★★
risk reduction	★★★
management	★★★★★
tax minimization	★★★★★
expense control	★★★★
symbol MUHLX	22 points
up-market performance	excellent
down-market performance	very good
predictability of returns	poor

Total Return   ★★★★★

Over the past five years, Muhlenkamp has taken $10,000 and turned it into $21,010 ($15,210 over three years and $48,070 over the past ten years). This translates into an annualized return of 16 percent over the past five years, 15 percent over the past three years, and 17 percent for the decade. Over the past five years, this fund has outperformed 96 percent of all mutual funds; within its general category, it has done better than 81 percent of its peers. Growth and income funds have averaged 9 percent annually over these same five years.

Risk/Volatility   ★★★

Over the past five years, Muhlenkamp has been safer than 12 percent of all growth and income funds. Over the past decade, the fund has had one negative year, while the S & P 500 has had two (off 9 percent in 2000 and 12 percent in 2001). The fund has underperformed the S & P 500 twice in the past ten years. Consistency of *over-performance* for this fund has been very good.

	past 5 years		past 10 years	
worst year	3.2%	1998	-7.2%	1994
best year	33.3%	1997	33.3%	1997

Over the past five years, the fund's three worst quarters have been third quarter 1998 (-21 percent), third quarter 2001 (-20 percent), and third quarter 1999 (-12 percent). During the same period, the three best quarters have been second quarter 1999 (20 percent), second quarter 1997 (15 percent), and third quarter 1997 (14 percent). In the past, Muhlenkamp has done better than more than 99 percent of its peer group during the most recent bull market and outperformed 58 percent of its peer group during the most recent bear market. Consistency, or predictability, of returns for Muhlenkamp can be described as poor. This fund's risk-related return ranks in the top quintile.

Management   ★★★★★

There are seventy-five stocks in this $540 million portfolio. The average growth and income fund today is $720 million in size. Close to 100 percent of the fund's holdings are in stocks. The stocks in this portfolio have an average p/e ratio of 22 and a median market capitalization of $2 billion. The ten largest holdings compose 37 percent of the fund's total assets. The three largest sector weightings are industrial cyclicals (23 percent), financials (21 percent), and durables (19 percent). The portfolio's equity holdings can be categorized as mid-cap and value-oriented issues.

Ronald Muhlenkamp has managed this fund for the past fourteen years. Manager Muhlenkamp uses a top-down approach, using macroeconomic and market data to help select companies that have hefty returns coupled with an inexpensive stock price. Muhlenkamp is the only fund within the Muhlenkamp family.

Tax Minimization   ★★★★★

During the past five years, a $10,000 initial investment grew to $20,380 after taxes, assuming a 40 percent income tax bracket (state and federal combined) and a capital gains rate of 20 percent. This means that investors in this fund were able to preserve 97 percent of their total returns. Compared to other equity funds in the same category, this fund's tax savings are considered to be exceptional.

Expenses   ★★★★

Muhlenkamp's expense ratio is 1.3 percent; it has averaged 1.3 percent annually over the past three calendar years. The average expense ratio for the 1,400 funds in this category is 1.3 percent. This fund's turnover rate over the past year has been 32 percent, while its peer group average has been 79 percent.

Summary

Muhlenkamp, a mid-cap value fund, has outperformed more than 96 percent of all mutual funds over the past five and ten years as well as 83 percent of its peer group. Risk-adjusted returns have also been superb over the past five and ten years. Within its peer group, the fund ranks number three in performance and number one when it comes to tax efficiency. This portfolio outperformed the S & P 500 in 2000 by over 34 percentage points. This portfolio's alpha, which measures excess returns per unit of risk taken, as measured against the fund's benchmark index, is appealing.

Profile

minimum initial investment $1,500	*IRA accounts available* . . . . yes
subsequent minimum investment . . . $50	*IRA minimum investment* $1,500
available in all 50 states. . . . . yes	*date of inception* . . . . Nov. 1988
telephone exchanges. . . . . yes	*dividend/income paid* . . . . annually
number of funds in family 1	*largest sector weighting* indust. cyclicals

Van Kampen Comstock A

One Parkview Plaza
Oakbrook Terrace, IL 60181
(800) 421-5666
www.vankampen.com

total return	★★★★
risk reduction	★★★★
management	★★★★
tax minimization	★★
expense control	★★★★
symbol ACSTX	18 points
up-market performance	fair
down-market performance	excellent
predictability of returns	good

Total Return   ★★★★

Over the past five years, Van Kampen Comstock A has taken $10,000 and turned it into $21,010 ($13,310 over three years and $37,080 over the past ten years). This translates into an annualized return of 16 percent over the past five years, 10 percent over the past three years, and 14 percent for the decade. Over the past five years, this fund has outperformed 97 percent of all mutual funds; within its general category, it has done better than 99 percent of its peers. Growth and income funds have averaged 9 percent annually over these same five years.

Risk/Volatility   ★★★★

Over the past five years, Van Kampen Comstock A has been safer than 89 percent of all growth and income funds. Over the past decade, the fund has had two negative years, while the S & P 500 has had two (off 9 percent in 2000 and 12 percent in 2001). The fund has underperformed the S & P 500 twice in the past ten years. Consistency of *overperformance* for this fund has been very good.

	past 5 years		past 10 years	
worst year	-1.8%	2001	-3.7%	1994
best year	31.9%	2000	36.2%	1995

Risk-adjusted returns have also been outstanding over the past five and ten years. Over the past five years, the fund's three worst quarters have been third quarter 2001 (- 14 percent), third quarter 1999 (-10 percent), and third quarter 1998 (-6 percent). During the same period, the three best quarters have been fourth quarter 1998 (15 percent), fourth quarter 2000 (15 percent), and third quarter 1997 (13 percent). In the past, Van Kampen Comstock A has done better than 27 percent of its peer group during the most recent bull market and outperformed 96 percent of its peer group during the most recent bear market. Consistency, or predictability, of returns for Van Kampen Comstock A can be described as good. This fund's risk-related return ranks in the top quintile.

Management
★★★★
There are 120 stocks in this $3.8 billion portfolio. The average growth and income fund today is $720 million in size. Close to 84 percent of the fund's holdings are in stocks. The stocks in this portfolio have an average p/e ratio of 25 and a median market capitalization of $17 billion. The ten largest holdings compose 40 percent of the fund's total assets. The three largest sector weightings are technology (16 percent), energy (15 percent), and industrials (14 percent). The portfolio's equity holdings can be categorized as large-cap and value-oriented issues.

A team has managed this fund for the past six years. Managers Baker, Leder, and Holt are contrarian investors who do not stray from a deep-value discipline. Lead manager Baker has an uncanny knack for finding stocks others have left for dead, only to see them rebound. There are 143 funds besides Comstock A within the Van Kampen family. Overall, the fund family's risk-adjusted performance can be described as good.

Tax Minimization
★★
During the past five years, a $10,000 initial investment grew to $14,080 after taxes, assuming a 40 percent income tax bracket (state and federal combined) and a capital gains rate of 20 percent. This means that investors in this fund were able to preserve 67 percent of their total returns. Compared to other equity funds in the same category, this fund's tax savings are considered to be fair.

Expenses
★★★★
Van Kampen Comstock A's expense ratio is 0.9 percent; it has averaged 0.9 percent annually over the past three calendar years. The average expense ratio for the 1,400 funds in this category is 1.3 percent. This fund's turnover rate over the past year has been 89 percent, while its peer group average has been 79 percent.

Summary
Van Kampen Comstock A, a large-cap value fund, has outperformed 97 percent of all mutual funds over the past five years as well as 99 percent of its peer group over the same period. Returns over shorter and longer periods have been equally impressive. Within its peer group, the fund ranks very highly in the areas of performance, low risk, and expense control. This portfolio outperformed the S & P 500 in 2000 by over 41 percentage points. This portfolio's alpha, which measures excess returns per unit of risk taken, as measured against the fund's benchmark index, is appealing.

Profile

minimum initial investment $1,000	*IRA accounts available* . . . . yes
subsequent minimum investment . . . $25	*IRA minimum investment* $500
available in all 50 states. . . . . yes	*date of inception* . . . . Oct. 1968
telephone exchanges. . . . . yes	*dividend/income paid* . . . . quarterly
number of funds in family 144	*largest sector weighting* . . . technology

Van Kampen Equity-Income A
One Parkview Plaza
Oakbrook Terrace, IL 60181
(800) 421-5666
www.vankampen.com

total return	★★
risk reduction	★★★★★
management	★★★★
tax minimization	★★★
expense control	★★★★
symbol ACEIX	18 points
up-market performance	fair
down-market performance	very good
predictability of returns	excellent

Total Return   ★★
Over the past five years, Van Kampen Equity-Income A has taken $10,000 and turned it into $18,430 ($12,950 over three years and $37,080 over the past ten years). This translates into an annualized return of 13 percent over the past five years, 9 percent over the past three years, and 14 percent for the decade. Over the past five years, this fund has outperformed 94 percent of all mutual funds; within its general category, it has done better than 98 percent of its peers. Growth and income funds have averaged 9 percent annually over these same five years.

Risk/Volatility   ★★★★★
Over the past five years, Van Kampen Equity-Income A has been safer than 80 percent of all growth and income funds. Over the past decade, the fund has had two negative years, while the S & P 500 has had two (off 9 percent in 2000 and 12 percent in 2001). The fund has underperformed the S & P 500 twice in the past ten years. Consistency of *overperformance* for this fund has been very good.

	past 5 years		past 10 years	
worst year	-2.2%	2001	-2.2%	2001
best year	24.1%	1997	32.6%	1995

Over the past five years, the fund's three worst quarters have been third quarter 1998 (-8 percent), first quarter 2001 (-6 percent), and third quarter 2001 (-6 percent). During the same period, the three best quarters have been second quarter 1997 (13 percent), fourth quarter 1998 (12 percent), and first quarter 1998 (11 percent). In the past, Van Kampen Equity-Income A has done better than just 8 percent of its peer group during the most recent bull market and outperformed 81 percent of its peer group during the most recent bear market. Consistency, or predictability, of returns for Van Kampen Equity-Income A can be described as excellent. This fund's risk-related return ranks in the top quintile.

Management   ★★★★
There are ninety stocks in this $2.3 billion portfolio. The average growth and income fund today is $720 million in size. Close to 60 percent of the fund's holdings are in stocks. The stocks in this portfolio have an average p/e ratio of 25 and a median market capitalization of $24 billion. The ten largest holdings compose 22 percent of the fund's total assets. The three largest sector weightings are financials (30 percent), industals (19 percent), and health (10 percent). The portfolio's equity holdings can be categorized as large-cap and value-oriented issues.

A team has managed this fund for the past five years. Management has excelled in good as well as bad times, favoring a mix of momentum investing while looking for companies with improving earnings. A modest weighting in convertibles helps reduce overall risk while increasing current income. There are 143 funds besides Equity-Income A within the Van Kampen family. Overall, the fund family's risk-adjusted performance can be described as good.

Tax Minimization   ★★★
During the past five years, a $10,000 initial investment grew to $13,450 after taxes, assuming a 40 percent income tax bracket (state and federal combined) and a capital gains rate of 20 percent. This means that investors in this fund were able to preserve 73 percent of their total returns. Compared to other equity funds in the same category, this fund's tax savings are considered to be good.

Expenses   ★★★★
Van Kampen Equity-Income A's expense ratio is 0.8 percent; it has averaged 0.8 percent annually over the past three calendar years. The average expense ratio for the 1,400 funds in this category is 1.3 percent. This fund's turnover rate over the past year has been 85 percent, while its peer group average has been 79 percent.

Summary
Van Kampen Equity-Income A, a large-cap value fund, has outperformed 94 percent of all mutual funds over the past five years as well as 98 percent of its peer group over the past five, ten, and fifteen years. Risk-adjusted returns have also been superb over the past five and ten years. Within its peer group, the fund ranks well in every category measured. It ranks number one for low risk and as having the most predictibable returns. This portfolio's alpha, which measures excess returns per unit of risk taken, as measured against the fund's benchmark index, is quite appealing.

Profile

minimum initial investment $1,000	IRA accounts available . . . . yes
subsequent minimum investment . . . $25	IRA minimum investment $500
available in all 50 states. . . . . yes	date of inception . . . . Aug. 1960
telephone exchanges. . . . . yes	dividend/income paid . . . . quarterly
number of funds in family 144	largest sector weighting . . . . financials

Health Care Funds

Sector funds, such as health care, technology, and utilities, allow investors the opportunity to invest in a particular area of the market without exposing their portfolios to the same risk as investing in just a few individual stocks. The health-care sector includes pharmaceuticals, medical products, medical services, and biotechnology.

People spend money on health care even in a slowing economy, and the segment of the population that spends the most on health care has grown every year since 1929. According to Pharmaceutical Research and Manufacturers of America, those age sixty-five and older spend nearly four times more on health care than those younger than sixty-five. In the United States, 35 million people are sixty-five or older; that number is expected to increase to 40 million by 2010, 46 million by 2015, and 54 million by 2020.

These companies that make up this broad sector offer attractive revenue and earnings visibility that is generally immune to economic cycles. At the same time, the sector is benefiting from an overwhelming demographic shift.

Across the United States, Europe, and Asia, the sizable baby-boom generation is aging and demanding more treatments to improve their lifestyles. This trend could drive tremendous industry demand growth over the next several decades. At the same time, groundbreaking discoveries in the biotechnology area are creating a multitude of exciting products to meet the demands of this aging population.

Biotechnology companies are developing advancements for medical, agricultural, and industrial application. A number of biotechnology companies have shown progressive leadership, but few have successfully marketed drugs or generated earnings. As a result, stocks in this area can be very volatile and highly sensitive to adverse news. It is for this reason that those health-care mutual funds that have exposure to this subsector and are concerned with risk have only modest exposure to biotechnology. Research companies in areas such as genomics represent the ultimate in risk and reward potential.

Over the past couple of years, mutual fund managers have been more selective, focusing on profitable biotechnology companies that have products in the pipeline or currently on the market. In response to this, these companies have forged alliances with drug firms to expand their product portfolio and enhance profitability.

The medical supplies subsector remains strong. Increased demand for defibrillators, pacemakers, and cancer treatments such as radioactive seed implants, coupled with new-product approvals at the federal level, have kept this area's growth vigorous.

On the positive side, it is expected that the Bush administration will encourage and embrace market-driven policies. On the negative side, looming patent expirations and rising competition from generic drug companies continue to

Annual Returns - Health Care Funds

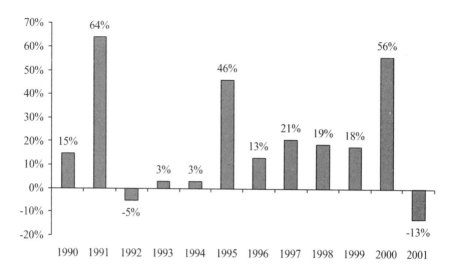

plague brand-dependent firms. The rising costs of brand-name drugs have prompted health maintenance organizations (HMOs) and preferred provider organizations (PPOs) to provide incentives for members to use less-expensive generic drugs. In response, brand-dependent firms have beefed up their research and development efforts by merging with other large drug firms.

The long-term growth prospects for health care are attractive and are largely based on three factors: People are living longer, products are coming to market faster, and the industry is benefiting from technological advances.

According to Data Resources, roughly 26 percent of the U.S. population is over fifty. By the year 2006, that number is expected to be 30 percent and close to 35 percent by the year 2015. Product approval cycles are shorter. According to the FDA, the mean number of approved products from 1989–1993 was twenty-five, with a mean approval time of twenty-nine months. Over the 1994–1998 period, the mean number increased to thirty-four and approval time dropped to seventeen months. Technological advances can also enhance profit potential.

There are just over 150 funds that make up the health-care category; total market capitalization for this group is roughly $46 billion. Over the past three years, the average turnover rate has been a rather high 178 percent. The price-earnings (p/e) ratio for health-care funds is 40. Dividend yield is close to zero. Over the past three years, these funds have averaged a 15.0 percent annualized gain per year with a standard deviation of 34.2 percent. For the past five and ten years, average annualized returns have been 15.2 percent; for the past fifteen years, annual returns have averaged 13.8 percent. The category has underperformed the S & P 500 in seven of the past ten years; yet for the entire ten-year period, average annual returns have been higher by nearly 1 percent.

Eaton Vance Worldwide Health A

255 State Street
Boston, MA 02109
(800) 225-6265
www.eatonvance.com

total return	★★★★★
risk reduction	★★★★
management	★★★★★
tax minimization	★★★★★
expense control	★★★
symbol ETHSX	22 points
up-market performance	excellent
down-market performance	good
predictability of returns	fair

Total Return   ★★★★★

Over the past five years, Eaton Vance Worldwide Health A has taken $10,000 and turned it into $28,160 ($20,980 over three years and $67,280 over the past ten years). This translates into an annualized return of 23 percent over the past five years, 28 percent over the past three years, and 21 percent for the decade. Over the past five years, this fund has outperformed 99 percent of all mutual funds; within its general category, it has done better than 97 percent of its peers. Health funds have averaged 15 percent annually over these same five years.

Risk/Volatility   ★★★★

Over the past five years, Eaton Vance Worldwide Health A has been safer than 52 percent of all health funds. Over the past decade, the fund has had two negative years, while the S & P 500 has had two (off 9 percent in 2000 and 12 percent in 2001); the Wilshire 5000 also fell twice (off 11 percent in 2000 and 11 percent in 2001). The fund has underperformed the S & P 500 twice and the Wilshire 5000 three times in the past ten years. Consistency of *overperformance* for this fund has been outstanding.

	past 5 years		past 10 years	
worst year	-6.6%	2001	-6.6%	2001
best year	81.6%	2000	81.6%	2000

Over the past five years, the fund's three worst quarters have been first quarter 2001 (-19 percent), fourth quarter 1997 (-11 percent), and second quarter 1998 (-6 percent). During the same period, the three best quarters have been first quarter 2000 (37 percent), fourth quarter 1998 (27 percent), and second quarter 2000 (20 percent). In the past, Eaton Vance Worldwide Health A has done better than 67 percent of its peer group during the most recent bull market and outperformed 57 percent of its peer group during the most recent bear market. Consistency, or predictability, of returns for Eaton Vance Worldwide Health A can be described as fair. This fund's risk-related return ranks in the top quintile.

Management ★★★★★
There are forty-five stocks in this $960 million portfolio. The average health fund today is $310 million in size. Close to 95 percent of the fund's holdings are in stocks. The stocks in this portfolio have an average p/e ratio of 43 and a median market capitalization of $17 billion. The ten largest holdings compose 46 percent of the fund's total assets. The portfolio's equity holdings can be categorized as large-cap and growth-oriented issues.

Samuel Isaly has managed this fund for thirteen years. He is atypical because of his larger-than-normal weighting in biotech companies. He also bucks the norm by including small- and mid-cap issues and a fairly large weighting in foreign equities. There are 181 funds besides Worldwide Health A within the Eaton Vance family. The fund family's risk-adjusted performance can be described as good.

Tax Minimization ★★★★★
During the past five years, a $10,000 initial investment grew to $26,745 after taxes, assuming a 40 percent income tax bracket (state and federal combined) and a capital gains rate of 20 percent. This means that investors in this fund were able to preserve 95 percent of their total returns. Compared to other equity funds in the same category, this fund's tax savings are considered to be exceptional.

Expenses ★★★
Eaton Vance Worldwide Health A's expense ratio is 1.7 percent; it has averaged 1.7 percent annually over the past three calendar years. The average expense ratio for the 155 funds in this category is 1.7 percent. This fund's turnover rate over the past year has been 24 percent, while its peer group average has been 178 percent.

Summary
Eaton Vance Worldwide Health A, a large-cap sector fund that invests in growth health-care stocks, has outperformed 99 percent of all mutual funds over the past three, five, ten, and fifteen years as well as 99 percent of its peer group. Returns over time have been equally impressive. Risk-adjusted returns have also been superb over the past three, five, and ten years. Within its peer group, the fund ties for first place as the best peformer over five years and is rated number one on a total return basis for the past three years. It also scores well in the areas of risk reduction and low turnover. The fund's performance has been in the top quartile of its group for each of the past three years—something not common with any fund in any category. This portfolio outperformed the S & P 500 in 2000 by over 90 percentage points. This portfolio's alpha, which measures excess returns per unit of risk taken, as measured against the fund's benchmark index, is extremely appealing.

Profile

minimum initial investment $1,000	IRA accounts available . . . . yes
subsequent minimum investment . . . $50	IRA minimum investment $50
available in all 50 states. . . . . yes	date of inception . . . . July 1985
telephone exchanges. . . . . yes	dividend/income paid . . . . annually
number of funds in family 182	largest sector weighting . . . . health

Vanguard Health Care

Vanguard Financial Centre
P.O. Box 2600
Valley Forge, PA 19482
(800) 662-7447
http://flagship.vanguard.com

total return	★★★★★
risk reduction	★★★★★
management	★★★★★
tax minimization	★★★★★
expense control	★★★
symbol VGHCX	22 points
up-market performance	poor
down-market performance	excellent
predictability of returns	excellent

Total Return   ★★★★★

Over the past five years, Vanguard Health Care has taken $10,000 and turned it into $28,160 ($16,020 over three years and $61,920 over the past ten years). This translates into an annualized return of 23 percent over the past five years, 17 percent over the past three years, and 20 percent for the decade. Over the past five years, this fund has outperformed 99 percent of all mutual funds; within its general category, it has done better than 94 percent of its peers. Health funds have averaged 15 percent annually over these same five years.

Risk/Volatility   ★★★★★

Over the past five years, Vanguard Health Care has been safer than 99 percent of all health funds. Over the past decade, the fund has had two negative years, while the S & P 500 has had two (off 9 percent in 2000 and 12 percent in 2001); the Wilshire 5000 also fell twice (off 11 percent in 2000 and 11 percent in 2001). The fund has underperformed the S & P 500 twice and the Wilshire 5000 three times in the past ten years. Consistency of *overperformance* for this fund has been outstanding.

	past 5 years		past 10 years	
worst year	-6.9%	2001	-6.9%	2001
best year	60.6%	2000	60.6%	2000

Over the past five years, the fund's three worst quarters have been first quarter 2001 (-13 percent), third quarter 1999 (-7 percent), and third quarter 1998 (-2 percent). During the same period, the three best quarters have been second quarter 2000 (19 percent), fourth quarter 1998 (19 percent), and second quarter 2000 (16 percent). In the past, Vanguard Health Care has done better than 65 percent of its peer group during the most recent bull market and outperformed 96 percent of its peer group during the most recent bear market. Consistency, or predictability, of returns for Vanguard Health Care can be described as excellent. This fund's risk-related return ranks in the top quintile.

Management   ★★★★★

There are 131 stocks in this $1.6 billion portfolio. The average health fund today is $310 million in size. Close to 90 percent of the fund's holdings are in stocks. The stocks in this portfolio have an average p/e ratio of 33 and a median market capitalization of $20 billion. The ten largest holdings compose 41 percent of the fund's total assets. The portfolio's equity holdings can be categorized as large-cap and growth-oriented issues.

Edward Owens has managed this fund for the past eighteen years. Manager Owens diversifies the portfolio well beyond the industry norm. He has never made a big bet on a single stock, which partially explains the fund's excellent risk versus return characteristics. There are 154 funds besides Health Care within the Vanguard family. Overall, the fund family's risk-adjusted performance can be described as very good.

Tax Minimization   ★★★★★

During the past five years, a $10,000 initial investment grew to $25,619 after taxes, assuming a 40 percent income tax bracket (state and federal combined) and a capital gains rate of 20 percent. This means that investors in this fund were able to preserve 91 percent of their total returns. Compared to other equity funds in the same category, this fund's tax savings are considered to be excellent.

Expenses   ★★★

Vanguard Health Care's expense ratio is 0.3 percent; it has averaged 0.4 percent annually over the past three calendar years. The average expense ratio for the 155 funds in this category is 1.7 percent. This fund's turnover rate over the past year has been 21 percent, while its peer group average has been 178 percent.

Summary

Vanguard Health Care, a large-cap growth fund, has outperformed 99 percent of all mutual funds over the past five, ten, and fifteen years as well as 99 percent of its peer group. Returns over other periods of time have been equally impressive. Risk-adjusted returns have also been superb over the past three, five, and ten years. By category, the fund ranks in the top quartile when it comes to returns versus risk. Within its peer group, the fund ranks number one when it comes to total returns, risk reduction, low expenses, and low turnover. This portfolio outperformed the S & P 500 in 2000 by more than 69 percentage points. This portfolio's alpha, which measures excess returns per unit of risk taken, as measured against the fund's benchmark index, is quite appealing.

Profile

minimum initial investment $25,000	*IRA accounts available* . . . . yes
subsequent minimum investment . . $100	*IRA minimum investment* $25,000
available in all 50 states. . . . . yes	*date of inception*. . . . . May 1984
telephone exchanges. . . . . yes	*dividend/income paid* . . . . annually
number of funds in family 155	*largest sector weighting* . . . . health

High-Yield Corporate Bond Funds

Sometimes referred to as "junk bond" funds, high-yield bond funds invest in corporate bonds rated lower than BBB or BAA. The world of bonds is divided into two general categories: investment grade and high-yield. Investment grade, sometimes referred to as "bank quality," means that the bond issue has been rated AAA, AA, A, or BAA (or BBB if the rating service is Standard and Poor's instead of Moody's). Certain institutions and fiduciaries are forbidden to invest their clients' monies in anything less than investment grade. Everything less than bank quality is considered junk.

Yet the world of bonds is not black and white. There are several categories of high-yield bonds. Junk bond funds contain issues that range from BB to C; a rating less than C means that the bond is in default, and payment of interest and/or principal is in arrears. High-yield bond funds perform best during good economic times. Traditional investors should avoid such issues during recessionary periods, since the underlying corporations may have difficulty making interest and principal payments when business slows down. However, these bonds, like common stocks, can perform very well during the second half of a recession.

Although junk bonds may exhibit greater volatility than their investment-grade peers, they are safer when it comes to interest-rate risk. Since junk issues have higher-yielding coupons and often shorter maturities than quality corporate bond funds, they fluctuate less in value when interest rates change. Thus, during expansionary periods in the economy when interest rates are rising, high-yield funds will generally drop less in value than high-quality corporate or government bond funds. Conversely, when interest rates are falling, government and corporate bonds will appreciate more in value than junk funds. High-yield bonds resemble equities at least as much as they do traditional bonds when it comes to economic cycles and certain important technical factors. Studies show that only 19 percent of the average junk fund's total return is explained by the up or down movement of the Lehman Brothers Government/Corporate Bond Index. To give an idea of how low this number is, 94 percent of a typical high-quality corporate bond fund's performance is explainable by movement in the same index. Indeed, even international bond funds have a higher correlation coefficient than junk, with 25 percent of their performance explained by the Lehman index.

The following table covers the five-year period ending December 31, 2001, and compares the total return of four well-known bond indexes: Credit Suisse High Yield Index (bonds rated BBB or lower), the Lehman Brothers Aggregate Bond Index (securities from the Lehman Government/Corporate, Mortgage-Backed Securities, and Asset-Backed Indexes), the Lehman Brothers Government Bond

Index (all publicly traded domestic debt of the U.S. government), and the Lehman Brothers Municipal Bond Index.

index	1 year	3 years	5 years	10 years
high-yield	5.8%	1.2%	3.2%	7.8%
aggregate	8.4%	6.3%	7.4%	7.2%
government	7.2%	5.9%	7.4%	7.1%
municipal	5.1%	4.8%	6.0%	6.6%

The high end of the junk bond market, those debentures rated BA and BB, have been able to withstand the general beating the junk bond market incurred during the late 1980s and early 1990s. Moderate and conservative investors who want high-yield bonds as part of their portfolio should focus on funds that have a high percentage of their assets in higher-rated bonds, BB or better.

According to Salomon Brothers, the people who are responsible for the Lehman Brothers corporate and government bond indexes used in this book, junk bond defaults averaged only 0.8 percent from 1980 to 1984. This rate almost tripled from 1985 to 1989 as defaults averaged 2.2 percent per year. Then, in 1990, defaults surged to 4.6 percent. Analysis based on historical data did not predict this huge increase in defaults. Bear in mind that BB-rated junk bonds can be expected to perform closer to high-quality bonds than will lower-rated junk. During 1990, for example, BB-rated bonds declined only slightly in price and actually delivered positive returns, whereas bonds rated CCC declined over 30 percent. During the mid-1990s, the default risk for the entire category had fallen to about 1.5 percent per year (well under 1 percent in the case of high-yield bond funds).

Over the past three and five years, high-yield corporate bond funds have had an average compound total return of negative 1.1 percent and 1.4 percent, respectively. The annual return for the past ten years has been 6.6 percent, and 6.6 percent for the past fifteen years (all figures as of December 31, 2001). The standard deviation for high-yield bond funds has been 8.6 percent over the past three years. This means that these funds have been less volatile than any equity fund category but have experienced over twice the return variances of other types of domestic bond funds. Turnover has averaged 95 percent. More than 350 funds make up the high-yield category. Total market capitalization of this category is $82 billion.

The majority of investors believe that the track record of high-yield bonds has been mixed, particularly in recent years. There was a crash in this market in 1990, but the overall track record has been quite good. These bond funds were up 13.4 percent in 1987, the year of the stock market crash. As the junk bond scare started in 1989, the fund category was still able to show a 12.8 percent return for the calendar year. The following year the group showed a negative return of 9.5 percent.

The 1990 loss was caused by regulatory agencies putting pressure on the insurance industry, formerly the largest owner of this investment category. This, together with the demise of Drexel Burnham, the largest issuer of junk bonds, caused high-yield bonds to suffer their biggest loss in recent memory. And yet the very next year, 1991, high-yield bond funds did better than ever before, up over 36.3 percent. The following two years were also quite good—up 17.0 percent in

Annual Returns - High Yield Corporate Bonds

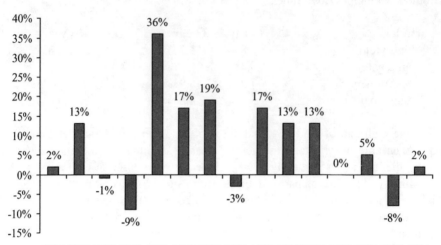

1992 and up 18.9 percent in 1993. The following year, 1994, these funds fell -3.0 percent, followed by gains of 16.7, 13.5, 13.0 percent the next 3 years; then flat in 1998; a gain of 4.7 percent in 1999; a loss of 7.8 percent in 2000; and a small gain of 1.6 percent in 2001.

American Funds High-Income Trust A

333 South Hope Street
Los Angeles, CA 90071
(800) 421-4120
www.americanfunds.com

total return	★★★
risk reduction	★★
management	★★★★
current income	★★★★★
expense control	★★★★★
symbol AHITX	19 points
up-market performance	excellent
down-market performance	poor
predictability of returns	good

Total Return   ★★★

Over the past five years, American Funds High-Income Trust A has taken $10,000 and turned it into $12,770 ($11,250 over three years and $21,590 over the past ten years). This translates into an annualized return of 5 percent over the past five years, 4 percent over the past three years, and 8 percent for the decade. Over the past five years, this fund has outperformed 43 percent of all mutual funds; within its general category, it has done better than 93 percent of its peers. High-yield bond funds have averaged 1 percent annually over these same five years.

During the past five years, a $10,000 initial investment grew to $10,780 after taxes, assuming a 40 percent income tax bracket (state and federal combined) and a capital gains rate of 20 percent. This means that investors in this fund were able to preserve 28 percent of their total returns. Compared to other funds in the same category, this fund's tax savings are considered to be good.

Risk/Volatility   ★★

Over the past five years, American Funds High-Income Trust A has been safer than 81 percent of all high-yield bond funds. Over the past decade, the fund has had two negative years, while the Lehman Brothers Aggregate Bond Index has had two (off 3 percent in 1994 and 1 percent in 1999); the Credit Suisse High-Yield Bond Index also fell twice (off 1 percent in 1994 and 5 percent in 2000). The fund has under-performed the Lehman Brothers Aggregate Bond Index twice and the Credit Suisse High-Yield Bond Index twice in the past ten years. Consistency of *overperformance* for this fund has been good.

	past 5 years		past 10 years	
worst year	-3.4%	2000	-5.1%	1994
best year	12.2%	1997	20.7%	1995

Over the past five years, the fund's three worst quarters have been third quarter 1998 (-8 percent), third quarter 2001 (-4 percent), and fourth quarter 2000 (-4 percent). During the same period, the three best quarters have been second quarter 1997 (6 percent), fourth quarter 1998 (6 percent), and fourth quarter 1999 (5 percent). In the past, American Funds High-Income Trust A has done better than 92 percent of its peer group during the most recent bull market and outperformed 76 percent of its peer group during the most recent bear market. Consistency, or predictability, of returns for American Funds High-Income Trust A can be described as good. This fund's risk-related return ranks in the top half.

Management   ★★★★
There are 380 fixed-income securities in this $3.1 billion portfolio. The average high-yield bond fund today is $220 million in size. Close to 85 percent of the fund's holdings are in bonds. The average maturity of the bonds in this account is nine years; the weighted coupon rate averages 7 percent. The portfolio's fixed-income holdings can be categorized as intermediate-term, low-quality debt.

A team has managed this fund for the past eleven years. Managers Barclay, Tolson, and Goldstine are defensive, cautious investors and for good reason. The below-investment-grade fixed-income marketplace is not always predictable and large losses on some individual securities are always possible. There are 103 funds besides High-Income Trust A within the American Funds family. Overall, the fund family's risk-adjusted performance can be described as very good.

Current Income   ★★★★★
Over the past year, American Funds High-Income Trust A had a twelve-month yield of 10 percent. During this same twelve-month period, the typical high-yield bond fund had a yield that averaged 10.9 percent.

Expenses   ★★★★★
American Funds High-Income Trust A's expense ratio is 0.8 percent; it has averaged 0.8 percent annually over the past three calendar years. The average expense ratio for the 400 funds in this category is 1.3 percent. This fund's turnover rate over the past year has been 46 percent, while its peer group average has been 95 percent.

Summary
American Funds High-Income Trust A, a low-quality, intermediate-term bond fund, has outperformed 57 percent of all mutual funds over the past ten years as well as 94 percent of its peer group over the same period. Returns over shorter periods have been equally impressive. Risk-adjusted returns have ranged between fair and good over the past decade. Within its peer group, the fund ranks number one when it comes to controlling expenses and limiting turnover. This offering is part of the American Funds group, a family that is frequently rated as the best in the country.

Profile

minimum initial investment $250	*IRA accounts available* . . . . yes
subsequent minimum investment . . . $50	*IRA minimum investment* $250
available in all 50 states. . . . . yes	*date of inception* . . . . Feb. 1988
telephone exchanges. . . . . yes	*dividend/income paid.* . . . . monthly
number of funds in family 104	*average credit quality* . . . . BB

Columbia High-Yield

1301 SW Fifth Avenue
P.O. Box 1350
Portland, OR 97207
(800) 547-1707
www.columbiafunds.com

total return	★★★★★
risk reduction	★★★★
management	★★★★★
current income	★★★
expense control	★★★★★
symbol CMHYX	22 points
up-market performance	good
down-market performance	excellent
predictability of returns	excellent

Total Return   ★★★★★

Over the past five years, Columbia High-Yield has taken $10,000 and turned it into $13,390 ($11,580 over three years). This translates into an annualized return of 6 percent over the past five years and 5 percent over the past three years. Over the past five years, this fund has outperformed 66 percent of all mutual funds; within its general category, it has done better than 98 percent of its peers. High-yield bond funds have averaged 1 percent annually over these same five years.

During the past five years, a $10,000 initial investment grew to $11,670 after taxes, assuming a 40 percent income tax bracket (state and federal combined) and a capital gains rate of 20 percent. This means that investors in this fund were able to preserve 49 percent of their total returns. Compared to other funds in the same category, this fund's tax savings are considered to be exceptional.

Risk/Volatility   ★★★★

Over the past five years, Columbia High-Yield has been safer than 96 percent of all high-yield bond funds. Over the past decade, the fund has had one negative year, while the Lehman Brothers Aggregate Bond Index has had two (off 3 percent in 1994 and 1 percent in 1999); the Credit Suisse High-Yield Bond Index also fell twice (off 1 percent in 1994 and 5 percent in 2000). The fund has underperformed the Lehman Brothers Aggregate Bond Index twice and the Credit Suisse High-Yield Bond Index twice in the past ten years. Consistency of *overperformance* for this fund has been very good.

	past 5 years		past 10 years	
worst year	2.4%	1999	-0.9%	1994
best year	6.6%	2001	19.1%	1995

Over the past five years, the fund's three worst quarters have been first quarter 2000 (-1 percent), third quarter 1998 (-1 percent), and third quarter 2001 (-1 percent). During the same period, the three best quarters have been second quarter 1997 (5 percent), first quarter 2001 (4 percent), and third quarter 1997 (4 percent). In the past, Columbia High-Yield has done better than 33 percent of its peer group during the most recent bull market and outperformed 94 percent of its peer group during the most recent bear market. Consistency, or predictability, of returns for Columbia High-Yield can be described as excellent. This fund's risk-related return ranks in the top third.

Management   ★★★★★

There are eighty fixed-income securities in this $210 million portfolio. The average high-yield bond fund today is $220 million in size. Close to 100 percent of the fund's holdings are in bonds. The average maturity of the bonds in this account is five years; the weighted coupon rate averages 9 percent. The portfolio's fixed-income holdings can be categorized as intermediate-term, low-quality debt.

Jeffrey Rippey has managed this fund for the past nine years. Managers Rippey and Havnaer are cautious, making sure that no holdings are rated below single B. There are nineteen funds besides High-Yield within the Columbia family. Overall, the fund family's risk-adjusted performance can be described as good to very good.

Current Income   ★★★

Over the past year, Columbia High-Yield had a twelve-month yield of 7.8 percent. During this same twelve-month period, the typical high-yield bond fund had a yield that averaged 10.9 percent.

Expenses   ★★★★★

Columbia High-Yield's expense ratio is 0.9 percent; it has averaged 0.9 percent annually over the past three calendar years. The average expense ratio for the 400 funds in this category is 1.3 percent. This fund's turnover rate over the past year has been 50 percent, while its peer group average has been 95 percent.

Summary

Columbia High-Yield, a low-quality, intermediate-term bond fund, has outperformed 65 percent of all mutual funds over the past three and five years as well as 98 percent of its peer group. Returns over shorter periods have been equally impressive. Risk-adjusted returns have been good. By category, the fund ranks in the top quintile when it comes to returns versus risk. Within its peer group, the fund ranks number one for performance, predictability of returns, and tax efficiency. It also receives top marks for controlling expenses and low turnover. Close to two-thirds of the portfolio are in bonds rated BB or higher. This portfolio's alpha, which measures excess returns per unit of risk taken, as measured against the fund's benchmark index, is quite appealing. On a total point basis, this is the number-one fund for its category.

Profile

minimum initial investment $1,000	*IRA accounts available* . . . . yes
subsequent minimum investment . . $100	*IRA minimum investment* $1,000
available in all 50 states. . . . . yes	*date of inception* . . . . Oct. 1993
telephone exchanges. . . . . yes	*dividend/income paid.* . . . . monthly
number of funds in family 20	*average credit quality* . . . . BB

Janus High-Yield

100 Fillmore Street, Suite 300
Denver, CO 80206
(800) 525-8983
http://ww4.janus.com

total return	★★★★
risk reduction	★★★
management	★★★
current income	★★★
expense control	★★
symbol JAHYX	15 points
up-market performance	very good
down-market performance	fair
predictability of returns	very good

Total Return   ★★★★

Over the past five years, Janus High-Yield has taken $10,000 and turned it into
$13,390 ($11,250 over three years). This translates into an annualized return of 6
percent over the past five years and 4 percent over the past three years. Over the
past five years, this fund has outperformed 55 percent of all mutual funds; within
its general category, it has done better than 95 percent of its peers. High-yield bond
funds have averaged 1 percent annually over these same five years.

During the past five years, a $10,000 initial investment grew to $10,820 after
taxes, assuming a 40 percent income tax bracket (state and federal combined) and
a capital gains rate of 20 percent. This means that investors in this fund were able
to preserve 24 percent of their total returns. Compared to other funds in the same
category, this fund's tax savings are considered to be good.

Risk/Volatility   ★★★

Over the past five years, Janus High-Yield has been safer than 94 percent of all
high-yield bond funds. Over the past decade, the fund has had no negative years,
while the Lehman Brothers Aggregate Bond Index has had two (off 3 percent in
1994 and 1 percent in 1999); the Credit Suisse High-Yield Bond Index also fell
twice (off 1 percent in 1994 and 5 percent in 2000). The fund has underperformed
the Lehman Brothers Aggregate Bond Index once and the Credit Suisse High-
Yield Bond Index once in the past ten years.

	past 5 years		past 10 years	
worst year	1.0%	1998	1.0%	1998
best year	15.5%	1997	24.0%	1996

Over the past five years, the fund's three worst quarters have been third
quarter 1998 (-6 percent), third quarter 2001 (-3 percent), and fourth quarter 2000
(-2 percent). During the same period, the three best quarters have been third quarter
1997 (6 percent), first quarter 1998 (5 percent), and fourth quarter 1999 (4 percent).
In the past, Janus High-Yield has done better than 48 percent of its peer group

during the most recent bull market and outperformed 87 percent of its peer group during the most recent bear market. Consistency, or predictability, of returns for Janus High-Yield can be described as very good. This fund's risk-related return ranks in the top third.

Management   ★★★
There are ninety-five fixed-income securities in this $440 million portfolio. The average high-yield bond fund today is $220 million in size. Close to 76 percent of the fund's holdings are in bonds. The average maturity of the bonds in this account is six years; the weighted coupon rate averages 9 percent. The portfolio's fixed-income holdings can be categorized as intermediate-term, low-quality debt.

Sandy Rufenacht has managed this fund for the past six years. Manager Rufenacht favors companies with hard assets and positive cash flow. There are forty-four funds besides Janus High-Yield within the Janus family. Overall, the fund family's risk-adjusted performance can be described as very good.

Current Income   ★★★
Over the past year, Janus High-Yield had a twelve-month yield of 8 percent. During this same twelve-month period, the typical high-yield bond fund had a yield that averaged 10.9 percent.

Expenses   ★★
Janus High-Yield's expense ratio is 1 percent; it has averaged 1 percent annually over the past three calendar years. The average expense ratio for the 400 funds in this category is 1.3 percent. This fund's turnover rate over the past year has been 295 percent, while its peer group average has been 95 percent.

Summary
Janus High-Yield, a low-quality, intermediate-term bond fund, has outperformed 55 percent of all mutual funds over the past five years as well as 95 percent of its peer group. Returns over shorter periods have been equally impressive. By category, the fund ranks in the top third when it comes to returns versus risk. Within its peer group, the fund ranks number two when it comes to returns and predictability of returns. At times, a large portion of the portfolio is in cash, awaiting buying opportunities. This portfolio's alpha, which measures excess returns per unit of risk taken, as measured against the fund's benchmark index, is quite appealing.

Profile

minimum initial investment $2,500	*IRA accounts available* . . . . yes
subsequent minimum investment . . $100	*IRA minimum investment* $500
available in all 50 states. . . . . yes	*date of inception*. . . . . Dec. 1995
telephone exchanges. . . . . yes	*dividend/income paid*. . . . . monthly
number of funds in family 45	*average credit quality* . . . . BB

Lord Abbett Bond-Debenture A

90 Hudson Street
Jersey City, NJ 07302
(800) 201-6984
www.lordabbett.com

total return	★★★
risk reduction	★★
management	★★★
current income	★★★★
expense control	★★★★
symbol LBNDX	16 points
up-market performance	very good
down-market performance	fair
predictability of returns	very good

Total Return   ★★★

Over the past five years, Lord Abbett Bond-Debenture A has taken $10,000 and turned it into $12,770 ($10,930 over three years and $21,590 over the past ten years). This translates into an annualized return of 5 percent over the past five years, 3 percent over the past three years, and 8 percent for the decade. Over the past five years, this fund has outperformed 38 percent of all mutual funds; within its general category, it has done better than 91 percent of its peers. High-yield bond funds have averaged 1 percent annually over these same five years.

During the past five years, a $10,000 initial investment grew to $10,950 after taxes, assuming a 40 percent income tax bracket (state and federal combined) and a capital gains rate of 20 percent. This means that investors in this fund were able to preserve 34 percent of their total returns. Compared to other funds in the same category, this fund's tax savings are considered to be very good.

Risk/Volatility   ★★

Over the past five years, Lord Abbett Bond-Debenture A has been safer than 92 percent of all high-yield bond funds. Over the past decade, the fund has had two negative years, while the Lehman Brothers Aggregate Bond Index has had two (off 3 percent in 1994 and 1 percent in 1999); the Credit Suisse High-Yield Bond Index also fell twice (off 1 percent in 1994 and 5 percent in 2000). The fund has underperformed the Lehman Brothers Aggregate Bond Index twice and the Credit Suisse High-Yield Bond Index twice in the past ten years. Consistency of *overperformance* for this fund has been good.

	past 5 years		past 10 years	
worst year	-0.9%	2000	-3.9%	1994
best year	4.9%	2001	17.5%	1995

Over the past five years, the fund's three worst quarters have been third quarter 1998 (-5 percent), third quarter 2001 (-3 percent), and fourth quarter 2000 (-3 percent). During the same period, the three best quarters have been second quarter 1997 (6 percent), fourth quarter 1998 (5 percent), and first quarter 1998 (4 percent). In the past, Lord Abbett Bond-Debenture A has done better than 43 percent of its peer group during the most recent bull market and outperformed 86 percent of its peer group during the most recent bear market. Consistency, or predictability, of returns for Lord Abbett Bond-Debenture A can be described as very good. This fund's risk-related return ranks in the top half.

Management   ★★★
There are 320 fixed-income securities in this $2.4 billion portfolio. The average high-yield bond fund today is $220 million in size. Close to 95 percent of the fund's holdings are in bonds. The average maturity of the bonds in this account is eleven years; the weighted coupon rate averages 8 percent. The portfolio's fixed-income holdings can be categorized as intermediate-term, low-quality debt.

Christopher Towle has managed this fund for the past eleven years. Manager Towle maintains a much larger portion of investment grade bonds than his peers. There are 100 funds besides Lord Abbett Bond-Debenture A within the Lord Abbett Family of Funds family. Overall, the fund family's risk-adjusted performance can be described as good.

Current Income   ★★★★
Over the past year, Lord Abbett Bond-Debenture A had a twelve-month yield of 9 percent. During this same twelve-month period, the typical high-yield bond fund had a yield that averaged 10.9 percent.

Expenses   ★★★★
Lord Abbett Bond-Debenture A's expense ratio is 1 percent; it has averaged 1 percent annually over the past three calendar years. The average expense ratio for the 400 funds in this category is 1.3 percent. This fund's turnover rate over the past year has been 66 percent, while its peer group average has been 95 percent.

Summary
Lord Abbett Bond-Debenture A, a low-quality, intermediate-term bond fund, has outperformed 50 percent of all mutual funds over the past fifteen years as well as 98 percent of its peer group over the same period. Returns over shorter periods have been equally impressive. Risk-adjusted returns have ranged between fair and good. By category, the fund ranks in the top third when it comes to returns versus risk. Within its peer group, the fund ranks well in every category measured. This portfolio will appeal to the more conservative junk bond investor. This portfolio's alpha, which measures excess returns per unit of risk taken, as measured against the fund's benchmark index, is appealing.

Profile

minimum initial investment $1,000	IRA accounts available . . . . yes
subsequent minimum investment $1	IRA minimum investment $250
available in all 50 states. . . . . yes	date of inception. . . . . Apr. 1971
telephone exchanges. . . . . yes	dividend/income paid. . . . . monthly
number of funds in family 101	average credit quality . . . . BB

T. Rowe Price High-Yield

100 East Pratt Street
Baltimore, MD 21202
(800) 638-5660
www.troweprice.com

total return	★★★
risk reduction	★★
management	★★★
current income	★★★★★
expense control	★★★★
symbol PRHYX	17 points
up-market performance	excellent
down-market performance	fair
predictability of returns	very good

Total Return   ★★★

Over the past five years, T. Rowe Price High-Yield has taken $10,000 and turned it into $12,770 ($10,620 over three years and $21,590 over the past ten years). This translates into an annualized return of 5 percent over the past five years, 2 percent over the past three years, and 8 percent for the decade. Over the past five years, this fund has outperformed 42 percent of all mutual funds; within its general category it has done better than 91 percent of its peers. High-Yield bond funds have averaged 1 percent annually over these same five years.

During the past five years, a $10,000 initial investment grew to $10,780 after taxes, assuming a 40 percent income tax bracket (state and federal combined) and a capital gains rate of 20 percent. This means that investors in this fund were able to preserve 28 percent of their total returns. Compared to other funds in the same category, this fund's tax savings are considered to be good.

Risk/Volatility   ★★

Over the past five years, T. Rowe Price High-Yield has been safer than 88 percent of all high-yield bond funds. Over the past decade, the fund has had two negative years, while the Lehman Brothers Aggregate Bond Index has had two (off 3 percent in 1994 and 1 percent in 1999); the Credit Suisse High-Yield Bond Index also fell twice (off 1 percent in 1994 and 5 percent in 2000). The fund has underperformed the Lehman Brothers Aggregate Bond Index twice and the Credit Suisse High-Yield Bond Index twice in the past ten years. Consistency of *overperformance* for this fund has been good.

	past 5 years		past 10 years	
worst year	-3.3%	2000	-8.0%	1994
best year	6.1%	2001	21.8%	1993

Over the past five years, the fund's three worst quarters have been third quarter 1998 (-5 percent), third quarter 2001 (-4 percent), and fourth quarter 2000 (-4 percent). During the same period, the three best quarters have been first quarter

2001 (5 percent), second quarter 1997 (5 percent), and third quarter 1997 (5 percent). In the past, T. Rowe Price High-Yield has done better than 74 percent of its peer group during the most recent bull market and outperformed 81 percent of its peer group during the most recent bear market. Consistency, or predictability, of returns for T. Rowe Price High-Yield can be described as very good. This fund's risk-related return ranks in the top third.

Management   ★★★
There are 250 fixed-income securities in this $1.5 billion portfolio. The average high-yield bond fund today is $220 million in size. Close to 85 percent of the fund's holdings are in bonds. The average maturity of the bonds in this account is ten years; the weighted coupon rate averages 9 percent. The portfolio's fixed-income holdings can be categorized as intermediate-term, low-quality debt.

Mark Vaselkiv has managed this fund for the past six years. Manager Vaselkiv frequently ventures into more lower-rated fixed-income than his typical competitor but he offsets this greater risk by keeping a respectible amount of the portfolio in cash. There are eighty-four funds besides High-Yield within the T. Rowe Price family. Overall, the fund family's risk-adjusted performance can be described as good to very good.

Current Income   ★★★★★
Over the past year, T. Rowe Price High-Yield had a twelve-month yield of 10.3 percent. During this same twelve-month period, the typical high-yield bond fund had a yield that averaged 10.9 percent.

Expenses   ★★★★
T. Rowe Price High-Yield's expense ratio is 0.8 percent; it has averaged 0.8 percent annually over the past three calendar years. The average expense ratio for the 400 funds in this category is 1.3 percent. This fund's turnover rate over the past year has been 76 percent, while its peer group average has been 95 percent.

Summary
T. Rowe Price High-Yield, a low-quality, intermediate-term bond fund, has outperformed 53 percent of all mutual funds over the past ten years as well as 91 percent of its peer group over the past five years. Returns over shorter and longer periods have been impressive. Risk-adjusted returns have ranged between fair and good. Within its peer group, the fund ranks well in every category measured and is number one when it comes to yield. Risk is further reduced by management's interest in broad diversification.

Profile

minimum initial investment $2,500	IRA accounts available . . . . yes
subsequent minimum investment . . $100	IRA minimum investment $1,000
available in all 50 states. . . . . yes	date of inception. . . . . Dec. 1984
telephone exchanges. . . . . yes	dividend/income paid. . . . . monthly
number of funds in family 85	average credit quality . . . . BB

Metals and Natural Resources Funds

As their name implies, metals funds purchase precious metals in one or more of the following forms: bullion, South African gold stocks, and non-South African mining stocks. The United States, Canada, and Australia are the three major stock-issuing producers of metals outside South Africa. Metals funds, also referred to as gold funds, often own minor positions in other precious metals stocks, such as silver and platinum.

The proportion and type of metal held by a fund can have a great impact on its performance and volatility. Outright ownership of gold bullion is almost always less volatile than owning stock in a gold mining company. Thus, much greater gains or losses occur in metals funds that purchase only gold stocks, compared to funds that hold high levels of bullion, coins, and stock. Silver, incidentally, has nearly twice the volatility of gold, yet has not enjoyed any greater returns over the long term.

Gold, or metals, funds can do well during periods of political uncertainty and inflationary concerns. Over the past several hundred years, gold and silver have served as hedges against inflation. Most readers will be surprised to learn that, historically, both metals have outperformed inflation by less than 1 percent annually.

Metals funds are one of the riskiest categories of mutual funds described in this book with a standard deviation of 28.9 (technology stocks are number one, with a standard deviation of 59.7). And yet, although this is certainly a high-risk investment when viewed on its own, ownership of a metals fund can sometimes reduce a portfolio's overall risk level. Why? Because gold usually has a negative correlation to other investments.

There are thirty-nine metals funds; total market capitalization is less than $2 billion. Turnover has averaged 67 percent. The price-earnings (p/e) ratio for metals funds is 22, while dividend yield is a little less than 1.3 percent. Over the past three years, these funds have averaged 1.7 percent per year, negative 11.7 percent for the past five years, negative 3.2 percent for the past decade, and negative 1.3 percent for the past fifteen years.

Natural resources funds invest in the stocks of companies that deal in the ownership, production, transmission, transportation, refinement, and/or storage of oil, natural gas, and timber. These funds also invest in companies that either own or are involved in real estate.

There are seventy-two natural resources funds; total market capitalization is under $6 billion. This group has had a standard deviation of 32.0 percent over the past three years. Beta, or market-related risk, is 0.73, but do not let this low number fool you. As you can see by the standard deviation, few equity categories are riskier. Annual turnover has averaged 256 percent. The p/e ratio for natural resources funds is 21; dividend yield is 0.9 percent. Over the past three years, these funds have averaged 1.8 percent, 3.1 percent for the past five years, 9.2 percent for the past ten years, and 8.6 percent for the past fifteen years.

Metals and natural resources funds should be avoided by anyone who cannot tolerate wide price swings in any single part of the portfolio. These funds are designed as an integral part of a diversified portfolio, for investors who look at the overall return of their holdings. Despite the potential benefits of diversification, metals funds are still not recommended for the vast majority of investors. The track record for metals funds is simply terrible except for an occasional great year (for example, +81.1 percent in 1993) and variations of return are frequently wild.

Annual Returns - Precious Metals Fund

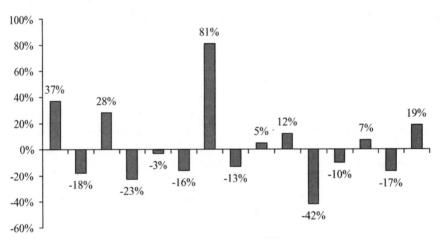

Annual Returns - Natural Resources Fund

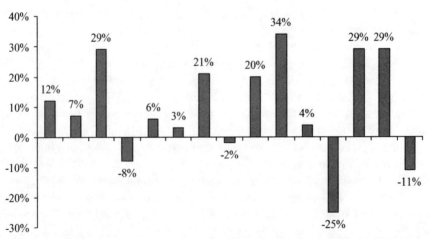

Excelsior Energy & Natural Resources
114 West 47th Street
New York, NY 10036
(800) 446-1012
www.excelsiorfunds.com

total return	★★★★★
risk reduction	★★★★
management	★★★★
tax minimization	★★★
expense control	★★★
symbol UMESX	19 points
up-market performance	poor
down-market performance	good
predictability of returns	good

Total Return   ★★★★★
Over the past five years, Excelsior Energy & Natural Resources has taken $10,000 and turned it into $15,390 ($15,610 over three years). This translates into an annualized return of 9 percent over the past five years and 16 percent over the past three years. Over the past five years, this fund has outperformed 74 percent of all mutual funds; within its general category, it has done better than 98 percent of its peers. Metals and natural resources funds have averaged -2 percent annually over these same five years.

Risk/Volatility   ★★★★
Over the past five years, Excelsior Energy & Natural Resources has been safer than 67 percent of all metals and natural resources funds. Over the past decade, the fund has had three negative years, while the S & P 500 has had two (off 9 percent in 2000 and 12 percent in 2001). The fund has underperformed the S & P 500 twice in the past ten years. Consistency of *overperformance* for this fund has been very good.

	past 5 years		past 10 years	
worst year	-15.7%	1998	-15.7%	1998
best year	42.5%	2000	42.5%	2000

Over the past five years, the fund's three worst quarters have been: third quarter 1998 (-14 percent), third quarter 2001 (-13 percent), and fourth quarter 1997 (-8 percent). During the same period, the three best quarters have been first quarter 2000 (21 percent), second quarter 1999 (20 percent), and third quarter 1997 (20 percent). In the past, Excelsior Energy & Natural Resources has done better than 41 percent of its peer group during the most recent bull market and outperformed 36 percent of its peer group during the most recent bear market. Consistency, or predictability, of returns for Excelsior Energy & Natural Resources can be described as good. This fund's risk-related return ranks in the top quintile.

Management   ★★★★
There are fifty-five stocks in this $115 million portfolio. The average metals and natural resources fund today is $70 million in size. Close to 86 percent of the fund's holdings are in stocks. The stocks in this portfolio have an average p/e ratio of 23 and a median market capitalization of $7 billion. The ten largest holdings compose 38 percent of the fund's total assets. The portfolio's equity holdings can be categorized as mid-cap and a blend of growth and value stocks.

Michael Hoover has managed this fund for the past seven years. Manager Hoover favors four main industry groups: large integrated oil companies, corporations involved with exploration and production, oil services, and pipeline and utilities. Management first accesses macroeconomic conditions in order to project energy prices as well as those subsectors with the most favorable fundamentals. There are twenty-nine funds besides Energy & Natural Resources within the Excelsior family. Overall, the fund family's risk-adjusted performance can be described as good to very good.

Tax Minimization   ★★★
During the past five years, a $10,000 initial investment grew to $11,540 after taxes, assuming a 40 percent income tax bracket (state and federal combined) and a capital gains rate of 20 percent. This means that investors in this fund were able to preserve 75 percent of their total returns. Compared to other equity funds in the same category, this fund's tax savings are considered to be good.

Expenses   ★★★
Excelsior Energy & Natural Resources's expense ratio is 1 percent; it has averaged 1 percent annually over the past three calendar years. The average expense ratio for the 115 funds in this category is 1.8 percent. This fund's turnover rate over the past year has been 138 percent, while its peer group average has been 195 percent.

Summary
Excelsior Energy & Natural Resources, a mid-cap sector fund that invests in both growth and value stocks, has outperformed 94 percent of all mutual funds over the past three years as well as 98 percent of its peer group over the past five years. Risk-adjusted returns have also been superb over the past five years. By category, the portfolio ranks in the top third when it comes to return versus risk. Within its peer group, the fund ranks number two when it comes to total return. The portfolio also does a very good job at risk reduction. This fund outperformed the S & P 500 by 52 percentage points in 2000. This portfolio's alpha, which measures excess returns per unit of risk taken, as measured against the fund's benchmark index, is quite appealing.

Profile

minimum initial investment $500	*IRA accounts available* . . . . yes
subsequent minimum investment . . . $50	*IRA minimum investment* $250
available in all 50 states. . . . . yes	*date of inception.* . . . . Dec. 1992
telephone exchanges. . . . . yes	*dividend/income paid* . . . . quarterly
number of funds in family 30	*largest sector weighting.* . . . . energy

INVESCO Energy Investor Shares
P.O. Box 173706
Denver, CO 80217
(800) 525-8085
www.invescofunds.com

total return	★★★★★
risk reduction	★★
management	★★★★
tax minimization	★★★
expense control	★
symbol FSTEX	15 points
up-market performance	very good
down-market performance	fair
predictability of returns	poor

Total Return ★★★★★
Over the past five years, INVESCO Energy Investor Shares has taken $10,000 and turned it into $16,110 ($18,610 over three years and $25,940 over the past ten years). This translates into an annualized return of 10 percent over the past five years, 23 percent over the past three years, and 10 percent for the decade. Over the past five years, this fund has outperformed 85 percent of all mutual funds; within its general category it has done better than 99 percent of its peers. Metals and natural resources funds have averaged -2 percent annually over these same five years.

Risk/Volatility ★★
Over the past five years, INVESCO Energy Investor Shares has been safer than 30 percent of all metals and natural resources funds. Over the past decade, the fund has had four negative years, while the S & P 500 has had two (off 9 percent in 2000 and 12 percent in 2001). The fund has underperformed the S & P 500 twice in the past ten years. Consistency of *overperformance* for this fund has been very good.

	past 5 years		past 10 years	
worst year	-27.8%	1998	-27.8%	1998
best year	58.2%	2000	58.2%	2000

Over the past five years, the fund's three worst quarters have been third quarter 1998 (-18 percent), third quarter 2001 (-17 percent), and fourth quarter 1997 (-14 percent). During the same period, the three best quarters have been third quarter 1997 (28 percent), second quarter 1999 (23 percent), and first quarter 2000 (21 percent). In the past, INVESCO Energy Investor Shares has done better than 69 percent of its peer group during the most recent bull market and outperformed just 12 percent of its peer group during the most recent bear market. Consistency, or predictability, of returns for INVESCO Energy Investor Shares can be described as poor. This fund's risk-related return ranks in the top quintile.

Management   ★★★★

There are thirty-five stocks in this $350 million portfolio. The average metals and natural resources fund today is $70 million in size. Close to 100 percent of the fund's holdings are in stocks. The stocks in this portfolio have an average p/e ratio of 21 and a median market capitalization of $4.8 billion. The ten largest holdings compose 50 percent of the fund's total assets. The portfolio's equity holdings can be categorized as mid-cap and value-oriented issues.

John Segner has managed this fund for the past five years. Manager Segner concentrates just on energy stocks. He has done a surprisingly good job at moving in and out of some of the sector's more volatile components. There are seventy-nine funds besides Energy Investor Shares within the INVESCO family. Overall, the fund family's risk-adjusted performance can be described as good.

Tax Minimization   ★★★

During the past five years, a $10,000 initial investment grew to $11,120 after taxes, assuming a 40 percent income tax bracket (state and federal combined) and a capital gains rate of 20 percent. This means that investors in this fund were able to preserve 69 percent of their total returns. Compared to other equity funds in the same category, this fund's tax savings are considered to be good.

Expenses   ★

INVESCO Energy Investor Shares's expense ratio is 1.4 percent; it has averaged 1.6 percent annually over the past three calendar years. The average expense ratio for the 115 funds in this category is 1.8 percent. This fund's turnover rate over the past year has been 166 percent, while its peer group average has been 195 percent.

Summary

INVESCO Energy, a mid-cap sector value fund, has outperformed 98 percent of all mutual funds over the past three years as well as 99 percent of its peer group over the past five years. Returns over shorter periods have been equally impressive. Risk-adjusted returns have also been superb over the past three, five, and ten years. By category, the portfolio ranks in the top quintile when it comes to return versus risk. Within its peer group, the fund easily ranks number one for total return. This fund outperformed the S & P 500 by 67 percentage points in 2000. This portfolio's alpha, which measures excess returns per unit of risk taken, as measured against the fund's benchmark index, is extremely appealing.

Profile

minimum initial investment $1,000	*IRA accounts available* . . . . yes
subsequent minimum investment . . . $50	*IRA minimum investment* $250
available in all 50 states. . . . . yes	*date of inception* . . . . Jan. 1984
telephone exchanges. . . . . yes	*dividend/income paid* . . . . annually
number of funds in family 80	*largest sector weighting*. . . . . . . energy

T. Rowe Price New Era
100 East Pratt Street
Baltimore, MD 21202
(800) 638-5660
www.troweprice.com

total return	★★★
risk reduction	★★★★★
management	★★★★
tax minimization	★
expense control	★★★★
symbol PRNEX	17 points
up-market performance	good
down-market performance	very good
predictability of returns	very good

Total Return   ★★★

Over the past five years, T. Rowe Price New Era has taken $10,000 and turned it into $14,030 ($14,050 over three years and $25,940 over the past ten years). This translates into an annualized return of 7 percent over the past five years, 12 percent over the past three years, and 10 percent for the decade. Over the past five years, this fund has outperformed 53 percent of all mutual funds; within its general category, it has done better than 82 percent of its peers. Metals and natural resources funds have averaged -2 percent annually over these same five years.

Risk/Volatility   ★★★★★

Over the past five years, T. Rowe Price New Era has been safer than 99 percent of all metals and natural resources funds. Over the past decade, the fund has had two negative years, while the S & P 500 has had two (off 9 percent in 2000 and 12 percent in 2001). The fund has underperformed the S & P 500 twice in the past ten years. Consistency of *overperformance* for this fund has been good.

	past 5 years		past 10 years	
worst year	-9.9%	1998	-9.9%	1998
best year	21.2%	1999	24.3%	1996

Over the past five years, the fund's three worst quarters have been third quarter 1998 (-12 percent), third quarter 2001 (-12 percent), and fourth quarter 1997 (-9 percent). During the same period, the three best quarters have been second quarter 1999 (15 percent), third quarter 1997 (11 percent), and second quarter 1997 (11 percent). In the past, T. Rowe Price New Era has done better than 64 percent of its peer group during the most recent bull market and outperformed 60 percent of its peer group during the most recent bear market. Consistency, or predictability, of returns for T. Rowe Price New Era can be described as very good. This fund's risk-related return ranks in the top third.

Management   ★★★★

There are 110 stocks in this $1 billion portfolio. The average metals and natural resources fund today is $70 million in size. Close to 97 percent of the fund's holdings are in stocks. The stocks in this portfolio have an average p/e ratio of 22 and a median market capitalization of $7 billion. The ten largest holdings compose 29 percent of the fund's total assets. The portfolio's equity holdings can be categorized as mid-cap and value-oriented issues.

Charles Ober has managed this fund for the past five years. Manager Ober has been able to largely avoid the cyclical downturns that plague this, as well as most other, sectors. Management believes in broad diversification, even more so than its peers. (Note: the portfolio's second largest holding is Wal-Mart.) There are eighty-four funds besides New Era within the T. Rowe Price family. Overall, the fund family's risk-adjusted performance can be described as good to very good.

Tax Minimization   ★

During the past five years, a $10,000 initial investment grew to $7,440 after taxes, assuming a 40 percent income tax bracket (state and federal combined) and a capital gains rate of 20 percent. This means that investors in this fund were able to preserve 53 percent of their total returns. Compared to other equity funds in the same category, this fund's tax savings are considered to be poor.

Expenses   ★★★★

T. Rowe Price New Era's expense ratio is 0.7 percent; it has averaged 0.7 percent annually over the past three calendar years. The average expense ratio for the 115 funds in this category is 1.8 percent. This fund's turnover rate over the past year has been 29 percent, while its peer group average has been 195 percent.

Summary

T. Rowe Price New Era, a mid-cap value sector fund, has outperformed 87 percent of all mutual funds over the past three years as well as 91 percent of its peer group over the past fifteen years. Returns over shorter periods have also been impressive. Risk-adjusted returns have ranged between fair and very good over the past three to ten years. Within its peer group, the fund ranks number one when it comes to low risk. This portfolio's alpha, which measures excess returns per unit of risk taken, as measured against the fund's benchmark index, is appealing.

Profile

minimum initial investment $2,500	IRA accounts available . . . . yes
subsequent minimum investment . . $100	IRA minimum investment $1,000
available in all 50 states. . . . . yes	date of inception . . . . Jan. 1969
telephone exchanges. . . . . yes	dividend/income paid . . . . annually
number of funds in family 85	largest sector weighting. . . . . . . energy

Vanguard Energy
Vanguard Financial Centre
P.O. Box 2600
Valley Forge, PA 19482
(800) 662-7447
www.vanguard.com

total return	★★★★
risk reduction	★★★★
management	★★★★
tax minimization	★★★
expense control	★★★★★
symbol VGENX	20 points
up-market performance	very good
down-market performance	very good
predictability of returns	good

Total Return   ★★★★

Over the past five years, Vanguard Energy has taken $10,000 and turned it into $14,700 ($16,020 over three years and $33,950 over the past ten years). This translates into an annualized return of 8 percent over the past five years, 17 percent over the past three years, and 13 percent for the decade. Over the past five years, this fund has outperformed 62 percent of all mutual funds; within its general category, it has done better than 87 percent of its peers. Metals and natural resources funds have averaged -2 percent annually over these same five years.

Risk/Volatility   ★★★★

Over the past five years, Vanguard Energy has been safer than 70 percent of all metals and natural resources funds. Over the past decade, the fund has had three negative years, while the S & P 500 has had two (off 9 percent in 2000 and 12 percent in 2001). The fund has underperformed the S & P 500 twice in the past ten years. Consistency of *overperformance* for this fund has been good.

	past 5 years		past 10 years	
worst year	-20.5%	1998	-20.5%	1998
best year	36.4%	2000	36.4%	2000

Over the past five years, the fund's three worst quarters have been third quarter 1998 (-14 percent), third quarter 2001 (-11 percent), and fourth quarter 1997 (-7 percent). During the same period, the three best quarters have been third quarter 1997 (16 percent), second quarter 1999 (15 percent), and first quarter 2000 (12 percent). In the past, Vanguard Energy has done better than 70 percent of its peer group during the most recent bull market and outperformed 59 percent of its peer group during the most recent bear market. Consistency, or predictability, of returns for Vanguard Energy can be described as good. This fund's risk-related return ranks in the top quintile.

Management   ★★★★

There are fifty stocks in this $1.3 billion portfolio. The average metals and natural resources fund today is $70 million in size. Close to 93 percent of the fund's holdings are in stocks. The stocks in this portfolio have an average p/e ratio of 21 and a median market capitalization of $9 billion. The ten largest holdings compose 41 percent of the fund's total assets. The portfolio's equity holdings can be categorized as mid-cap and value-oriented issues.

Ernst von Metzsch has managed this fund for the past eighteen years. Manager von Metzsch has a conservative, diversified approach for this portfolio. There are 154 funds besides Energy within the Vanguard family. Overall, the fund family's risk-adjusted performance can be described as very good.

Tax Minimization   ★★★

During the past five years, a $10,000 initial investment grew to $11,320 after taxes, assuming a 40 percent income tax bracket (state and federal combined) and a capital gains rate of 20 percent. This means that investors in this fund were able to preserve 77 percent of their total returns. Compared to other equity funds in the same category, this fund's tax savings are considered to be good.

Expenses   ★★★★★

Vanguard Energy's expense ratio is 0.5 percent; it has averaged 0.5 percent annually over the past three calendar years. The average expense ratio for the 115 funds in this category is 1.8 percent. This fund's turnover rate over the past year has been 18 percent, while its peer group average has been 195 percent.

Summary

Vanguard Energy, a mid-cap value sector fund, has outperformed 80 percent of all mutual funds over the past fifteen years as well as 99 percent of its peer group over the same period. Returns over shorter periods have been equally impressive. Risk-adjusted returns have ranged from outstanding to fair over the past three to ten years. By category, the portfolio ranks in the top third when it comes to return versus risk. Within its peer group, the fund ranks number one when it comes to low expenses plus has an incredibly low turnover rate. Total return and risk reduction figures are also very appealing. Energy represents a very small portion of the S & P 500. This fund will help the typical investor become more diversified. This fund outperformed the S & P 500 by 46 percentage points in 2000. This portfolio's alpha, which measures excess returns per unit of risk taken, as measured against the fund's benchmark index, is quite appealing. On a total point basis, this is the number-one fund for its category.

Profile

minimum initial investment $3,000	IRA accounts available . . . . yes
subsequent minimum investment . . $100	IRA minimum investment $1,000
available in all 50 states. . . . . yes	date of inception. . . . . May 1984
telephone exchanges. . . . . yes	dividend/income paid . . . . annually
number of funds in family 155	largest sector weighting. . . . . . . energy

Vanguard Precious Metals
Vanguard Financial Centre
P.O. Box 2600
Valley Forge, PA 19482
(800) 662-7447
www.vanguard.com

total return	★★
risk reduction	★★
management	★★★
tax minimization	★★★★★
expense control	★★★★
symbol VGPMX	16 points
up-market performance	excellent
down-market performance	very good
predictability of returns	poor

Total Return   ★★
Over the past five years, Vanguard Precious Metals has taken $10,000 and turned it into $8,160 ($14,050 over three years and $11,050 over the past ten years). This translates into an annualized return of -4 percent over the past five years, 12 percent over the past three years, and 1 percent for the decade. Over the past five years, this fund has outperformed 3 percent of all mutual funds; within its general category, it has done better than 99 percent of its peers. Metals and natural resources funds have averaged -2 percent annually over these same five years.

Risk/Volatility   ★★
Over the past five years, Vanguard Precious Metals has been safer than 69 percent of all metals and natural resources funds. Over the past decade, the fund has had seven negative years, while the S & P 500 has had two (off 9 percent in 2000 and 12 percent in 2001). The fund has underperformed the S & P 500 twice in the past ten years. Consistency of *overperformance* for this fund has been good.

	past 5 years		past 10 years	
worst year	-38.9%	1997	-38.9%	1997
best year	28.8%	1999	93.4%	1994

Over the past five years, the fund's three worst quarters have been fourth quarter 1997 (-29 percent), first quarter 2000 (-19 percent), and second quarter 1998 (-15 percent). During the same period, the three best quarters have been second quarter 2001 (24 percent), third quarter 1999 (19 percent), and second quarter 1999 (12 percent). In the past, Vanguard Precious Metals has done better than 94 percent of all metals funds during the most recent bull market and outperformed 62 percent of its peer group during the most recent bear market. Consistency, or predictability, of returns for Vanguard Precious Metals can be described as poor. This fund's risk-related return ranks in the top quintile.

Management   ★★★
There are thirty stocks in this $375 million portfolio. The average metals and nat-ural resources fund today is $70 million in size. Close to 95 percent of the fund's holdings are in stocks. The stocks in this portfolio have an average p/e ratio of 21 and a median market capitalization of $2 billion. The ten largest holdings compose 74 percent of the fund's total assets. The portfolio's equity holdings can be cate-gorized as mid-cap and a blend of growth and value stocks.

Graham French has managed this fund for the past six years. Manager French has put together a portfolio that is appealing in an otherwise very unappealing cat-egory, metals. Management likes to have roughly a third of the portfolio in metals besides gold, such as palladium and platinum. There are 154 funds besides Precious Metals within the Vanguard family. Overall, the fund family's risk-adjusted performance can be described as very good.

Tax Minimization   ★★★★★
During the past five years, a $10,000 initial investment grew to $8,160 after taxes, assuming a 40 percent income tax bracket (state and federal combined) and a cap-ital gains rate of 20 percent. This means that investors in this fund were able to pre-serve 100 percent of their losses. Compared to other equity funds in the same category, this fund's tax efficiency is considered to be excellent.

Expenses   ★★★★
Vanguard Precious Metals's expense ratio is 0.7 percent; it has averaged 0.8 per-cent annually over the past three calendar years. The average expense ratio for the 115 funds in this category is 1.8 percent. This fund's turnover rate over the past year has been 17 percent, while its peer group average has been 195 percent.

Summary
Vanguard Precious Metals, a mid-cap sector fund that invests in both growth and value stocks, has outperformed 87 percent of all mutual funds over the past three years as well as 99 percent of its peer group over the past three and five years. Returns over longer periods have also been impressive. Risk-adjusted returns have ranged from superb to fair over the past three to ten years. By category, the port-folio ranks in the top quintile when it comes to return versus risk. As a metals fund, this portfolio ranks number one in virtually every imaginable category. Most years, this offering lands in the top quartile of performance—a rarity for any fund in any category. If you are going to own any metals fund, this is the one you should have. This portfolio's alpha, which measures excess returns per unit of risk taken, as measured against the fund's benchmark index, is extremely appealing.

Profile
minimum initial investment $3,000	*IRA accounts available* . . . . yes
subsequent minimum investment . . $100	*IRA minimum investment* $1,000
available in all 50 states. . . . . yes	*date of inception*. . . . . May 1984
telephone exchanges. . . . . yes	*dividend/income paid* . . . . annually
number of funds in family 155	*largest sector weighting* indust. cyclicals

Money Market Funds

Money market funds invest in securities that mature in less than one year. They are made up of one or more of the following instruments: Treasury bills, certificates of deposit, commercial paper, repurchase agreements, Eurodollar CDs, and notes. There are four different categories of money market funds: all-purpose, government-backed, federally tax-free, and double tax-exempt.

All-purpose funds are the most popular and make up the bulk of the money market universe. Fully taxable, they are composed of securities such as CDs, commercial paper, and T-bills.

Government-backed money funds invest only in short-term paper, directly or indirectly backed by the U.S. government. These funds are technically safer than the all-purpose variety, but only one money market fund has ever defaulted (a fund set up by a bank for banks). The yield on government-backed funds is somewhat lower than that of its all-purpose peers.

Federally tax-free funds are made up of municipal notes. Investors in these funds do not have to pay federal income taxes on the interest earned. The before-tax yield on federally tax-free funds is certainly lower than that of all-purpose and government-backed funds, but the after-tax return can be greater for the moderate- or high-tax-bracket investor.

Double tax-exempt funds invest in the municipal obligations of a specific state. To avoid paying state income taxes on any interest earned, you must be a resident of that state. Nonresident investors will still receive a federal tax exemption.

All money market funds are safer than any other mutual fund or category of funds in this book. They have a perfect track record (if you exclude the one money market fund set up for banks)—investors can only make money in these interest-bearing accounts. The rate of return earned in a money market depends on the average maturity of the fund's paper, the kinds of securities held, the quality rating of that paper, and how efficiently the fund is operated. A lean fund will almost always outperform a similar fund with high operating costs.

Investments such as U.S. Treasury bills and, for all practical purposes, money market funds, are often referred to as "risk-free." These kinds of investments are free from price swings and default risk because of their composition. However, as we have come to learn, there is more than one form of risk. Money market funds should never be considered as a medium- or long-term investment. The *real return* on this investment is poor. An investment's real return takes into account the effects of inflation and income taxes. During virtually every period of time, the after-tax, after-inflation return on all money market funds has been near zero or even negative.

Over the past fifty years, Treasury bills—an index often used as a substitute for money market funds—have outperformed inflation on average 80 percent of the time over one-, five-, and ten-year periods and 100 percent over any given twenty-year period of time. These figures are not adjusted for income taxes. Money market funds have rarely, if ever, outperformed inflation on an *after-tax* basis when looking at three-, five-, ten-, fifteen-, or twenty-year holding positions.

Investors often look back to the good old days of the early 1980s, when money market funds briefly averaged 18 percent, and wish such times would come again. Well, those were not good times. During the early 1980s the top tax bracket, state and federal combined, was 55 percent. If you began with an 18-percent return and deducted taxes, many taxpayers saw their 18-percent return knocked down to about 9 percent. This may look great, especially for a "risk-free" investment, but we are not through yet. During the partial year in which money market accounts paid 18 percent, inflation was 12 percent. Now, if you take the 9-percent return and subtract 12 percent for inflation; the real return was actually minus 3 percent for the year—so much for the good old days.

Money market funds and ultra-short-term bond funds are the best places to park your money while you are looking at other investment alternatives or if you will be using the money during the next year. These funds can provide the convenience of check writing and a yield that is highly competitive with interest rates in general. These incredibly safe funds should only be considered for short-term periods or for regular expenditures, the way you would use a savings or checking account.

Since money market funds only came into existence for the general public in the mid-1970s, those who wish to analyze the performance of these funds over a long period often use Treasury bills as a substitute. The results are instructive. Over the past half-century (1952–2001), a dollar invested in T-bills grew to $13.17 by the end of 2001. By the end of 2001, you would have needed $6.67 to equal the purchasing power of a dollar at the beginning of 1952. This means that T-bills have outperformed inflation by roughly a two-to-one margin on a pretax basis over the past fifty years. If income taxes were factored in, using the then highest marginal rates, an investor would not have kept pace with inflation over the last half-century.

To give you a better sense of the cumulative effects of inflation, consider what a $100,000 investment in a money market fund would have to yield at the beginning of 2002 to equal the same purchasing power as the interest (or yield) from a $100,000 investment in a money market fund twenty years ago (1982). At the beginning of 2002, for instance, a $100,000 account held since 1982 would need to generate $19,744 to equal the same purchasing power as a $100,000 account yielding approximately 10.5 percent in 1982 (the average interest rate for money market accounts that year). The reality, however, is that at the beginning of 2002, money market funds were yielding less than 4 percent (less than $4,000 a year versus the $19,744 that would be required to maintain purchasing power).

You may have avoided stock investing in the past because "stocks are too risky." Yet, it all depends on how you define risk. As an example, in 1969 a $100,000 CD generated enough interest ($7,900) to buy a new, fully loaded Cadillac ($5,936) and take a week's cruise. As of the beginning of 1997, that same $100,000 CD would not generate enough income (CD rates were 4.95 percent) to buy an eighth of the Cadillac ($4,950 versus $43,000 for the cost of a 1997 Cadillac Hardtop Sedan De Ville).

Over the past one, three, five, and ten years, ending December 31, 2001, money market funds have averaged 3.6 percent, 4.7 percent, 4.9 percent, and 4.5 percent, respectively The standard deviation for money market funds is roughly a quarter of 1 percent, a figure much lower than any other mutual fund category. This means that these funds have had fewer return variances than any other group. Close to 1,300 funds make up the money market category. Total market capitalization of this category is over $2.3 trillion, making this the largest fund category by a wide margin.

Elfun Money Market

3003 Summer Street
P.O. Box 120074
Stamford, CT 06912
(800) 242-0134
www.elfun.org

total return	★★★★★
risk reduction	★★★★★
management	★★★★★
expense control	★★★★★
symbol ELMXX	20 points

Total Return ★★★★★

Over the past five years, Elfun Money Market has taken $10,000 and turned it into $12,770 ($11,580 over three years). This translates into an average annual return of 5 percent over five years and 5 percent over the past three years. This is the number-eleven performing taxable money market fund over the past five years and number six for the past three years.

Risk/Volatility ★★★★★

During the past three and five years, the fund's standard deviation has been 0.2 percent.

	past 5 years		past 10 years	
worst year	4.1%	2001	3.3%	1993
best year	6.4%	2000	6.4%	2000

Management ★★★★★

The average maturity of the paper in the portfolio is approximately forty-two days. Robert MacDougall has managed the fund since June 1990. The fund has outperformed its peer group average over the past one, three, five, and ten years.

Expenses ★★★★★

The expense ratio for this $380 million fund is 0.2 percent. This means that for every $1,000 invested, $2 goes to paying overhead.

Summary

Elfun Money Market is highly recommended.

Profile

minimum initial investment	$500	*IRA accounts available*	yes
subsequent minimum investment	$100	*IRA minimum investment*	$100
available in all 50 states	yes	*date of inception*	1990
telephone exchanges	yes	*dividend/income paid*	daily
number of funds in family	362		

Fidelity U.S. Government Reserves

82 Devonshire Street
Mailzone F 9A
Boston, MA 02109
(800) 522-7297
www.fidelity.com

total return	★★★★★	
risk reduction	★★★★★	
management	★★★★★	
expense control	★★★★★	
symbol FGRXX	20 points	

Total Return ★★★★★

Over the past five years, Fidelity U.S. Government Reserves has taken $10,000 and turned it into $12,770 ($11,580 over three years). This translates into an average annual return of 5 percent over five years and 5 percent over the past three years. This is the number-fourteen performing government money market fund over the past five years and number four for the past three years.

Risk/Volatility ★★★★★

	past 5 years		past 10 years	
worst year	4.1%	2001	2.6%	1993
best year	6.1%	2000	6.1%	2000

Management ★★★★★

The average maturity of the paper in the portfolio is approximately forty-eight days. Robert Litterst has managed the fund since April 1997. The fund has outperformed its peer group average over the past one, three, five, and ten years.

Expenses ★★★★★

The expense ratio for this $2.3 billion fund is 0.4 percent. This means that for every $1,000 invested, $4 goes to paying overhead.

Summary

Fidelity U.S. Government Reserves is highly recommended.

Profile

minimum initial investment $2,500
subsequent minimum investment . . $250
available in all 50 states. . . . . yes
telephone exchanges. . . . . yes
number of funds in family 155

IRA accounts available . . . . yes
IRA minimum investment $500
date of inception. 1981
dividend/income paid . . . . daily

Glenmede Government Cash

One Liberty Place
1650 Market Street, Suite 1200
Philadelphia, PA 19103
(800) 442-8299
www.glenmede.com

total return	★★★★★
risk reduction	★★★★★
management	★★★★★
expense control	★★★★★
symbol GTGXX	20 points

Total Return   ★★★★★

Over the past five years, Glenmede Government Cash has taken $10,000 and turned it into $12,763 ($11,576 over three years). This translates into an average annual return of 5 percent over five years and 5 percent over the past three years. This is the number-two performing government money market fund over the past five years and number one for the past three years.

Risk/Volatility   ★★★★★

During the past three and five years, the fund's standard deviation has been 0.2 percent.

	past 5 years		past 10 years	
worst year	4.2%	2001	3.2%	1993
best year	6.4%	2000	6.4%	2000

Management   ★★★★★

The average maturity of the paper in the portfolio is approximately thirty-eight days. Mary Ann Wirts has managed the fund since November 1996. The fund has outperformed its peer group average over the past one, three, five, and ten years.

Expenses   ★★★★★

The expense ratio for this $430 million fund is 0.1 percent. This means that for every $1,000 invested, $1 goes to paying overhead.

Summary

Glenmede Government Cash is highly recommended.

Profile

minimum initial investment $25,000
subsequent minimum investment . $1,000
available in all 50 states. . . . . yes
telephone exchanges. . . . . yes
number of funds in family 12

IRA accounts available . . . . yes
IRA minimum investment $2,000
date of inception. 1988
dividend/income paid . . . . daily

Janus Tax-Exempt Money Market Service

100 Fillmore Street, Suite 300
Denver, CO 80206
(8000 525-3713
www.janus.com

total return	★★★★★
risk reduction	★★★★★
management	★★★★★
expense control	★★★★★
symbol JATXX	20 points

Total Return   ★★★★★
Over the past five years, Janus Tax-Exempt Money Market Service has taken $10,000 and turned it into $11,600 ($10,930 over three years). This translates into an average annual return of 3 percent over five years and 3 percent over the past three years. This is the number-five performing tax-free money market fund over the past five years and number two for the past three years.

Risk/Volatility   ★★★★★
During the past three and five years, the fund's standard deviation has been 0.2 percent.

	past 5 years		since inception	
worst year	2.9%	2001	2.9%	2001
best year	4.0%	2000	4.0%	2000

Management   ★★★★★
The average maturity of the paper in the portfolio is approximately fifty-seven days. Sharon Pichler has managed the fund since November 1996. The fund has outperformed its peer group average over the past one, three, and five years.

Expenses   ★★★★★
The expense ratio for this $290 million fund is 0.4 percent. This means that for every $1,000 invested, $4 goes to paying overhead.

Summary
Janus Tax-Exempt Money Market Service is highly recommended.

Profile

minimum initial investment $2,500	*IRA accounts available* . . . . n/a
subsequent minimum investment . . $100	*IRA minimum investment* . . . . n/a
available in all 50 states . . . . yes	*date of inception* 1996
telephone exchanges . . . . yes	*dividend/income paid* . . . . daily
number of funds in family 45	

Scudder Premium Money Market

Two International Place
Boston, MA 02110
(800) 621-1048
www.scudder.com

total return	★★★★★
risk reduction	★★★★★
management	★★★★★
expense control	★★★★★
symbol SPMXX	20 points

Total Return ★★★★★
Over the past five years, Scudder Premium Money Market has taken $10,000 and turned it into $ ($11,580 over three years). This translates into a return of 5 percent over the past three years. This is the number-ten performing taxable money market fund over the past three years.

Risk/Volatility ★★★★★
During the past three years, the fund's standard deviation has been 0.2 percent.

	past 3 years		since inception	
worst year	3.9%	2001	3.9%	1993
best year	6.4%	2000	6.4%	2000

Management ★★★★★
The average maturity of the paper in the portfolio is approximately thirty-three days. David Wines has managed the fund since July 1997. The fund has outperformed its peer group average over the past one and three years.

Expenses ★★★★★
The expense ratio for this $950 million fund is 0.2 percent. This means that for every $1,000 invested, $2 goes to paying overhead.

Summary
Scudder Premium Money Market is highly recommended.

Profile

minimum initial investment $2,500	*IRA accounts available* . . . . yes
subsequent minimum investment . . $100	*IRA minimum investment* $500
available in all 50 states. . . . . yes	*date of inception*. 1999
telephone exchanges. . . . . yes	*dividend/income paid* . . . . daily
number of funds in family 199	

Strong Municipal Money Market
100 Heritage Reserve
Menomonee Falls, WI 53051
(800) 368-383
www.estrong.com

total return	★★★★★
risk reduction	★★★★★
management	★★★★★
expense control	★★★★★
symbol SXFXX	20 points

Total Return ★★★★★
Over the past five years, Strong Municipal Money Market has taken $10,000 and turned it into $12,170 ($10,930 over three years). This translates into an average annual return of 4 percent over five years and 3 percent over the past three years. This is the number-one performing tax-free money market fund over the past five years and number two for the past three years.

Risk/Volatility ★★★★★
During the past three and five years, the fund's standard deviation has been 0.2 percent.

	past 5 years		past 10 years	
worst year	2.9%	2001	2.5%	1993
best year	4.2%	2000	4.2%	2000

Management ★★★★★
The average maturity of the paper in the portfolio is approximately thirty-seven days. John Bonnell has managed the fund since March 2000. The fund has outperformed its peer group average over the past one, three, five, and ten years.

Expenses ★★★★★
The expense ratio for this $3.1 billion fund is 0.6 percent. This means that for every $1,000 invested, $6 goes to paying overhead.

Summary
Strong Municipal Money Market is highly recommended.

Profile
minimum initial investment $2,500
subsequent minimum investment . . . $50
available in all 50 states. . . . . yes
telephone exchanges. . . . . yes
number of funds in family 102

IRA accounts available . . . . n/a
IRA minimum investment . . . . n/a
date of inception. 1986
dividend/income paid . . . . daily

Trust for Credit Union Money Market

4900 Sears Tower
Chicago, IL 60606
(800) 621-2550
www.goldmansachs.com

total return	★★★★★
risk reduction	★★★★★
management	★★★★★
expense control	★★★★★
symbol TCUXX	20 points

Total Return   ★★★★★

Over the past five years, Trust for Credit Union Money Market has taken $10,000 and turned it into $12,770 ($11,580 over three years). This translates into an average annual return of 5 percent over five years and 5 percent over the past three years. This is the number-four performing taxable money market fund over the past five years and number four for the past three years.

Risk/Volatility   ★★★★★

During the past three and five years, the fund's standard deviation has been 0.2 percent.

	past 5 years		past 10 years	
worst year	4.3%	2001	3.1%	1993
best year	6.4%	2000	6.4%	2000

Management   ★★★★★

The average maturity of the paper in the portfolio is approximately eighteen days. A team has managed the fund since May 1988. The fund has outperformed its peer group average over the past one, three, five, and ten years.

Expenses   ★★★★★

The expense ratio for this $2 billion fund is 0.1 percent. This means that for every $1,000 invested, $1 goes to paying overhead.

Summary

Trust for Credit Union Money Market is highly recommended.

Profile

minimum initial investment $1	*IRA accounts available* . . . . yes
subsequent minimum investment $1	*IRA minimum investment* $1
available in all 50 states. . . . . yes	*date of inception.* 1988
telephone exchanges. . . . . yes	*dividend/income paid* . . . . daily
number of funds in family 3	

USAA Tax-Exempt Money Market
USAA Building
San Antonio, TX 78288
(800) 531-8722
www.usaa.com

total return	★★★★★
risk reduction	★★★★★
management	★★★★★
expense control	★★★★★
symbol USEXX	20 points

Total Return   ★★★★★
Over the past five years, USAA Tax-Exempt Money Market has taken $10,000 and turned it into $11,600 ($10,930 over three years). This translates into an average annual return of 3 percent over five years and 3 percent over the past three years. This is the number-nine performing tax-free money market fund over the past five years and number eight for the past three years.

Risk/Volatility   ★★★★★
During the past three and five years, the fund's standard deviation has been 0.2 percent.

	past 5 years		past 10 years	
worst year	2.6%	2001	2.4%	1993
best year	3.9%	2000	3.9%	2000

Management   ★★★★★
The average maturity of the paper in the portfolio is approximately thirty-seven days. Anthony Era has managed the fund since February 2000. The fund has out-performed its peer group average over the past one, three, and five years.

Expenses   ★★★★★
The expense ratio for this $1.9 billion fund is 0.4 percent. This means that for every $1,000 invested, $4 goes to paying overhead.

Summary
USAA Tax-Exempt Money Market is highly recommended.

Profile

minimum initial investment $3,000	IRA accounts available . . . . n/a
subsequent minimum investment . . . $50	IRA minimum investment . . . . n/a
available in all 50 states. . . . . yes	date of inception. 1984
telephone exchanges. . . . . yes	dividend/income paid . . . . daily
number of funds in family 33	

Vanguard Federal Money Market
Vanguard Financial Center
P.O. Box 2600
Valley Forge, PA 19482
(800) 662-2739
www.vanguard.com

total return	★★★★★
risk reduction	★★★★★
management	★★★★★
expense control	★★★★★
symbol VMFXX	20 points

Total Return   ★★★★★
Over the past five years, Vanguard Federal Money Market has taken $10,000 and turned it into $12,770 ($11,580 over three years). This translates into an average annual return of 5 percent over five years and 5 percent over the past three years. This is the number-six performing government money market fund over the past five years and number five for the past three years.

Risk/Volatility   ★★★★★
During the past three and five years, the fund's standard deviation has been 0.2 percent.

	past 5 years		past 10 years	
worst year	4.2%	2001	3.0%	1993
best year	6.2%	2000	6.2%	2000

Management   ★★★★★
The average maturity of the paper in the portfolio is approximately sixty-two days. Robert Auwaerter has managed the fund since November 1981. The fund has out-performed its peer group average over the past one, three, five, and ten years.

Expenses   ★★★★★
The expense ratio for this $7 billion fund is 0.3 percent. This means that for every $1,000 invested, $3 goes to paying overhead.

Summary
Vanguard Federal Money Market is highly recommended.

Profile
minimum initial investment $3,000
subsequent minimum investment . . $100
available in all 50 states. . . . . yes
telephone exchanges. . . . . yes
number of funds in family 155

IRA accounts available . . . . yes
IRA minimum investment $100
date of inception. 1981
dividend/income paid . . . . daily

Wells Fargo Money Market Trust

525 Market Street, 12th Floor
San Francisco, CA 94105
(800) 222-8222
www.wellsfargo.com

total return	★★★★★
risk reduction	★★★★★
management	★★★★★
expense control	★★★★★
symbol SCCME	20 points

Total Return   ★★★★★
Over the past five years, Wells Fargo Money Market Trust has taken $10,000 and turned it into $12,770 ($11,580 over three years). This translates into an average annual return of 5 percent over five years and 5 percent over the past three years. This is the number-two performing taxable money market fund over the past five years and number two for the past three years.

Risk/Volatility   ★★★★★
During the past three and five years, the fund's standard deviation has been 0.2 percent.

	past 5 years		past 10 years	
worst year	4.3%	2001	2.8%	1993
best year	6.5%	2000	6.5%	2000

Management   ★★★★★
The average maturity of the paper in the portfolio is approximately seventy-two days. A team has managed the fund since September 1990. The fund has outperformed its peer group average over the past one, three, five, and ten years.

Expenses   ★★★★★
The expense ratio for this $2 billion fund is 0.2 percent. This means that for every $1,000 invested, $2 goes to paying overhead.

Summary
Wells Fargo Money Market Trust is highly recommended.

Profile

minimum initial investment $1	IRA accounts available . . . . yes
subsequent minimum investment $1	IRA minimum investment $1
available in all 50 states. . . . . yes	date of inception. 1990
telephone exchanges. . . . . yes	dividend/income paid . . . . daily
number of funds in family 123	

Wells Fargo National Tax-Free Money Market Trust

525 Market Street, 12th Floor
San Francisco, CA 94105
(800) 222-8222
www.wellsfargo.com

total return	★★★★★
risk reduction	★★★★★
management	★★★★★
expense control	★★★★★
symbol SEATE	20 points

Total Return   ★★★★★

Over the past five years, Wells Fargo National Tax-Free Money Market Trust has taken $10,000 and turned it into $11,600 ($10,930 over three years). This translates into an average annual return of 3 percent over five years and 3 percent over the past three years. This is the number-eight performing tax-free money market fund over the past three years.

Risk/Volatility   ★★★★★

During the past three years, the fund's standard deviation has been 0.2 percent.

	past 5 years		past 10 years	
worst year	2.7%	2001	2.7%	1993
best year	4.1%	2000	4.1%	2000

Management   ★★★★★

The average maturity of the paper in the portfolio is approximately fifty-five days. Kevin Shaughnessy has managed the fund since November 1997. The fund has outperformed its peer group average over the past one and three years.

Expenses   ★★★★★

The expense ratio for this $433 million fund is 0.2 percent. This means that for every $1,000 invested, $2 goes to paying overhead.

Summary

Wells Fargo National Tax-Free Money Market Trust is highly recommended.

Profile

minimum initial investment $1	*IRA accounts available* . . . . n/a
subsequent minimum investment $1	*IRA minimum investment* . . . . n/a
available in all 50 states. . . . . yes	*date of inception*. 1997
telephone exchanges. . . . . yes	*dividend/income paid* . . . . daily
number of funds in family 123	

Municipal Bond Funds

Municipal bond funds invest in securities issued by municipalities, political subdivisions, and U.S. territories. The type of security issued is either a note or bond, both of which are interest-bearing instruments that are exempt from federal income taxes. There are three different categories of municipal bond funds: national, state-free, and high-yield.

National municipal bond funds are made up of debt instruments issued by a wide range of states. These funds are exempt from federal income taxes only. To determine what small percentage is also exempt from state income taxes, consult the fund's prospectus and look for the weighting of U.S. territory issues (U.S. Virgin Islands, Guam, Puerto Rico), District of Columbia items, and obligations from your state of residence.

State-free municipal bond funds, sometimes referred to as "double tax-free funds," invest only in bonds and notes issued in a particular state. To avoid paying state income taxes on the fund's return, you must be a legal resident of that state. For example, most California residents who are in a high tax bracket will only want to consider purchasing a municipal bond fund that has the name "California" in it. Residents of New York who purchase a California tax-free fund will escape federal income taxes but not state taxes.

High-yield tax-free funds invest in the same kinds of issues found in a national municipal bond fund but with one important difference. By seeking higher returns, high-yield funds look for lower-rated or nonrated notes and bonds. A municipality may decide not to obtain a rating for its issue because of the costs involved compared to the relatively small size of the bond or note being floated. Many nonrated issues are very safe. High-yield municipal bond funds are relatively new but should not be overlooked by the tax-conscious investor. These kinds of tax-free funds have demonstrated less volatility and higher return than their other tax-free counterparts.

Prospective investors need to compare tax-free bond yields to after-tax yields on corporate or government bond funds. To determine which of these three fund categories is best for you, use your marginal tax bracket, subtract this amount from one, and multiply the resulting figure by the taxable investment. For instance, suppose you were in the 35 percent bracket, state and federal combined. By subtracting this figure from 1, you are left with 0.65. Multiply 0.65 by the fully taxable yield you could get; let us say, 9 percent—65 percent of 9 percent is 5.85 percent. The 5.85 percent represents what you get on a 9-percent investment after you have paid state and federal income taxes on it. This means that if you can get 5.85 percent or higher from a tax-free investment, take it.

Annual Returns - Municipal Bond Funds

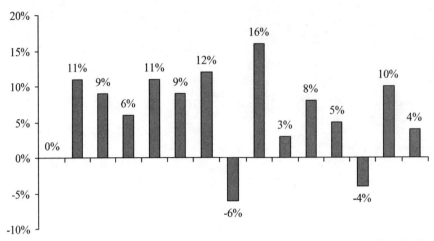

Interest paid on tax-free investments is generally lower than interest paid on taxable investments like corporate bonds and bank CDs. But you should compare the yields on tax-free investments to taxable investments only after you have considered the municipal bond fund's tax-free advantage. The result will be the taxable equivalent yield—the yield you will have to get on a similar taxable investment to equal the tax-free yield.

Municipal bond funds are not for investors who are in a low tax bracket. If such investors want to be in bonds, they would be better off in corporate or government issues. Furthermore, municipals should never be used in a retirement plan. There is only one way to make tax-free income taxable and that is to put it into a traditional IRA, pension, or profit-sharing plan. Everything that comes out of these plans is fully taxable by the federal government.

Over the past three and five years, the typical municipal bond fund has had an average compounded annual return of 3.4 and 4.8 percent, respectively. They have averaged a total annual return (current yield plus bond appreciation or minus bond depreciation) of 5.8 percent over the past ten years and 6.3 percent annually for the past fifteen years. Municipal bond fund returns have been fairly stable over the past three years, having a standard deviation of 4.0 percent.

Nearly 1,900 funds make up the municipal bond category. Total market capitalization of all municipal bond funds is $296 billion. Close to 99 percent of a typical municipal bond fund's portfolio is in tax-free bonds, with the balance in tax-free money market instruments. Close to 1,250 of the 1,849 municipal bond funds offered are single-state funds.

The typical municipal bond fund yields 4.4 percent in tax-free income each year. The average weighted maturity is 16.5 years. Expenses for this category are 1.1 percent each year.

As you read through the descriptions of the municipal bond funds selected, you will notice a paragraph in each describing the tax efficiency of the portfolio. This may surprise you, because municipal bonds are supposed to be tax-free. Keep in mind that only the income (current yield) from these instruments is free from federal income taxes (and often state income taxes, depending on the fund in question and your state of residence). Since bond funds generally have a high turnover rate (which triggers a potential capital gain or loss upon each sale of a security by the portfolio manager), there are capital gains considerations with municipal bonds.

American Century California High-Yield Municipal Investor Shares

4500 Main Street
P.O. Box 64141
Kansas City, MO 64141
(800) 345-2021
www.americancentury.com

total return	★★★★★
risk reduction	★★★★
management	★★★★★
current income	★★★★★
expense control	★★★★
symbol BCHYX	23 points
up-market performance	good
down-market performance	very good
predictability of returns	good

Total Return   ★★★★★

Over the past five years, American Century California High-Yield Municipal Investor Shares has taken $10,000 and turned it into $13,390 ($11,250 over three years and $19,680 over the past ten years). This translates into an annualized return of 6 percent over the past five years, 4 percent over the past three years, and 7 percent for the decade. Over the past five years, this fund has outperformed 56 percent of all mutual funds; within its general category, it has done better than 95 percent of its peers. Municipal bond funds have averaged 5 percent annually over these same five years.

During the past five years, a $10,000 initial investment grew to $13,330 after taxes, assuming a 40 percent income tax bracket (state and federal combined) and a capital gains rate of 20 percent. This means that investors in this fund were able to preserve 98 percent of their total returns. Compared to other funds in the same category, this fund's tax savings are considered to be excellent.

Risk/Volatility   ★★★★

Over the past five years, American Century California High-Yield Municipal Investor Shares has been safer than 95 percent of all municipal bond funds. The fund has underperformed the Lehman Brothers Aggregate Bond Index twice and the Lehman Brothers Municipal Bond Index twice in the past ten years. Consistency of *overperformance* for this fund has been outstanding.

	past 5 years		past 10 years	
worst year	-3.3%	1999	-5.4%	1994
best year	12.5%	2000	18.3%	1995

In the past, American Century California High-Yield Municipal Investor Shares has done better than 90 percent of its peer group during the most recent bull market and outperformed 55 percent of its peer group during the most recent bear market. Consistency, or predictability, of returns for this fund can be described as good. This fund's risk-related return ranks in the top quintile.

Management   ★★★★★
There are 150 fixed-income securities in this $330 million portfolio. The average municipal bond fund today is $160 million in size. Close to 100 percent of the fund's holdings are in bonds. The average maturity of the bonds in this account is twenty years; the weighted coupon rate averages 6 percent. The portfolio's fixed-income holdings can be categorized as medium quality, intermediate-term.

A team has managed this fund for the past fifteen years. Management's success has been due to what it has gone after (e.g., land-secured bonds) as well as what it has stayed away from (e.g., pollution control bonds). There are 109 funds besides California High-Yield Municipal Investor Shares within the American Century family. Overall, the fund family's risk-adjusted performance can be described as very good.

Current Income   ★★★★★
Over the past year, American Century California High-Yield Municipal Investor Shares had a twelve-month yield of 5.2 percent. During this same twelve-month period, the typical municipal bond fund had a yield that averaged 4.4 percent.

Expenses   ★★★★
American Century California High-Yield Municipal Investor Shares's expense ratio is 0.5 percent; it has averaged 0.5 percent annually over the past three calendar years. The average expense ratio for the 2,000 funds in this category is 1.1 percent. This fund's turnover rate over the past year has been 47 percent, while its peer group average has been 45 percent.

Summary
American Century California High-Yield Municipal Investor Shares, a medium-quality, long-term tax-free bond fund, has outperformed 62 percent of all mutual funds over the past three years as well as 95 percent of its peer group over the past five years. Returns over shorter and longer periods have been equally impressive. Risk-adjusted returns have also been outstanding over the past three, five, and ten years. Within its peer group, the fund ranks number one when it comes to performance and also receives high marks in every other area measured. This fund overall rates as one of the very best whether it is compared to other single-state issues or municipal bonds in general. As a side note, this is the only California fund in the book. On a total point basis, this is the number-one fund for its category.

Profile

minimum initial investment $5,000	*IRA accounts available.* . . . . no
subsequent minimum investment . . . $50	*IRA minimum investment* . . . . n/a
available in all 50 states. . . . . yes	*date of inception.* . . . . Dec. 1986
telephone exchanges. . . . . yes	*dividend/income paid.* . . . . monthly
number of funds in family 110	*average credit quality* . . . . AAA

American Funds Tax-Exempt Bond Fund A

333 South Hope Street
Los Angeles, CA 90071
(800) 421-4120
www.americanfunds.com

total return	★★★★
risk reduction	★★★★
management	★★★★
current income	★★★★
expense control	★★★★
symbol AFTEX	20 points
up-market performance	fair
down-market performance	excellent
predictability of returns	very good

Total Return   ★★★★

Over the past five years, American Funds Tax-Exempt Bond Fund A has taken $10,000 and turned it into $13,390 ($11,250 over three years and $17,910 over the past ten years). This translates into an annualized return of 6 percent over the past five years, 4 percent over the past three years, and 6 percent for the decade. Over the past five years, this fund has outperformed 48 percent of all mutual funds; within its general category, it has done better than 89 percent of its peers. Municipal bond funds have averaged 5 percent annually over these same five years.

During the past five years, a $10,000 initial investment grew to $13,330 after taxes, assuming a 40 percent income tax bracket (state and federal combined) and a capital gains rate of 20 percent. This means that investors in this fund were able to preserve 98 percent of their total returns. Compared to other funds in the same category, this fund's tax savings are considered to be excellent.

Risk/Volatility   ★★★★

Over the past five years, American Funds Tax-Exempt Bond Fund A has been safer than 58 percent of all municipal bond funds. Over the past decade, the fund has had two negative years, while the Lehman Brothers Aggregate Bond Index has had two (off 3 percent in 1994 and 1 percent in 1999); the Lehman Brothers Municipal Bond Index also fell twice (off 5 percent in 1994 and 2 percent in 1999). The fund has underperformed the Lehman Brothers Aggregate Bond Index twice and the Lehman Brothers Municipal Bond Index twice in the past ten years. Consistency of *overperformance* for this fund has been very good.

	past 5 years		past 10 years	
worst year	-2.3%	1999	-4.8%	1994
best year	9.7%	2000	17.3%	1995

Over the past five years, the fund's three worst quarters have been second quarter 1999 (-2 percent), third quarter 1999 (0 percent), and fourth quarter 1999 (-1 percent). During the same period, the three best quarters have been second quarter

1997 (3 percent), third quarter 1997 (3 percent), and fourth quarter 2000 (4 percent). In the past, American Funds Tax-Exempt Bond Fund A has done better than 37 percent of its peer group during the most recent bull market and outperformed 90 percent of its peer group during the most recent bear market. Consistency, or predictability, of returns for American Funds Tax-Exempt Bond Fund A can be described as very good. This fund's risk-related return ranks in the top third.

Management   ★★★★
There are 673 fixed-income securities in this $2.3 billion portfolio. The average municipal bond fund today is $160 million in size. Close to 98 percent of the fund's holdings are in bonds. The average maturity of the bonds in this account is eleven years; the weighted coupon rate averages 6 percent. The portfolio's fixed-income holdings can be categorized as intermediate-term, medium-quality debt.

A team has managed this fund for the past eleven years. Management tends to operate conservatively, sticking with medium-term maturities, which represent the "sweet spot" of the bond market (the best risk-adjusted return statistics). There are 103 funds besides Tax-Exempt Bond Fund A within the American Funds family. Overall, the fund family's risk-adjusted performance can be described as very good.

Current Income   ★★★★
Over the past year, American Funds Tax-Exempt Bond Fund A had a twelve-month yield of 4.9 percent. During this same twelve-month period, the typical municipal bond fund had a yield that averaged 4.4 percent.

Expenses   ★★★★
American Funds Tax-Exempt Bond Fund A's expense ratio is 0.7 percent; it has averaged 0.7 percent annually over the past three calendar years. The average expense ratio for the 2,000 funds in this category is 1.1 percent. This fund's turnover rate over the past year has been 29 percent, while its peer group average has been 45 percent.

Summary
This medium-quality, intermediate-term municipal bond fund, has outperformed 61 percent of all mutual funds over the past three years (note: the percentage figure would be much higher if after-tax return figures were used) and 98 percent of its peer group over the past ten years. Returns over shorter and longer periods have also been impressive. Risk-adjusted returns have been very good over the past three, five, and ten years. Within its peer group, the fund scores very highly in every category measured.

Profile

minimum initial investment $250	*IRA accounts available* .... no
subsequent minimum investment ... $50	*IRA minimum investment* .... n/a
available in all 50 states .... yes	*date of inception* .... Oct. 1979
telephone exchanges .... yes	*dividend/income paid* .... monthly
number of funds in family 104	*average credit quality* .... A

Calvert Tax-Free Reserves Limited-Term A

4550 Montgomery Avenue, Suite 1000N
Bethesda, MD 20814
(800) 368-2748
www.calvertgroup.com

total return	★★★
risk reduction	★★★★★
management	★★★★
current income	★★★
expense control	★★★
symbol CTFLX	18 points
up-market performance	very good
down-market performance	fair
predictability of returns	excellent

Total Return   ★★★

Over the past five years, Calvert Tax-Free Reserves Limited-Term A has taken $10,000 and turned it into $12,170 ($11,250 over three years and $14,810 over the past ten years). This translates into an annualized return of 4 percent over the past five years, 4 percent over the past three years, and 4 percent for the decade. Over the past five years, this fund has outperformed 21 percent of all mutual funds; within its general category, it has done better than 18 percent of its peers. Municipal bond funds have averaged 5 percent annually over these same five years.

During the past five years, a $10,000 initial investment grew to $12,170 after taxes, assuming a 40 percent income tax bracket (state and federal combined) and a capital gains rate of 20 percent. This means that investors in this fund were able to preserve 100 percent of their total returns. Compared to other funds in the same category, this fund's tax savings are considered to be excellent.

Risk/Volatility   ★★★★★

Over the past five years, Calvert Tax-Free Reserves Limited-Term A has been safer than 99 percent of all municipal bond funds. Over the past decade, the fund has had no negative years, while the Lehman Brothers Aggregate Bond Index has had two (off 3 percent in 1994 and 1 percent in 1999); the Lehman Brothers Municipal Bond Index also fell twice (off 5 percent in 1994 and 2 percent in 1999). The fund has underperformed the Lehman Brothers Aggregate Bond Index twice and the Lehman Brothers Municipal Bond Index twice in the past ten years. Consistency of *overperformance* for this fund has been good.

	past 5 years		past 10 years	
worst year	2.9%	1999	2.4%	1994
best year	4.5%	2000	5.6%	1995

In the past, Calvert Tax-Free Reserves Limited-Term A has done better than over 99 percent of its peer group during the most recent bull market and outperformed just 3 percent of its peer group during the most recent bear market.

Consistency, or predictability, of returns for Calvert Tax-Free Reserves Limited-Term A can be described as excellent. This fund's risk-related return ranks in the top quintile.

Management   ★★★★

There are seventy fixed-income securities in this $670 million portfolio. The average municipal bond fund today is $160 million in size. Close to 80 percent of the fund's holdings are in bonds. The average maturity of the bonds in this account is 0.7 years; the weighted coupon rate averages 5 percent. The portfolio's fixed-income holdings can be categorized as short-term, medium-quality debt.

A team has managed this fund for the past fourteen years. Managers Rochat, Martini, and Dailey have put together a portfolio that has virtually no volatility by sticking with fixed-income securities that are close to maturing, thereby making the portfolio much less susceptible to interest-rate risk. There are forty-three funds besides Tax-Free Reserves Limited-Term A within the Calvert family. Overall, the fund family's risk-adjusted performance can be described as good to very good.

Current Income   ★★★

Over the past year, Calvert Tax-Free Reserves Limited-Term A had a twelve-month yield of 4.1 percent. During this same twelve-month period, the typical municipal bond fund had a yield that averaged 4.4 percent.

Expenses   ★★★

Calvert Tax-Free Reserves Limited-Term A's expense ratio is 0.7 percent; it has averaged 0.7 percent annually over the past three calendar years. The average expense ratio for the 2,000 funds in this category is 1.1 percent. This fund's turnover rate over the past year has been 82 percent, while its peer group average has been 45 percent.

Summary

Calvert Tax-Free Reserves Limited-Term Portfolio A, a medium-quality, short-term municipal bond fund, has outperformed 51 percent of all mutual funds over the past three years (note: the percentage figure would be much higher if after-tax return figures were used) as well as half of its peer group over the same period. Risk-adjusted returns have been superb over the past three and five years. Within its peer group, the fund easily ranks number one when it comes to low risk and predictability of returns (the price paid for lower yields). It would be difficult to find a better choice for the tax-conscious investor who wants a higher return than money market accounts but does not want to take on much more risk.

Profile

minimum initial investment $2,000	*IRA accounts available* . . . . no
subsequent minimum investment . . $250	*IRA minimum investment* . . . . n/a
available in all 50 states . . . . yes	*date of inception* . . . . Mar. 1981
telephone exchanges . . . . yes	*dividend/income paid* . . . . monthly
number of funds in family 44	*average credit quality* . . . . A

Limited Term New York Municipal A
350 Linden Oaks
Rochester, NY 14625
(800) 525-7048
www.oppenheimerfunds.com

total return	★★★★
risk reduction	★★★★★
management	★★★★★
current income	★★★★
expense control	★★★★
symbol LTNYX	22 points
up-market performance	good
down-market performance	good
predictability of returns	excellent

Total Return   ★★★★

Over the past five years, Limited Term New York Municipal A has taken $10,000 and turned it into $12,770 ($11,250 over three years and $17,910 over the past ten years). This translates into an annualized return of 5 percent over the past five years, 4 percent over the past three years, and 6 percent for the decade. Over the past five years, this fund has outperformed 39 percent of all mutual funds; within its general category, it has done better than 99 percent of its peers. Municipal bond funds have averaged 5 percent annually over these same five years.

During the past five years, a $10,000 initial investment grew to $12,770 after taxes, assuming a 40 percent income tax bracket (state and federal combined) and a capital gains rate of 20 percent. This means that investors in this fund were able to preserve 100 percent of their total returns. Compared to other funds in the same category, this fund's tax savings are considered to be excellent.

Risk/Volatility   ★★★★★

Over the past five years, Limited Term New York Municipal A has been safer than 55 percent of all municipal bond funds. Over the past decade, the fund has had two negative years, while the Lehman Brothers Aggregate Bond Index has had two (off 3 percent in 1994 and 1 percent in 1999); the Lehman Brothers Municipal Bond Index also fell twice (off 5 percent in 1994 and 2 percent in 1999). The fund has underperformed the Lehman Brothers Aggregate Bond Index twice and the Lehman Brothers Municipal Bond Index twice in the past ten years. Consistency of overperformance for this fund has been good.

	past 5 years		past 10 years	
worst year	-0.9%	1999	-0.9%	1999
best year	8.0%	1997	10.6%	1992

Over the past five years, the fund's three worst quarters have been second quarter 1999 (-1 percent), fourth quarter 1999 (0 percent), and third quarter 1999 (0 percent). In the past, Limited Term New York Municipal A has done better than

94 percent of its peer group during the most recent bull market and outperformed just 19 percent of its peer group during the most recent bear market. Consistency, or predictability, of returns for Limited Term New York Municipal A can be described as excellent. This fund's risk-related return ranks in the top quintile.

Management ★★★★★
There are 850 fixed-income securities in this $1.1 billion portfolio. The average municipal bond fund today is $160 million in size. Close to 100 percent of the fund's holdings are in bonds. The average maturity of the bonds in this account is thirteen years; the weighted coupon rate averages 6 percent. The portfolio's fixed-income holdings can be categorized as long term, medium quality.

Ronald Fielding and Anthony Tanner have managed this fund for the past ten years. Managers Fielding and Tanner concentrate on current yield and stability of principal. Instead of trying to guess the direction of interest rates, management looks for "unearthed value" (mispriced bonds). Lead manager Fielding is not afraid to load up on higher-yielding callable bonds, correctly reasoning that the costs to the issuer to call in a bond, coupled with unsophisticated treasurers, are such that any risk in this area is minimal. There are six funds besides Limited Term New York Municipal A within the Rochester family. Overall, the fund family's risk-adjusted performance can be described as very good. Rochester has been part of the Oppenheimer group of funds for a number of years. Oppenheimer is a huge fund family.

Current Income ★★★★
Over the past year, Limited Term New York Municipal A had a twelve-month yield of 4.8 percent. During this same twelve-month period, the typical municipal bond fund had a yield that averaged 4.4 percent.

Expenses ★★★★
Limited Term New York Municipal A's expense ratio is 0.8 percent; it has averaged 0.8 percent annually over the past three calendar years. The average expense ratio for the 2,000 funds in this category is 1.1 percent. This fund's turnover rate over the past year has been 37 percent, while its peer group average has been 45 percent.

Summary
Limited Term New York Municipal A, a medium-quality, long-term municipal bond fund, has outperformed close to half of all mutual funds over the past three and five years as well as 99 percent of its peer group over the past five and ten years. Risk-adjusted returns have also been outstanding over the past three, five, and ten years. This is the only New York fund in the book.

Profile
minimum initial investment $1,000	IRA accounts available. . . . . no
subsequent minimum investment . . . $25	IRA minimum investment . . . . n/a
available in all 50 states. . . . . yes	date of inception . . . . Sept. 1991
telephone exchanges. . . . . yes	dividend/income paid. . . . . monthly
number of funds in family 7	average credit quality . . . . AAA

Scudder High-Yield Tax-Free S

Two International Place
Boston, MA 02110
(800) 621-1048
www.scudder.com

total return	★★★★★
risk reduction	★★★★
management	★★★★★
current income	★★★★★
expense control	★★★
symbol SHYTX	22 points
up-market performance	fair
down-market performance	excellent
predictability of returns	very good

Total Return   ★★★★★

Over the past five years, Scudder High-Yield Tax-Free S has taken $10,000 and turned it into $13,390 ($11,250 over three years and $19,680 over the past ten years). This translates into an annualized return of 6 percent over the past five years, 4 percent over the past three years, and 7 percent for the decade. Over the past five years, this fund has outperformed 57 percent of all mutual funds; within its general category, it has done better than 97 percent of its peers. Municipal bond funds have averaged 5 percent annually over these same five years.

During the past five years, a $10,000 initial investment grew to $13,390 after taxes, assuming a 40 percent income tax bracket (state and federal combined) and a capital gains rate of 20 percent. This means that investors in this fund were able to preserve 100 percent of their total returns. Compared to other funds in the same category, this fund's tax savings are considered to be excellent.

Risk/Volatility   ★★★★

Over the past five years, Scudder High-Yield Tax-Free S has been safer than 92 percent of all municipal bond funds. Over the past decade, the fund has had two negative years, while the Lehman Brothers Aggregate Bond Index has had two (off 3 percent in 1994 and 1 percent in 1999); the Lehman Brothers Municipal Bond Index also fell twice (off 5 percent in 1994 and 2 percent in 1999). The fund has underperformed the Lehman Brothers Aggregate Bond Index twice and the Lehman Brothers Municipal Bond Index twice in the past ten years. Consistency of *overperformance* for this fund has been very good.

	past 5 years		past 10 years	
worst year	-2.2%	1999	-8.4%	1994
best year	12.0%	1997	19.3%	1995

In the past, Scudder High-Yield Tax-Free S has done better than 31 percent of its peer group during the most recent bull market and outperformed 79 percent of its peer group during the most recent bear market. Consistency, or predictability, of returns for Scudder High-Yield Tax-Free S can be described as very good. This fund's risk-related return ranks in the top quintile.

Management   ★★★★★

There are 185 fixed-income securities in this $540 million portfolio. The average municipal bond fund today is $160 million in size. Close to 100 percent of the fund's holdings are in bonds. The average maturity of the bonds in this account is twelve years; the weighted coupon rate averages 5 percent. The portfolio's fixed-income holdings can be categorized as long-term, medium-quality debt.

Philip Condon and Rebecca Wilson have managed this fund for the past ten years. Managers Condon and Wilson have not sacrificed total return for current income. There are 198 funds besides High-Yield Tax-Free S within the Scudder family. Overall, the fund family's risk-adjusted performance can be described as good.

Current Income   ★★★★★

Over the past year, Scudder High-Yield Tax-Free S had a twelve-month yield of 5.5 percent. During this same twelve-month period, the typical municipal bond fund had a yield that averaged 4.4 percent.

Expenses   ★★★

Scudder High-Yield Tax-Free S's expense ratio is 0.9 percent; it has averaged 0.9 percent annually over the past three calendar years. The average expense ratio for the 2,000 funds in this category is 1.1 percent. This fund's turnover rate over the past year has been 62 percent, while its peer group average has been 45 percent.

Summary

Scudder High-Yield Tax-Free S, a medium-quality, short-term municipal bond fund, has outperformed 55 percent of all mutual funds over the past five years (note: the percentage figure would be much higher if after-tax return figures were used) as well as 97 percent of its peer group over the past five and ten years. Returns over shorter periods have also been impressive. Risk-adjusted returns have ranged between very good and exceptional over the past three, five, and ten years. Within its peer group, the fund comes very close to tying for first place for total return. It also scores well in the areas of low risk and predictability of returns. For current income, the fund ranks number one. The portfolio has a very high yield, yet its underlying principal has not been jeopardized. This is a surprisingly small fund, given its exemplary track record.

Profile

minimum initial investment $2,500	*IRA accounts available* . . . . yes
subsequent minimum investment . . $100	*IRA minimum investment* $1,000
available in all 50 states . . . . yes	*date of inception* . . . . Jan. 1987
telephone exchanges . . . . yes	*dividend/income paid* . . . . monthly
number of funds in family 199	*average credit quality* . . . . A

T. Rowe Price Tax-Free Short-Intermediate

100 East Pratt Street
Baltimore, MD 21202
(800) 638-5660
www.troweprice.com

total return	★★★★
risk reduction	★★★★★
management	★★★★★
current income	★★★
expense control	★★★★
symbol PRFSX	21 points
up-market performance	good
down-market performance	very good
predictability of returns	excellent

Total Return   ★★★★

Over the past five years, T. Rowe Price Tax-Free Short-Intermediate has taken $10,000 and turned it into $12,770 ($11,250 over three years and $16,290 over the past ten years). This translates into an annualized return of 5 percent over the past five years, 4 percent over the past three years, and 5 percent for the decade. Over the past five years, this fund has outperformed 31 percent of all mutual funds; within its general category, it has done better than 82 percent of its peers. Municipal bond funds have averaged 5 percent annually over these same five years.

During the past five years, a $10,000 initial investment grew to $12,750 after taxes, assuming a 40 percent income tax bracket (state and federal combined) and a capital gains rate of 20 percent. This means that investors in this fund were able to preserve 99 percent of their total returns. Compared to other funds in the same category, this fund's tax savings are considered to be excellent.

Risk/Volatility   ★★★★★

Over the past five years, T. Rowe Price Tax-Free Short-Intermediate has been safer than 51 percent of all municipal bond funds. Over the past decade, the fund has had no negative years, while the Lehman Brothers Aggregate Bond Index has had two (off 3 percent in 1994 and 1 percent in 1999); the Lehman Brothers Municipal Bond Index also fell twice (off 5 percent in 1994 and 2 percent in 1999). The fund has underperformed the Lehman Brothers Aggregate Bond Index twice and the Lehman Brothers Municipal Bond Index twice in the past ten years. Consistency of *overperformance* for this fund has been very good.

	past 5 years		past 10 years	
worst year	1.0%	1999	0.3%	1994
best year	6.8%	2000	8.1%	1995

Over the past five years, the fund's three worst quarters have been second quarter 1999 (-1 percent), fourth quarter 1999 (0 percent), and first quarter 1997 (0 percent). During the same period, the three best quarters have been fourth quarter

2000 (2 percent), first quarter 2001 (2 percent), and third quarter 2001 (2 percent). In the past, T. Rowe Price Tax-Free Short-Intermediate has done better than 97 percent of its peer group during the most recent bull market and outperformed 32 percent of its peer group during the most recent bear market. Consistency, or predictability, of returns for T. Rowe Price Tax-Free Short-Intermediate can be described as excellent. This fund's risk-related return ranks in the top quintile.

Management   ★★★★★
There are 180 fixed-income securities in this $450 million portfolio. The average municipal bond fund today is $160 million in size. Close to 100 percent of the fund's holdings are in bonds. The average maturity of the bonds in this account is four years; the weighted coupon rate averages 6 percent. The portfolio's fixed-income holdings can be categorized as short-term, high-quality debt.

Manager Charles Hill looks for underappreciated issues while maintaining a conservative approach. There are eighty-four funds besides Tax-Free Short-Intermediate within the T. Rowe Price family. Overall, the fund family's risk-adjusted performance can be described as good to very good.

Current Income   ★★★
Over the past year, T. Rowe Price Tax-Free Short-Intermediate had a twelve-month yield of 4 percent. During this same twelve-month period, the typical municipal bond fund had a yield that averaged 4.4 percent.

Expenses   ★★★★
T. Rowe Price Tax-Free Short-Intermediate's expense ratio is 0.5 percent; it has averaged 0.5 percent annually over the past three calendar years. The average expense ratio for the 2,000 funds in this category is 1.1 percent. This fund's turnover rate over the past year has been 41 percent, while its peer group average has been 45 percent.

Summary
T. Rowe Price Tax-Free Short-Intermediate, a high-quality, short-term municipal bond fund, has outperformed 60 percent of all mutual funds over the past three years (note: the percentage figure would be much higher if after-tax return figures were used) as well as 94 percent of its peer group over the same period. Risk-adjusted returns have also been superb over the past three and five years. Within its peer group, the fund ranks number one when it comes to predictability of returns and low risk. Expense control is also quite good. The fund family has a number of highly regarded tax-free offerings.

Profile

minimum initial investment $2,500	IRA accounts available . . . . yes
subsequent minimum investment . . $100	IRA minimum investment $1,000
available in all 50 states. . . . . yes	date of inception. . . . . Dec. 1983
telephone exchanges. . . . . yes	dividend/income paid. . . . . monthly
number of funds in family 85	average credit quality. . . . . AA

USAA Tax-Exempt Short-Term

USAA Building
San Antonio, TX 78288
(800) 382-8722
www.usaa.com

total return	★★★★
risk reduction	★★★★★
management	★★★★★
current income	★★★
expense control	★★★★★
symbol USSTX	22 points
up-market performance	good
down-market performance	good
predictability of returns	excellent

Total Return   ★★★★

Over the past five years, USAA Tax-Exempt Short-Term has taken $10,000 and turned it into $12,770 ($11,250 over three years and $16,290 over the past ten years). This translates into an annualized return of 5 percent over the past five years, 4 percent over the past three years, and 5 percent for the decade. Over the past five years, this fund has outperformed 32 percent of all mutual funds; within its general category, it has done better than 87 percent of its peers. Municipal bond funds have averaged 5 percent annually over these same five years.

During the past five years, a $10,000 initial investment grew to $12,770 after taxes, assuming a 40 percent income tax bracket (state and federal combined) and a capital gains rate of 20 percent. This means that investors in this fund were able to preserve 100 percent of their total returns. Compared to other funds in the same category, this fund's tax savings are considered to be excellent.

Risk/Volatility   ★★★★★

Over the past five years, USAA Tax-Exempt Short-Term has been safer than 85 percent of all municipal bond funds. Over the past decade, the fund has had no negative years, while the Lehman Brothers Aggregate Bond Index has had two (off 3 percent in 1994 and 1 percent in 1999); the Lehman Brothers Municipal Bond Index also fell twice (off 5 percent in 1994 and 2 percent in 1999). The fund has underperformed the Lehman Brothers Aggregate Bond Index twice and the Lehman Brothers Municipal Bond Index twice in the past ten years. Consistency of *overperformance* for this fund has been good.

	past 5 years		past 10 years	
worst year	1.8%	1999	0.8%	1994
best year	6.0%	2000	8.1%	1995

In the past, USAA Tax-Exempt Short-Term has done better than 97 percent of its peer group during the most recent bull market and outperformed just 13 percent of its peer group during the most recent bear market. Consistency, or predictability, of returns for USAA Tax-Exempt Short-Term can be described as excellent. This fund's risk-related return ranks in the top quintile.

Management ★★★★★

There are 235 fixed-income securities in this $1.1 billion portfolio. The average municipal bond fund today is $160 million in size. Close to 95 percent of the fund's holdings are in bonds. The average maturity of the bonds in this account is two years; the weighted coupon rate averages 5 percent. The portfolio's fixed-income holdings can be categorized as short-term, high-quality debt.

Clifford Gladson has managed this fund for the past eight years. Manager Gladson is able to get quite a high current yield from a short-term fund; his secret is owning quite a bit of single A and BBB rated paper. There are thirty-two funds besides Tax-Exempt Short-Term within the USAA family. Overall, the fund family's risk-adjusted performance can be described as good to very good.

Current Income ★★★

Over the past year, USAA Tax-Exempt Short-Term had a twelve-month yield of 4.1 percent. During this same twelve-month period, the typical municipal bond fund had a yield that averaged 4.4 percent.

Expenses ★★★★★

USAA Tax-Exempt Short-Term's expense ratio is 0.4 percent; it has averaged 0.4 percent annually over the past three calendar years. The average expense ratio for the 2,000 funds in this category is 1.1 percent. This fund's turnover rate over the past year has been 19 percent, while its peer group average has been 45 percent.

Summary

USAA Tax-Exempt Short-Term, a high-quality, short-term municipal bond fund, has outperformed 91 percent of all mutual funds over the past three years (note: the percentage figure would be much higher if after-tax return figures were used) as well as 91 percent of its peer group over the same period. Returns over longer periods have also been impressive. Risk-adjusted returns have also been superb over the past three, five, and ten years. Within its peer group, the fund ranks number two when it comes to low risk and number one when it comes to pre-dictability of returns. Total return and expense ratio figures are also very good. This is one of the most consistent tax-free offerings to be found anywhere. Most years, the fund's performance puts it in the top quartile of its group—a pretty amazing accomplishment when you consider that this short-term portfolio is competing against some very long-term offerings.

Profile

minimum initial investment $3,000	IRA accounts available. . . . . no
subsequent minimum investment . . . $50	IRA minimum investment . . . . n/a
available in all 50 states. . . . . yes	date of inception. . . . . Mar. 1982
telephone exchanges. . . . . yes	dividend/income paid. . . . . monthly
number of funds in family 33	average credit quality. . . . . AA

Vanguard Florida Insured Long-Term Tax-Exempt

Vanguard Financial Centre
P.O. Box 2600
Valley Forge, PA19482
(800) 662-7447
www.vanguard.com

total return	★★★★★
risk reduction	★★★
management	★★★★★
current income	★★★★
expense control	★★★★★
symbol VFLTX	22 points
up-market performance	fair
down-market performance	excellent
predictability of returns	good

Total Return   ★★★★★

Over the past five years, Vanguard Florida Insured Long-Term Tax-Exempt has taken $10,000 and turned it into $13,390 ($11,580 over three years). This translates into an annualized return of 6 percent over the past five years and 5 percent over the past three years. Over the past five years, this fund has outperformed 55 percent of all mutual funds; within its general category, it has done better than 98 percent of its peers. Municipal bond funds have averaged 5 percent annually over these same five years.

During the past five years, a $10,000 initial investment grew to $13,370 after taxes, assuming a 40 percent income tax bracket (state and federal combined) and a capital gains rate of 20 percent. This means that investors in this fund were able to preserve 99 percent of their total returns. Compared to other funds in the same category, this fund's tax savings are considered to be excellent.

Risk/Volatility   ★★★

Over the past five years, Vanguard Florida Insured Long-Term Tax-Exempt has been safer than 30 percent of all municipal bond funds. Over the past decade, the fund has had two negative years, while the Lehman Brothers Aggregate Bond Index has had two (off 3 percent in 1994 and 1 percent in 1999); the Lehman Brothers Municipal Bond Index also fell twice (off 5 percent in 1994 and 2 percent in 1999). The fund has underperformed the Lehman Brothers Aggregate Bond Index twice and the Lehman Brothers Municipal Bond Index twice in the past ten years. Consistency of *overperformance* for this fund has been outstanding.

	past 5 years		past 10 years	
worst year	-2.8%	1999	-4.7%	1994
best year	13.2%	2000	17.7%	1995

In the past, Vanguard Florida Insured Long-Term Tax-Exempt has done better than 43 percent of its peer group during the most recent bull market and outperformed

95 percent of its peer group during the most recent bear market. Consistency, or predictability, of returns for Vanguard Florida Insured Long-Term Tax-Exempt can be described as good. This fund's risk-related return ranks in the top third.

Management   ★★★★★

There are 180 fixed-income securities in this $810 million portfolio. The average municipal bond fund today is $160 million in size. Close to 100 percent of the fund's holdings are in bonds. The average maturity of the bonds in this account is twelve years; the weighted coupon rate averages 5 percent. The portfolio's fixed-income holdings can be categorized as long-term, high-quality debt.

Ian MacKinnon and Reid Smith have managed this fund for the past ten years. Managers MacKinnon and Smith keep overhead costs so low that they are able to boost shareholder returns by almost an entire percentage point each year. By investing in insured bonds, management has pretty much eliminated any default risk, yet total return and yield have not suffered. There are 154 funds besides Florida Insured Long-Term Tax-Exempt within the Vanguard family. Overall, the fund family's risk-adjusted performance can be described as very good.

Current Income   ★★★★

Over the past year, Vanguard Florida Insured Long-Term Tax-Exempt had a twelve-month yield of 4.8 percent. During this same twelve-month period, the typical municipal bond fund had a yield that averaged 4.4 percent.

Expenses   ★★★★★

Vanguard Florida Insured Long-Term Tax-Exempt's expense ratio is 0.2 percent; it has averaged 0.2 percent annually over the past three calendar years. The average expense ratio for the 2,000 funds in this category is 1.1 percent. This fund's turnover rate over the past year has been 34 percent, while its peer group average has been 45 percent.

Summary

Vanguard Florida Insured Long-Term Tax-Exempt, a high-quality, long-term municipal bond fund, has outperformed 67 percent of all mutual funds over the past three years as well as 99 percent of its peer group over the same period. Returns over longer periods have been equally impressive. Risk-adjusted returns have been very good. Within its peer group, the fund ties for first place, along with another Vanguard offering, for the fund with the lowest expenses; turnover is extremely small also. The fund also receives the highest marks possible for returns.

Profile

minimum initial investment $3,000	*IRA accounts available* . . . . yes
subsequent minimum investment . . $100	*IRA minimum investment* $1,000
available in all 50 states. . . . . yes	*date of inception* . . . . Sept. 1992
telephone exchanges. . . . . yes	*dividend/income paid.* . . . . monthly
number of funds in family 155	*average credit quality* . . . . AAA

Vanguard Intermediate-Term Tax-Exempt

Vanguard Financial Centre
P.O. Box 2600
Valley Forge, PA 19482
(800) 662-7447
www.vanguard.com

total return	★★★★
risk reduction	★★★★
management	★★★★
current income	★★★★
expense control	★★★★★
symbol VWITX	21 points
up-market performance	fair
down-market performance	excellent
predictability of returns	very good

Total Return   ★★★★

Over the past five years, Vanguard Intermediate-Term Tax-Exempt has taken $10,000 and turned it into $12,770 ($11,250 over three years and $17,910 over the past ten years). This translates into an annualized return of 5 percent over the past five years, 4 percent over the past three years, and 6 percent for the decade. Over the past five years, this fund has outperformed 42 percent of all mutual funds; within its general category, it has done better than 79 percent of its peers. Municipal bond funds have averaged 5 percent annually over these same five years.

During the past five years, a $10,000 initial investment grew to $12,750 after taxes, assuming a 40 percent income tax bracket (state and federal combined) and a capital gains rate of 20 percent. This means that investors in this fund were able to preserve 99 percent of their total returns. Compared to other funds in the same category, this fund's tax savings are considered to be exceptional.

Risk/Volatility   ★★★★

Over the past five years, Vanguard Intermediate-Term Tax-Exempt has been safer than 81 percent of all municipal bond funds. Over the past decade, the fund has had two negative years, while the Lehman Brothers Aggregate Bond Index has had two (off 3 percent in 1994 and 1 percent in 1999); the Lehman Brothers Municipal Bond Index also fell twice (off 5 percent in 1994 and 2 percent in 1999). The fund has underperformed the Lehman Brothers Aggregate Bond Index twice and the Lehman Brothers Municipal Bond Index twice in the past ten years. Consistency of *overperformance* for this fund has been outstanding.

	past 5 years		past 10 years	
worst year	-0.5%	1999	-2.1%	1994
best year	9.2%	2000	13.6%	1995

Over the past five years, the fund's three worst quarters have been second quarter 1999 (-2 percent), first quarter 1997 (0 percent), and fourth quarter 1999

(0 percent). During the same period, the three best quarters have been fourth quarter 2000 (3 percent), second quarter 1997 (3 percent), and third quarter 1998 (3 percent). In the past, Vanguard Intermediate-Term Tax-Exempt has done better than 61 percent of its peer group during the most recent bull market and outperformed 65 percent of its peer group during the most recent bear market. Consistency, or predictability, of returns for Vanguard Intermediate-Term Tax-Exempt can be described as very good. This fund's risk-related return ranks in the top quintile.

Management   ★★★★
There are 1,050 fixed-income securities in this $6.7 billion portfolio. The average municipal bond fund today is $160 million in size. Close to 98 percent of the fund's holdings are in bonds. The average maturity of the bonds in this account is twelve years; the weighted coupon rate averages 6 percent. The portfolio's fixed-income holdings can be categorized as intermediate-term, high-quality debt.

Ian MacKinnon and Christopher Ryon have managed this fund for the past thirteen years. Managers MacKinnon and Ryon work within a self-imposed, fairly narrow, interest-rate range in order to make sure that there are no surprises. There are 154 funds besides Intermediate-Term Tax-Exempt within the Vanguard family. Overall, the fund family's risk-adjusted performance can be described as very good.

Current Income   ★★★★
Over the past year, Vanguard Intermediate-Term Tax-Exempt had a twelve-month yield of 4.8 percent. During this same twelve-month period, the typical municipal bond fund had a yield that averaged 4.4 percent.

Expenses   ★★★★★
Vanguard Intermediate-Term Tax-Exempt's expense ratio is 0.2 percent; it has averaged 0.2 percent annually over the past three calendar years. The average expense ratio for the 2,000 funds in this category is 1.1 percent. This fund's turnover rate over the past year has been 17 percent, while its peer group average has been 45 percent.

Summary
Vanguard Intermediate-Term Tax-Exempt, a high-quality, medium-term municipal bond fund, has outperformed 64 percent of all mutual funds over the past three years as well as 88 percent of its peer group over the same period. Returns over longer periods have been equally impressive. Risk-adjusted returns have also been superb. Within its peer group, the fund ranks number one when it comes to low expenses and low turnover. For tax-free income investors, this is one of the best choices.

Profile

minimum initial investment $3,000	*IRA accounts available* . . . . yes
subsequent minimum investment . . $100	*IRA minimum investment* $1,000
available in all 50 states. . . . . yes	*date of inception* . . . . Sept. 1977
telephone exchanges. . . . . yes	*dividend/income paid*. . . . . monthly
number of funds in family 155	*average credit quality*. . . . . AA

Real Estate Funds

Real estate, financial, health care, metals, natural resources, and technology represent some of the most popular sectors for investors. These industry-specific mutual funds hone in on a particular group of stocks and invest accordingly. Each sector has its pluses and minuses; certain sectors, such as technology and metals, are much more volatile than others, such as utilities and natural resources. In the case of real estate, a potential problem for prospective investors is overweighting; that is, committing too much of an overall portfolio to one particular asset group. With this particular sector, defining one's holdings can be difficult.

Securities investors who own residential property must ask themselves if they view their home as an investment, a place to live, or both. Since most people would describe their home as their largest or second-largest asset, the decision as to whether it is "an investment" becomes important. If you view your home as an investment, real estate funds are probably not for you. Similarly, if you own any vacant land or income-producing property, you may already have enough, or even too much, in this one category. However, the case could be made that a real-estate fund would provide a homeowner with broad diversification within the category. Real estate funds invest in real estate investment trusts (REITs) that are diversified by category (shopping centers, medical buildings, apartment buildings, etc.) or location (the West, the South, etc.). In addition, if a portfolio were to be weighted too much in any category, real estate would be more desirable than most other sectors.

The risk level for REITs and real estate funds vary significantly. A fund that specializes in mortgages is usually going to be more stable than one that owns land that is yet to be developed. A portfolio comprised of properties from one geographical area is conceptually at greater risk than one that owns land across the country. A fund that owns triple net leased properties is more conservative than a portfolio of apartment buildings.

Over the past fifteen years (ending December 31, 2001), real estate funds have underperformed common stocks by 4.8 percent per year, as measured by the Standard & Poor's 500 Stock Index. From 1987 through 2001, real estate funds averaged 8.9 percent, while common stocks averaged 13.7 percent compounded per year. A $10,000 investment in real estate funds grew to $403,672 over the past fifteen years; a similar initial investment in the S & P 500 grew to $68,900.

During the past three years, real estate funds have outperformed the S & P 500 by 11.2 percent per year. Over the past five years, this fund category has underperformed the S & P 500 by an average of 4.5 percent per year. Average turnover during the past three years has been 56 percent.

The price-earnings (p/e) ratio is 20 for the typical real estate fund, versus 31 for the S & P 500. The typical stock in these portfolios is only four percent the size of the average stock in the S & P 500. The average beta is 0.2, which means the group has a market-related risk that is 80 percent lower than the S & P 500. There is more than $335 billion in all real estate funds combined. The average real estate fund has an annual income stream of 4 percent. The typical annual expense ratio for this group is 1.7 percent.

Over the past three years, real estate funds have had an average compound return of 10.1 percent per year. The annual return has been 6.2 percent for the past five years, 10.0 percent for the past decade, and 8.9 percent per year for the past fifteen years. The standard deviation for this category has been 15 percent over the past three years, versus 17 percent for the S & P 500.

Columbia Real Estate Equity
1301 SW Fifth Avenue
P.O. Box 1350
Portland, OR 97207
(800) 547-1707
www.columbiafunds.com

total return	★★★★
risk reduction	★★★★★
management	★★★★★
tax minimization	★★★★
expense control	★★★★★
symbol CREEX	23 points
up-market performance	good
down-market performance	good
predictability of returns	excellent

Total Return   ★★★★
Over the past five years, Columbia Real Estate Equity has taken $10,000 and turned it into $14,700 ($13,310 over three years). This translates into an annualized return of 8 percent over the past five years and 10 percent over the past three years. Over the past five years, this fund has outperformed 82 percent of all mutual funds; within its general category, it has done better than 90 percent of its peers. Real estate funds have averaged 6 percent annually over these same five years.

Risk/Volatility   ★★★★★
Over the past five years, Columbia Real Estate Equity has been safer than 71 percent of all real estate funds. Over the past decade, the fund has had two negative years, while the S & P 500 has had two (off 9 percent in 2000 and 12 percent in 2001); the Wilshire REIT Index also fell twice (off 3 percent in 1999 and 17 percent in 1998). The fund has underperformed the S & P 500 twice and the Wilshire REIT Index twice in the past ten years. Consistency of *overperformance* for this fund has been good.

	past 5 years		past 10 years	
worst year	-11.9%	1998	-11.9%	1998
best year	29.3%	2000	40.2%	1996

Over the past five years, the fund's three worst quarters have been third quarter 1998 (-8 percent), third quarter 1999 (-8 percent), and second quarter 1998 (-5 percent). During the same period, the three best quarters have been third quarter 1997 (14 percent), second quarter 2000 (11 percent), and second quarter 2001 (10 percent). In the past, Columbia Real Estate Equity has done better than 68 percent of its peer group during the most recent bull market and outperformed 20 percent of its peer group during the most recent bear market. Consistency, or predictability, of returns for Columbia Real Estate Equity can be described as excellent. This fund's risk-related return ranks in the top third.

Management   ★★★★★
There are thirty stocks in this $500 million portfolio. The average real estate fund today is $86 million in size. Close to 100 percent of the fund's holdings are in stocks. The stocks in this portfolio have an average p/e ratio of 19 and a median market capitalization of $3 billion. The ten largest holdings compose 63 percent of the fund's total assets. The portfolio's equity holdings can be categorized as mid-cap and value-oriented issues.

David Jellison has managed this fund for the past eight years. Manager Jellison is loyal to his portfolio holdings, using price declines to increase holdings of his favorite equities. There are nineteen funds besides Real Estate Equity within the Columbia family. Overall, the fund family's risk-adjusted performance can be described as good to very good.

Tax Minimization   ★★★★
During the past five years, a $10,000 initial investment grew to $13,480 after taxes, assuming a 40 percent income tax bracket (state and federal combined) and a capital gains rate of 20 percent. This means that investors in this fund were able to preserve 74 percent of their total returns. Compared to other equity funds in the same category, this fund's tax savings are considered to be very good.

Expenses   ★★★★★
Columbia Real Estate Equity's expense ratio is 1 percent; it has averaged 1 percent annually over the past three calendar years. The average expense ratio for the 150 funds in this category is 1.7 percent. This fund's turnover rate over the past year has been 25 percent, while its peer group average has been 56 percent.

Summary
Columbia Real Estate Equity, a mid-cap value fund, has outperformed 86 percent of all mutual funds over the past three years as well as 90 percent of its sector peer group over the past five years. Risk-adjusted returns have been very good over the past three and five years. Within its peer group, the fund ranks number one when it comes to predictability of returns, low expenses, and low turnover. This portfolio outperformed the S & P 500 in 2000 by 38 percentage points. This portfolio's alpha, which measures excess returns per unit of risk taken, as measured against the fund's benchmark index, is slightly negative.

Profile
minimum initial investment $1,000	*IRA accounts available* . . . . yes
subsequent minimum investment . . $100	*IRA minimum investment* $1,000
available in all 50 states. . . . . yes	*date of inception* . . . . Apr. 1994
telephone exchanges. . . . . yes	*dividend/income paid* . . . . quarterly
number of funds in family 20	*largest sector weighting* . . . . financials

Security Capital U.S. Real Estate
11 South LaSalle Street
2nd Floor
Chicago, IL 60603
(888) 732-8748
www.securitycapital.com

total return	★★★★★
risk reduction	★★★★★
management	★★★★★
tax minimization	★★★★★
expense control	★★★
symbol SUSIX	23 points
up-market performance	good
down-market performance	excellent
predictability of returns	excellent

Total Return   ★★★★★
Over the past five years, Security Capital U.S. Real Estate has taken $10,000 and turned it into $16,110 ($14,820 over three years). This translates into an annualized return of 10 percent over the past five years and 14 percent over the past three years. Over the past three years, this fund has outperformed 93 percent of all mutual funds; within its general category, it has done better than 98 percent of its peers. Real estate funds have averaged 6 percent annually over these same five years.

Risk/Volatility   ★★★★★
Over the past three years, Security Capital U.S. Real Estate has been safer than 71 percent of all real estate funds. Over the past decade, the fund has had one negative year, while the S & P 500 has had two (off 9 percent in 2000 and 12 percent in 2001); the Wilshire REIT Index also fell twice (off 3 percent in 1999 and 17 percent in 1998). The fund has underperformed the S & P 500 twice and the Wilshire REIT Index twice in the past ten years. Consistency of *overperformance* for this fund has been good.

	past 5 years		past 10 years	
worst year	-11.9%	1998	-11.9%	1998
best year	35.8%	2000	35.8%	2000

Over the past five years, the fund's three worst quarters have been third quarter 1998 (-10 percent), third quarter 1999 (-8 percent), and second quarter 1998 (-6 percent). During the same period, the three best quarters have been third quarter 1997 (17 percent), second quarter 1999 (14 percent), and second quarter 2000 (12 percent). In the past, Security Capital U.S. Real Estate has done better than just 16 percent of its peer group during the most recent bull market and outperformed 88 percent of its peer group during the most recent bear market. Consistency, or predictability, of returns for Security Capital U.S. Real Estate can be described as excellent. This fund's risk-related return ranks in the top quintile.

Management ★★★★★

There are twenty-five stocks in this $160 million portfolio. The average real estate fund today is $86 million in size. Close to 95 percent of the fund's holdings are in stocks. The stocks in this portfolio have an average p/e ratio of 22 and a median market capitalization of $3 billion. The ten largest holdings compose 66 percent of the fund's total assets. The portfolio's equity holdings can be categorized as mid-cap and value-oriented issues.

A team has managed this fund for the past six years. Managers Manno, Statz, and Bedell look for companies with clean balance sheets and properties with high market barriers to entry in order to deter competiton. There is one other fund besides U.S. Real Estate within the Security Capital family.

Tax Minimization ★★★★★

During the past five years, a $10,000 initial investment grew to $15,080 after taxes, assuming a 40 percent income tax bracket (state and federal combined) and a capital gains rate of 20 percent. This means that investors in this fund were able to preserve 83 percent of their total returns. Compared to other equity funds in the same category, this fund's tax savings are considered to be very good.

Expenses ★★★

Security Capital U.S. Real Estate's expense ratio is 1.4 percent; it has averaged 1.3 percent annually over the past three calendar years. The average expense ratio for the 150 funds in this category is 1.7 percent. This fund's turnover rate over the past year has been 91 percent, while its peer group average has been 56 percent.

Summary

Security Capital U.S. Real Estate, a mid-cap value fund, has outperformed 93 percent of all mutual funds over the past three years as well as 98 percent of its sector peer group over the same period. Risk-adjusted returns have also been superb over the past three years. By category, the fund ranks in the top quartile when it comes to returns versus risk. Within its peer group, the fund ranks number one when it comes to returns and risk reduction. The fund's focus on high-quality properties and companies has earned it a great reputation within the real estate industry. Performance on a year-by-year basis is almost always in the top quartile—a rarity for any fund in any category. This portfolio outperformed the S & P 500 in 2000 by 45 percentage points. This portfolio's alpha, which measures excess returns per unit of risk taken, as measured against the fund's benchmark index, is appealing.

Profile

minimum initial investment $1,000
subsequent minimum investment . . $100
available in all 50 states. . . . . yes
telephone exchanges. . . . . yes
number of funds in family 2

IRA accounts available . . . . yes
IRA minimum investment $500
date of inception. . . . . Dec. 1996
dividend/income paid . . . . quarterly
largest sector weighting . . . . financials

Technology Funds

Consider the following statistics: The first desktop PC was introduced in 1984, the World Wide Web was invented in Switzerland in 1989, 46 million U.S. adults had Net access in 1997, 98 million U.S. adults had Net access in 1999, and the World Wide Web surpassed 1 billion unique pages in the year 2000. Just five years ago, it would have taken forty-seven minutes to download 1,000 pages; today this transmission takes just seconds.

Around the world, consumers who are rapidly embracing existing hardware and software in areas such as electronics, information technology, and cellular technology are driving the burgeoning need for technology. Technologies once considered highly advanced are now seen as household essentials—with progressively lower prices as a result of mass marketing. Because of intense global competition, lack of pricing flexibility, and tight labor markets, corporations seeking to maintain their profit margins are increasingly investing in technology to enhance productivity.

However, technology stocks are also inherently more volatile and, consequently, riskier than the broad market as well as most, if not all, industry sectors. To demonstrate, let us examine standard deviation, the most common measure of performance volatility, or its tendency to move up or down. The higher the fund's standard deviation, the greater the fund's swings in performance. According to Morningstar, Inc., the standard deviation of returns for technology funds typically is roughly three times that of the S & P 500 Index.

Not all technology stocks are created equal. At the very basic level, Internet-related companies and general, non-Internet technology companies (those that make computers, chips, hard drives, or software) are at very different stages in their evolution. Internet companies are where regular technology companies were ten to fifteen years ago. The instability of Internet companies is what has made these stocks so volatile and so susceptible to momentum. As an example, Morgan Stanley's MOX Index of Internet stocks gained a staggering 514 percent between the end of 1998 and its peak on March 9, 2000, only to give up close to half of those gains over the next several weeks.

Technology stocks represent one of the fastest growing and largest contributors to the S & P 500 Index. At year-end 1999, technology stocks represented 30 percent of the S & P 500 Index (dropping to less than 20 percent by the middle of 2000; currently about 19 percent of the S & P 500) and accounted for 80 percent of the Index's overall growth. Eight of the ten largest contributors to the S & P 500's 1999 return were technology companies.

Annual Returns - Technology Funds

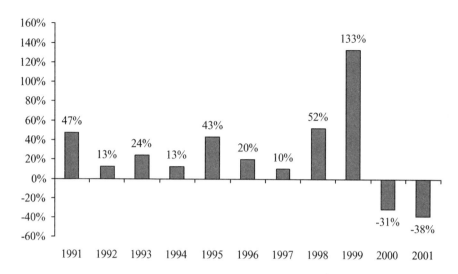

Technology fund investing can be quite complex. Not only are there more than 350 funds that are specifically in the technology sector, but hundreds more in other categories are also heavily technology oriented. And this may not be the whole story. Just defining technology can be a challenging endeavor.

There are 360-plus funds in this $143 billion category. Since 1986, the technology sector has underperformed the S & P 500 in the following years: 1986 by 11.1 percent, 1987 by 5.7 percent, 1988 by 9.8 percent, 1989 by 10.0 percent, 1996 by 2.6 percent, 1997 by 23.6 percent, by 22.3 percent in 2000, and by 26.2 percent in 2001 However, in 1999, technology funds outperformed the S & P 500 by 112 percent.

The typical technology fund is divided as follows: 78 percent in technology stocks, 12 percent in service, 5 percent in health, and 2 percent in industrials. The average technology fund is divided as follows: 84 percent in common stocks, 8 percent in foreign equities, and 7 percent in cash. The typical price-earnings (p/e) ratio for stocks in this category is 46 and they have a standard deviation of 59.7 percent.

Firsthand Technology Value

125 South Market Street, Suite 1200
San Jose, CA 95113
(888) 884-2675
www.firsthandfunds.com

total return	★★★
risk reduction	★★★★
management	★★★★
tax minimization	★★★★★
expense control	★★
symbol TVFQX	18 points
up-market performance	excellent
down-market performance	good
predictability of returns	fair

Total Return   ★★★

Over the past five years, Firsthand Technology Value has taken $10,000 and turned it into $19,260 ($14,820 over three years). This translates into an annualized return of 14 percent over the past five years and 14 percent over the past three years. Over the past five years, this fund has outperformed 95 percent of all mutual funds; within its general category, it has done better than 80 percent of its peers. Technology funds have averaged 9 percent annually over these same five years.

Risk/Volatility   ★★★★

Over the past five years, Firsthand Technology Value has been safer than 24 percent of all technology funds. Over the past decade, the fund has had two negative years, while the NASDAQ Index has had three (off 3 percent in 1994, 39 percent in 2000, and 21 percent in 2001); the Russell 2000 also fell three times (off 2 percent in 1994, 3 percent in 1998, and 3 percent in 2000). The fund has underperformed the NASDAQ Index twice and the Russell 2000 twice in the past ten years. Consistency of *overperformance* for this fund has been very good.

	past 5 years		past 10 years	
worst year	-44.0%	2001	-44.0%	2001
best year	190.4%	1999	190.4%	1999

Over the past five years, the fund's three worst quarters have been first quarter 2001 (-42 percent), third quarter 2001 (-40 percent), and fourth quarter 2000 (-34 percent). During the same period, the three best quarters have been fourth quarter 1998 (61 percent), fourth quarter 1999 (53 percent), and second quarter 1999 (47 percent). In the past, Firsthand Technology Value has done better than 77 percent of its peer group during the most recent bull market and outperformed 44 percent of its peer group during the most recent bear market. Consistency, or predictability, of returns for Firsthand Technology Value can be described as fair. This fund's risk-related return ranks in the top third.

Management   ★★★★
There are fifty stocks in this $4.6 billion portfolio. The average technology fund today is $180 million in size. Close to 80 percent of the fund's holdings are in stocks. The stocks in this portfolio have an average p/e ratio of 45 and a median market capitalization of $3 billion. The ten largest holdings compose 54 percent of the fund's total assets. The portfolio's equity holdings can be categorized as mid-cap and growth-oriented issues.

Kevin Landis has managed this fund for the past eight years. Manager Landis has had more than his share of ups and downs, but the fund has not been disappointing for the patient investor. There are five funds besides Technology Value within the Firsthand family. Overall, the fund family's risk-adjusted performance can be described as fair to good.

Tax Minimization   ★★★★★
During the past five years, a $10,000 initial investment grew to $17,329 after taxes, assuming a 40 percent income tax bracket (state and federal combined) and a capital gains rate of 20 percent. This means that investors in this fund were able to preserve 90 percent of their total returns. Compared to other equity funds in the same category, this fund's tax savings are considered to be excellent.

Expenses   ★★
Firsthand Technology Value's expense ratio is 1.8 percent; it has averaged 1.9 percent annually over the past three calendar years. The average expense ratio for the 380 funds in this category is 1.8 percent. This fund's turnover rate over the past year has been 59 percent, while its peer group average has been 201 percent.

Summary
Firsthand Technology Value, a mid-cap growth fund, has outperformed 95 percent of all mutual funds over the past five years as well as 88 percent of its peer group over the past three years. Risk-adjusted returns have been very good. This portfolio outperformed the S & P 500 in 1999 by an amazing 169 percentage points. This portfolio's alpha, which measures excess returns per unit of risk taken, as measured against the fund's benchmark index, is extremely appealing.

Profile

minimum initial investment $10,000	*IRA accounts available* . . . . yes
subsequent minimum investment . . . $50	*IRA minimum investment* $2,000
available in all 50 states. . . . . yes	*date of inception.* . . . . May 1994
telephone exchanges. . . . . yes	*dividend/income paid* . . . . annually
number of funds in family 6	*largest sector weighting* . . . technology

North Track PSE Tech 100 Index A
215 North Main Street
West Bend, WI 53095
(800) 826-4600
www.northtrackfunds.com

total return	★★★★★
risk reduction	★★★★★
management	★★★★★
tax minimization	★★★★★
expense control	★★★★★
symbol PPTIX	25 points
up-market performance	good
down-market performance	excellent
predictability of returns	very good

Total Return ★★★★★
Over the past five years, North Track PSE Tech 100 Index A has taken $10,000 and turned it into $28,160 ($15,210 over three years). This translates into an annualized return of 23 percent over the past five years and 15 percent over the past three years. Over the past five years, this fund has outperformed 99 percent of all mutual funds; within its general category, it has done better than 96 percent of its peers. Technology funds have averaged 9 percent annually over these same five years.

Risk/Volatility ★★★★★
Over the past five years, North Track PSE Tech 100 Index A has been safer than 96 percent of all technology funds. Over the past decade, the fund has had two negative years, while the NASDAQ Index has had three (off 3 percent in 1994, 39 percent in 2000, and 21 percent in 2001); the Russell 2000 also fell three times (off 2 percent in 1994, 3 percent in 1998, and 3 percent in 2000). The fund has underperformed the NASDAQ Index twice and the Russell 2000 twice in the past ten years. Consistency of *overperformance* for this fund has been outstanding.

	past 5 years		past 10 years	
worst year	-17.2%	2000	-17.2%	2000
best year	114.6%	1999	114.6%	1999

Over the past five years, the fund's three worst quarters have been third quarter 2001 (-29 percent), fourth quarter 2000 (-22 percent), and first quarter 2001 (-19 percent). During the same period, the three best quarters have been fourth quarter 1999 (54 percent), fourth quarter 1998 (40 percent), and second quarter 1999 (20 percent). In the past, North Track PSE Tech 100 Index A has done better than 44 percent of its peer group during the most recent bull market and outperformed 89 percent of its peer group during the most recent bear market. Consistency, or predictability, of returns for North Track PSE Tech 100 Index A can be described as very good. This fund's risk-related return ranks in the top quintile.

Management   ★★★★★
There are 100 stocks in this $280 million portfolio. The average technology fund today is $180 million in size. Close to 100 percent of the fund's holdings are in stocks. The stocks in this portfolio have an average p/e ratio of 43 and a median market capitalization of $11 billion. The ten largest holdings compose 26 percent of the fund's total assets. The portfolio's equity holdings can be categorized as large-cap and growth-oriented issues.

Jay Ferrara has managed this fund for the past six years. There are twenty funds besides PSE Tech 100 Index A within the North Track family. Overall, the fund family's risk-adjusted performance can be described as fair to good.

Tax Minimization   ★★★★★
During the past five years, a $10,000 initial investment grew to $24,500 after taxes, assuming a 40 percent income tax bracket (state and federal combined) and a capital gains rate of 20 percent. This means that investors in this fund were able to preserve 87 percent of their total returns. Compared to other equity funds in the same category, this fund's tax savings are considered to be excellent.

Expenses   ★★★★★
North Track PSE Tech 100 Index A's expense ratio is 0.7 percent; it has averaged 0.7 percent annually over the past three calendar years. The average expense ratio for the 380 funds in this category is 1.8 percent. This fund's turnover rate over the past year has been 40 percent, while its peer group average has been 201 percent.

Summary
North Track PSE Tech 100 Index A, a large-cap growth fund, has outperformed 99 percent of all mutual funds over the past five years as well as 96 percent of its peer group over the same period. Returns over shorter periods have been equally impressive. Risk-adjusted returns have also been outstanding over the past three and five years. By category, the fund ranks in the top quartile when it comes to returns versus risk. Within its peer group, the fund ranks number one when it comes to returns, risk reduction, expense control, and low turnover. This portfolio's alpha, which measures excess returns per unit of risk taken, as measured against the fund's benchmark index, is extremely appealing. On a total point basis, this is the number-one fund for its category and is the only fund in the book to receive a perfect score, 25 out of 25 possible points.

Profile
minimum initial investment $1,000
subsequent minimum investment . . . $50
available in all 50 states. . . . . yes
telephone exchanges. . . . . yes
number of funds in family 21

IRA accounts available . . . . yes
IRA minimum investment $500
date of inception. . . . . June 1996
dividend/income paid . . . . quarterly
largest sector weighting . . . technology

Utility Stock Funds

Utility stock funds look for both growth and income, investing in common stocks of utility companies across the country. Somewhere between one-third and one-half of these funds' total returns come from common stock dividends. Utility funds normally stay away from speculative issues, focusing instead on well-established companies with solid histories of paying good dividends. The goal of most of these funds is long-term growth.

Utility, metals, natural resources, and, health care/biotech, and technology funds are the only sector, or specialty, fund categories in this book. Most investors should avoid funds that invest in a single industry, or sector, for two reasons. First, you limit the fund manager's ability to find attractive stocks or bonds if he or she is only able to choose securities from one particular geographic area or industry. Second, the track record of sector funds as a whole is pretty bad. In fact, as a general category, these specialty funds represent the worst of both worlds: above-average risk and substandard returns. If you find the term *aggressive growth* unappealing, then the words *sector fund* should positively appall you.

Utility funds are the one exception. They sound safe and they are safe. In fact, over the past ten years (ended December 31, 2001), this category has only experienced two down years (-9.0 percent in 1994 and -21 percent in 2001). Any category of stocks that somewhat relies on dividends generated automatically has a built-in safety cushion. A comparatively high dividend income means that you have to worry less about the appreciation of the underlying issues.

Four factors generally determine the profitability of a utility company: (1) how much it pays for energy, (2) the general level of interest rates, (3) its expected use of nuclear power, and (4) the political climate.

The prices of oil and gas are passed directly to the consumer, but the utility companies are sensitive to this issue. Higher fuel prices mean that the utility industry has less latitude to increase its profit margins. Thus, higher fuel prices can mean smaller profits and/or dividends to investors.

Next to energy costs, interest expense is the industry's greatest expense. Utility companies are heavily debt-laden. Their interest costs directly affect their profitability. When rates go down and companies are able to refinance their debt, the savings can be staggering. Paying 7 percent interest on a couple of hundred million dollars' worth of bonds each year is much more appealing than having to pay 9 percent on the same amount of debt. A lower interest-rate environment translates into more money being left over for shareholders.

Depending on how you look at it, nuclear power has been an issue or problem for the United States for a few decades now. Other countries seem to have come to grips with the matter, yet we remain divided. Although new power plants have not been successfully proposed or built in this country for several years, no one knows what the future may hold. Venturing into nuclear power always seems to be much more expensive than anticipated by the utility companies and the independent experts they rely on for advice. Because of these uncertainties, mutual fund managers try to seek out utility companies that have no foreseeable plans to develop any or more nuclear power facilities. Whether this will help the nation in the long run remains to be seen, but such avoidance keeps share prices more stable and predictable.

Finally, the political climate is an important concern when calculating whether utility funds should be part of your portfolio. The Public Utilities Commission (PUC) is a political animal and can directly reflect the views of a state's government. Utility bills are something most of us are concerned with and aware of; the powers that be are more likely to be re-elected if they are able to keep rate increases to a minimum. Modest, or minimum, increases can be healthy for the utility companies; freezing rates for a couple of years is a bad sign.

Nearly 100 funds make up the utilities category. Total market capitalization of this category is $21 billion. Over 85 percent of a typical utility fund's portfolio is in common stocks, with the balance in bonds, convertibles, and money market instruments. The typical utility fund has about 7 percent of its holdings in foreign stocks.

Over the past three years, utility funds have had an average compound return of negative 0.6 percent per year; the annual return for the past five years has been 8.0 percent. For the past ten and fifteen years, these funds have averaged 9.2 percent and 10.0 percent, respectively. The standard deviation for utility funds has been 15.5 percent over the past three years. This means that these funds have been less volatile than any other stock category except equity-income funds, which have exhibited almost identical volatility. The average annual expense ratio for this category is 1.5 percent.

Standard Deviation of the Different Stock (Equity) Categories over the Past Three Years (Ending December 31, 2001)

category	standard deviation	category	standard deviation
technology	59.7%	growth	24.4%
aggressive growth	36.9%	world stock	21.3%
metals	28.9%	growth & income	17.1%
health care	34.2%	utilities	15.5%
natural resources	32.0%		

Usually, utility stock prices closely follow the long-term bond market. If long-term interest rates go up, utility stock prices are likely to go down. Utility stocks are also vulnerable to a general stock market decline, although they are considered less risky than other types of common stock because of their dividends and the monopoly position of most utilities. Typically, utilities have fallen about two-thirds as much as other common stocks during market downturns.

Annual Returns - Utility Stock Funds

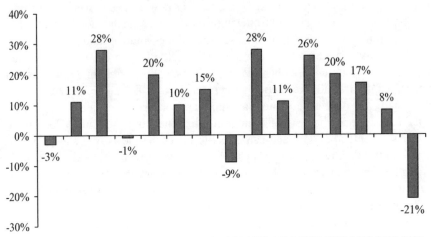

Worldwide, there is a tremendous opportunity for growth in this industry. The average per-capita production of electricity in many developing countries is only one-fifth that of the United States. The electrical output per capita in the United States is 12,100 kilowatt-hours, compared to 2,500 kilowatt-hours for developing nations. This disparity may well be on the way out. All over the world, previously underdeveloped countries are making economic strides as they move toward free market systems.

When emerging countries become developed economically, their citizens demand higher standards of living. As a result, their requirements for electricity, water, and telephones tend to rise dramatically. Moreover, many countries are selling their utility companies to public owners, opening a new arena for investors. The net result of all of this for you, the investor, is that fund groups are beginning to offer global utility funds. This increased diversification—allowing a fund to invest in utility companies all over the world instead of just in the United States—coupled with tremendous long-term growth potential should make this a dynamic industry group. Utility funds are a good choice for the investor who wants a hedge against inflation but is still afraid or distrustful of the stock market in general.

Beta, which measures the market-related risk of a stock, is only 0.5 for utility funds as a group (compared to 1.0 for the S & P 500). This means that when it comes to stock market risk, utilities have only 50 percent the risk of the S & P 500. Keep in mind, however, that other risks, such as rising interest rates, also need to be evaluated whenever utilities are being considered.

AXP Utilities Income A

IDS Tower 10
Minneapolis, MN 55440
(800) 328-8300
www.americanexpress.com

total return	★★★★
risk reduction	★★★★★
management	★★★★★
tax minimization	★★★★
expense control	★★★★★
symbol INUTX	23 points
up-market performance	good
down-market performance	very good
predictability of returns	excellent

Total Return   ★★★★

Over the past five years, AXP Utilities Income A has taken $10,000 and turned it into $16,110 ($10,310 over three years and $28,400 over the past ten years). This translates into an annualized return of 10 percent over the past five years, 1 percent over the past three years, and 11 percent for the decade. Over the past five years, this fund has outperformed 81 percent of all mutual funds; within its general category, it has done better than 65 percent of its peers. Utility stock funds have averaged 8 percent annually over these same five years.

Risk/Volatility   ★★★★★

Over the past five years, AXP Utilities Income A has been safer than 66 percent of all utility stock funds. Over the past decade, the fund has had two negative years, while the S & P 500 has had two (off 9 percent in 2000 and 12 percent in 2001). The fund has underperformed the S & P 500 twice in the past ten years. Consistency of *overperformance* for this fund has been very good.

	past 5 years		past 10 years	
worst year	-20.1%	2001	-20.1%	2001
best year	29.0%	1997	29.0%	1997

Over the past five years, the fund's three worst quarters have been third quarter 2001 (-11 percent), first quarter 2001 (-6 percent), and third quarter 1999 (-5 percent). During the same period, the three best quarters have been third quarter 2000 (18 percent), fourth quarter 1997 (14 percent), and fourth quarter 1998 (13 percent). In the past, AXP Utilities Income A has done better than just 2 percent of its peer group during the most recent bull market and outperformed 79 percent of its peer group during the most recent bear market. Consistency, or predictability, of returns for AXP Utilities Income A can be described as excellent. This fund's risk-related return ranks in the top third.

Management   ★★★★★

There are fifty stocks in this $1.4 billion portfolio. The average utility stock fund today is $220 million in size. Close to 87 percent of the fund's holdings are in stocks. The stocks in this portfolio have an average p/e ratio of 19 and a median market capitalization of $12 billion. The ten largest holdings compose 46 percent of the fund's total assets. The portfolio's equity holdings can be categorized as large-cap and value-oriented issues.

Bern Fleming has managed this fund for the past seven years. Manager Fleming has a somewhat conservative approach to equity selection. When he finds speculative plays that are appealing, he buys the underlying convertible instead of the common stock, thereby reducing risk. There are 170 funds besides Utilities Income A within the American Express Financial family. Overall, the fund family's risk-adjusted performance can be described as good.

Tax Minimization   ★★★★

During the past five years, a $10,000 initial investment grew to $11,440 after taxes, assuming a 40 percent income tax bracket (state and federal combined) and a capital gains rate of 20 percent. This means that investors in this fund were able to preserve 71 percent of their total returns. Compared to other equity funds in the same category, this fund's tax savings are considered to be very good.

Expenses   ★★★★★

AXP Utilities Income A's expense ratio is 1 percent; it has averaged 1 percent annually over the past three calendar years. The average expense ratio for the 100 funds in this category is 1.5 percent. This fund's turnover rate over the past year has been 85 percent, while its peer group average has been 107 percent.

Summary

AXP Utilities Income, a large-cap value sector fund, has outperformed 81 percent of all mutual funds over the past five years as well as 84 percent of its peer group over the past decade. Risk-adjusted returns have been good over the past three, five, and ten years. Within its peer group, the fund ranks number one when it comes to controlling overhead costs and low turnover; the fund also scores well in the areas of low risk, predictability of returns, and total return. This portfolio's alpha, which measures excess returns per unit of risk taken, as measured against the fund's benchmark index, is negative.

Profile

minimum initial investment $2,000	*IRA accounts available* . . . . yes
subsequent minimum investment . . $100	*IRA minimum investment* $1
available in all 50 states. . . . . yes	*date of inception* . . . . Aug. 1988
telephone exchanges. . . . . yes	*dividend/income paid* . . . . quarterly
number of funds in family 171	*largest sector weighting* . . . . . . utilities

MFS Utilities A
P.O. Box 2281
Boston, MA 02107
(800) 637-2929
www.mfs.com

total return	★★★★
risk reduction	★★★★★
management	★★★★
tax minimization	★★
expense control	★★★★
symbol MMUFX	19 points
up-market performance	very good
down-market performance	good
predictability of returns	very good

Total Return ★★★★
Over the past five years, MFS Utilities A has taken $10,000 and turned it into $16,110 ($10,620 over three years). This translates into an annualized return of 10 percent over the past five years and 2 percent over the past three years. Over the past five years, this fund has outperformed 88 percent of all mutual funds; within its general category, it has done better than 82 percent of its peers. Utility stock funds have averaged 8 percent annually over these same five years.

Risk/Volatility ★★★★★
Over the past five years, MFS Utilities A has been safer than 74 percent of all utility stock funds. Over the past decade, the fund has had two negative years, while the S & P 500 has had two (off 9 percent in 2000 and 12 percent in 2001). The fund has underperformed the S & P 500 twice in the past ten years. Consistency of *overperformance* for this fund has been outstanding.

	past 5 years		past 10 years	
worst year	-25.0%	2001	-25.0%	2001
best year	31.8%	1999	32.5%	1995

Over the past five years, the fund's three worst quarters have been third quarter 2001 (-17 percent), second quarter 2000 (-6 percent), and second quarter 2001 (-5 percent). During the same period, the three best quarters have been fourth quarter 1999 (22 percent), second quarter 1997 (12 percent), and first quarter 1998 (11 percent). In the past, MFS Utilities A has done better than 69 percent of its peer group during the most recent bull market and outperformed 34 percent of its peer group during the most recent bear market. Consistency, or predictability, of returns for MFS Utilities A can be described as very good. This fund's risk-related return ranks in the top third.

Management   ★★★★
There are sixty-five stocks in this $740 million portfolio. The average utility stock fund today is $220 million in size. Close to 75 percent of the fund's holdings are in stocks. The stocks in this portfolio have an average p/e ratio of 19 and a median market capitalization of $8 billion. The ten largest holdings compose 28 percent of the fund's total assets. The portfolio's equity holdings can be categorized as large-cap and value-oriented issues.

Maura Shaughnessy has managed this fund for the past ten years. Manager Shaughnessy is different from the crowd because she keeps this portfolio in utilities, sticking with the more traditional gas, telephone, and water stocks. Management has a strong attention to diversification and is not afraid to go into cash when there are no buying opportunities. There are 196 funds besides Utilities A within the MFS family. Overall, the fund family's risk-adjusted performance can be described as good to very good.

Tax Minimization   ★★
During the past five years, a $10,000 initial investment grew to $9,180 after taxes, assuming a 40 percent income tax bracket (state and federal combined) and a capital gains rate of 20 percent. This means that investors in this fund were able to preserve 57 percent of their total returns. Compared to other equity funds in the same category, this fund's tax savings are considered to be fair.

Expenses   ★★★★
MFS Utilities A's expense ratio is 1 percent; it has averaged 1 percent annually over the past three calendar years. The average expense ratio for the 100 funds in this category is 1.5 percent. This fund's turnover rate over the past year has been 113 percent, while its peer group average has been 107 percent.

Summary
MFS Utilities A, a large-cap value sector fund, has outperformed 88 percent of all mutual funds over the past five years as well as 82 percent of its peer group over the same period. Risk-adjusted returns have ranged from good to very good over the past three to five years. By category, the fund ranks in the top third when it comes to returns versus risk. Within its peer group, the fund ties for first place in risk reduction. Its rating in all other categories measured is also quite good. This portfolio's alpha, which measures excess returns per unit of risk taken, as measured against the fund's benchmark index, is slightly negative.

Profile
minimum initial investment $1,000	*IRA accounts available* . . . . yes
subsequent minimum investment . . . $50	*IRA minimum investment* $250
available in all 50 states. . . . . yes	*date of inception* . . . . Feb. 1992
telephone exchanges. . . . . yes	*dividend/income paid*. . . . . monthly
number of funds in family 197	*largest sector weighting* . . . . . . utilities

Morgan Stanley Global Utilities B

P.O. Box 2798
Boston, MA 02208
(800) 869-3863
www.deanwitter.com

total return	★★★★
risk reduction	★★★★★
management	★★★★★
tax minimization	★★★★★
expense control	★★★
symbol GUTBX	22 points
up-market performance	good
down-market performance	very good
predictability of returns	very good

Total Return   ★★★★

Over the past five years, Morgan Stanley Global Utilities B has taken $10,000 and turned it into $16,860 ($10,000 over three years). This translates into an annualized return of 11 percent over the past five years and 0 percent over the past three years. Over the past five years, this fund has outperformed 88 percent of all mutual funds; within its general category it has done better than 85 percent of its peers. Utility stock funds have averaged 8 percent annually over these same five years.

Risk/Volatility   ★★★★★

Over the past five years, Morgan Stanley Global Utilities B has been safer than 45 percent of all utility stock funds. Over the past decade, the fund has had one negative year, while the S & P 500 has had two (off 9 percent in 2000 and 12 percent in 2001). The fund has underperformed the S & P 500 twice in the past ten years. Consistency of *overperformance* for this fund has been very good.

	past 5 years		past 10 years	
worst year	-24.3%	2001	-24.3%	2001
best year	37.6%	1998	37.6%	1998

Over the past five years, the fund's three worst quarters have been third quarter 2001 (-12 percent), first quarter 2001 (-10 percent), and second quarter 2000 (-7 percent). During the same period, the three best quarters have been first quarter 1998 (20 percent), fourth quarter 1999 (19 percent), and fourth quarter 1998 (17 percent). In the past, Morgan Stanley Global Utilities B has done better than 42 percent of its peer group during the most recent bull market and outperformed 39 percent of its peer group during the most recent bear market. Consistency, or predictability, of returns for Morgan Stanley Global Utilities B can be described as very good. This fund's risk-related return ranks in the top third.

Management   ★★★★★
There are fifty stocks in this $625 million portfolio. The average utility stock fund today is $220 million in size. Close to 90 percent of the fund's holdings are in stocks. The stocks in this portfolio have an average p/e ratio of 17 and a median market capitalization of $8 billion. The ten largest holdings compose 36 percent of the fund's total assets. The portfolio's equity holdings can be categorized as large-cap and value-oriented issues.

Edward Gaylor has managed this fund for the past eight years. Manager Gaylor tends to favor telecommunications as well as foreign equities much more than his peers. There are 218 funds besides Global Utilities B within the Morgan Stanley family. Overall, the fund family's risk-adjusted performance can be described as good.

Tax Minimization   ★★★★★
During the past five years, a $10,000 initial investment grew to $13,320 after taxes, assuming a 40 percent income tax bracket (state and federal combined) and a capital gains rate of 20 percent. This means that investors in this fund were able to preserve 79 percent of their total returns. Compared to other equity funds in the same category, this fund's tax savings are considered to be excellent.

Expenses   ★★★
Morgan Stanley Global Utilities B's expense ratio is 1.7 percent; it has averaged 1.7 percent annually over the past three calendar years. The average expense ratio for the 100 funds in this category is 1.5 percent. This fund's turnover rate over the past year has been 31 percent, while its peer group average has been 107 percent.

Summary
Morgan Stanley Global Utilities B, a large-cap value sector fund, has outperformed 88 percent of all mutual funds over the past five years as well as 85 percent of its peer group. Risk-adjusted returns have ranged between good and very good over the past three and five years. Within its peer group, the fund's ratings range from good to exceptional in every category measured. The fund ranks number one in its category when it comes to tax efficiency. This portfolio's alpha, which measures excess returns per unit of risk taken, as measured against the fund's benchmark index, is negative.

Profile

minimum initial investment $1,000	*IRA accounts available* . . . . yes
subsequent minimum investment . . $100	*IRA minimum investment* $1,000
available in all 50 states. . . . . yes	*date of inception.* . . . . June 1994
telephone exchanges. . . . . yes	*dividend/income paid* . . . . quarterly
number of funds in family 219	*largest sector weighting* . . . . . . utilities

Strong Dividend Income

P.O. Box 2936
Milwaukee, WI 53201
(800) 368-1030
www.strongfunds.com

total return	★★★★★
risk reduction	★★★★★
management	★★★★★
tax minimization	★★★★★
expense control	★★★★
symbol SDVIX	24 points
up-market performance	good
down-market performance	excellent
predictability of returns	very good

Total Return   ★★★★★

Over the past five years, Strong Dividend Income has taken $10,000 and turned it into $17,630 ($11,250 over three years). This translates into an annualized return of 12 percent over the past five years and 4 percent over the past three years. Over the past five years, this fund has outperformed 92 percent of all mutual funds; within its general category it has done better than 94 percent of its peers. Utility stock funds have averaged 8 percent annually over these same five years.

Risk/Volatility   ★★★★★

Over the past five years, Strong Dividend Income has been safer than 91 percent of all utility stock funds. Over the past decade, the fund has had two negative years, while the S & P 500 has had two (off 9 percent in 2000 and 12 percent in 2001). The fund has underperformed the S & P 500 twice in the past ten years. Consistency of *overperformance* for this fund has been very good.

	past 5 years		past 10 years	
worst year	-11.2%	2001	-11.2%	2001
best year	27.6%	1997	37.0%	1995

Over the past five years, the fund's three worst quarters have been first quarter 1999 (-7 percent), third quarter 2001 (-6 percent), and first quarter 2001 (-5 percent). During the same period, the three best quarters have been third quarter 2000 (16 percent), second quarter 1999 (14 percent), and fourth quarter 1997 (12 percent). In the past, Strong Dividend Income has done better than 38 percent of its peer group during the most recent bull market and outperformed 92 percent of its peer group during the most recent bear market. Consistency, or predictability, of returns for Strong Dividend Income can be described as very good. This fund's risk-related return ranks in the top third.

Management ★★★★★
There are thirty-five stocks in this $240 million portfolio. The average utility stock fund today is $220 million in size. Close to 92 percent of the fund's holdings are in stocks. The stocks in this portfolio have an average p/e ratio of 15 and a median market capitalization of $12 billion. The ten largest holdings compose 65 percent of the fund's total assets. The portfolio's equity holdings can be categorized as large-cap and value-oriented issues.

A team has managed this fund for the past nine years. Management's current and future goal is to make this sector portfolio more diversified than the typical utilities fund. There are 101 funds besides Dividend Income within the Strong family. Overall, the fund family's risk-adjusted performance can be described as good.

Tax Minimization ★★★★★
During the past five years, a $10,000 initial investment grew to $13,750 after taxes, assuming a 40 percent income tax bracket (state and federal combined) and a capital gains rate of 20 percent. This means that investors in this fund were able to preserve 78 percent of their total returns. Compared to other equity funds in the same category, this fund's tax savings are considered to be excellent.

Expenses ★★★★
Strong Dividend Income's expense ratio is 1 percent; it has averaged 1 percent annually over the past three calendar years. The average expense ratio for the 100 funds in this category is 1.5 percent. This fund's turnover rate over the past year has been 107 percent, while its peer group average has been 107 percent.

Summary
Strong Dividend Income, a large-cap value sector fund, has outperformed 92 percent of all mutual funds over the past five years as well as 94 percent of its peer group. Returns over shorter periods have been equally impressive. Risk-adjusted returns have been very good over the past three and five years. By category, the fund ranks in the top third when it comes to returns versus risk. Within its peer group, the fund ranks number one when it comes to performance by a hefty margin. It ties as the best utilities fund when it comes to low risk. The portfolio also receives very high marks in all other areas measured. This portfolio outperformed the S & P 500 in 2000 by 36 percentage points. This portfolio's alpha, which measures excess returns per unit of risk taken, as measured against the fund's benchmark index, is slightly negative. On a total point basis, Strong Dividend Income is the number-one fund for its category.

Profile
minimum initial investment $2,500	*IRA accounts available* . . . . yes
subsequent minimum investment . . . $50	*IRA minimum investment* $250
available in all 50 states. . . . . yes	*date of inception* . . . . July 1993
telephone exchanges. . . . . yes	*dividend/income paid* . . . . quarterly
number of funds in family 102	*largest sector weighting* . . . . . . utilities

World Bond Funds

Global, or world, funds invest in securities issued all over the world, including the United States. A global bond fund usually invests in bonds issued by stable governments from a handful of countries. These funds try to avoid purchasing foreign government debt instruments from politically or economically unstable nations. Foreign, also known as international, bond funds invest in debt instruments from countries other than the United States.

International funds purchase securities issued in a foreign currency, such as the Japanese yen or the British pound. Prospective investors need to be aware of the potential changes in the value of the foreign currency relative to the U.S. dollar. As an example, if you were to invest in U.K. pound-denominated bonds with a yield of 15 percent and the British currency appreciated 12 percent against the U.S. dollar, your total return for the year would be 27 percent. If the British pound declined by 20 percent against the U.S. dollar, your total return would be -5 percent (15 percent yield minus 20 percent).

Since foreign markets do not necessarily move in tandem with U.S. markets, each country represents varying investment opportunities at different times. According to Salomon Brothers, the current value of the world bond market is estimated to be over $24 trillion. About 40 percent of this bond marketplace is made up of U.S. bonds; Japan ranks a distant second.

Assessing the economic environment to evaluate its effects on interest rates and bond values requires an understanding of two important factors: inflation and supply. During inflationary periods, when there is too much money chasing too few goods, government tightening of the money supply helps create a balance between an economy's cash resources and its available goods. Money supply refers to the amount of cash made available for spending, borrowing, or investing. Controlled by the central banks of each nation, the money supply is the primary tool used to manage inflation, interest rates, and economic growth.

A prudent tightening of the money supply can help bring on disinflation—decelerated loan demand, reduced durable goods orders, and falling prices. During disinflationary times, interest rates also fall, strengthening the underlying value of existing bonds. While such factors ultimately contribute to a healthier economy, they also mean lower yields for government bond investors. A trend toward disinflation currently exists in markets around the world.

As the United States and other governments implement policies designed to reduce inflation, interest rates are stabilizing. This disinflation can be disquieting to the individual who specifically invests for high monthly income. In reality, falling interest rates mean higher bond values, and investors seeking long-term growth or high total returns can therefore benefit from declining rates. Inflation, which drives interest rates higher, is the true enemy of bond investors. It diminishes bond values and, in addition, erodes the buying power of the interest income investors receive.

Income-seeking investors need to find economies in which inflation is coming under control, yet interest rates are still high enough to provide favorable bond yields. An investor who has only U.S. bonds is not taking advantage of such opportunities. If global disinflationary trends continue, those who remain invested only in the United States can lose out on opportunities for high income and total return elsewhere. The gradually decreasing yields on U.S. bonds compel the investor who seeks high income to think globally.

While not all bond markets will peak at the same level, they do tend to follow patterns. Targeting those countries in which interest rates are at peak levels and inflation is falling not only results in higher income but also creates significant potential for capital appreciation as rates ultimately decline and bond prices increase.

Each year since 1984, at least three government bond markets have provided yields higher than those available in the United States. With over 60 percent of the world's bonds found outside the United States, investors must look beyond U.S. borders to find bonds offering yields and total returns that meet their investment objectives.

According to Salomon Brothers, over the past three years, international bonds have underperformed U.S. bonds by an average of 9.6 percent per year; the figure drops to 7.3 percent over the past five years. Over the past ten years, the figure drops to an average of 2.3 percent per year and then falls to just 0.6 percent per year over the past fifteen years (all periods ending December 31, 2001).

Even with high income as the primary goal (these funds have a typical yield of roughly 5.7 percent annually), investors must consider credit and market risk. By investing primarily in mutual funds that purchase government-guaranteed bonds from the world's most creditworthy nations, you can get an extra measure of credit safety for payment of interest and repayment of principal. By diversifying across multiple markets, fund managers can significantly reduce market risk as well. Diversification is a proven technique for controlling market risk.

The long-term success of a global bond manager depends on expertise in assessing economic trends from country to country, as well as protecting the U.S. valuation of foreign holdings. The most effective way to protect the U.S. dollar value of international holdings is through active currency management. Although its effects over a ten-year period are nominal at best, currency fluctuations can help returns over a one-, three-, or five-year period.

In the simplest terms, effective currency management provides exposure to bond markets worldwide, while reducing the effects of adverse currency changes that can lower bond values. If a portfolio manager anticipates that the U.S. dollar will strengthen, he or she can lock in a currency exchange rate to protect the fund against a decline in the value of its foreign holdings. (A strong dollar means that other currencies are declining in value.) This strategy is commonly referred to as hedging the exposure of the portfolio. If, on the other hand, the manager expects the

Annual Returns - World Bond Funds

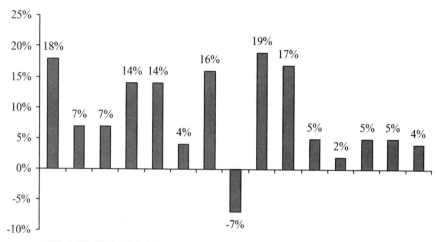

U.S. dollar to weaken, the fund can stay unhedged to allow it to benefit from the increasing value of foreign currencies. As good as hedging sounds, there is a cost to hedging and, on balance, this cost over time more than wipes out any benefit.

Investing in global bonds gives you the potential for capital appreciation during periods of declining interest rates. An inverse relationship exists between bond values and interest rates. When interest rates fall, as is the case in most bond markets in the world today, existing bond values climb. Conversely, as interest rates rise, the value of existing bonds declines (they are less desirable since "new" bonds have a higher current yield).

Over the past three and five years, global bond funds have had an average compound return of 4.4 and 3.1 percent per year, respectively; the annual returns for the past ten and fifteen years have been 4.7 and 6.3 percent, respectively. The standard deviation for global bond funds has been 7.9 percent over the past three years. This means that these funds have been less volatile than any equity fund but more volatile than government bond funds (standard deviation of 3.4 percent). Just 184 funds make up the global bond category. Total market capitalization of this category is approximately $17 billion.

Global bond funds, particularly those with high concentrations in foreign issues, are an excellent risk-reduction tool that should be utilized by a wide range of investors.

Alliance North American Government Income A

P.O. Box 1520
Secaucus, NJ 07086
(800) 227-4618
www.alliancecapital.com

total return	★★★★★
risk reduction	★★★
management	★★★★
current income	★★★★
expense control	★★
symbol ANAGX	18 points
up-market performance	poor
down-market performance	excellent
predictability of returns	very good

Total Return   ★★★★★

Over the past five years, Alliance North American Government Income A has taken $10,000 and turned it into $16,110 ($12,600 over three years). This translates into an annualized return of 10 percent over the past five years and 8 percent over the past three years. Over the past five years, this fund has outperformed 84 percent of all mutual funds; within its general category, it has done better than 99 percent of its peers. World bond funds have averaged 3 percent annually over these same five years.

During the past five years, a $10,000 initial investment grew to $13,000 after taxes, assuming a 40 percent income tax bracket (state and federal combined) and a capital gains rate of 20 percent. This means that investors in this fund were able to preserve 49 percent of their total returns. Compared to other funds in the same category, this fund's tax savings are considered to be very good.

Risk/Volatility   ★★★

Over the past five years, Alliance North American Government Income A has been safer than 34 percent of all world bond funds. Over the past decade, the fund has had two negative years, while the Lehman Brothers Aggregate Bond Index has had two (off 3 percent in 1994 and 1 percent in 1999); the Salomon Brothers World Government Bond Index fell four times (off 4 percent in 1997, 5 percent in 1999, 3 percent in 2000, and 4 percent in 2001). The fund has underperformed the Lehman Brothers Aggregate Bond Index twice and the Salomon Brothers World Government Bond Index four times in the past ten years. Consistency of *overperformance* for this fund has been very good.

	past 5 years		past 10 years	
worst year	-0.1%	2001	-30.2%	1994
best year	18.5%	2000	31%	1995

Over the past five years, the fund's three worst quarters have been third quarter 1998 (-4 percent), second quarter 1999 (-1 percent), and third quarter 2001 (-1 percent).

During the same period, the three best quarters have been second quarter 1997 (8 percent), first quarter 2000 (8 percent), and fourth quarter 1998 (7 percent). In the past, Alliance North American Government Income A has done better than just 2 percent of its peer group during the most recent bull market but outperformed 71 percent of its peer group during the most recent bear market. Consistency, or predictability, of returns for Alliance North American Government Income A can be described as very good. This fund's risk-related return ranks in the top half.

Management   ★★★★

There are twenty fixed-income securities in this $980 million portfolio. The average world bond fund today is $95 million in size. Close to 93 percent of the fund's holdings are in bonds. The average maturity of the bonds in this account is fifteen years; the weighted coupon rate averages 10 percent. The portfolio's fixed-income holdings can be categorized as long-term, medium-quality debt.

Wayne Lyski has managed this fund for the past ten years. Predictability of return figures are also impressive. Manager Lyski only invests in the Western Hemisphere, paying particular attention to Mexico and Argentina. Management's quirky, offbeat approach has certainly paid off. There are 152 funds besides North American Government Income A within the Alliance family. Overall, the fund family's risk-adjusted performance can be described as good.

Current Income   ★★★★

Over the past year, Alliance North American Government Income A had a twelve-month yield of 10.3 percent. During this same twelve-month period, the typical world bond fund had a yield that averaged 5.7 percent.

Expenses   ★★

Alliance North American Government Income A's expense ratio is 1.3 percent; it has averaged 1.3 percent annually over the past three calendar years. The average expense ratio for the 190 funds in this category is 1.4 percent. This fund's turnover rate over the past year has been 234 percent, while its peer group average has been 231 percent.

Summary

Alliance North American Government Income Trust A, a mid-quality, long-term world bond fund, has outperformed roughly 85 percent of all mutual funds over the past three and five years, plus 98 percent of its peers. Risk-adjusted returns have ranged from good to fair over the past three to five years. Within its peer group, the fund easily ranks number one when it comes to total return. This remains one of the finest offerings in its category.

Profile

minimum initial investment $250	*IRA accounts available* . . . . yes
subsequent minimum investment . . . $50	*IRA minimum investment* $250
available in all 50 states. . . . . yes	*date of inception*. . . . . Mar. 1992
telephone exchanges. . . . . yes	*dividend/income paid*. . . . . monthly
number of funds in family 153	*average credit quality* . . . . A

Fidelity New Markets Income
82 Devonshire Street
Boston, MA 02109
(800) 544-8888
www.100fidelity.com

total return	★★★★
risk reduction	★★
management	★★★★
current income	★★★★★
expense control	★★★
symbol FNMIX	18 points
up-market performance	excellent
down-market performance	fair
predictability of returns	fair

Total Return   ★★★★
Over the past five years, Fidelity New Markets Income has taken $10,000 and
turned it into $18,390 ($16,860 over three years). This translates into an annualized
return of 9 percent over the past five years and 19 percent over the past three years.
Over the past five years, this fund has outperformed 77 percent of all mutual funds;
within its general category, it has done better than 97 percent of its peers. World
bond funds have averaged 3 percent annually over these same five years.

During the past five years, a $10,000 initial investment grew to $13,700 after
taxes, assuming a 40 percent income tax bracket (state and federal combined) and
a capital gains rate of 20 percent. This means that investors in this fund were able
to preserve 44 percent of their total returns. Compared to other funds in the same
category, this fund's tax savings are considered to be very good.

Risk/Volatility   ★★
Over the past five years, Fidelity New Markets Income has been safer than 76 percent of all world bond funds. Over the past decade, the fund has had two negative
years, while the Lehman Brothers Aggregate Bond Index has had two (off 3 percent in 1994 and 1 percent in 1999); the Salomon Brothers World Government
Bond Index fell four times (off 4 percent in 1997, 5 percent in 1999, 3 percent in
2000, and 4 percent in 2001). The fund has underperformed the Lehman Brothers
Aggregate Bond Index once and the Salomon Brothers World Government Bond
Index six times in the past ten years. Consistency of *overperformance* for this fund
has been good.

	past 5 years		past 10 years	
worst year	-22.4%	1998	-22.4%	1998
best year	36.7%	1999	41.4%	1996

Over the past five years, the fund's three worst quarters have been third
quarter 1998 (-29 percent), second quarter 1998 (-7 percent), and third quarter 2001
(-5 percent). During the same period, the three best quarters have been fourth

quarter 1999 (16 percent), fourth quarter 1998 (12 percent), and second quarter 1997 (12 percent). In the past, Fidelity New Markets Income has done better than 84 percent of its peer group during the most recent bull market and outperformed 39 percent of its peer group during the most recent bear market. Consistency, or predictability, of returns for Fidelity New Markets Income can be described as fair. This fund's risk-related return ranks in the top third.

Management ★★★★
There are 115 fixed-income securities in this $300 million portfolio. The average world bond fund today is $95 million in size. Close to 85 percent of the fund's holdings are in bonds. The average maturity of the bonds in this account is fourteen years. The portfolio's fixed-income holdings can be categorized as low quality, long term.

John Carlson has managed this fund for the past seven years. Manager Carlson prefers U.S. dollar-denominated Brady bonds instead of fixed-income priced in local currencies. There are 154 funds besides New Markets Income within the Fidelity family. Overall, the fund family's risk-adjusted performance can be described as very good.

Current Income ★★★★★
Over the past year, Fidelity New Markets Income had a twelve-month yield of 11.1 percent. During this same twelve-month period, the typical world bond fund had a yield that averaged 5.7 percent.

Expenses ★★★
Fidelity New Markets Income's expense ratio is 1 percent; it has averaged 1 percent annually over the past three calendar years. The average expense ratio for the 190 funds in this category is 1.4 percent. This fund's turnover rate over the past year has been 278 percent, while its peer group average has been 231 percent.

Summary
Fidelity New Markets Income, a low-quality, long-term world bond fund, has outperformed 96 percent of all mutual funds over the past three years as well as 97 percent of its peer group over the past five years. Risk-adjusted returns have ranged from exceptional to fair during the past three to five years. Within its peer group, the fund ranks number two when it comes to performance and number one, by a wide margin, when it comes to current income. This is one of the safer emerging market debt plays. This fund outperformed the Lehman Brothers Aggregate Bond Index by 38 percentage points in 1999.

Profile

minimum initial investment $2,500	*IRA accounts available* . . . . yes
subsequent minimum investment . . $250	*IRA minimum investment* $500
available in all 50 states. . . . . yes	*date of inception.* . . . . May 1993
telephone exchanges. . . . . yes	*dividend/income paid.* . . . . monthly
number of funds in family 155	*average credit quality* . . . . BB

Payden & Rygel Global Fixed-Income R
333 South Grand Avenue, 32nd Floor
Los Angeles, CA 90071
(800) 572-9336
www.payden.com

total return	★★★
risk reduction	★★★★★
management	★★★★
current income	★★
expense control	★★★★★
symbol PYGFX	19 points
up-market performance	good
down-market performance	excellent
predictability of returns	excellent

Total Return ★★★
Over the past five years, Payden & Rygel Global Fixed-Income R has taken $10,000 and turned it into $14,030 ($11,580 over three years). This translates into an annualized return of 7 percent over the past five years and 5 percent over the past three years. Over the past five years, this fund has outperformed 69 percent of all mutual funds; within its general category, it has done better than 90 percent of its peers. World bond funds have averaged 3 percent annually over these same five years.

During the past five years, a $10,000 initial investment grew to $12,300 after taxes, assuming a 40 percent income tax bracket (state and federal combined) and a capital gains rate of 20 percent. This means that investors in this fund were able to preserve 57 percent of their total returns. Compared to other funds in the same category, this fund's tax savings are considered to be excellent.

Risk/Volatility ★★★★★
Over the past five years, Payden & Rygel Global Fixed-Income R has been safer than 82 percent of all world bond funds. Over the past decade, the fund has had two negative years, while the Lehman Brothers Aggregate Bond Index has had two (off 3 percent in 1994 and 1 percent in 1999); the Salomon Brothers World Government Bond Index fell four times (off 4 percent in 1997, 5 percent in 1999, 3 percent in 2000, and 4 percent in 2001). The fund has underperformed the Lehman Brothers Aggregate Bond Index twice and the Salomon Brothers World Government Bond Index four times in the past ten years. Consistency of *overperformance* for this fund has been very good.

	past 5 years		past 10 years	
worst year	-0.5%	1999	-3.0%	1994
best year	11.7%	1998	18%	1995

Risk-adjusted returns have also been superb over the past three, five, and ten years. Over the past five years, the fund's three worst quarters have been second quarter 1999 (-1 percent), first quarter 1997 (-1 percent), and second quarter 2001

(0 percent). During the same period, the three best quarters have been third quarter 1998 (6 percent), fourth quarter 2000 (4 percent), and second quarter 1997 (4 percent). In the past, Payden & Rygel Global Fixed-Income R has done better than 41 percent of its peer group during the most recent bull market and outperformed 76 percent of its peer group during the most recent bear market. Consistency, or predictability, of returns for Payden & Rygel Global Fixed-Income R can be described as excellent. This fund's risk-related return ranks in the top quintile.

Management   ★★★★
There are forty-five fixed-income securities in this $350 million portfolio. The average world bond fund today is $95 million in size. Close to 86 percent of the fund's holdings are in bonds. The average maturity of the bonds in this account is nine years; the weighted coupon rate averages 5 percent. The portfolio's fixed-income holdings can be categorized as intermediate-term, high-quality debt.

A team has managed this fund for the past seven years. Management maintains an average credit rating of AAA within the portfolio; currency hedging is also used to reduce risk. There are nineteen funds besides Global Fixed-Income R within the Payden & Rygel family. Overall, the fund family's risk-adjusted performance can be described as good to very good.

Current Income   ★★
Over the past year, Payden & Rygel Global Fixed-Income R had a twelve-month yield of 8.4 percent. During this same twelve-month period, the typical world bond fund had a yield that averaged 5.7 percent.

Expenses   ★★★★★
Payden & Rygel Global Fixed-Income R's expense ratio is 0.5 percent; it has averaged 0.5 percent annually over the past three calendar years. The average expense ratio for the 190 funds in this category is 1.4 percent. This fund's turnover rate over the past year has been 131 percent, while its peer group average has been 231 percent.

Summary
Payden & Rygel Global Fixed-Income R, a high-quality, intermediate-term world bond fund, has outperformed 70 percent of all mutual funds over the past five years as well as 90 percent of its peer group over the same period. Returns over shorter periods have also been quite good. Within its peer group, the fund easily ranks number one when it comes to predictability of returns, low risk, and low expense. It is also the most tax efficient of its group. On a total point basis, this is the number-one fund for its category.

Profile

minimum initial investment $5,000	*IRA accounts available* . . . . yes
subsequent minimum investment . $1,000	*IRA minimum investment* $2,000
available in all 50 states. . . . . yes	*date of inception* . . . . Sept. 1992
telephone exchanges. . . . . yes	*dividend/income paid.* . . . . monthly
number of funds in family 20	*average credit quality* . . . . AAA

T. Rowe Price Emerging Markets Bond

100 East Pratt Street
Baltimore, MD 21202
(800) 638-5660
www.troweprice.com

total return	★★★
risk reduction	★★
management	★★★
current income	★★★★★
expense control	★★★★
symbol PREMX	17 points
up-market performance	excellent
down-market performance	good
predictability of returns	fair

Total Return   ★★★

Over the past five years, T. Rowe Price Emerging Markets Bond has taken $10,000 and turned it into $14,030 ($15,610 over three years). This translates into an annualized return of 7 percent over the past five years and 16 percent over the past three years. Over the past five years, this fund has outperformed 63 percent of all mutual funds; within its general category, it has done better than 66 percent of its peers. World bond funds have averaged 3 percent annually over these same five years.

During the past five years, a $10,000 initial investment grew to $11,130 after taxes, assuming a 40 percent income tax bracket (state and federal combined) and a capital gains rate of 20 percent. This means that investors in this fund were able to preserve 28 percent of their total returns. Compared to other funds in the same category, this fund's tax savings are considered to be fair.

Risk/Volatility   ★★

Over the past five years, T. Rowe Price Emerging Markets Bond has been safer than 80 percent of all world bond funds. Over the past decade, the fund has had one negative year, while the Lehman Brothers Aggregate Bond Index has had two (off 3 percent in 1994 and 1 percent in 1999); the Salomon Brothers World Government Bond Index fell four times (off 4 percent in 1997, 5 percent in 1999, 3 percent in 2000, and 4 percent in 2001). The fund has underperformed the Lehman Brothers Aggregate Bond Index once and the Salomon Brothers World Government Bond Index five times in the past ten years. Consistency of *overperformance* for this fund has been good.

	past 5 years		past 10 years	
worst year	-23.1%	1998	-23.1%	1998
best year	23.0%	1999	36.8%	1996

Over the past five years, the fund's three worst quarters have been third quarter 1998 (-30 percent), second quarter 1998 (-8 percent), and fourth quarter 1997 (-5 percent). During the same period, the three best quarters have been fourth quarter 1999 (14 percent), fourth quarter 1998 (13 percent), and second quarter 1997 (12 percent). In the past, T. Rowe Price Emerging Markets Bond has done better than 86 percent of its peer group during the most recent bull market and outperformed 46 percent of its peer group during the most recent bear market. Consistency, or predictability, of returns for T. Rowe Price Emerging Markets Bond can be described as fair. This fund's risk-related return ranks in the top half.

Management   ★★★
There are fifty fixed-income securities in this $150 million portfolio. The average world bond fund today is $95 million in size. Close to 97 percent of the fund's holdings are in bonds. The average maturity of the bonds in this account is twelve years; the weighted coupon rate averages 7.9 percent. The portfolio's fixed-income holdings can be categorized as intermediate-term, low-quality debt.

A team has managed this fund for the past six years. Managers Rothery, Conelius, and Kelson believe more in developing market diversity than their brethren. Management prefers sovereign debt instead of the less reliable corporate paper. No more than a fifth of the portfolio is in any one country. There are eighty-four funds besides Emerging Markets Bond within the T. Rowe Price family. Overall, the fund family's risk-adjusted performance can be described as good to very good.

Current Income   ★★★★★
Over the past year, T. Rowe Price Emerging Markets Bond had a twelve-month yield of 11.2 percent. During this same twelve-month period, the typical world bond fund had a yield that averaged 5.7 percent.

Expenses   ★★★★
T. Rowe Price Emerging Markets Bond's expense ratio is 1.2 percent; it has averaged 1.2 percent annually over the past three calendar years. The average expense ratio for the 190 funds in this category is 1.4 percent. This fund's turnover rate over the past year has been 70 percent, while its peer group average has been 231 percent.

Summary
T. Rowe Price Emerging Markets Bond, a low-quality, intermediate-term world bond fund, has outperformed 94 percent of all mutual funds over the past three years as well as 66 percent of its peer group over the past five years. Risk-adjusted returns have ranged from very good to poor over the past three to five years. This fund outperformed the Lehman Brothers Aggregate Bond Index by 24 percentage points in 1999. This portfolio's alpha, which measures excess returns per unit of risk taken, as measured against the fund's benchmark index, is quite appealing.

Profile

minimum initial investment $2,500	*IRA accounts available* . . . . yes
subsequent minimum investment . . $100	*IRA minimum investment* $1,000
available in all 50 states. . . . . yes	*date of inception*. . . . . Dec. 1994
telephone exchanges. . . . . yes	*dividend/income paid*. . . . . monthly
number of funds in family 85	*average credit quality* . . . . BB

XII.
Summary

Aggressive Growth Funds
    Fidelity Low-Priced Stock
    Fremont U.S. Micro-Cap
    Meridian Growth
    Merrill Lynch Small Cap Value B
    Quaker Aggressive Growth A
    Reserve Small-Cap Growth R
    Royce Micro-Cap Investor Shares
    Smith Barney Aggressive
      Growth A
    Tocqueville Small Cap Value
    Wasatch Small Cap Growth

Balanced Funds
    Calamos Convertible A
    Calamos Convertible Growth &
      Income A
    Dodge & Cox Balanced
    First Eagle SoGen Global A
    Gabelli ABC
    Nations Convertible Securities
      Investor A
    Oakmark Equity & Income I
    Oppenheimer Global Growth &
      Income A

Corporate Bond Funds
    Dodge & Cox Income
    FPA New Income
    Fremont Bond
    Harbor Bond
    Stein Roe Intermediate Bond
    Strong Advantage Investor Class

Financial Funds
    Century Shares Trust
    Davis Financial A

Global Equity (Stock) Funds
    Artisan International
    First Eagle SoGen Overseas A
    Merrill Lynch Global Small Cap D
    Oppenheimer Global A
    Pilgrim International Small Cap A
    Tweedy, Browne Global Value
    William Blair International
      Growth N

Government Bond Funds
    Franklin U.S. Government
      Securities A
    Pilgrim GNMA Income A
    Sit U.S. Government Securities
    Strong Government Securities
      Investor Shares
    Vanguard GNMA

Growth Funds
    Calamos Growth A
    FMI Focus
    Fountainhead Special Value
    Hartford Capital Appreciation A
    Lord Abbett Mid-Cap Value A
    Meridian Value
    Olstein Financial Alert C
    Parnassus
    Thompson Plumb Growth
    Wasatch Core Growth

Growth and Income Funds
American Century Equity Income
Investor Shares
Ameristock
Dodge & Cox Stock
FPA Perennial
MFS Value A
Muhlenkamp
Van Kampen Comstock A
Van Kampen Equity-Income A

Health Care Funds
Eaton Vance Worldwide Health A
Vanguard Health Care

High-Yield Corporate Bond Funds
American Funds High-Income
Trust A
Columbia High-Yield
Janus High-Yield
Lord Abbett Bond-Debenture A
T. Rowe Price High-Yield

Metals and Natural Resources Funds
Excelsior Energy & Natural
Resources
INVESCO Energy Investor Shares
T. Rowe Price New Era
Vanguard Energy
Vanguard Precious Metals

Money Market Funds
Elfun Money Market
Fidelity U.S. Government Reserves
Glenmede Government Cash
Janus Tax-Exempt Money
Market Service
Scudder Premium Money Market
Strong Municipal Money Market
Trust for Credit Union Money
Market
USAA Tax-Exempt Money Market
Vanguard Federal Money Market
Wells Fargo Money Market Trust
Wells Fargo National Tax-Free
Money Market Trust

Municipal Bond Funds
American Century California High-
Yield Municipal Investor Shares
American Funds Tax-Exempt
Bond Fund A
Calvert Tax-Free Reserves
Limited-Term A
Limited Term New York
Municipal A
Scudder High-Yield Tax-Free S
T. Rowe Price Tax-Free Short-
Intermediate
USAA Tax-Exempt Short-Term
Vanguard Florida Insured Long-
Term Tax-Exempt
Vanguard Intermediate-Term Tax-
Exempt

Real Estate Funds
Columbia Real Estate Equity
Security Capital U.S. Real Estate

Technology Funds
Firsthand Technology Value
North Track PSE Tech 100 Index A

Utility Stock Funds
AXP Utilities Income A
MFS Utilities A
Morgan Stanley Global Utilities B
Strong Dividend Income

World Bond Funds
Alliance North American
Government Income A
Fidelity New Markets Income
Payden & Rygel Global Fixed-
Income R
T. Rowe Price Emerging
Markets Bond

Appendix A
Glossary of Mutual Fund Terms

advisor—The individual or organization employed by a mutual fund to give professional advice on the fund's investments and asset management practices (also called the "investment advisor").

asked or offering price—The price at which a mutual fund's shares can be purchased. The asked, or offering, price means the current net asset value per share plus sales charge, if any.

BARRA Growth Index—An index of 152 large-capitalization stocks that are all part of the Standard & Poor's 500, specifically those with above-average sales and earnings growth.

BARRA Value Index—An index of 363 large-capitalization stocks that are all part of the Standard & Poor's 500, specifically those with above-average dividend yields and relatively low prices considering their book values.

bid or sell price—The price at which a mutual fund's shares are redeemed (bought back) by the fund. The bid or redemption price usually means the current net asset value per share.

board certified—Designation given to someone who has become certified in insurance, estate planning, income taxes, securities, mutual funds, or financial planning. To obtain additional information about the board-certified programs or to get the name of a board-certified advisor in your area, call (800) 848-2029.

bottom up—Refers to a type of security analysis. Management that follows the bottom-up approach is more concerned with the company than with the economy in general. Analysis is based on things such as a company's financial strength, competitive strength, and potential for growth in earnings and cash flow. (For a contrasting style, see **top down**.)

broker/dealer—A firm that buys and sells mutual fund shares and other securities to the public.

capital gains distributions—Payments to mutual fund shareholders of profits (long-term gains) realized on the sale of the fund's portfolio securities. These amounts are usually paid once a year.

capital growth—An increase in the market value of a mutual fund's securities, as reflected in the net asset value of fund shares. This is a specific long-term objective of many mutual funds.

cash reserves—Short-term, interest-bearing securities that can easily and quickly be converted to cash. Some funds keep cash levels at a minimum and always remain in stocks and/or bonds; other funds hold up to 25 percent or more of their assets in cash reserves (money market instruments) as either a defensive play or as a buying opportunity to be used when securities become depressed in price.

CFS—Also known as Certified Fund Specialist, this is the only designation awarded to brokers, financial planners, CPAs, insurance agents, and other investment advisors who either recommend or sell mutual funds. Fewer than 7,000 people across the country have passed this certification program. To obtain additional information about the CFS program or to get the name of a CFS in your area, call (800) 848-2029.

CPI—The Consumer Price Index (CPI) is the most commonly used yardstick for measuring the rate of inflation in the United States.

custodian—The organization (usually a bank) that keeps custody of securities and other assets of a mutual fund.

derivatives—A financial contract whose value is based on, or "derived," from a traditional security, such as a stock or bond. The most common examples of derivatives are futures contracts and options.

diversification—The policy of all mutual funds to spread investments among a number of different securities in order to reduce the risk inherent in investing.

dollar-cost averaging—The practice of investing equal amounts of money at regular intervals regardless of whether securities markets are moving up or down. This procedure reduces average share costs to the investor, who acquires more shares during periods of lower securities prices and fewer shares during periods of higher prices.

EAFE—An equity index (EAFE stands for Europe, Australia, and the Far East) used to measure stock market performance outside the United States. The EAFE is a sort of Standard & Poor's 500 Index for overseas or foreign stocks. As of the middle of 1997, the EAFE was weighted as follows: 59.5 percent Europe, 28.8 percent Japan, 10.6 percent Pacific Rim, and 1.1 percent "other."

exchange privilege—An option enabling mutual fund shareholders to transfer their investment from one fund to another within the same fund family as their needs or objectives change. Typically, funds allow investors to use the exchange privilege several times a year for a low fee or no fee per exchange.

expense ratio—A figure expressed as a percentage of a fund's assets. The main element is the management fee. Administrative fees cover a fund's day-to-day operations, including printing materials, keeping records, paying staff, and renting office space. Sometimes administrative fees are included in the management fee; a number of funds list such fees separately. Roughly half of all funds charge a 12b-1 fee, which pays for a fund's distribution and advertising costs. The 12b-1 fee can be higher than the management or administrative fee.

indexing—In contrast to the traditional approach to investing that tries to outperform market averages, index investing is a strategy that seeks to match the performance of a group of securities that form a recognized market measure, known as an index.

investment company—A corporation, trust, or partnership that invests pooled funds of shareholders in securities appropriate to the fund's objective. Among the benefits of investment companies, compared to direct investments, are professional management and diversification. Mutual funds (also known as open-ended and close-ended investment companies) are the most popular type of investment company.

investment objective—The goal that the investor and mutual fund pursue together (e.g., growth of capital or current income).

large-cap stocks—Equities issued by companies with a net worth of at least $7.5 billion.

long-term funds—An industry designation for funds that invest primarily in securities with remaining maturities of more than one year. In this book, the term means fifteen years or more. Long-term funds are broadly divided into bond and income funds.

management fee—The amount paid by a mutual fund to the investment advisor for its services. The average annual fee industrywide is about 0.7 percent of fund assets.

"market-neutral" funds—A strategy that seeks to neutralize market movements by running two portfolios simultaneously: One buys stocks that are predicted to rise, and the other invests an equal amount in a similar assortment of other stocks that are predicted to decline.

mid-cap stocks—Equities issued by companies with a net worth between $1 billion and $7.5 billion.

mutual fund—An investment company that pools money from shareholders and invests in a variety of securities, including stocks, bonds, and money market instruments. A mutual fund stands ready to buy back (redeem) its shares at their current net asset value; this value depends on the market value of the fund's portfolio securities at the time of redemption. Most mutual funds continuously offer new shares to investors.

net asset value per share—The market worth of one share of a mutual fund. This figure is derived by taking a fund's total assets—securities, cash, and any accrued earnings—deducting liabilities, and dividing by the number of shares outstanding.

no-load fund—A mutual fund selling its shares at net asset value without the addition of sales charges.

passive management—A portfolio that tries to match the performance of a target index, such as the Standard & Poor's 500.

portfolio—A collection of securities owned by an individual or an institution (such as a mutual fund). A fund's portfolio may include a combination of stocks, bonds, and money market securities.

portfolio diversification—The average U.S. stock fund has about 30 percent of its assets invested in its ten largest holdings.

prospectus—The official booklet that describes a mutual fund; it must be furnished to all investors. The prospectus contains information required by the U.S. Securities and Exchange Commission on subjects such as the fund's investment objectives, services, and fees. A more detailed document, known as "Part B" of the prospectus or the "Statement of Additional Information," is available at no charge on request.

redemption price—The amount per share (shown as the "bid" in newspaper tables) that mutual fund shareholders receive when they cash in the shares. The value of the shares depends on the market value of the fund's portfolio securities at the time. This value is the same as net asset value per share.

reinvestment privilege—An option available to mutual fund shareholders in which fund dividends and capital gains distributions are automatically turned back into the fund to buy new shares, without charge (meaning no sales fee or commission), thereby increasing holdings.

Russell 2000—An index that represents 2,000 small domestic companies (less than 8 percent of the U.S. equity market).

sales charge—An amount charged to purchase shares in many mutual funds sold by brokers or other sales agents. The maximum charge is 8.5 percent of the initial investment; the vast majority of funds now have a maximum charge of 4.75 percent or less. The charge is added to the net asset value per share when determining the offering price.

short-term funds—An industry designation for funds that invest primarily in securities with maturities of less than one year; the term means five years or less in this book. Short-term funds include money market funds and certain municipal bond funds.

small-cap stocks—Equities issued by companies with a net worth of less than $1 billion.

top down—Refers to a type of security analysis. Management that follows the top-down approach is very concerned with the general level of the economy and any fiscal policy being followed by the government. (see **bottom up**.)

transfer agent—The organization employed by a mutual fund to prepare and maintain records relating to the accounts of its shareholders. Some funds serve as their own transfer agents.

turnover—The percentage of a fund's portfolio that is sold during the year, a percentage rate that can range from 0 percent to 300 percent or more. The average turnover rate for U.S. stock funds is approximately 80 percent (10 percent for domestic stock index funds).

12b-1 fee—The distribution fee charged by some funds, named after a federal government rule. Such fees pay for marketing costs, such as advertising and dealer compensation. The fund's prospectus outlines 12b-1 fees, if applicable.

underwriter—The organization that acts as the distributor of a mutual fund's shares to broker/dealers and investors.

value stocks—Stocks that most investors view as unattractive for some reason. They tend to be priced low relative to some measure of the company's worth, such as earnings, book value, or cash flow. Value stock managers try to identify companies whose prices are depressed for temporary reasons, and that may bounce back strongly if investor sentiment improves.

■ ■ ■

The Securities Act of 1933 requires a fund's shares to be registered with the Securities and Exchange Commission (SEC) prior to their sale. In essence, the Securities Act ensures that the fund provides potential investors with a current prospectus. This law also limits the types of advertisements that may be used by a mutual fund.

The Securities Exchange Act of 1934 regulates the purchase and sale of all types of securities, including mutual fund shares.

The Investment Advisors Act of 1940 is a body of law that regulates certain activities of the investment advisors with regard to mutual funds.

The Investment Company Act of 1940 is a highly detailed regulatory statute applying to mutual fund companies. This act contains numerous provisions designed to prevent self-dealing by employees of the mutual fund company, as well as other conflicts of interest. It also provides for the safekeeping of fund assets and prohibits the payment of excessive fees and charges by the fund and its shareholders.

Appendix B
Who Regulates Mutual Funds?

Mutual funds are highly regulated businesses that must comply with some of the toughest laws and rules in the financial services industry. All funds are regulated by the U.S. Securities and Exchange Commission (SEC). With its extensive rule-making and enforcement authority, the SEC oversees mutual fund compliance chiefly by relying on the four major federal securities statutes mentioned in Appendix A.

Fund assets must generally be held by an independent custodian. There are strict requirements for fidelity bonding to ensure against the misappropriation of shareholder monies. In addition to federal statutes, almost every state has its own set of regulations governing mutual funds.

Although federal and state laws cannot guarantee that a fund will be profitable, they are designed to ensure that all mutual funds are operated and managed in the interests of their shareholders. Here are some specific investor protections that every fund must follow:

- Regulations concerning what may be claimed or promised about a mutual fund and its potential
- Requirements that vital information about a fund be made readily available (such as a prospectus, the "Statement of Additional Information," also known as "Part B" of the prospectus, and annual and semiannual reports)
- Requirements that a fund operate in the interest of its shareholders, rather than any special interests of its management
- Rules dictating diversification of the fund's portfolio over a wide range of investments to avoid too much concentration in a particular security

Appendix C
Dollar-Cost Averaging

Investors often believe that the market will go down as soon as they get in. For these people, and anyone concerned with reducing risk, the solution is dollar-cost averaging.

Dollar-cost averaging is a simple yet effective way to reduce risk, whether you are investing in stocks or bonds. The premise behind dollar-cost averaging (DCA) is that if several purchases of a fund are made over an extended period, the unpredictable highs and lows will average out. The investor ends up buying some shares at a comparatively low price, others at perhaps a much higher price.

DCA assumes that investors are willing to sacrifice the possibility that they bought all their shares at the lowest price for the certainty that they did not buy every share at the highest price. In short, investors are willing to accept a compromise—a sort of *risk-adjusted* decision.

DCA is based on investing a fixed amount of money in a given fund at specific intervals. Typically, an investor will put a few hundred dollars at the beginning of each month into the XYZ mutual fund. DCA works best if you invest and continue to invest on an established schedule, *regardless of price fluctuations*. You will be buying more shares when the price is down than when it is up. Most investors do not mind buying shares when prices are increasing, since this means that their existing shares are also going up. When this program is followed, losses during market declines are limited, while the ability to participate in good markets is maintained.

Another advantage is that DCA increases the likelihood that you will follow an investment program. As with other aspects of our life, it is important to have goals. However, DCA is not something that should be universally recommended. Whether you should use dollar-cost averaging depends on your risk level.

From its beginnings well over one hundred years ago, the stock market has always had an upward bias in performance. More often than not, the market goes up, not down. Therefore, it hardly makes sense to apply dollar-cost averaging to an investment vehicle, knowing that historically you would be paying a higher and higher price per share over time.

Studies done by the Institute of Business & Finance (800-848-2029) show that over the past fifty years, a dollar-cost averaging program produced inferior returns compared to a lump-sum investment. The institute's studies conclude the following: (1) a DCA program is a good idea for a conservative investor (the person or couple who gives more weight or importance to risk than reward); (2) for investors whose risk level is anything but conservative (an immediate, one-time investment resulted in better returns the great majority of the time); and (3) there

have certainly been periods when a DCA program would have benefited even the
extremely aggressive investor—but such periods have not been very common over
the past half-century and have been quite rare over the past twenty, fifteen, ten,
five, and three years.

Example of Dollar-Cost Averaging
($1,000 invested per period)

period (1)	cost per share (2)	number of shares bought with $1,000 (3)	total shares owned (4)	current total amount invested (5)	net gain value of shares (2) x (4) (6)	or loss (percentage) (6) x (5) (7)
1	$100	10.0	10.0	$1,000	$1,000	0
2	$80	12.5	22.5	$2,000	$1,800	-10.0
3	$70	14.3	36.8	$3,000	$2,576	-14.1
4	$60	16.7	53.5	$4,000	$3,210	-19.7
5	$50	20.0	73.5	$5,000	$3,675	-26.5
6	$70	14.3	87.8	$6,000	$6,146	+2.4
7	$80	12.5	100.3	$7,000	$8,024	+14.6
8	$100	10.0	110.3	$8,000	$11,030	+37.9

Appendix D
Systematic Withdrawal Plan

A systematic withdrawal plan (SWP) allows a check for a specified amount to be sent monthly or quarterly to you, or to anyone you designate, from your mutual fund account. There is no charge for this service.

This method of getting monthly checks is ideal for the income-oriented investor. It is also a risk reduction technique—a kind of dollar-cost averaging in reverse. A set amount is sent to you each month. In order to send you a check for a set amount, shares of one or more of your mutual funds must be sold, which, in turn, will most likely trigger a taxable event, but only for those shares redeemed.

When the market is low, the number of mutual fund shares being liquidated will be higher than when the market is high, since the fund's price per share will be lower. If you need $500 a month and the fund's price is $25 per share, twenty shares must be liquidated; if the price per share is $20 per share, twenty-five shares must be sold.

Here is an example of a SWP from the Investment Company of America (ICA), a conservative growth and income fund featured in previous editions of this book. The example assumes an initial investment of $100,000 in the fund at its inception, the beginning of 1934. A greater or smaller dollar amount could be used. The example shows what happens to the investor's principal over a sixty-eight-year period (January 1, 1934, through March 31, 2002). It assumes that $10,000 is withdrawn from the fund at the end of the first year. At the end of the first year, the $10,000 withdrawal *is increased by 4 percent each year thereafter* to offset the effects of inflation, which averaged less than 4 percent during this sixty-seven-year period. This means that the withdrawal for the second year was $10,400 ($10,000 multiplied by 1.04), for the third year $10,816 ($10,400 multiplied by 1.04), and so on.

Compare this example to what would have happened if the money had been placed in an average fixed-income account at a bank. The $100,000 depositor who took out only $9,000 each year would be in a far different situation. His (or her) original $100,000 was fully depleted by the end of 1948. All the principal and interest payments could not keep up with an annual withdrawal of $9,000.

The difference between ICA and the savings account is over $13 million. The savings account had a total return of $26,300 (plus distribution of the original $100,000 principal); the ICA account had a total return of $13,580,211 ($3,349,211 distributed over sixty-eight years plus a remaining principal, or account balance, of $10,231,000). This difference becomes even more disturbing when you consider that the bank depositor's withdrawals were not increasing each year to offset the effects of inflation. The interest rates used in this example came from the *U.S. Savings & Loan League Fact Book*.

SWP from the Investment Company of America (ICA)
initial investment: $100,000
annual withdrawals of: $10,000 (10 percent)
the first check is sent: 12/31/34
withdrawals annually increased by: 4 percent

date	amount withdrawn	value of remaining shares
12/31/34	$10,000	$109,000
12/31/35	$10,400	$185,000
12/31/40	$12,700	$153,000
12/31/45	$15,400	$247,000
12/31/50	$18,700	$212,000
12/31/55	$22,800	$374,000
12/31/60	$27,700	$465,000
12/31/65	$33,700	$679,000
12/31/70	$41,000	$742,000
12/31/75	$50,000	$669,000
12/31/80	$60,700	$1,007,000
12/31/85	$73,900	$1,790,000
12/31/86	$76,900	$2,104,000
12/31/87	$79,900	$2,136,000
12/31/88	$83,100	$2,336,000
12/31/89	$86,500	$2,936,000
12/31/90	$89,900	$2,865,000
12/31/91	$93,500	$3,525,000
12/31/92	$86,500	$3,673,000
12/31/93	$101,200	$3,997,000
12/31/94	$105,200	$3,897,000
12/31/95	$109,400	$4,981,000
12/31/96	$113,780	$5,830,000
12/31/97	$118,330	$7,448,000
12/31/98	$123,060	$9,026,000
12/31/99	$127,987	$10,386,000
12/31/00	$133,107	$10,649,000
12/31/01	$138,431	$10,159,100
3/31/02	————	$10,231,100

If the ICA systematic withdrawal plan were 8 percent annually instead of 10 percent (but still increased by 4 percent each year to offset the effects of inflation), the investor would have ended up with remaining shares worth nearly $100 million, plus withdrawals that totaled $2.7 million.

So, the next time some broker or banker tells you that you should be buying bonds or CDs for current income, tell him or her about a systematic withdrawal plan (SWP), a program designed to maximize your income and offset something the CD, T-bill, and bond advocates never mention: inflation.

Appendix E
Load or No-Load—Which Is Right for You?

As the amount of information available on mutual funds continues to grow almost exponentially, the load versus no-load debate has intensified. What makes the issue difficult to evaluate is the continued absence of neutrality on either side. Before you learn the real truth, let us first examine who is advocating what, what their biases are, and how each side argues its point.

A number of publications, including *Money*, *Forbes*, *Fortune*, *Kiplinger Personal Investor*, and *BusinessWeek*, favor the no-load camp. Although these publications appear neutral, they are not. First, each one derives the overwhelming majority of its mutual fund advertisements from funds that charge no commission. Second, these publications are trying to increase readership; they are in the business of selling copy, not information. A good way to increase or maintain a healthy circulation is by having their readership rely on them for advice—instead of going to a broker or investment advisor.

On the other side is the financial services industry, whose most vocal load supporters include the brokerage, banking, and insurance industries. That's not much of a surprise. These groups are also biased. Like the publication that only makes money by getting you to purchase a copy or having an editorial board whose policy favors no-load funds, much of the financial services community supports a sales charge because that is how they are compensated.

No-load proponents argue that a fund that charges any kind of commission or ongoing marketing fee (which is known as a 12b-1 charge) inherently cannot be as good as a similar investment that has no entry or exit fee or ongoing 12b-1 charge. On the surface, this argument appears logical. After all, if one investor starts off with a dollar invested and the other starts off with somewhere between 99 and 92 cents (commissions range from 1 to 8.5 percent; most are in the 3 to 5 percent range), all other things being equal, the person who has all of his money working for him will do better than the person who has an initial deduction. The press and the no-load funds say that there is no reason to pay a commission because you can do as well or better than the broker or advisor whose job it is to provide you with suggestions and guidance.

The commission-oriented community says you should pay a sales charge because you get what you pay for—good advice and ongoing service. After all, brokers, financial planners, banks that include mutual fund desks, and insurance agents are all highly trained professionals who know things you do not. Moreover, they study the markets on a continuous basis, ensuring that they have more information than any weekend investor. In short, they ask, Do you want someone managing your money who has experience and works full-time in this area, or someone such as yourself who has no formal training and whose time and resources are limited?

There is no clear-cut solution. Both sides raise valid points. To gain more insight into what course of action (or type of fund) is best for you, let us take a neutral approach. I believe I can give you valid reasons both kinds of funds make sense, because I have no hidden agenda. True, I am a licensed broker and branch manager of a national securities firm; however, the great majority of my compensation is based on a fee for service, meaning that clients who invest solely in no-load funds pay me an annual management fee.

First, you should never pay a commission to someone who knows no more about investing than you do. There is no value added in such a situation, except perhaps during uncertain or negative periods in the market. (This point will be discussed later.) After all, if your broker's advice and mutual fund experience are based solely on the same financial publications you have access to, you are not getting your money's worth by paying a sales charge. I raise this point first because the financial services industry is filled with a tremendous number of inexperienced and ignorant brokers. These people may make a lot of money, but this is usually the result of their connections (they know a lot of people) or marketing skills (they know how to get new business)—neither of which has anything to do with your money.

Brokerage firms, banks, and insurance companies hire stockbrokers based on their sales ability, not on their knowledge or analytical ability. The financial analysts at the home office are the ones involved in research and managing money. The fact that your broker has a couple of dozen years' experience in the securities industry or is a vice president may actually be hazardous to your financial health. Extensive experience could mean that the advisor is less inclined to learn about new products or studies, because she already has an established client base. Brokers obtain titles such as "vice president" because they outsell their peers. Contests (awards, trips, prizes, and enhanced payouts) are based on how much is sold, period. There has never been an instance of a brokerage firm, bank, or insurance company giving an award to someone based on knowledge or how well a client's account performed.

Second, if your investment time horizon is less than a couple of years, it is a mistake to pay anything more than a nominal fee, something in the 1 percent range. Even though the advice you are receiving may be great, it is hard to justify a 3 to 5 percent commission over the short haul. Sales charges in this range can only be rationalized if they can be amortized over a number of years. Thus, worthwhile advice becomes a bargain if you stay with the investment, or within the same family of mutual funds, for at least three years.

Third, if you are purchasing a fund that charges a fee, find out what you are getting for your money. Question the advisor; find out about his or her training, experience, education, and designations. Equally important, get a clear understanding about what you will be receiving on an ongoing basis. What kind of continuing education does the broker engage in (attending conferences, reading books, seeking a designation, and so forth)? Finally, make sure your advisor or broker tells you how your investments will be monitored. It is important to know how often you will be contacted and how a buy, hold, or sell decision will be made.

So far, it looks as if I've been pretty tough on my fellow brokers. Well, believe me, I'm even harder on about 99 percent of those do-it-yourself investors. I have been in this business for close to twenty years, and I can tell you that I have rarely met an investor who was better off on his or her own. Here's why.

First, it is extremely difficult to be objective about your own investments. Decisions based on what you have read from a newsletter or magazine or what you learned at a seminar are often a response to current news, such as trade relations with Japan, the value of the U.S. dollar, the state of the economy, or the direction of interest rates. This kind of knee-jerk reaction has proved to be wrong in most cases.

Mind you, out of fairness to those who manage their own investments, amateurs aren't the only ones who make investment errors. As an example, the majority of the major brokerage firms gave a sell signal just before the war in the Persian Gulf. It turned out that this would have been about the perfect time to buy. E. F. Hutton was forced to merge with another brokerage firm because they incorrectly predicted the direction of interest rates (and lost tens of millions of dollars in their own portfolio).

The mutual fund industry itself deserves a healthy part of the blame, as evidenced by their timing of new funds. Take my advice: When you see a number of new mutual funds coming out with the same timely theme (government plus or optioned-enhanced bond funds in the mid-1980s, Eastern European funds after German reunification, health-care funds a few years ago, derivatives and hedge funds last year), run for cover. By the time these funds come out, the party is about to end. Investors who got into these funds often do well for a number of months but soon face devastating declines.

Your favorite financial publications are also to blame. Their advice is based on a herd instinct: What do our readers think? Instead of providing leadership, they simply reinforce what is most likely incorrect information. For example, for over a year after the 1987 stock market crash, the most popular of these mainstream publications, *Money*, had cover stories that recommended (and extolled the virtues of) safe investments. For almost a year and a half after the crash, this magazine was giving out bad advice. When something goes on sale (stocks, in this case) you should be a buyer, not a seller. Since *Money* routinely surveys (or polls) their readers for feature articles, such behavior (the herd instinct) is understandable but not forgivable.

Besides the lack of objectivity and the constant bombardment of what I call "daily noise" (what the market is doing at the moment, comments from the financial gurus, etc.), there is also the question of your competence. Presumably, you and I could figure out how to fix our own plumbing, sew our own clothes, fix the car when it breaks down, or avoid paying a lawyer by purchasing "do-it-yourself" books. The question then becomes whether it is worth going through the learning curve, and, even supposing we are successful, whether the task would have been better accomplished by someone else—perhaps for less money or better use of our own time. I think the answer is obvious. Each of us has his or her own area or areas of expertise or skill. You and I rely on others either because they know more than we do about the topic or task at hand or because having someone else help is a more efficient use of our time.

If you're going to seek the services of an investment advisor or broker, it should be because he or she knows more than you do, because he or she is more objective, or because you can make more money doing whatever you do than taking the time to make complex investment decisions yourself. This is what makes sense. The fact that there are brokers and advisors who put their interests before yours is simply a reality that you must deal with. And the proper way to deal with these conflicts of interest or ignorant counselors is by doing your homework. Ask questions. Just as there are great plumbers, mechanics, lawyers, and doctors, so, too, are there exceptional investment advisors and brokers. Your job is to find them.

Eliminating load or no-load funds from your investing universe is not the answer. If you are determined never to pay a commission, then you may miss out on the next John Templeton (the Franklin-Templeton family of funds), Peter Lynch (Fidelity Magellan Fund), or Jean-Marie Eveillard (SoGen Funds). You will also miss out on some of the very best mutual fund families: American Funds (large), Fidelity-Advisor (medium), and SoGen (small). A better way to proceed is to try to separate good funds from bad ones. After all, an investor is clearly far better off in a good load fund than in a bad no-load one.

The bottom line is that performance, as well as *risk-adjusted returns*, for load funds often exceeds the returns on no-load funds, and vice versa. The "top ten" list (or whatever number you want to use) for one period may have been dominated by funds that charge a commission, but in just a year or two the top ten list may be heavily populated by mutual funds with no sales charge or commission.

It might seem strange to be questioning the benefits of financial planning when our society places professions like law and accountancy in such high regard. And certainly I am not suggesting that investors should consider only load funds. But with all the load-fund bashing in recent years, it is important to recognize that no-load funds are not the perfect answer for a large percentage of investors. Approaching the mutual fund industry with an "us versus them" mentality results in a great deal of misleading information and unfairly discredits the work of skilled financial planners and brokers.

Appendix F
The U.S. Market Compared to Foreign Markets

Investing worldwide gives you exposure to different stages of economic market cycles, which has given international investors an advantage in the past. Foreign equities and bonds have generally offered higher levels of short-, intermediate-, and long-term growth than their domestic counterparts. Not once during the past fourteen years was the U.S. stock market the world's top performer (all figures are in U.S. dollars).

Historically, Europeans have invested most of their money in gold and bonds. Today, lower interest rates, the privatization of state assets, and pension reform are providing renewed interest in common stocks for the Continent, where levels of equity ownership are a very small percentage of what they are in the United States and the United Kingdom.

Top-Performing World Stock Markets: A Fourteen-Year Review: 1987–2000

year	1st	2nd	3rd	4th	5th
2000	Denmark 22%	Switzerland 16%	Venezuela 12%	Ireland 7%	Norway 2%
1999	Finland 153%	Malaysia110%	Singapore 99%	Sweden 80%	Japan 62%
1998	Finland 121%	Belgium 68%	Italy 52%	Spain 50%	France 42%
1997	Portugal 47%	Switzerland 45%	Italy 36%	Denmark 35%	USA 34%
1996	Spain 37%	Sweden 35%	Finland 32%	Hong Kong 29%	Ireland 29%
1995	Switzerland 44%	USA 37%	Sweden 33%	Spain 30%	Netherlands 28%
1994	Finland 52%	Norway 24%	Japan 22%	Sweden 19%	Ireland 15%
1993	Malaysia 114%	Hong Kong 110%	Finland 101%	Singapore 62%	Ireland 60%
1992	Hong Kong 37%	Switzerland 17%	USA 6%	Singapore 6%	France 3%
1991	Hong Kong 43%	Australia 39%	USA 30%	Singapore 23%	France 16%
1990	United Kingdom 6%	Austria 5%	Hong Kong 4%	Norway (1%)	Denmark (2%)
1989	Austria 105%	Germany 49%	Norway 46%	Denmark 45%	Singapore 42%
1988	Belgium 54%	Denmark 53%	Sweden 48%	Norway 42%	France 38%
1987	Japan 43%	Spain 41%	United Kingdom 35%	Canada 14%	Denmark 13%

The U.S. stock market has ranked among the five top performers only four times in the past fourteen years. During this same period, the U.S. bond market has never claimed the number-one spot against other world markets.

For the 2000 calendar year, the five worst-performing stock markets were Indonesia (-56 percent), Thailand (-51 percent), Taiwan (-45 percent), Greece (-42 percent), and New Zealand (-32 percent).

Appendix G
The Power of Dividends

The following table shows how important common stock dividends can be. The figures assume a one-time investment of $100,000 in the Standard & Poor's 500 at the beginning of 1977. The table shows that dividends have increased for fourteen of the past twenty-four years.

Viewed from a different perspective, if you were strictly income-oriented and invested $100,000 in the S & P 500 at the beginning of 1977, you would have received a 4.3 percent return on your investment ($4,310 divided by $100,000) for the calendar year. For the 2000 calendar year, this same investment returned 13.5 percent for the year ($18,838 divided by the original $100,000); for 2001 the figure decreases to 12.8 percent ($12,823 divided by $100,000). These figures assume that dividends received each year were spent and not reinvested. Moreover, these numbers do not include the over *ninefold* growth of capital (the original $100,000 grew to $1,068,594 without dividends) that also took place.

As a point of comparison for the figures described in the previous paragraph, consider what would have happened if the same investor had invested in a twenty-five-year U.S. government bond in 1977. By the end of 2001, twenty-five years later, the original $100,000 worth of bonds would have matured and had an ending value of $100,000. Additionally, the investor would have received approximately 7 percent for each of these twenty-five years—a far cry from the increased dividend stream and capital appreciation the S & P 500 experienced over the same period. Perhaps more important, the bond investor could have taken her $100,000 at the beginning of 2002 and invested the money for another twenty to thirty years, getting a 5 percent return for each of those years (versus the S & P 500 investor who just finished receiving over 12.8 percent and presumably will be receiving even greater dividend returns for most of the next twenty years).

The reason the dividend income stream appears to be so large, even though it was just 1.2 percent in 2001 (and 1.1 percent in 2000), is that the yields are based on the yearly value and growth of the S & P 500. Starting off with a negative return in 1977 (the S & P 500 was down 11.5 percent, excluding dividends), a $100,000 investment at the beginning of 1977 grew to $1,068,594 by the end of 2001 (assuming all dividends were spent each year). Thus, 1.2 percent (the dividend yield for 2001) multiplied by $1,068,594 equals $12,823 (shown here). As a side note, if no dividends were taken out, and were instead reinvested, a $100,000 investment made at the beginning of 1977 in the S & P 500 grew to $2,516,037 by the end of 2001 ($2,855,387 by the end of 2000).

Annual Dividends from $100,000 Invested in the S & P 500 (1977–2000)

year	S & P 500 dividend
1977	$3,857
1978	$4,821
1979	$5,800
1980	$7,321
1981	$5,640
1982	$7,280
1983	$7,761
1984	$7,177
1985	$10,141
1986	$8,525
1987	$8,465
1988	$10,901
1989	$12,808
1990	$10,445
1991	$11,897
1992	$12,428
1993	$12,427
1994	$12,192
1995	$16,873
1996	$17,254
1997	$19,275
1998	$19,440
1999	$18,838
2000	$13,518
2001	$12,823

Appendix H
Growth Stocks versus Value Stocks

Throughout the different equity sections (growth, growth and income, global equity, etc.), the end of each stock fund's "Management" paragraph often mentions whether the fund manager seeks out "growth" or "value" issues. The differences and possible consequences of these two forms of equity selection are shown in the following table.

Value means that the stocks are inexpensive relative to their earnings potential. *Growth* refers to stocks of companies whose earnings per share are expected to grow significantly faster than the market average.

As you can see by the table, the performance of these two types of stocks can vary from year to year. On a monthly or quarterly basis, the difference is often much more significant than on an annual basis.

The following table shows performance of the S & P Barra Value Index and the S & P Barra Growth Index (dividends reinvested in both indexes). Over the past eleven years, an investment in both growth stocks and value stocks would have been less volatile than an investment in only one equity style.

year	growth stocks	value stocks	year	growth stocks	value stocks
1991	29.7%	22.6%	1996	19.5%	22.5%
1992	6.0%	13.3%	1997	27.5%	-33.6%
1993	7.7%	16.0%	1998	26.4%	4.8%
1994	-3.1%	-1.0%	1999	25.5%	6.0%
1995	31.5%	33.9%	2000	-4.1%	18.3%
			2001	-7.3%	2.8%

Source: S & P 500 Barra Value Index and the S & P 500 Barra Growth Index.

Although growth stocks have outperformed value stocks during most of the 1990s, value has been the winner in five of the past seven decades. The following figures are average annual returns for each of the past seven decades.

decade	growth	value	decade	growth	value
1930s	1.9%	-4.6%	1970s	3.8%	20.8%
1940s	7.3%	17.9%	1980s	14.7%	20.8%
1950s	17.9%	21.8%	1990s	19.4%	15.3%
1960s	8.0%	12.3%			

Appendix I
Stock Market Declines

If you are a relatively new investor, you may not have had firsthand experience with a bear market. Since corrections are a natural part of the stock market cycle, it is important to ask yourself how you would react. Would you panic or would you be patient? It is difficult to know for sure. Stock market fire drills do not really work, because it is one thing to ponder your reaction to a market meltdown—another to live through one with your financial goals at stake. However, a historical perspective may help you gain a better perspective and, even more important, remain patient.

The following table shows all of the periods when the U.S. stock market dropped 15 percent or more from 1953 through the end of 2000 (a "bear market" is defined as a drop of 20 percent or more; a "correction" is a decline of 10 percent or more). Of these fourteen down markets, the worst took place during the 1973–1974 recession, resulting in the greatest loss since the Great Depression. Surprisingly, half of the 48 percent loss that took place during the 1973–1974 decline was recovered within five months after the drop.

U.S. Market Declines of 15% or More (1953–2000)

bear year	% decline	# of down months	months to recovery
1953	15%	9	6
1956–1957	16%	6	5
1957	20%	3	12
1961–1962	29%	6	14
1966	22%	9	6
1968–1970	37%	18	22
1973–1974	48%	21	64
1975	15%	2	4
1977–1978	18%	14	6
1978	17%	2	10
1980	22%	2	4
1981–1982	22%	13	3
1987	34%	2	23
1990	20%	3	23
1998	15%	2	5
2000	13%	3	?
average	23%	7	14

During the 1998 calendar year, the S & P 500 dropped 15.4 percent from the end of June through the end of August. It took just four months (end of November) for the market to recover this loss and move on to yet another high. For 1999, the market had a positive return of 21 percent, but it had a negative return of 9.1 percent for the 2000 calendar year, followed by a loss of 11.9 in 2001.

One possible strategy to avoiding market declines is to sit on the sidelines until the volatility passes. According to a study by the University of Michigan, this is a bad idea. An investor who was on the sidelines during the best 1 percent of all trading days from 1963 to 2000 missed 95 percent of the market's gains. According to figures from Micropal, missing the best fifteen months of the market from June 1980 to June 2000 resulted in foregoing 75 percent of the market's gain (as measured by the S & P 500). A $100 investment in the S & P 500 grew to $613 if all fifteen months were missed, versus $100 growing to $2,456 if one were fully invested from June 1980 to June 2000.

These included investors who were sidelined in 1995 by the poor showing in 1994 for both stocks and bonds as well as those stock market investors who bailed out in 1996 because the 38 percent gain in 1995 made them nervous about a downturn. Investors who bailed out in 1997 because the 23 percent gain in 1996 made them nervous missed a 29 percent gain in 1998 and a 21 percent gain in 1999!

Being in the market when it falls is not the greatest risk most stock investors face; it is being out of the market when it soars. The best strategy is to keep investing through any market environment.

The problem is that no one rings a bell when the market hits bottom. Similarly, there is no advance notice that the market is turning around. Stocks tend to gain significant ground in short periods; missing out on the first, brief phase of a recovery can be costly. For example, when the stock market took off in August 1982, ending years of mediocre performance, the market jumped 42 percent in just three months. From the October low of the 1987 crash to the end of December, just two months later, stocks rebounded 22 percent. And in the four months after the October 1990 Gulf War low, with the United States still mired in recession, the stock market shot up more than 30 percent.

Trying to get out of the market and get back in calls for two right decisions. There is no evidence that professional investors, market timers, brokers, financial analysts, or anyone else can get these calls right with any degree of consistency. One bad market timing call can seriously handicap lifetime performance.

The question then becomes, If stock prices fall hard, should you cut your losses and play it safe? Of all the options that investors have, this one may be the worst solution and the most devastating. An investment of $10,000 in common stocks, as measured by the S & P 500, on the day before the October 1987 crash would have fallen to $7,995 in a single day. Leaving the account intact would have resulted in a whopping 746 percent gain through December 31, 2001. Taking the $7,995 and reinvesting it in U.S. Treasury bills would have resulted in a gain of just 98 percent over the same period.

Moving from the S & P 500 to the Dow Jones Industrial Average, and changing the perspective somewhat, a review of the declines in the Dow may be an insightful comparison. Since 1990, a "routine" decline (a loss of 5 percent or more) has happened about three times a year, and it has taken about forty-eight days for half of the decline to be recouped. A "moderate" decline (a loss of 10 percent or more) has happened about once a year, and it has taken about 114 days for half of the decline to be recouped. A "severe" decline (a loss of 15 percent or more) has happened about once every two years and it has taken about 219 days for half of the decline to be recouped. A "bear market" decline (a loss of 20 percent or more) has happened about once every three and a half years and it has taken about 340 days for half of the decline to be recouped.

Appendix J
A Reason Not to Index

Appendix D showed a systematic withdrawal program (SWP) for Investment Company of America (ICA), a growth and income portfolio from the American Funds Group, starting with its first full year through the first three months of 2002. Let us now look at two more examples of a SWP, comparing results from the S & P 500 versus Washington Mutual, another growth and income fund offered through the American Funds Group.

For this example, a different time frame (January 1, 1973 through March 31, 2001) will be used, showing radically different results. Like the ICA example, it is assumed that a single $100,000 investment is made and that all capital gains and dividend payments are automatically reinvested into the fund. Also less money is taken out in this example (8 percent, or $8,000 per year).

As you can see, applying an SWP to the S & P 500 results in the investor being flat broke by December 1996 (all of the $100,000 and its resulting growth has been depleted). Yet, by using professional management like that found with Washington Mutual (abbreviated as WM), not only are the cumulative distributions greater ($232,000 versus $188,700), so is the remaining principal ($859,550 versus zero).

**Systematic Withdrawal Program Using a
Growth & Income Fund (Washington Mutual) versus the S & P 500
$100,000 Invested in Each Portfolio on January 1, 1973**

date	cumulative withdrawal from WM	cumulative withdrawal from S & P 500	remaining value of Washington Mutual (WM)	remaining value of S & P 500
01/01/73	0	0	$100,000	$100,000
12/31/73	$8,000	$8,000	$79,280	$76,890
12/31/74	$16,000	$16,000	$57,460	$48,370
12/31/75	$24,000	$24,000	$74,830	$58,050
12/31/80	$64,000	$64,000	$89,980	$52,930
12/31/85	$104,000	$104,000	$170,740	$42,890
12/31/90	$144,000	$144,000	$260,020	$28,520
12/31/95	$184,000	$184,000	$503,180	$3,910
12/31/96	$192,000	$188,700	$596,530	$0
12/31/97	$200,000	$787,050		
12/31/98	$208,000	$931,140		
12/31/99	$216,000	$933,800		
12/31/00	$224,000	$1,009,930		
12/31/01	$232,000	$829,440		
03/31/02	——————	$859,550		

For the S & P 500, the average annual total return for this illustration was 6.0 percent (January 1, 1973 through December 15, 1996 when the money ran out). For Washington Mutual Fund (WM), the average annual total return for this illustration was 12 percent (January 1, 1973 through March 31, 2002).

Two conclusions can be reached from this illustration. First, there is a benefit to professional management versus a passively managed portfolio such as the S & P 500 (which as an index fund is also considered to be a growth and income fund). Second, moderate gains or advances in some early years can make a great difference later on (compare the value of both portfolios at the end of 1974 and 1975 with what happened in later years, such as 1980 and 1985, when the gaps become huge due to earlier gains by Washington Mutual).

Appendix K
A Benefit of Balanced Funds

Prudence can pay off. Even though stocks usually outperform bonds, there have been extensive periods when a balanced portfolio (30 percent to 70 percent in bonds and the balance in stocks) can be a better way to go than a pure stock portfolio (represented by the S & P 500 here)—especially when current income is needed.

The following table shows a systematic withdrawal program (SWP) for Income Fund of America (a balanced portfolio from the American Funds Group) versus a similar SWP using the S & P 500. Both withdrawal programs assume a one-time investment of $200,000 made on January 1, 1974, annual withdrawals made at the end of each year, and a first-year withdrawal of $15,000 (7.5 percent of $200,000) that is then increased by 3.5 percent for each subsequent year (in order to offset the effects of inflation). As you can see, the balanced fund comes out ahead.

Systematic Withdrawal Program Using a Balanced Fund (IFA) and the S & P 500 ($200,000 Invested in Each Portfolio on January 1, 1972)

date	cumulative withdrawal from IFA	cumulative withdrawal from S & P 500	remaining value of IFA	remaining value of S & P 500
01/01/74	0	0	$200,000	$200,000
12/31/74	$15,000	$15,000	$165,240	$131,834
12/31/75	$30,525	$30,525	$208,287	$164,740
12/31/76	$46,593	$46,593	$265,307	$187,368
12/31/80	$116,691	$116,691	$248,709	$191,095
12/31/85	$219,029	$219,029	$488,588	$221,773
12/31/90	$340,574	$340,574	$632,843	$257,400
12/31/95	$484,932	$484,932	$1,067,108	$347,972
12/31/96	$516,905	$516,905	$1,197,075	$394,987
12/31/97	$549,997	$549,997	$1,428,937	$493,109
12/31/98	$584,247	$584,247	$1,529,268	$597,424
12/31/99	$619,696	$619,696	$1,501,077	$686,033
12/31/00	$656,385	$656,385	$1,612,601	$586,516
12/31/01	$679,360	$679,360	$1,596,644	$493,746

For the S & P 500, the average annual total return for this illustration was 13 percent (January 1, 1974 through December 31, 2001) and 14 percent for the past ten years. For Income Fund of America (IFA), the average annual total return for this illustration was 13 percent and 11 percent for the past ten years.

Appendix L
Asset Categories: Total Returns for the Past Fourteen Years

The following table shows the year-by-year returns for eight different asset categories. All of the returns are in U.S. dollars, expressed as percentages, and include the reinvestment of any dividends, interest, and capital gains. The boldface type indicates the best-performing category for the year.

category	'87	'88	'89	'90	'91	'92	'93	'94	'95	'96	'97	'98	'99	'00	'01
S & P 500	5	17	32	-3	31	8	10	1	**38**	**23**	**33**	**29**	21	-9	-12
small U.S. stocks	-9	25	16	-20	**46**	**18**	19	-2	28	17	22	-3	30	-4	**23**
foreign stocks (EAFE)	25	28	11	-24	12	-12	33	**8**	11	6	2	20	27	-14	-21
emerging market stocks	14	**58**	**55**	-30	18	0	**68**	-1	-13	8	-15	-25	**74**	-31	-4
U.S. government/ corporate bonds	3	8	15	9	16	7	10	-3	19	4	10	10	-1	12	8
high-yield bonds	5	13	1	-10	**46**	16	17	-1	19	11	13	4	5	-5	6
foreign government bonds	**35**	2	-3	**15**	16	5	15	6	20	4	-4	18	3	-3	-4
U.S. T-bills	6	7	8	8	5	4	3	4	5	5	5	5	5	6	4

Source: Micropal

Appendix M
Stock Gains, Losses, and Averages

In the five calendar years ending December 1932, the S & P 500 had a cumulative loss of almost 49 percent. Although this is quite a depressing figure (particularly since similar losses took place during the 1973–1974 recession), basing your stock market strategy on a couple of terrible periods is foolish.

To get a better feel for the likely range of returns you will experience, let us examine what happens when you throw out the worst 10 percent and best 10 percent of the years and then look at performance for the remaining 80 percent of the time. Here is what you would find, looking at rolling calendar-year periods from 1871 through 1998 (all figures are from *Stocks for the Long Run* by Jeremy Siegel and the Institute of Business and Finance):

- For five-year periods (124 observations) and then eliminating the twelve best and twelve worst such periods, annualized returns ranged from 0.1 percent to 18.5 percent
- For ten-year periods (119 observations), annualized returns ranged from 2.8 percent to 15.9 percent
- for twenty-year periods (109 observations), annualized returns ranged from 5.3 percent to 13.8 percent
- for thirty-year periods (99 observations), annualized returns ranged from 6.0 percent to 11.8 percent

Note: If you earned 5.3 percent per year for twenty years, your money would grow 181 percent. If you earned 6.0 percent per year for thirty years, you would end up with 474 percent.

Looking at returns and variability from a different perspective, Jeffrey Schwartz, a senior consultant at Ibbotson, provides an even wider range of returns. According to his figures, since the end of World War II (throwing out the best 5 percent and the worst 5 percent of the years):

- Five-year returns vary from 2.5 percent to 22.7 percent per year
- Ten-year returns vary from 4.0 percent to 20.4 percent per year
- Twenty-year returns vary from 6.0 percent to 15.8 percent a year

The Siegel and Schwartz figures are slightly more positive if you include 1999 and 2000 figures.

Appendix N
Individual Stocks versus Mutual Funds

If you believe recent headlines, you might think that mutual funds are a thing of the past, and that today's investors prefer to choose individual stocks for their portfolio. However, as you will see in the following table, funds are more relevant now than they were in 1924, when MFS invented the mutual fund. Unlike individual stocks, funds provide active management with the risk-reduction benefit of diversification. Perhaps no other investment has provided a better balance of risk and return.

Did you know:

- Over the past five years, from September 30, 1995 to September 30, 2000, **39 percent** of stocks produced negative annualized total returns as compared to **less than 1 percent** of equity mutual funds?
- In 1999, the standard deviation of individual stocks was **229**, while it was only **37.3** for equity mutual funds?
- Historically, individual stocks have had higher annualized average returns over the one-year period, but equity mutual funds produced higher returns over the **three-, five-,** *and* **ten**-year periods ending September 30, 2000?

individual U.S. stocks	**1 year** (2000)	**3 years** (1998–2000)	**5 years** (1996–2000)	**10 years** (1991–2000)
# stocks in existence	6,375	5,424	4,408	2,524
average annualized return	32%	-3%	5%	12%
highest return per year	5,569%	395%	179%	94%
lowest return per year	-97%	-83%	-76%	-35%
# stocks with negative annualized return	3,137	3,103	1,711	420
% stocks with negative annualized return	49%	57%	39%	17%

U.S. equity mutual funds	**1 year** (2000)	**3 years** (1998–2000)	**5 years** (1996–2000)	**10 years** (1991–2000)
# funds in existence	2,683	2,110	1,565	778
average annualized return	28%	14%	17%	17%
highest return per year	264%	88%	56%	41%
lowest return per year	-75%	-18%	-17 %	-8%
# funds with negative annualized return	116	140	13	1
% funds with negative annualized return	2%	3%	0%	0%

Appendix O
Decades at a Glance (1930–1999)

The following text and figures cover the past seven decades (1930–1999). The summary information is useful in gaining a historical perspective of the market. Perhaps more important, it shows that despite a number of catastrophic events, the U.S. stock market has continued to trend upward.

DECADE AT A GLANCE (the 1930s)

Economic distress swept the nation after the October 1929 stock market crash. The Great Depression, which lasted from 1930 to 1936, bottomed in 1933, when *one-fourth* of the civilian labor force was unemployed.

index	average annual total return
Standard & Poor's 500 Index	-0.1%
long-term U.S. government bonds	4.9%
U.S. Treasury bills	0.6%
	average for the decade
short-term interest rates	1.5%
annual inflation rate	-2.1%
unemployment rate	18.2%

DECADE AT A GLANCE (the 1940s)

Japan's attack on Pearl Harbor on December 7, 1941, thrust the United States into World War II and a wartime economy. In the midst of price controls and consumer goods shortages, upward trends marked the stock market from 1943 to 1946, with a vigorous bull market in 1945 as the war ended.

index	average annual total return
Standard & Poor's 500 Index	9.2%
long-term U.S. government bonds	3.2%
U.S. Treasury bills	0.4%
	average for the decade
short-term interest rates	1.6%
annual inflation rate	5.4%
unemployment rate	5.2%

DECADE AT A GLANCE (the 1950s)

While Eisenhower guided America through the early years of the Cold War, the stock market made gains, and by year-end 1954, stock prices had reached their highest levels since 1929. This exuberance was followed by a bear market lasting eighteen months, from April 1956 through October 1957, during which the S & P 500 declined 19.4 percent.

index	average annual total return
Standard & Poor's 500 Index	19.4%
long-term U.S. government bonds	0.1%
U.S. Treasury bills	1.9%
	average for the decade
short-term interest rates	3.2%
annual inflation rate	2.2%
unemployment rate	4.5%

DECADE AT A GLANCE (the 1960s)

American culture, long restrained by the sense of team spirit and conformity induced by the crises of depression, war, and the ongoing Cold War, broke loose in a multitude of swift changes. The economy was equally turbulent, and the stock market cycles recorded three bear markets. In 1963, President Kennedy submitted a federal budget with the largest deficit in history, $10 billion.

index	average annual total return
Standard & Poor's 500 Index	7.8%
long-term U.S. government bonds	1.5%
U.S. Treasury bills	3.9%
	average for the decade
short-term interest rates	5.3%
annual inflation rate	2.5%
unemployment rate	4.8%

DECADE AT A GLANCE (the 1970s)

When the Organization of Petroleum Exporting Countries (OPEC) quintupled oil prices in 1973, a deep recession hit America. The stock market plunged 45.1 percent, from January 1973 through December 1974. Unemployment reached 8.7 percent in March 1975, the highest level since 1941. In 1979, commercial banks raised their prime rates to a whopping 15.7 percent.

index	average annual total return
Standard & Poor's 500 Index	5.9%
long-term U.S. government bonds	5.5%
U.S. Treasury bills	6.3%
	average for the decade
short-term interest rates	8.1%
annual inflation rate	7.4%
unemployment rate	6.2%

DECADE AT A GLANCE (the 1980s)

President Reagan signed extensive budget- and tax-cutting legislation in 1981, and sweeping tax-reform legislation in 1986. The Black Monday stock market crash of October 19, 1987, became the largest one-day stock market decline on record, as the Dow Jones Industrial Average fell an astounding 508.32 points.

index	average annual total return
Standard & Poor's 500 Index	17.6%
long-term U.S. government bonds	12.6%
U.S. Treasury bills	8.9%
	average for the decade
short-term interest rates	11.8%
annual inflation rate	5.1%
unemployment rate	7.3%

DECADE AT A GLANCE (the 1990s)

From November 1990 through the end of 1999, stock market investors were rewarded by the longest bull market in history. "The current bull market has added about $7.2 trillion to households' balance sheets." The Asian Economic Crisis briefly shook U.S. investor confidence as the Dow Jones Industrial Average experienced the single-biggest point loss ever on October 27, 1997. The decade ended with technology stocks fueling the NASDAQ Index to its highest close ever on December 31, 1999.

index	average annual total return
Standard & Poor's 500 Index	18.2%
long-term U.S. government bonds	8.8%
U.S. Treasury bills	4.9%
	average for the decade
short-term interest rates	8.0%
annual inflation rate	2.9%
unemployment rate	5.8%

About the Author

Gordon K. Williamson, JD, MBA, MS, CFS, CLU, ChFC, AEP, CSA, CLTC, RP, is one of the most highly trained investment counselors in the United States. Williamson, a former tax attorney, is a Certified Fund Specialist and branch manager of a national brokerage firm. He has been admitted to the Registry of Financial Planning Practitioners, the highest honor one can attain as a financial planner. He holds the two highest designations in the life insurance industry: Chartered Life Underwriter and Chartered Financial Consultant. Gordon is an Accredited Estate Planner, Certified Senior Advisor, and certified in long-term care. He is also a real estate broker with an MBA in real estate.

Mr. Williamson is the founder and executive director of the Institute of Business & Finance, a fourteen-year-old professional education program that leads to the designations "CFS" and "Board Certified" (800-848-2029).

He is also the author of more than thirty books, including *Building & Managing an Investment Portfolio, Making the Most of Your 401(k), The 100 Best Annuities You Can Buy, All about Annuities, How You Can Survive and Prosper in the Clinton Years, Investment Strategies under Clinton/Gore, The Longman Investment Companion, Investment Strategies, Survey of Financial Planning, Tax Shelters, Advanced Investment Vehicles and Techniques, Your Living Trust, Sooner Than You Think, Getting Started in Annuities, Big Decisions—Small Investor, Building & Managing an Investment Portfolio, Low Risk Investing,* and *First Time Investor.* He has been the financial editor of various magazines and newspapers and a stock market consultant for a television station.

Gordon K. Williamson is located in La Jolla, California. The firm specializes in financial planning and investments for individuals and institutions ($100,000 minimum account size). Additional information can be obtained by phoning (800) 748-5552 or (858) 454-3938.

100 BEST STOCKS YOU CAN BUY, 2003

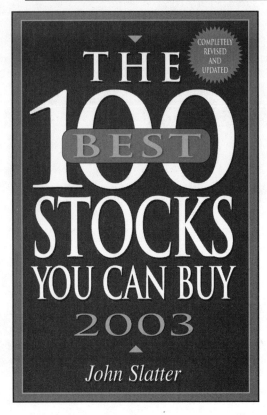

Stocks remain the most popular form of investment. However, in today's volatile climate choosing the right stock isn't easy. In fact, it can be a risky, stressful, and time-consuming experience.

In *The 100 Best Stocks You Can Buy, 2003*, investment analyst John Slatter helps you minimize your risk by narrowing the options down to the 100 stocks you can't afford to miss. Mr. Slatter has painstakingly researched thousands of stocks to bring you those that demonstrate the best potential for both long- and short-term growth. The 100 best are companies with innovative marketing, great products, cutting-edge research, sound management, financial strength, and consistent growth.

The 100 Best Stocks You Can Buy, 2003 brings you the best choices for the following investment strategies:

✦ Income
✦ Conservative Growth
✦ Growth
✦ Aggressive Growth

Each stock listing includes invaluable background on the company, contact information, stock and ticker symbols, Web site address, S & P rating, plus insider tips on reasons to buy, potential shortcomings to bear in mind, and a snapshot of company financials. *The 100 Best Stocks You Can Buy, 2003* is the guide you'll rely on—year after year.

Trade Paperback, $14.95
6" x 9 ¼" 368 pages
ISBN: 1-58062-753-6